THE LURE OF AUTHORITARIANISM

INDIANA SERIES IN MIDDLE EAST STUDIES

Mark Tessler, editor

THE LURE OF AUTHORITARIANISM

The Maghreb after the Arab Spring

Edited by
Stephen J. King and
Abdeslam M. Maghraoui

With an Afterword by
Hicham Alaoui

INDIANA UNIVERSITY PRESS

This book is a publication of

Indiana University Press
Office of Scholarly Publishing
Herman B Wells Library 350
1320 East 10th Street
Bloomington, Indiana 47405 USA

iupress.indiana.edu

© 2019 by Indiana University Press

Manufactured in the United States of America

Library of Congress Cataloging-in-Publication Data

Names: King, Stephen J. (Stephen Juan), [date] editor. | Maghraoui, Abdeslam, editor. | Moulay Hicham, Prince of Morocco, [date] writer of afterword.
Title: The lure of authoritarianism : the Maghreb after the Arab Spring / edited by Stephen J. King and Abdeslam M. Maghraoui ; with an afterword by Hicham Alaoui.
Description: Bloomington, Indiana, USA : Indiana University Press, 2019. | Series: Indiana series in Middle East studies | Includes bibliographical references and index.
Identifiers: LCCN 2018049709 (print) | LCCN 2019001809 (ebook) | ISBN 9780253040893 (e-book) | ISBN 9780253040855 (cl : alk. paper) | ISBN 9780253040862 (pb : alk. paper)
Subjects: LCSH: Authoritarianism—Africa, North. | Africa, North—Politics and government—21st century. | Arab Spring, 2010- | Islam and politics—Africa, North.
Classification: LCC JQ3198.A58 (ebook) | LCC JQ3198.A58 L87 2019 (print) | DDC 320.530961—dc23
LC record available at https://lccn.loc.gov/2018049709

1 2 3 4 5   24 23 22 21 20 19

To the people in the region yearning for justice
and the end of oppression

CONTENTS

THE LURE OF AUTHORITARIANISM

INTRODUCTION

The Lure of Authoritarianism

Abdeslam M. Maghraoui

A CROSS THE MAGHREB, AUTHORITARIAN TENDENCIES ARE REEMERGING UNAPOLOGETICALLY and with new vigor. Except in Tunisia, commitment to power sharing in politics and the idea of cultural diversity in society have all but disappeared. In Mauritania, Morocco, and Algeria, weak opposition parties either boycott the political process or remain subservient to the regimes. At the same time, observers note the increasing role of the police, the dependent judiciary, and local authorities deploying the old methods of political control. In Libya, the hope of bringing the country together after a decade of bloody civil war rests on the shoulders of yet another military strongman. Likewise, the authoritarian temptation at the societal level has outlived the Arab Spring uprisings. Despite persistent popular demands for social justice and better living conditions across the Maghreb countries, the domestic forces for democratic change remain weak. Social protests like the *Haratine* movement in Mauritania, the *Hirak* in the Moroccan Rif, or austerity strikes in Algeria have failed to galvanize popular support around a democratic agenda. As if the Arab Spring never happened, the military, Islamist parties, or populist leaders remain the main credible political alternatives in most of the Maghreb today. Even in Tunisia, the only country that made promising steps toward democracy, worrisome restrictions on freedom of expression and individual rights are compromising progress.[1]

The rejuvenation of authoritarianism in the Maghreb, and in other parts of the Arab world, is not surprising. The political and economic liberalization reforms since the 1980's didn't converge on a serious process of democratic transition where actors abide by transparent democratic rules. But the depth and breadth of the temptation is puzzling. During the last fifteen years, scholars of Middle East politics shifted the focus of their research from the conditions that make democratic transition possible to the study of institutions that allow authoritarianism to "upgrade" and even prosper.[2] Thanks to the privatization of state enterprises and liberalization of the economy, autocratic regimes across the region were able to tap into new resources and create new clientelist networks to shore up their support. Scholarly interest in the role of authoritarian institutions in the Middle East was partly a reaction to the discrepancy between political reforms and what the transition paradigm predicted would happen;[3] and partly due to the paradoxical role of constitutions, parties, elections, and legislatures in authoritarian rejuvenation.[4] Rather than dismissing semidemocratic institutions as mere window-dressing, scholars began to study them on their own merit: as part of the authoritarian regimes' strategy to form winning coalitions, broaden popular support, co-opt elites, marginalize opposition, create new resources, and adapt to domestic and external challenges. This edited volume takes the study of authoritarianism in the Maghreb a step further to highlight the broader appeal of authoritarianism.

In a survey of North African politics after the 2011 popular uprisings, the volume paves the way for another paradigmatic shift in approaching the region's politics. Beyond the regimes' use of institutions, support for authoritarianism *tout court* in the name of order and stability is providing the regimes with a potent source of legitimacy. The reinvigoration of authoritarian tendencies in the region cannot be reduced to cultural attributes, though these may play a role. Rather, the volume demonstrates that the Arab Spring and its chaotic aftermath are renormalizing the temptation of authoritarianism for regime elites, civil society, and the people at large. Notably, we do not claim that the trend is socially uniform, politically consistent, or ideologically coherent at this point. As the chapters in this volume illustrate, the trend is not entirely new or unopposed, and there are significant variations across countries and political spheres. Nonetheless, the phenomenon is more readily observable now, and it is wiping out the hopes for democratic transformation.

The shift from "upgraded" to unapologetic authoritarianism is observable first and foremost in the regimes' official discourse. In the late 1990s, except for Gulf state's rulers, virtually all Arab autocrats jumped on the bandwagon of democracy, human rights, and civil society even as they used every tool at their disposal to derail democratic change.[5] The autocratic regimes' sponsorship of a flurry of national and international workshops on political reform, economic liberalization, human rights, or transparent governance was of course self-serving.[6] The perfect illustration of this tactic was Tunisia's hosting of the 2005 World Summit on the Information Society when the regime of Zine El Abidine Ben Ali was one of the most repressive of internet use in the world. However, the frequent and widely publicized increase in prodemocracy stunts in Arab capitals reflected a global and domestic normative change that the authoritarian regimes could not afford to ignore. In the post–Arab Spring era, such a display of phony democratic sentiments has all but disappeared. While governments continue to take advantage of selective reforms that shore up their power, very few bother to justify them in the name of democratic change anymore.

Moroccans were baffled when King Mohammed VI, a trusted Western ally and reputed democracy sympathizer, castigated the West's push for reform in the Arab world in high-profile forums, including one at the United Nations annual meetings.[7] In Egypt, General Abdel Fattah el-Sisi justified a brutal campaign against the Muslim Brotherhood in the name of order and stability. He declared that the Egyptian people have different priorities and conceptions of democracy and human rights than the West. After a meeting with Donald Trump in September 2016, el-Sisi had high praise for the Republican nominee's commitment to fighting terrorism. The next day, senior Egyptian officials blasted Hillary Clinton's democracy designs for the Middle East.[8] And in Jordan, by 2014 the regime's narrative shifted abruptly from the National Dialogue Committee's recommendations for democratic reforms to fighting ISIS and passing antiterrorism laws. King Abdullah declared that the monarchy's long-standing "social contract" with tribes, Bedouins, entrepreneurs, and governorates' leaders is akin to democratic participation. These examples are significant because the leaders of the three countries depend on Western aid, investments, and political support. But the Arab regimes' pushback against democracy is much broader, which partly explains the governments' enthusiasm for the new Trump administration.[9]

Beyond reversals at the official level, negative public views of democracy and popular support for strong leaders seem to be growing. It is difficult to know exactly what people think of democracy and even more difficult to gauge changing public attitudes in an authoritarian context.[10] But findings from longitudinal and cross-country surveys about public support for democracy in the Arab world during the 1999–2010 period indicate deepening skepticism.[11] For example, while many people express a preference for democratic governance, they have widely divergent interpretations of what democracy means or what it is supposed to deliver. In general, survey results show that people associate democracy with what they consider just social and economic orders as postulated in Islamic principles rather than with a set of political rights and freedoms. Hence, overwhelming majorities see no contradiction between Islam and democracy because most believe that Islam subsumes modern democracy. And although people support modern democratic institutions, including competitive elections and legislative oversight, unelected strong leaders remain surprisingly popular.

Desire for strong, autocratic leadership may have to do with other survey findings: participants associate democracy with economic risks, social instability, and political disorder. More recent research finds that while people still view democratic ideals positively, they don't find it suitable for their own country.[12] This is hardly surprising when the freest and most competitive elections in the Arab world, arguably in Algeria in 1991, Iraq in 2005, and Libya and Egypt in 2012, led to bloodshed. Even in Morocco, where elections are relatively free and competitive and the alternation of power is peaceful, trust in the political process and rates of political participation have been steadily declining over the decades.[13] In sum, although the Arab Spring demonstrated the region's yearning for justice, social equality, and transparent governance, the uprisings stirred deeply rooted skepticism about democracy and revived authoritarian temptations.

A third significant indication of warming attitudes toward authoritarian rule in the Maghreb is the Arab democrats' receptiveness to the regimes' backpedaling on democratic reforms. In the troubling aftermaths of the popular uprisings, Arab democracy advocates were forced to choose between the majoritarian and unpredictable Islamists and the more familiar relics of autocratic rule. They tilted toward the latter even though "the devil they know" has no reason to be accommodating, given growing domestic skepticism about democracy and weakening external pressure for democratic change.

The gloomiest illustration of the political dynamic between Islamists, liberals, and autocrats is post-Mubarak Egypt.[14] Egypt's secular democrats, socialist groups, and civil society liberals marched in the streets along youths and Islamists to demand free elections and democracy. But divided, leaderless, and with no societal depth, they lost badly to the more experienced and disciplined Islamist or nationalist parties in the 2011–12 legislative elections. Frustrated, they dubbed the anti–Muslim Brotherhood street protest and the 2013 military coup a "June Revolution," which in their view echoed the ideals of the 2011 "January Revolution." Even if the embrace was tactical, Egyptian liberal reformers stand today divided and powerless in the face of the regime's media campaign of denigration and hounding by the security services.[15]

But the liberals' warming up to authoritarian rule in the region goes beyond Egypt and has deeper roots. Independently of the Arab Spring, two interrelated factors explain the shift: structural weaknesses and the ever-growing shadow of political Islam. Across the region, Arab secular parties in Morocco, Algeria, Egypt, Kuwait, and Yemen have been unable to articulate a credible democratic alternative to autocracy and political Islam.[16] And despite enthusiasm about growing civil activism, technological sophistication, and social deepening in many Arab countries, civil society's ability to drive meaningful and sustainable democratic change remains uncertain.[17] Together, these trends point to a departure from the authoritarian model where top-down, incremental reforms permitted authoritarianism's opponents to chip away at the coalitions and institutions that kept authoritarian regimes running and, under certain conditions, opened up meaningful democratic spaces.

The only notable exceptions to deepening authoritarianism in the Maghreb are women's rights and Amazigh (or Berber) activism. The two movements hold the most promising potential for countering the authoritarian slide we tackle in this volume. As such, we believe they deserve a separate full treatment in a later work. Notwithstanding structural hurdles and looming confrontations with the state, women's groups and Amazigh minorities across North Africa have been more successful than any other social groups in achieving gains through grassroots activism. Three interrelated factors might explain this success in spite of the movements' political divisions, lack of broad societal support, and, for the Amazigh, geographic and linguistic dispersion. Ideologically, the demands of women's legal equality and Amazigh minority rights have been consistently in tune with universal human rights values, which maximizes the two movements' international audience. Strategically, the movements are tied to Western European resources and networks of power, which gives them a considerable tactical and political advantage. And domestically, the women and Amazigh movements' general opposition to conservative and domineering political Islam opens up fresh bargaining possibilities vis-à-vis the authoritarian state. Broadly speaking, women's rights groups have been fighting the state's and society's discriminating laws, norms, and institutions, especially in civil matters. Amazigh activism emerged in reaction to forced Arabization and the denial of Amazigh culture, identity, and languages by Maghrebi postcolonial states. But only in Algeria and Morocco can we really speak of a significant social movement with critical mass to challenge majoritarian-authoritarian tendencies in the region.

Contributors to this volume explore the key features of the negative transformation in North Africa after the Arab Spring. The volume is divided into two parts. The six chapters in part I examine cross-regional trends clustered around three broad topics: the normative or ideological foundations of authoritarianism, the social and economic drivers of authoritarianism, and the security justifications of authoritarianism.

In chapter 1, "Religious Conservatism, Religious Extremism, and Secular Civil Society in North Africa," Marina Ottaway highlights the subordination of ideological and political debates to fierce religious battles in Morocco, Algeria, Tunisia, and Egypt. The protagonists are state religious authorities, semi-independent traditional Islam, modern political Islam, and various splintered Salafi groups. None of the actors is preoccupied with substantive democratic principles. Islamic groups, parties, and organizations are bent on Islamizing society from below, peacefully or through violence and coercion. The regimes' main preoccupation is not to assert the primacy of political rights over religious domination but rather to reclaim monopoly over the religious sphere in the name of fighting religious extremism and terrorism. In chapter 2, "Do Political and Economic Grievances Foster Support for Political Islam in the Post–Arab Spring Maghreb?," Mark Tessler examines the microbehavioral dimension of the same phenomenon. At the center of his exploration is the question of who supports political Islam and why. Across the region, when free elections are held, Islamist parties tend to win overwhelmingly. Surveys reveal that socioeconomic considerations, education, age, gender, faith, and politics can all drive support for political Islam. In a study of attitudes toward political Islam in Morocco, Algeria, and Tunisia after the Arab Spring, Tessler finds no conclusive evidence that political and economic discontents drive support for political Islam. Personal religiosity and social conservatism may play a greater role in fostering political Islam than previously suspected. This finding gibes with Ottaway's ideological conservatism argument and the overall deepening authoritarian tendencies depicted in this volume.

The second cluster of chapters tackles the socioeconomic underpinnings of the new authoritarian turn. In chapter 3, "Demographic Pressure,

Social Demands, and Instability in the Maghreb," Wai Mun Hong explains how social demands will continue to be the main source of social mobilization and political instability for years to come. Detailing demographic pressure, youth unemployment, and uneven human development in Morocco, Algeria, Tunisia, and Egypt, the chapter provides statistical evidence of why immediate social priorities and social justice issues are likely to trump democratic aspirations for the foreseeable future. In chapter 4, "Shifting Courses: Economies of the Maghreb after 2011," Karen Pfeifer examines new impediments to economic growth that could propel and support democratic transitions. While neoliberalism never performed as well as hoped, in previous decades, authoritarian governments took advantage of expanding global markets and global trade by liberalizing their economies to create new resources. That lifeline may be breaking as the world economy has entered a period of stagnation, and demand from North Africa's economic partners is subsiding. Slow economic growth in the region coupled with steady demographic pressure and a stagnant job market greatly limits the benefits liberalized autocracies draw from economic opening. Given prevailing conditions, Pfeifer argues that the best way to have an accountable government that actually serves the goals of the Arab Spring—bread, freedom, and socioeconomic justice—is to generate a new democratically negotiated social contract encompassing an economic program that does not isolate the country from the rest of the world, but is able to pursue national policies that are not subservient to the dictates of foreign capital and the international financial institutions.

The last two chapters in part I detail the central piece of unapologetic authoritarianism: domestic security and regional instability. Since the 1990s, authoritarian regimes in North Africa, regardless of their ideological orientation or institutional fabric, adopted political reform as a principle. The pace and areas of reforms varied from country to country, but the "security state" had loosened its grip. Chapters 5 and 6 detail how the threat of terrorism and the collapse of authority in Libya and parts of the Levant are bringing back the security state. In chapter 5, "Geopolitical Evolutions in North Africa after the Arab Spring," Pierre Razoux argues that, to the detriment of NATO and the European Union, the Maghreb has become increasingly ensnared in the geopolitics of the Machrek. For the purpose of this volume, such an evolution is significant because alliances with Eastern regional powers (Saudi Arabia, Iran, Turkey, or even Russia) further undermines inter-Maghrebi cooperation and weakens the prospects of democratic pressure from the European Union. In chapter 6, "Jihadism in the Post–Arab Spring Maghreb," Daveed Gartenstein-Ross asserts that jihadist groups have flourished in postrevolutionary North Africa by capitalizing on state weakness to carve out several spheres of influence. Libya's descent into civil war has provided a further boost to jihadist groups in every Maghrebi country.

The five chapters in part II of the volume explore authoritarian retrenchment in each North African country since the Arab Spring began. Initially, the Arab Spring seemed destined to definitively end the effectiveness of authoritarian upgrading. How could Arab autocrats manage the shocking and unprecedented region-wide popular upsurge? Diverse layers of society had come together to support each other's efforts toward democracy. Arab autocrats everywhere were on the defensive. However, the Moroccan, Mauritanian, and Algerian case studies in part II demonstrate how the normative, socioeconomic, and security dynamics of the Arab Spring discussed in part I ultimately fed into a reconfiguring of authoritarian rule in those countries. Experiencing both a bloody revolution to remove Qaddafi and a subsequent civil war, the Libyan case has had a chilling impact on the desire for democratic transitions across the region. Instead, it has become powerful fodder for authoritarian "downgrading" (toward unapologetic authoritarianism). The Tunisian case, on the other hand, has demonstrated the potential of democratic impulses in the region. Authoritarian upgrading (and downgrading) in the Arab world has it limits. Still, even in Tunisia's democratic transition, the lure of authoritarian stability has not been completely defeated.

In chapter 7, "Elections before and after the Arab Spring in North Africa," Stephen J. King analyzes the role of competitive elections in authoritarian context. He argues that while elections in Morocco, Mauritania, and Algeria inadvertently open democratic spaces, people vote for primarily clientelist purpose. Elections after the Arab Spring in Libya and Tunisia were freer and more competitive but marred with regional and religious conflict (Libya) and undermined by a returned to elite politics (Tunisia). In chapter 8, "Tunisia Triggers the Arab Spring," Stephen J. King assesses the stunning, historic, and admirable achievements of a mass uprising that set regional political change in motion in late 2010 and early 2011. By keeping the military out of politics, maintaining relative stability, and getting Tunisian parties to compete according to the rules of political democracy, Tunisians have ensured significant regime change in their own country and inspired mass uprisings against authoritarianism across the region. However, six years after the Arab Spring began, the lure of authoritarian stability continues to touch Tunisians as well. The security sector, powerful under former president Ben Ali, has been slow to change from a brutal instrument of internal repression to a professional and neutral public authority that protects citizens' rights and safety. Judicial sector reforms have been slow as well. Based on its role under Ben Ali, the judiciary is still commonly viewed as an instrument of authoritarian repression.

Libya has conducted two free and fair elections since Qaddafi's fall, yet the country is mired in a low-simmering civil war, the state has collapsed, and there are three operating governments, each claiming national legitimacy. In chapter 9, "Social and External Origins of State Collapse, the Crisis of Transition, and Strategies for Political and Institutional Reconstruction in Libya," Ali Ahmida describes a revolution hijacked by Islamic extremists, armed militias, and warlords who publicly oppose rebuilding a national army and police force. Instead of continued hope for democracy, in this climate many Libyans are looking to a military strongman, General Khalifa Haftar, for salvation.

In chapter 10, "From Authoritarian Pluralism to Centralized Autocracy in Morocco," Abdeslam Maghraoui captures a critical moment of authoritarian metamorphosis under the monarchy. The case of Morocco is illuminating because the regime sees itself and is seen by others as a model in the region for steady, incremental, and peaceful reforms that could lead to full-fledged democratization. Yet Morocco's political progress, economic dynamism, and dependence on Western aid did not prevent the country from succumbing to the new, unapologetic authoritarian pulse described in this volume.

In chapter 11, "The Politics of Mauritania's Arab Uprising and Aftermath," Matt Buehler and Mehdi Ayari identify familiar techniques of authoritarian upgrading taken by the country's military strongman, Mohamed Ould Abdel Aziz. General Aziz was able to demobilize an important part of Mauritania's February 25 movement by co-opting participants from the "white Arab" northern tribes that are the core base of support for his regime. So-called democratic reforms were turned into opportunities for authoritarian maintenance. Minor constitutional changes were manipulated to Abdel Aziz's advantage. Less-than-competitive legislative and presidential elections were used to dress up continued military authoritarian rule. Persistent opposition was met with regime repression. That these old techniques produced some popular support speaks volumes about a desire for stability in a post–Arab Spring context.

In chapter 12, "Algeria: Economic Austerity, Political Stagnation, and the Gathering Storm," Azzedine Layachi describes a country traumatized by the "Algerian Spring" of the late 1980s and early 1990s and the dark decade of bloodshed and destruction that followed it. The winds of change during the Arab Spring never seriously tempted the Algerian population. There were organized protests, but mobilization was weak and short-lived. The lure of authoritarian stability was enhanced by the civil war in neighboring Libya and the chaos and bloodshed of Algeria's own recent history.

ABDESLAM M. MAGHRAOUI is Associate Professor of Practice of Political Science at Duke University. He is author of *Liberalism without Democracy: Nationhood and Citizenship in Egypt, 1922–1936.*

Notes

1. Amnesty International, "Tunisia: Severe Restrictions on Liberty and Movement Latest Symptoms of Repressive Emergency Laws," press release, March 17, 2016, https://www.amnesty.org/en/press-releases/2016/03/tunisia-severe-restrictions-on-liberty-and-movement-latest-symptoms-of-repressive-emergency-law/.

2. Steven Heydemann, "Upgrading Authoritarianism in the Arab World," *Analysis Paper*, no. 13 (October 2007), Brookings Institution.

3. Daniel Brumberg, "Liberalization versus Democracy: Understanding Arab Political Reform," Carnegie Papers, no. 37 (May 2003), Carnegie Endowment for International Peace; Marsha Pripstein Posusney, "Enduring Authoritarianism: Middle East Lesson for Comparative Theory," special issue, *Comparative Politics*, January 2004.

4. Nathan J. Brown, *Constitutions in a Nonconstitutional World: Arab Basic Laws and the Prospects for Accountable Government* (Albany: SUNY Press, 2002); Ellen Lust-Okar, *Structuring Conflict in the Arab World: Incumbents, Opponents and Institutions* (New York: Cambridge University Press, 2005); Jennifer Gandhi, *Political Institutions under Dictatorship* (New York: Cambridge University Press, 2008); Jason Brownlee, *Authoritarianism in the Age of Democratization* (New York: Cambridge University Press, 2008); Stephen King, *The New Authoritarianism in the Middle East and North Africa* (Bloomington: Indiana University Press, 2009).

5. The proliferation of Arab official sponsoring and participation in democracy-related events is documented in the *Arab Reform Bulletin* archives (2003–11) hosted by the Carnegie Endowment for International Peace. Since 2011, the site changed its name to *Sada*, or "reverberation" in Arabic, to reflect simmering pressure from below.

6. Heydemann, "Upgrading Authoritarianism," 5–10.

7. Youssef Ait Akdim, "Maroc: le virage anti-occidental de Mohammed VI," *Le Monde*, April 26, 2016.

8. Editorial Board, "The Stark Difference between Trump's and Clinton's Meeting with a Dictator," *Washington Post*, September 22, 2016.

9. Robin Wright, "President Trump's Surprisingly Warm Welcome in the Middle East," *New Yorker*, November 10, 2016.

10. Timur Kuran, *Private Truths, Public Lies: The Social Consequences of Preference Falsification* (Cambridge: Harvard University Press, 1995).

11. See, for example, Mark Tessler, "Do Islamic Orientations Influence Attitudes toward Democracy in the Arab World? Evidence from Egypt, Jordan, Morocco, and Algeria," *International Journal of Comparative Sociology* 2 (Spring 2003); Mark Tessler and Eleanor Gao, "Gauging Arab Support for Democracy," *Journal of Democracy* 16 (July 2005); Mark Tessler, Mansour Moaddel, and Ronald Ingelehart, "Getting to Arab Democracy: What Do Iraqis Want?," *Journal of Democracy* 17 (January 2006); Amaney Jamal, "Reassessing Support of Democracy and Islam in the Arab World: Evidence from Egypt and Jordan," *World Affairs*, no. 169 (Fall 2006); Amaney Jamal and Mark Tessler, "The Democracy Barometers: Attitudes in the Arab World," *Journal of Democracy* 19 (January 2008); Lindsay Benstead, "Why Do Some Arab Citizens See Democracy as Unsuitable for Their Country?," *Democratization* 22 (2015).

12. Benstead, "Unsuitable for Their Country."

13. Bernabé López García and Miguel Hernando de Larramendi, "Las elecciones legislativas de Marruecos de 2016: contexto y lecturas," Real Instituto Elcano, November 30, 2016, http://www.realinstitutoelcano.org/wps/portal/rielcano_es.

14. See, for example, Daanish Faruqi and Dalia F. Fahmi, eds., *Egypt and the Contradictions of Liberalism: Illiberal Intelligentsia and the Future of Egyptian Democracy* (London: Oneworld, 2017).

15. Muhammad Mansour, "Why Sisi Fears Egypt's Liberals: Behind the Recent Crackdown on Civil Society," *Foreign Affairs*, May 18, 2016.

16. Marina Ottaway and Amr Hamzawy, "Fighting on Two Fronts: Secular Parties in the Arab World," *Carnegie Papers*, no. 85 (May 2007), Carnegie Endowment for International Peace.

17. Sean Yom, "Civil Society and Democratization: Critical Views from the Middle East," *Middle East Review of International Affairs* 9, no. 4 (2005); Vickie Langohr, "Too Much Civil Society, Too Little Politics? Egypt and Other Liberalizing Arab Regimes," in *Authoritarianism in the Middle East*, ed. Marsha Pripstein Posusney and Michele Penner Angrist (Boulder: Lynne Rienner, 2005), 193–220.

PART I

AUTHORITARIAN TRENDS

1

RELIGIOUS CONSERVATIVISM, RELIGIOUS EXTREMISM, AND SECULAR CIVIL SOCIETY IN NORTH AFRICA

Marina Ottaway

THE COUNTRIES OF NORTH AFRICA ARE BEING PULLED in different directions, ideologically and politically. At the ideological level, a traditional, moderately conservative Islam competes with jihadi extremism and, to a much lesser extent, with modern tolerant interpretations of Islam and with secular, liberal democratic values. This battle of ideas is reflected at the political level in the competition among organizations: an official Islamic religious leadership largely on the payroll of the government; legally recognized Islamist parties that participate in the legal and political systems of their countries; Salafi organizations that focus on the betterment of their members and, more broadly, their society, while shunning politics; jihadi organizations that do not hesitate to advocate and use violence to achieve their ideal of an Islamic state; and secular civil society organizations that try to function in the narrow available political space.[1]

Ideologically and politically, the countries of North Africa are diverse, with various trends well rooted in their respective segments of society. The authoritarian tendencies that have characterized North African regimes in recent decades thus cannot be attributed to the underlying characteristics of the societies or to the characteristics of North African Islam. The societies are inherently pluralistic; autocratic regimes fear the consequences of pluralism and seek to keep it from gaining political expression. It is also important to keep in mind that authoritarianism in North Africa, except in Morocco, has never relied on religion to justify itself. Rather, authoritarianism in North Africa has been and continues to be predominantly secular in orientation. Gamal Abdel Nasser, Hosni Mubarak, and now Abdel Fattah el-Sisi in Egypt; Habib Bourguiba and Zine El Abidine Ben Ali in Tunisia; and the National Liberation Front (FLN) personalities that have dominated Algeria since the days of independence were all essentially secular leaders for whom religion was only occasionally a convenient tool. Religion, in all its forms, is important in North Africa and affects politics, but it does not explain authoritarian tendencies.

The outcome of the ideological tensions throughout the region remains uncertain. North African societies are changing rapidly and often in unexpected directions. Countries once considered secularized have turned into hotbeds of religious extremism. The secular, modern civil society organizations that Western analysts believe will pave the way to liberalism and democracy are thriving in some countries in the sense that they are allowed to exist, but they do not have a substantial impact on policies or the political and social climate: most North African countries have become more visibly religious than they were a generation ago, and it is unclear whether or when the pendulum will swing back.

Describing and documenting these changes in detail, let alone providing an explanation of why they are taking place backed up by theory, accurate methodology, and exhaustive data goes far beyond what can be accomplished in a single analysis covering four countries stretching from Morocco to Egypt. Instead, this chapter sketches a broad picture of the relationships among religious conservativism, religious extremism, and secular civil society and provides tentative explanations in the hope they can become a starting point for discussion.

The dynamics of religious extremism, religious conservativism, and secular civil society differ significantly across Morocco, Algeria, Tunisia, and Egypt. Secular civil society, for example, has a greater impact in Morocco than elsewhere, whereas in Egypt even seemingly strong nongovernmental organizations have remained ineffectual. Many Salafis in Algeria and Tunisia are attracted to violent extremism; in Morocco and Egypt, they are more inclined to seek political integration or focus on the reform of society. Yet the four countries also share common characteristics in terms of dominant religious beliefs, similar external influences, and the historical trends to which they all have been exposed. That the outcomes are so different is due largely to distinctive leadership in government and society and to the strength of particular civil organizations.

The four countries share a similar approach to Islam. As practiced by the majority, Islam is by and large moderate—these are not countries where rigid and puritanical interpretations are imposed on the population. Sufi influences, particularly in Morocco and Algeria, have introduced an element of mysticism at the ideological level, as well as a popular tradition of venerating saints through pilgrimages to their tombs and ceremonies that soften the strictures of religious practice. Also, except in Egypt, where the indigenous Christian Coptic population may be as high as 15 percent of the total, the population in these countries is almost completely Sunni Muslim, with only small numbers of Christians, minute and literally dying Jewish communities, and a few Shias. This homogeneity allows people to take their religious identity for granted, rather than having to affirm it against that of others. In other words, nothing in the traditional religious makeup of these countries would seem to predispose them to religious extremism.

All four countries have also been exposed over the years to strong secularizing influences, some of them imposed, some freely accepted. Contact with European countries contributed to the spread of secular ideas in the nineteenth and early twentieth centuries—in Algeria, France even sought to limit and regulate religious practice. But the most widespread force for secularization came from the region itself in the 1950s and 1960s, when the ideas of Arab nationalism and Arab socialism spread throughout the region and beyond in the wake of Gamal Abdel Nasser's rise to power in Egypt. Arab nationalism and socialism were not anti-Islamic or militantly secularistic—Nasser was pragmatic on this issue—but offered a project for Arab countries and an identity to their citizens that was not based on religion.

After Nasser's death in 1971, governments seeking to distance themselves from his legacy and an antidote to the lingering influence of his ideas turned to religion, particularly in Egypt. During the 1970s and 1980s, North African countries underwent a process of re-Islamization of their elites as a result of deliberate government policy and efforts by Islamic organizations that became freer to operate. Governments in all four countries in our study allowed Islamist organizations to reappear. The re-Islamization of these societies was highly visible because it influenced the citizens' manner of dressing. Headscarves became the norm even in milieus where they had largely been cast aside. Families that had not respected the Ramadan fasting obligation for decades, considering it to be an obsolete practice not worthy of modernizing countries, went back to it, often at the instigation of their younger members.

Re-Islamization as a cultural phenomenon was accompanied (and in part caused) by the reappearance of the Muslim Brotherhood in Egypt and organizations inspired by it in other countries.[2] It is important to underline that re-Islamization was not only the direct consequence of the rise of the Brotherhood but also a change instigated by government-controlled religious authorities. As will be discussed later, in Egypt re-Islamization owed more to the relationship between the Mubarak regime and Al-Azhar University than to the Muslim Brotherhood.

Since its founding by Hassan al-Banna in 1928, the Muslim Brotherhood has had a long-term political goal: the restoration of a state governed by Islamic precepts. The issue of how this goal was to be attained split the organization and led to the emergence of many Islamist trends, all of which are still present in North Africa.[3] Al-Banna believed Arab societies had strayed too far from the precepts of Islam and were too corrupt to provide the underpinnings for a true Islamic state. He thought that the organization must seek to reform society before attempting to reform the state and should thus concentrate on *dawa*, or preaching. Inevitably, not everybody was satisfied with this long view of the process. Some believed in forcing the change, using violence if necessary, rather than waiting for society to be ready. Sayyid Qutb, a major advocate of this trend, was imprisoned by Nasser and executed in 1966. Many see him as the inspiration for radical Islamic groups in Egypt and beyond—Ayman al-Zawahiri, who succeeded Osama Bin Laden as leader of al-Qaeda, was apparently influenced by Qutb's ideas. The mainstream of the Muslim Brotherhood, on the other hand, was committed to nonviolence and by and large respected that commitment after clashes with Nasser.

During the 1980s and 1990s, a third school of thought developed within the Muslim Brotherhood, led by people who thought the organization should not limit itself to *dawa* but should work to change the state through legal political participation, not violence. In this view, even if conditions did not yet exist for the formation of a true Islamic state, Muslims could bring about incremental reforms by participating peacefully in the politics of their countries wherever they could. Democratic participation was an acceptable means to the end of creating Islamic states. This trend gained acceptance in all four countries under discussion, all of which have (or, in the case of Egypt, had until 2013) political parties rooted in the thinking of the Muslim Brotherhood represented in the parliament or even in the cabinet.[4]

The final development that greatly affected the dynamics of religious conservativism, religious extremism, and secular civil society in the four countries was the rise of Salafism in its more violent, radical form. Salafism is an approach to Islam that calls for a return to its pure, uncorrupted form as practiced by Muhammad and his companions, "the pious ancestors." Inevitably, there are many interpretations of what this pure form of Islam entails. One frequently drawn distinction is that between "scientific" Salafism and "jihadi" Salafism. The former is essentially an attempt to strip Islam of the interpretations that have piled up over the centuries and take it back to a purer form. Scientific Salafism puts less emphasis on changing the state than on changing individuals and creating communities of people who help each other lead their lives according to the precepts of the original religion. In general, governments have been tolerant of scientific Salafism, because it does not call for political action. On the contrary, it calls for submission to the ruler, as long as he is a Muslim.

Scientific Salafism has existed in North Africa for a long time, and even included a modernist reform movement that sought in Islam the source for rational thought and change.[5] But Saudi efforts to spread their form of Salafism by financing mosques and madrasas and training preachers led to the rapid diffusion of a very conservative form of Salafism during the 1980s and 1990s. The Saudis never intended Salafism to become political. The Wahhabi Salafism they support is based on a strict separation between political and religious authority, with the royal family giving the religious establishment complete control over religious teaching and social norms—which makes women's driving a theological issue, for example—in return for the religious establishment leaving politics and government to the royal family. Things did not go as planned. As we will see later at greater length, governments in North Africa discovered that alongside the politically docile Salafism, they had allowed and even unintentionally encouraged the violent jihadi Salafism that would become the hallmark of al-Qaeda and the Islamic State of Iraq and al-Shams (ISIS).

The secular element of society did not disappear in this kaleidoscope of Islamist trends, but it was put at a definite disadvantage, despite the proliferation of donor-assisted nongovernmental organizations (NGOs) beginning in the 1990s. To be sure, the entire range of secular political ideas—from liberalism to Marxism—is still alive in North Africa, with leftist ideas particularly strong in Morocco and Tunisia, where they appear hardwired in the labor union movement. But at present many secularists, particularly among liberals, do not want to be considered secular, fearing that the term can be interpreted as denoting lack of piety, or even hostility to Islam.[6] Re-Islamization has put many people who would not have hesitated to call themselves secular in the past on the defensive. On the other hand, foreign aid in the name of democracy promotion has led to the emergence of many organizations that are becoming the visible face of secular civil society, although they are not well embedded in the broader society.

Against this common background, I will try to explore the dynamics of religious conservatism, extremism, and secular civil society in Morocco, Algeria, and Tunisia. Because of ongoing civil strife and political instability, Libya does not lend itself easily to the type of analysis I pursue. To illustrate the broad significance of the trend, I added the case of Egypt.

Morocco: Conservativism, Extremism, and Co-optation

In Morocco, religion pervades the political sphere, not because Moroccan society is more pious than others in North Africa, but because the main political forces in Morocco are embedded in one or another aspect of Islam. At the same time, Morocco has a lively and fairly influential secular civil society organized in urban-based NGOs. Moroccan politics is pluralistic, and religion-influenced organizations are part of this pluralism. Morocco is not a democratic country, however, because of the overwhelming power of the monarchy and the elusiveness of constitutional limits on the king's power.

Islam in Morocco is strongly associated with the monarchy, contributing to its moderation and political quietism. The king, considered to be a descendant of Prophet Muhammad, carries the title of "commander of the faithful"; thus, he is a spiritual as well as a political leader. Any political organization that wants to obtain legal recognition must acknowledge not only the political authority of the king, but also his religious role. The Muslim Brotherhood–inspired Party for Justice and Development (PJD) has accepted the religious role of the king and is now the major party in the governing coalition. The al-Adl wal-Ihsan Islamist movement, which possibly has a following larger than the PJD's, adamantly refuses to recognize the king as commander of the faithful; thus, this movement is not legal and remains politically ineffectual.

Because of the symbiotic relation between traditional Moroccan Islam and the monarchy, the latter has a vested interest in making sure that religion remains a conservative force and a factor of stability. Religion-oriented parties, particularly the conservative, monarchist Istiqlal party, existed in Morocco even under the French protectorate, opening the way for the acceptance of the PJD as a legal party in 2002. But the monarchy also seeks to prevent Islam from becoming a source of opposition and extremism by controlling how it is being preached and taught. For that purpose, it has undertaken a large-scale program to train imams. It is now also trying to export its moderate form of Islam, and in March 2015 it opened a training center for foreign preachers that recruits students from Africa, Europe, and Asia. In a move that departs from tradition in order to better influence the population, Morocco has also been training women to be spiritual guides to other women.

The conservative religious environment has helped Morocco contain the rise of religious extremism more successfully than supposedly more secular countries. The regime has succeeded in fully integrating the PJD into the political establishment, marginalizing the more challenging al-Adl wal-Ihsan and containing the Salafis, who in any case never gained as much traction in Morocco as in other Maghreb countries.[7] The conservative religious climate and the role of the king as commander of the faithful by themselves were not enough to guarantee such an outcome. Morocco was also helped by skillful leadership from the palace and restraint from the rising Islamist organizations.

Morocco was not immune to the rise of political movements rooted in Islam that affected the entire North African area, however, particularly in the 1970s and 1980s. At the outset, the palace tried to counter these movements in two ways: by arresting their leaders and trying to suppress the organizations, as it did with all regime opponents regardless of political orientation; and by allowing Saudi Arabia to finance the building of mosques and the staffing of them with preachers spreading Wahabi Salafism. Socially conservative and respectful of the authority of Muslim rulers, Wahabism was seen by the Moroccan monarchy as a useful tool to strengthen its position and authority. The palace was only partially correct on this point, however: together with the Salafism that supported the status quo and the monarchy, a more militant and jihadi Wahabi Salafism that did not hesitate to turn to violence was taking hold in Morocco. By the time the Moroccan authorities became aware of the problem and tried to curb the spread of Salafism, they had a problem on their hands, although never as serious as that faced by other countries in the region. In May 2003, a series of five suicide bombings occurring almost simultaneously shook Casablanca, revealing the existence of a significant jihadi network. A government crackdown on extremist groups, resulting in hundreds of arrests, significantly decreased the threat but did not eliminate it completely. New attacks were thwarted in Casablanca in 2007, but an attack in Marrakesh in 2011 succeeded in killing seventeen people. A rough measure of the influence of jihadi ideas in Morocco is provided by the estimate of young Moroccans recruited by ISIS to fight in Syria and Iraq: Morocco sent an estimated twelve to fifteen hundred, more than any other North African country except Tunisia, which sent four times as many.[8]

In the end, however, Morocco was spared the protracted confrontation between Islamist movements and the regime that the rest of North Africa experienced. A mixture of repression, the willingness to embrace moderate Islamists, the enactment of political reforms, good leadership both from the palace and from some of the Islamist movements, and probably a measure of luck explains the relative success. While working to track down and dismantle the jihadi networks and organizations seeking to entice young Moroccans to go fight with al-Qaeda and later ISIS, the Moroccan government left the door open to other Islamists, who responded by becoming ever more moderate. The country's two major Islamist movements, the forerunner of PJD and al-Adl wal-Ihsan, were both committed to a peaceful political process. Al-Adl wal-Ihsan continued to oppose the monarchy and denounce the manipulation of elections but did not turn to violence. The other movement worked for years to gain acceptance as a legitimate political actor and in 2003 succeeded in legally registering the PJD. The acceptance of the PJD was facilitated by reforms introduced gradually by the aging King Hassan II in the 1990s, which included a more accommodating approach toward all opposition. In previous decades, particularly in the 1960s and 1970s, which Moroccans refer to as the *années de plomb* (the "lead years" or the "years of the bullets"), the palace had responded to its opponents brutally, imprisoning and torturing them and causing many to disappear. In the 1990s, the palace started to curb human rights violations, slightly enhance the role of the parliament, and allow greater space for political parties and organizations of civil society to function in. In this new climate, the organization that eventually gave rise to the PJD gained strength but also moderation.

After Hassan II's death in 1999, the reformist trend continued under his son, King Mohammed VI. The party that would become the PJD, running under the name MPDC (Popular and Constitutional Democratic Movement), gained the third highest number of seats in the 2002 parliamentary elections. Despite the Casablanca terrorist attacks in 2007 and the subsequent crackdown on extremists, the PJD continued to be accepted as a legitimate political organization and to behave as one. In 2011, it gained the largest number of seats in the parliamentary elections, and the king named its leader, Abdelilah Benkirane, as prime minister. After the 2016 elections, the king again tasked Benkirane with forming the government, but he revoked the mandate in April 2017 after a five-month political impasse. Even al-Adl wal-Ihsan was tolerated, although it remained illegal because of its refusal to recognize the religious authority of the king. Seen at one point as a potential major challenge to both the PJD and the regime, it slowly faded in importance. Rejecting both violence and electoral participation, it failed to develop an effective path to power or influence. Eventually, the regime even adopted a more tolerant position vis-à-vis Salafis, whose ranks had been depleted by arrests and imprisonment after the Casablanca attacks.[9]

I have explained the avoidance of confrontation between the regime and Islamists as the result of political choices made by the palace and the PJD, the failure of al-Adl wal-Ihsan to develop a viable path to political relevance, and the Salafis' inability to find a way forward after Casablanca. In other words, it was political dynamics, not the nature of Moroccan society, that shaped the outcome. The religious conservativism of Morocco is the background against which this political game unfolded, rather than an active element in avoiding the confrontation. Even the secular segment of civil society remained relatively unimportant. Moroccans never took to the streets in large numbers to demand change. On February 20, 2011, a large demonstration in Casablanca threatened to turn into an uprising, but the unrest quickly fizzled because of extremely skillful manipulations by the palace. The king immediately announced that a new constitution would be drafted, and by the summer the constitution was approved in a referendum, followed by new elections. The problems that caused the crowds to protest were not solved, but the February 20 movement never managed to seize the initiative again.

A study in early 2016 concluded that activists were channeling their efforts away from direct political demands to cultural activities, making large-scale protest even less likely.[10] Civil society organizations that essentially accept the monarchy and power structure have at times been able to influence the political process, but only when and as far as the king has been willing to accept them. Women's rights groups, for example, worked with the king to bring about an important reform to the personal status code that strengthened recognition of the rights of women. But secular civil society has not been the driver of change, nor has it been a bulwark against religious extremism. The driver of change was the king, and the barriers to extremism were religious conservatism and political participation by moderate Islamists. Moroccan authoritarianism has remained rather benevolent, particularly when compared to the forms it took in other North African countries.

Algeria: Religious Extremism in an Unsettled Society

Algeria presents a stark contrast to Morocco: its society is much more secular, yet religious extremism became the central determinant of its political and social dynamics in the 1990s. The government has addressed and continues to address challenges through repression and confrontation rather than accommodation and co-optation. Organized civil society has been stifled. After a ferocious ten-year war between the government and Islamic extremists during the 1990s, jihadi extremism seems to have largely disappeared from the society, although professional extremist groups, including al-Qaeda in the Islamic Maghreb, continue to battle in remote parts of the country. While a resurgence of religious extremism cannot be ruled out in Algeria, overall the nation seems to be following a trajectory quite different from that of neighboring countries.

On the surface, the tradition of popular Islam in Algeria is not very different from Morocco's. It is not puritanical, and it is heavily influenced by Sufism. The Algerian landscape is dotted with the whitewashed tombs of "saints" that are the destination of pilgrimages and places of religious celebration. There is, however, a different twist to the popular religion in Algeria. Whereas in Morocco the practice of Islam has never been challenged and has always been encouraged by the authorities, religion in Algeria was both suppressed and manipulated during the 130 years of French occupation. The French believed it important to show nominal respect for Islam, lest it become a focal point for anticolonial opposition as it had been at the beginning of the conquest, but they also tried to control it. As a result, at independence in 1962, many Algerians turned to religion in order to affirm their identity and make a political statement. The beginning of radical Islamism goes back to the immediate postindependence period, although analysts at the time, this writer included, overlooked the importance of this trend, focusing instead on the more visible attempt at socialist transformation launched by the government.[11] Even if not extremist in terms of its dominant ideas, Islam in postcolonial Algeria was a point of contention, not just a comfortable tradition people could take for granted.

Algerian society was radicalized by other experiences as well. While the first was the colonial experience, which lasted longer and affected the society more deeply than in most other countries, the war for independence was also a radicalizing experience. Lasting from 1954 to 1962, it was brutal. Algerians were not granted their independence by a colonial power that had accepted the days of empire were over; they had to fight for it. France considered Algeria, where over one million French settlers lived, as a department of metropolitan France and was determined to maintain control over it. The war was bitter and divided Algerian society between the nationalists in the FLN and some four hundred fifty thousand harkis (native Muslim Algerians) who served on the side of France. Many of these collaborators were killed in the chaotic months after independence, but most stayed on in Algeria.

Algeria was further traumatized by the sudden departure of virtually all settlers at independence, which left a vacuum in the economy. This disruption was compounded by a socialist experiment that created a lasting problem of sluggish growth and state domination of the economy. Although the more doctrinaire phase of the socialist experiment ended with the 1965 coup d'état that deposed President Ahmed Ben Bella and installed Houari Boumediene in his place, state control over the economy continued. So did the grip on the government of the FLN and of the generation that fought the war for independence—Abdelaziz Bouteflika, the current president, was one of the early leaders of the FLN. Because of the country's complicated and trauma-laden history, Algerian society did not have a comfortable tradition, religious or secular, to rely on. Everything required a choice, and all choices were contested. And there was no broadly accepted religious authority with a claim to legitimacy.

As part of the postindependence efforts to reclaim Algeria's religious and cultural traditions, the al-Qiyam organization was formed in 1964, advocating the rejection of values that did not stem from Islam. The Boumediene regime tried to suppress al-Qiyam as an independent organization but also embraced some of its ideas. The regime promoted the teaching of Arabic, and in 1976 it declared Islam the state religion. French policies had left Algeria short of teachers of Arabic and religion, so Algeria had to import them from other countries. Many came from Egypt, and among them were Muslim Brothers who brought with them not only Arabic and religion but also political Islam. Radical ideas took hold easily in a country with a troubled past and a tumultuous present. Although oil and gas provided Algeria with a ready source of revenue, the government was extremely slow to invest money to improve the lives of its citizens, devoting funds and efforts instead to the launching of ambitious industrialization schemes that failed. For a long time it neglected housing, services, and the most basic urban infrastructure such as waterworks, creating widespread discontent that could find no outlet in political activity, which was tightly controlled by the government.

In the single-party system that was enforced in Algeria from independence until 1989, when the constitution was amended, religious ideas and organizations provided an alternative for people dissatisfied with the status quo. During the 1980s an estimated two thousand five hundred Algerians flocked to Afghanistan to join the American-backed mujahideen (Afghan jihadists) in their fight against the Soviet Union. As in other countries, the return of the fighters—the Afghan Arabs, as they were dubbed—reinforced the spread of jihadi ideas. Many Algerians readily embraced the use of violence: the war of independence had prepared them to see violence as a tool for success, while nothing in the character of the regime suggested that a purely political battle could bring about change. Whereas in Morocco the government's willingness to legalize Islamist parties and the latter's determination to be recognized as legitimate political participants created a virtuous circle of moderation, in Algeria the combination of government inflexibility and the societal tradition of violence created a vicious circle culminating in the civil war of the 1990s.

The precipitating factor was the government's 1989 decision to amend the constitution, abolishing the single-party system and allowing multi-party elections. This decision was prompted by growing unrest, including riots triggered by the hardship imposed on the country by a lethal combination of mismanagement and the collapse of oil prices. The sudden opening had unexpected consequences. When the ban on political organizing was lifted, Islamists were the first to take advantage of the political space. Such a scenario has become familiar since the 2011 uprisings, but it was not then and caught the government unaware. The Islamic Salvation Front (Front

Islamique du Salut, or FIS) was formed in September 1989. In June 1990, it won a large majority in local elections. In December 1991, it won 47 percent of the vote in the first round of the parliamentary elections, leaving the FLN a distant second with 23 percent of the vote. At that point the military intervened, cancelled the election, and de facto seized power with the full backing of secularists who were alarmed by the extreme statements coming from the FIS, which suggested that there would be no place for them in an FIS-ruled country.

Algeria was at war for the next ten years, with atrocities committed by all sides. The extremism of jihadi organizations was matched by the extreme repression by the military. Proponents of moderation and reconciliation had no hope of being heard, while rival armed Islamic groups proliferated, the most important of which were the Armed Islamic Movement (Mouvement Islamique Armé, or MIA), the Islamic Salvation Army (Armée Islamique du Salut, or AIS, the FIS's armed wing), the Armed Islamic Group (Group Islamique Arme, or GIA), and the Salafist Group for Preaching and Combat (Groupe Islamiste pour la Predication et le Combat, or GSPC).

Repeated government attempts to negotiate with the FIS, seen as the most moderate of the jihadi groups, failed until 1997, when the weakened organization reached a truce with the government. Nevertheless, fighting did not stop completely until the election of President Abdelaziz Bouteflika in 1999. He immediately launched an initiative to pacify the country not by force but by a policy of forgiving and forgetting.[12] The initiative called for amnesty for all who had fought in jihadi organizations and in the military, with no attempt to investigate what had happened or hold perpetrators accountable. The initiative, much criticized abroad by human rights organizations, restored peace but without justice or accountability. The most radical Islamist elements never surrendered, becoming instead the nucleus of al-Qaeda in the Islamic Maghreb (AQIM), which operates to this day.[13]

There is little indication that the appeal of extremist jihadi ideas remains widespread. For example, Algeria has apparently contributed only 200 to 250 fighters to ISIS in Syria and Iraq.[14] The lingering conflict in Algeria itself is limited to remote mountains in the east and in border areas deep in the Sahara, where AQIM operates across borders, smuggling weapons and drugs, kidnapping for ransom, and establishing links to organizations in countries of the Sahel. In fact, there is little indication that most Algerians, who have been prone to violence and extremism for decades, are inclined to turn to violence or even to extralegal politics at this point. Alone among the North African countries, Algeria did not experience an uprising in 2011, not even one as modest as Morocco's. It is difficult to explain why this is the case. Some have suggested that the extreme violence of the 1990s has taught Algerians a lesson about the danger of extremism. Whatever the explanation, jihadi organizations in Algeria have become highly specialized groups of professionals fighting against the military. It is also possible that Algerians, governed by an aging, sick president, are simply waiting for his death before they act.

Since the end of the civil war, Algeria has reached a stability of sorts under a government that respects the form of electoral democracy by holding regular multiparty elections. But political parties are weak, including several Islamic parties that have embraced electoral politics and are allowed to legally participate in elections. In fact, one of them, the Movement for a Society of Peace (MSP), has been part of the cabinet but has never had any influence over its decisions, as party leaders readily admit. As a result, the MSP eventually withdrew from the coalition and joined the opposition instead. But the party later rejoined the government, having apparently concluded that being part of a feckless opposition was not an avenue to influence, either.[15]

Secular civil society organizations struggle in Algeria, as in the rest of the region, under restrictive legislation, shortage of funds, and limited experience.[16] The government, furthermore, has not seen the need to partner with them, as has been the case in Morocco, in order to strengthen its democratic credentials—democracy is not one of its concerns. Prodemocracy and human rights organizations that, if influential, could provide an ideological rallying point in the battle against Islamic extremism and autocratic government, remain marginal. Broad social movements have failed to emerge in Algeria, either on the side of extremism or on the side of democracy. Algerian society is still unsettled but also appears unorganized.

Algeria thus remains a country controlled from the top down. Religion, either in its conservative popular form or in the form of the radical organizations that plunged the country into violence in the 1990s, does not explain the persistence of authoritarianism. Rather, with radical Islamist organizations crushed militarily and then silenced by amnesty, weak political parties without ideologies, struggling civil society groups, and a population that appears largely passive at present, the country is authoritarian almost by default, and this allows an octogenarian president in extremely poor health to remain the linchpin of the system.

Tunisia: The Backlash against Secular Authoritarianism

Tunisia, a country not usually considered riddled with extremism, has sent more people to fight with jihadi movements than any other country in North Africa. As of late 2015, the number of Tunisian fighters joining extremist groups in Syria and Iraq was estimated at six to seven thousand, the highest number for any country, although the population of Tunisia is less than eleven million.[17] The dynamics of religious conservativism, extremism, and secular civil society in Tunisia are particularly complex and at times baffling. In part, this is because Tunisia is often represented as a "modern" secular and moderate country with a growing economy, where extremism is represented more by leftist labor unions and political parties than by Islamic extremism. The reality is more complicated.

As in the rest of North Africa, traditional Islam in Tunisia is not extreme or bound by puritanical, rigid doctrine. Traditionally, it has been the religion of a peasant population and has also been influenced by Sufism, although to a lesser extent than in Morocco and Algeria. The roots of religious extremism thus are not buried in ancient history and an entrenched culture.

After independence in 1956, Tunisia was governed by secular leaders who did not try to control religious practices. The constitution enacted under Habib Bourguiba, the first president, did not mention sharia as a guide for all legislation, as Arab constitutions tend to do, but simply recognized that Islam was the religion of the country, just as Arabic was its language. Bourguiba did defy traditional Islam by outlawing polygamy and going further than any other Arab leader at the time in recognizing the rights of women. He also occasionally defied Islamic tenets, such as by provocatively sipping juice while delivering a talk on TV during the Ramadan fast. But people were free to practice religion as they wanted, and the state continued to pay imams and finance the upkeep of mosques. By and large, the relation between the state and religion was one of live and let live. The spread of religious extremism thus cannot be explained as a reaction to a state-led effort to impose secularism under Bourguiba.

Bourguiba's successor, Zine El Abidine Ben Ali, who came to power in 1989, tried to follow the same moderate approach on the issue of religion, but he confronted a different situation. The process of re-Islamization was underway. Tunisians, like their neighbors in the entire region, were returning more openly to religious practices. More people observed the Ramadan fast, and more women wore the head scarf. Ben Ali, who was not a devout Muslim according to all accounts, went along with the trend, going to the mosque on major holidays and allowing one of his daughters to wear the head scarf. But he drew a very firm line when the return to Islam took on a political character, becoming a threat to his power. The emergence of radicalism in Tunisian society is explained in part by the political battles between an emerging political Islamist trend and an unyielding authoritarian regime.

An organization called the Movement of Islamic Tendency was launched in 1981, when Bourguiba was still in power, and the government immediately labeled it a dangerous radical group. When movement members joined bread riots in 1984, the government carried out a wave of arrests, but the movement survived. Some of its leaders and members, foremost the present chairman of the Ennahda Party, Rachid Ghannouchi, were far from radical. In fact, they were advocates for moderate Islamism, rejecting violence and accepting democracy, pluralism, and dialogue with the West. Ghannouchi published major and influential works on these issues and influenced reformist thinking across the region. But even moderate Islamists were political, criticized the regime, and wanted change. This automatically made them dangerous in the eyes of the regime. When the Movement of Islamic Tendency, renamed Ennahda or Renaissance, was not allowed to participate in the 1989 elections, it still managed to compete by running independent candidates and won 10–17 percent of the vote, according to official estimates that probably played down the success of Ennahda. This demonstration of popularity made the moderate movement even more suspicious in the eyes of the Ben Ali regime. By 1992 most of the party's leadership was in prison or in exile, and the movement disappeared from sight. But enough of the organization survived for Ennahda to revive instantaneously in 2011, when the uprising forced Ben Ali into exile and political prisoners were released. In October of the same year, the party had reestablished itself well enough to win the plurality of votes in the election for the constituent assembly.

Not all Islamists were willing to follow Ghannouchi and the founders of Ennahda in the acceptance of democratic politics and moderation. As early as 1988, a Tunisian Islamic Front broke off from the Movement of Islamic Tendency. Many of its members were imprisoned or exiled, and some went to fight with the mujahideen in Afghanistan. Others embraced scientific Salafism and became quickly visible in the immediate aftermath of the uprising, even registering a political party, the Reform Front, in 2012.

The violent jihadi trend also quickly gained ground after the uprising. Rachid Ghannouchi himself explained the rise of Salafism as partly the consequence of the absence of Ennahda and its moderating influence from Tunisia during the years of imprisonment or exile. But even after reestablishing itself in Tunisia, Ennahda did not have much influence on radical Salafis, who represented a younger generation, radicalized by the US intervention in Iraq and the Palestinian Intifada.[18] Tunisia's main jihadi organization, Ansar al-Sharia, emerged from this younger group in 2011, but it did not immediately get the attention it deserved. Most Tunisian and foreign observers tended to focus on the presence in Tunisia of scientific Salafis, who were not considered particularly dangerous.

Rachid Ghannouchi was among the many who did not initially appreciate the severity of the jihadist problem, arguing that even extremists were "our children," misguided and in need of being educated, and that he would not inflict on them the extreme repression Ben Ali had used against Ennahda. Many analysts fell into the same trap of dismissing radicals as a small minority. A December 2013 study, for example, estimated the number of jihadi Salafists in Tunisia at no more than five thousand, implying that they did not constitute a serious danger.[19] In reality the number was much greater, and in any case five thousand jihadists do not represent a small danger. Even the Tunisian security services, in disarray after the fall of Ben Ali, did not appear to have taken much notice of the growing jihadi trend initially.

But by early 2013, the extent of the jihadi presence could not be ignored, and Ghannouchi was forced to admit that gentle persuasion would not convince the radicals to change their ways. The Chaambi Mountains in western Tunisia had become a no-go area, and a serious attack in July 2014 showed that security forces cold not easily contain the problem. Terrorist attacks increased, targeting tourist destinations, such as the Bardo Museum in Tunis and beach resorts on the coast, and inflicting serious damage on an important source of income.

Tunisia's problem with Islamic extremists, which originally grew out of a mixture of social and economic neglect and political repression, was further compounded by what was happening all around, particularly in Libya and the Sahel countries, creating a region of chaos where arms and people moved freely across borders. At the same time, the rise of ISIS in Syria and

Iraq also provided both a model of militant jihadism and an appealing destination for young Tunisians anxious to practice their ideals and seek adventure.

Secular civil society in Tunisia, while growing steadily since the uprising in 2011, has not been an effective counterweight to the spread of radicalism in this historically moderate country. Neither have the established political parties, including Ennahda. It is not that Tunisia does not have civil society organizations. The problem is that these organizations are not rooted in the social milieus where young people are recruited and radicalized and where jihadism has its greatest appeal. Secular civil society simply belongs to a different world. Furthermore, in Tunisia most young people, not just the jihadists, are disaffected by the political system: participation by young voters in the 2014 parliamentary and presidential elections was extremely low, according to all observers, with many young people openly professing scorn for all participating parties and organizations.

One segment of secular Tunisian civil society that has played an important part in the post-2011 Tunisian transition is the labor union movement, which has its roots in the French labor movement and still has a strong socialist orientation—there is more than a whiff of Marxist analysis in the discourse of the older Tunisian General Labour Union (UGTT) cadres. Despite its radicalism, the UGTT does not move in the same milieu as the jihadists. The unions cater to what some Marxist scholars have called a labor aristocracy, people who have regular jobs in the formal sector and are oblivious to the problems that afflict people with precarious jobs in the informal sector. And the labor movement, according to all available information, is not where jihadists do their recruiting or find most of their followers. Unions appear to be as divorced from radical Islam as the civil society of educated, westernized people that attracts the attention and the financing of democracy promoters in the West. Younger radicals in Tunisia appear to be turning to Islam, not to Marx and Lenin, for inspiration.

Egypt: The Military-Muslim Brotherhood Clash

President Abdel Fattah el-Sisi likes to represent Egypt as a country that has undergone two revolutions—in 2011 and again in 2013. In reality, Egypt is probably the least changed among the North African countries. Despite the now familiar, dramatic scenes of the huge crowds demonstrating in Tahrir Square for the overthrow of President Hosni Mubarak in January and

February 2011, power always remained firmly in the hands of the military, where it resides to this day. Far from being revolutionary, the country can be best characterized as centrist. The political parties are all grouped in the center of the political spectrum. Parties of the left are essentially nonexistent. The Muslim Brotherhood and the Party for Justice and Development that the Brotherhood set up in 2011 were also moderate centrist organizations, despite the current government's accusation that they were terrorist. Even Salafis mostly opted for peaceful political participation by forming the al-Nour Party, and when that road was closed, they turned to quietism rather than violence. Jihadi Salafists do exist, of course, and Ansar Beit al-Maqdisi, the major violent, jihadi organization, has even declared its allegiance to ISIS and proclaimed Sinai to be a province of the Islamic State. Nevertheless, violent extremism in Egypt appears to be concentrated in and controlled by organized groups, rather than widespread through the society.

The interplay of violent extremism, religious conservativism, and secular forces in Egypt unfolds against the background of a predominant moderate and centrist tradition, which has been able to amalgamate many cultural trends over the decades, but has essentially rejected radicalism. Part of the Egyptian elite embraced secularism already in the early twentieth century, and liberal ideas and feminism took hold among the educated. Egypt experienced a second secularizing experience during the Nasser period, with the enormous popularity of Arab nationalism and socialism, which emphasized the Arab rather than Muslim identity of Egypt and made the Arab world, rather than the Islamic umma, the frame of reference. Despite these influences, most Egyptians remained deeply religious, indeed unquestioningly so because no events challenged either the Muslim or the Egyptian identity of the population. In a 2011 survey carried out by the Arab Barometer, only 2 percent of respondents classified themselves as nonreligious. Even among Copts, identity appeared to be based more on tradition than on a deliberate affirmation of a separate identity.

This paradox of a society that went through several secularizing influences but remained unquestioningly religious can be most easily understood by considering the class structure of Egyptian society. This structure consists of a small, educated elite quite divorced from the rest of the population and a large, barely schooled population only marginally affected by new political and cultural trends. Even today Egypt has an illiteracy rate of about 25 percent (and undoubtedly a much higher rate of functional illiteracy). The rate was around 75 percent overall (and 90 percent for women) when Nasser came to power in 1952. This has left many Egyptians on the margins of cultural influences.

All Egyptian presidents, from Gamal Abdel Nasser to Abdel Fattah el-Sisi, have recognized that religion is a central feature of the Egyptian identity and have tried to harness it to their advantage. Nasser did not try to impose secularism on the country, but he made sure to have the religious establishment under his control and thus on his side. He put religious institutions, and the land that was part of their endowments, under a new Ministry of Religious Endowments, which also gained jurisdiction over Al-Azhar University, the ancient center of Islamic learning. On the other hand, he repressed the Muslim Brotherhood, not because it was religious, but because it was political and he could not bring it under his control.

Anwar al-Sadat also recognized the importance of religious institutions and kept them under government control. But he tried to enlist the Muslim Brotherhood in his project to rid the country of the Nasserist influence, which he saw as an obstacle to the consolidation of his own power. He thus allowed the Brotherhood and Islamist groups in general to resume operating, although unofficially. (The Muslim Brotherhood was only legalized in 2011 and banned again in September 2013.) The consequences were much more far-reaching than Sadat had envisaged. Culturally, there was a visible re-Islamization of the society, manifested in the way people dressed, originally as a result of the distribution of free Islamic garb to impoverished university students and then of escalating social pressure. Such pressure induced many young people from secular families to defy their parents by returning to religious practices, which in turn often convinced parents to do the same.

The most dramatic result of the easing of the restriction on Islamist movements was not cultural but political. The Muslim Brotherhood proper reemerged as a socially conservative organization, intent on proselytizing but also determined to participate openly in the legal political process. A number of Muslim Brotherhood leaders elaborated theories about why political participation was desirable even if the conditions for an Islamist state did not exist yet, and accepted the ideas of democracy and pluralism.[20] These ideas, similar to those of Rachid Ghannouchi in Tunisia, gained considerable acceptance. When Sadat's reforms reopened the way to multiparty elections, the Muslim Brotherhood, still a banned organization officially, found ways to participate by putting candidates on other party's lists or having them run as independent. In 2005, the Brotherhood obtained its most important political victory yet by winning 20 percent of parliamentary seats. In the 2012 election, the only one in which it could participate legally, it gained 37.5 percent of the vote. The Salafi al-Nour Party won 27.8 percent.

The easing of restrictions on Islamists under Sadat revived the Brotherhood but also allowed the radical Islamists to organize. This was certainly not the intention of the president, but two major extremist groups, Gama'a al-Islamiyya and Islamic Jihad, were formed. They became even angrier and more radicalized when, in a sudden move, Sadat opened contacts with the Israeli government, traveling to Jerusalem in 1977 and signing the Camp David Accord in September 1978. Egypt's omnipresent security services knew of the existence of the radical movements, and in February 1981 they conducted a wave of arrests that aimed at dismantling them. However, they missed the presence of extremist cells in the military. The full extent of the problem became dramatically evident on October 6, 1981, when Sadat was assassinated by members of an Islamist cell, who opened fire on him during the yearly military parade commemorating Egypt's success in crossing the Suez Canal into Israel-occupied Sinai in the 1973 war.

During the thirty years of the presidency of Hosni Mubarak, Sadat's successor, Islam in Egypt continued to become more political, but it evolved in several different directions against the background of the conservative, moderate, and largely apolitical traditional Islam to which much of the population adheres. First, the religious establishment, represented by Al-Azhar University, Dar al-Ifta (the organization officially entitled to issue fatwas), and the Ministry of Religious Endowments with its control over mosques and imams, gained both more autonomy from the government and more influence over it. Since Nasser's days, Egyptian governments relied on the religious establishment to burnish their Islamic credentials and increase their legitimacy, but they also turned religious institutions into state agencies. Nasser, for example, decided Al-Azhar should become a full-fledged modern university as well as a venerable center of Islamic learning and introduced modern faculties such as economics, business, medicine, and agriculture without consulting its leaders. Under Mubarak the relation changed somewhat. Confronted with the growth of Islamist organizations, he needed the religious establishment's backing to maintain his legitimacy, and in return he allowed Al-Azhar to acquire more influence on the society. The visible re-Islamization of Egyptian society that many opponents blamed on the

Muslim Brotherhood was also, possibly more, the result of the greater influence gained by the religious establishment.[21]

Second, the Muslim Brotherhood continued to develop, turning into a strong organization capable of asserting itself politically even while banned. The Brotherhood reach was extended beyond the confines of its rigid hierarchy with strict rules for membership, thanks to a vast network of charitable, educational, and health associations that constituted a veritable Muslim civil society. Mubarak's policy toward the Muslim Brotherhood was highly ambiguous. The organization was illegal, and Mubarak did not trust it, but he also saw it as a useful tool in the fight against extremists. As the Brotherhood grew in strength, government concern mounted and repression increased, with thousands of Brothers, including the top leadership, constantly rotating in and out of jail. At the same time, the organization participated openly in parliamentary elections and those for the leadership of the professional syndicates, which it came to dominate. Nor did Muslim Brothers try to disguise their identity. It was always striking to an outsider how openly the identity of Muslim Brothers was acknowledged and even accepted. There were clearly redlines to what the organization could and could not do, but the redlines were not obvious, and members operated openly.

Third, scientific Salafi organizations also became stronger. They were tolerated and even initially encouraged by the government because they seemed to be focusing on *dawa* and on creating communities where their members could support each other in living their lives according to sharia precepts. As a result, they were not talked about much in Mubarak's Egypt, and most people, including the Muslim Brothers, were caught by surprise when the Salafi al-Nour Party was launched, participated in the 2011–12 elections, and placed a strong second.

The fourth development that took place in this period concerns jihadi Salafism, and it is the most difficult to explain. The regime's policy toward the jihadi groups was clear: members were to be imprisoned and the network destroyed. Leaders who recanted while in jail were eventually rehabilitated—in 2011, after Mubarak's overthrow, Gama'a al-Islamiyya even formed a party, called Building and Development, and went on to contest the elections. Although jihadi groups continued to exist, their presence and activities were muted, for reasons about which I can only speculate. Security services were certainly strong in Egypt—but they had also missed the military cell that assassinated Sadat. Some jihadi leaders imprisoned after Sadat's assassination repented and tried to convince their followers to do the same. A leader of Islamic Jihad, Ayman al-Zawahiri, went on to join al-Qaeda, which he now leads, and took his battles outside Egypt. After the uprising, when extremists in other countries became more active, Egyptian jihadists were quiet, possibly waiting to see what would happen with the Muslim Brotherhood controlling the government. What is clear, though, is that the coup d'état that deposed President Mohammed Morsi in July 2013 suddenly brought jihadi Salafists into the open again. Ansar Beit al-Maqdisi, the major jihadi organization in Egypt, has been at war with the security forces in Sinai since that time, and violent attacks take place more sporadically in Cairo, other cities, and even the western desert.

Yet religious extremism does not appear to have penetrated deeply into Egyptian society. There are organizations, to be sure, and they are active and dangerous. Security forces cannot bring the Sinai under control. But contrary to government propaganda, which portrays all members and sympathizers of the Muslim Brotherhood as violent extremists, Egyptians are not responding in large numbers to the call for jihad. Egypt has a population of over ninety million, yet it has sent only six hundred to one thousand young men to fight with ISIS. The apparent lack of penetration of the jihadi message in Egypt might be explained by the degree to which jihadi Salafism competes in Egypt with the Salafism of the al-Nour Party, the Islam of the Muslim Brotherhood, and the proregime Islam of the religious establishment, not to mention the relaxed popular Islam. Although the explanation is elusive, the facts are clear. But it is possible that extremist Islamists will spread in the future as a result of the government's repression of all forms of Islam other than what is controlled by the state.

Certainly, there is no reason to believe that the lack of penetration by jihadi Salafism in Egypt is the result of the strength of its secular civil society or its secular political parties. Egypt has a number of active, dedicated, courageous organizations that have been working to defend human rights and women's rights for decades, operating under difficult conditions. Laws regulating civil society organizations have always been restrictive, and successive attempts to revise them have resulted in even more restrictions, including the recent banning of all foreign funding. But these organizations do not have a popular base or widespread appeal.

Labor unions, which were a conspicuous and influential component of secular civil society in Tunisia, never liberated themselves of government control in Egypt, essentially remaining part of the state apparatus. A parallel movement to develop independent labor unions hardly had the time to get established before the 2013 coup d'état brought down new restrictions on it. We can only speculate whether more time would have allowed the independent unions to grow or whether government restrictions on all independent activity would have made it unlikely. In any event, it did not happen. Workers, who never ceased to protest on their own, outside the control of labor unions, did their best to appear apolitical in the hope of gaining at least some economic concessions. Human rights organizations penetrated Egyptian society even less than labor unions did. The same is true of secular political organizations, which were never able to build strong popular constituencies. Secular civil and political societies were always outbid for influence by traditional Islam, the religious establishment, and the Muslim Brotherhood.

The Different Worlds of Religious and Secular Civil Society

One of the major challenges confronting North Africa has been the spread of Islamic extremism. It is by no means the only challenge and, arguably, it may not even be the most serious, but it is the one addressed in this broad overview.

Although the countries differ considerably from each other, a few overall conclusions can be drawn. First, the spreading of extremism is not related to the character of traditional Islam, which in all four countries is conservative but moderate, free of dogmatism, and open in various degrees to Sufi influence. But if extremist ideas are not rooted in Islam as traditionally practiced in these countries, the conservative tradition has not stopped the appeal of extremist ideas, either.

Second, the acceptance of extremism is rooted in politics, not in religion. Extremist ideas have a stronger appeal as an alternative to the status quo when there are no peaceful avenues for change. This conclusion, hardly original but worth highlighting, is suggested by the fact that Morocco has been more successful in containing and even reintegrating jihadi Salafists than its neighbors, and by the fact that the explosion of violence perpetrated by extremist groups in Egypt followed the closure of the political space that resulted from the July 2013 military coup d'état. The case of Tunisia, however, contradicts this conclusion, in that jihadi Salafism seems to have penetrated the society deeply despite the relative openness of the postuprising governments.

Third, it appears that Islamic extremism does not need to be deeply rooted in the society to be a threat. In Tunisia, extremism has penetrated the society at the popular and cultural level, so that young people are attracted to the call for jihad in high numbers. But in Egypt, jihadi Salafism does not appear to have penetrated deeply, as seen by the small number of young people going to fight with the Islamic State in Iraq and Syria. The threat posed by radical Islamists still exists, but it comes from well-organized groups of professional jihadists.

Fourth, the reasons why extremist ideas resonate vary widely from country to country. North Africa shares a background of poverty, government mismanagement, social inequities, and lack of dignity, but that is not a sufficient explanation. Such conditions exist in the majority of countries in the world, and yet most of the time people do not turn to extremism.[22] And when people revolt, they can embrace different ideologies. Even in the Muslim Middle East, radical ideas until the 1970s were Arab socialism and nationalism, not jihadi Salafism. It is possible to identify specific reasons why a certain country becomes radicalized—for example, in the case of Algeria, being a society traumatized by successive experiences and never at peace with itself and its identity made radicalization easier—but these are ad hoc explanations from which it is difficult to derive overall conclusions.

A striking conclusion concerning all four countries is that, in the battle against religious extremism, secular civil society does not appear to be a factor. This is a harsh conclusion, and it goes against the deeply held liberal assumption that supporting the development of a strong secular civil society can help stem the diffusions of religious extremism. The four countries offer no evidence to support this assumption. Secular civil society organizations move in a different world from the one where radical Islamist groups operate. They talk to different publics and in different languages. In some cases, secular civil society organizations simply despise the people who are more open to Islamist appeals—this is very evident, for example, in the case of women's rights organizations from Morocco to Egypt. This harsh conclusion about the influence of secular civil society organizations on the spreading of radical Islamist ideas should not be construed as a condemnation of secular civil society in general. It is important to recognize the courage and determination of many individuals and organizations that fight against serious odds in recording and denouncing abuses and pushing for reforms. And serious discussion is needed on the issue of secular civil society in North Africa, but this goes well beyond the scope of this chapter. The conclusions here are restricted to the impact of secular civil society on the spread of religious radicalism.

Finally, it is difficult to find direct links between the character of Islam and the nature of civil society in the Maghreb and the authoritarianism that remains in evidence everywhere, even in somewhat less repressive countries such as Tunisia and Morocco. Islam in the region is not particularly rigid, nor is it monolithic. Rather, traditional Islam is fairly tolerant, softened by Sufi practices. The radical interpretations of Islam are the ideology of political movements, not necessarily deeply embedded in the societies of Maghreb countries, and always in competition with the interpretations of Islam of the religious establishments, the governments, and even popular views. Secular civil society is more homogeneous ideologically, although it is organizationally fragmented and capable of reaching out to only a small portion of the population. But there is enough cultural diversity in all Maghreb countries to potentially sustain pluralistic political systems. The explanation for the persistence of authoritarianism thus should be sought not in the character of religion or of secular civil society, but in the political dynamics of the countries—an issue that goes far beyond what is discussed in this chapter.

MARINA OTTAWAY is a Middle East scholar at the Woodrow Wilson International Center for Scholars. Among her numerous books are *Algeria: The Politics of a Socialist Revolution* and *Democracy Challenged: The Rise of Semi-authoritarianism.*

Notes

1. I am using the term *civil society* in the way it is normally used by organizations seeking to promote democracy: modern civil society encompasses the world of professional nongovernmental organizations, often receiving financing from outside the country. This definition is narrow and excludes organizations that can be influential, but this is not the place for a broader discussion.

2. The name Muslim Brotherhood is used in this article to refer to a specific Egyptian organization by that name, rejecting the recent practice by the Egyptian government to label all Islamist organizations as "Muslim Brotherhood," because such use confuses discussions. Organizations in countries other than Egypt that share many of the ideas are referred to here as "Muslim Brotherhood–inspired organizations."

3. Because some of these trends are violent and extremist, some consider the entire organization to be so.

4. In the late 1990s and early 2000s, Islamist political organizations or parties were openly participating in politics in seven Arab countries: Morocco, Algeria, Egypt, Jordan, Kuwait, Bahrain, and Yemen.

5. Anouar Boukhars, "The Politics of North African Salafism," *Orient* 2 (2016): 52–60.

6. The author had endless discussions with Arab politicians and activists who strongly objected to her use of the term *secular* in *Getting to Pluralism*, edited by Marina Ottaway and Amr Hamzawy (Washington, DC: Carnegie Endowment for International Peace, 2009). Interestingly, nobody could offer an alternative other than *leftists* or *liberals*, which do not cover the variety of secular organizations.

7. Marina Ottaway and Meredith Riley, "Morocco: From Top-Down Reform to Political Transition?," Carnegie Papers, no. 71 (September 2006), Carnegie Endowment for International Peace, https://carnegieendowment.org/files/cp71_ottaway_final.pdf.

8. *Foreign Fighters: An Updated Assessment of the Flow of Foreign Fighters into Syria and Iraq* (New York: Soufan Group, December 2015), http://soufangroup.com/wp-content /uploads/2015/12/TSG_ForeignFightersUpdate_FINAL3.pdf.

9. Salim Hmimnat, "Recalibrating Morocco's Approach to Salafism," *Sada*, January 14, 2016, Carnegie Endowment for International Peace, http://carnegieendowment.org/sada/62463.

10. Dörthe Engelcke, "Morocco's Changing Civil Society," *Sada*, January 7, 2016, Carnegie Endowment for International Peace, http://carnegieendowment.org/sada/62417.

11. David Ottaway and Marina Ottaway, *Algeria: The Politics of a Socialist Revolution* (Berkeley and Los Angeles: University of California Press, 1970).

12. Human Rights Watch, *Impunity in the Name of Reconciliation: Algerian President's Peace Plan Faces National Vote September 29* (September 2005), www.hrw.org/backgrounder /mena/algeria0905/index.htm.

13. Christopher Chivvis and Andrew Liepman, *North Africa's Menace: AQIM's Evolution and the U.S. Policy Response* (RAND Corporation, 2013), https://www.rand.org/content/dam /rand/pubs/research_reports/RR400/RR415/RAND_RR415.pdf.

14. *Foreign Fighters: An Updated Assessment of the Flow of Foreign Fighters into Syria and Iraq* (New York: Soufan Group, December 2015), http://soufangroup.com/wp-content /uploads/2015/12/TSG_ForeignFightersUpdate_FINAL3.pdf.

15. Dalia Ghanem-Yazbeck, "The Future of Algeria's Main Islamist Party," April 14, 2014, Carnegie Endowment for International Peace, http://carnegie-mec.org/2015/04/14/future-of -algeria-s-main-islamist-party-pub-59769.

16. Foundation for the Future, "Mapping of Civil Society Organizations in Algeria," September 2012, www.foundationforthefuture.org.

17. Ibid.

18. Fabio Merone and Francesco Cavatorta, "The Emergence of Salafism in Tunisia," *Jadaliyya*, August 17, 2012.

19. Christopher Alexander, "Tunisia's Islamists II: The Salafis," December 2013, Woodrow Wilson International Center for Scholars, https://www.wilsoncenter.org/article /tunisias-islamists-ii-the-salafis.

20. Nathan Brown, Amr Hamzawy, and Marina Ottaway, "Islamist Movements and the Democratic Processes in the Arab World: Exploring the Grey Zones," Carnegie Papers, no. 67 (March 2006), Carnegie Endowment for International Peace, https://carnegieendowment .org/files/cp_67_grayzones_final.pdf.

21. Steven Barraclough, "Al-Azhar between the Government and the Islamists," *Middle East Journal* 52, no. 2 (Spring 1998); Bassma Kodmani, "The Danger of Political Exclusion: Egypt's Islamist Problem," Carnegie Papers, no. 63 (October 2005), Carnegie Endowment for International Peace, https://carnegieendowment.org/files/CP63.Kodmani.FINAL.pdf.

22. This point was argued cogently by Barrington Moore Jr. in *Injustice: The Social Bases of Obedience and Revolt* (London: Palgrave Macmillan, 1978).

2

DO POLITICAL AND ECONOMIC GRIEVANCES FOSTER SUPPORT FOR POLITICAL ISLAM IN THE POST–ARAB SPRING MAGHREB?

Mark Tessler

Should Islamic institutions, officials, and laws play a central role, or at least a very important role, in government and political affairs? To what extent and in what ways should they influence these affairs? These are among the most important and most contested questions pertaining to governance in the North Africa and the rest of the Middle East at the present time. As the question was put in the title of a May 2011 lecture by Hamadi Jebali, the secretary-general of Tunisia's Islamist al-Nahda Party, "What Kind of Democracy for the New Tunisia: Islamic or Secular?"[1] Jebali asked this question after the fall of the Ben Ali regime but before the October 2011 parliamentary election that his party won. Writing during this period, Olivier Roy, a prominent student of political Islam, made clear that the salience of questions about Islam's political role are not limited to Tunisia. What is at stake, he wrote, "is the reformulation of religion's place in the public sphere." Considering the role of Islamic law in particular, he noted that there exists "broad agreement that constitutions should announce the 'Muslim' identity of society and the state. Yet there is similar agreement on the proposition that Shari'a is not an autonomous and complete system of law that can replace 'secular' law."[2]

As these observations affirm, the place of Islam in government and political affairs, however contested it may be, is an important element in the political systems taking shape in the post–Arab Spring Maghreb and the broader Arab world. The region's political leaders, ranging from quasi-authoritarian to quasi-democratic, for the most part have no choice but to consider Islamist movements and ideologies in their political calculations and strategies. They may choose either to incorporate or to marginalize political figures with Islamist commitments—those who proclaim that their engagement in political affairs is under the banner of Islam. Or they may seek to divide and conquer, offering an opening to some Islamists while seeking to deny any political space to others. The latter was the strategy of the Moroccan monarchy during an earlier period, as described by Ellen Lust-Okar;[3] and it has also been the approach of Algerian authorities when deciding which Islamist parties to permit to run candidates in elections.[4] And still another option, currently being discussed with respect to several Maghreb and other Arab countries, is to develop, manage, and employ an "official" political Islam as a counterweight to a more threatening "extremist" political Islam.[5] In each of these cases, political Islam and its advocates cannot be ignored by incumbent regimes. They are a force that has to be recognized and dealt with in one way or another.

Political Islam would perhaps be less relevant if the countries of the Maghreb were prepared to follow the course currently charted by the authoritarian regimes in Egypt and several Arab countries further to the east. In these cases, advocates of political Islam have been suppressed, often brutally and without any distinction between genuine extremists and those prepared to work within the political system to advance an Islamist agenda. Whether and to what extent the perceived short-term stability of these authoritarian governments will appeal to countries in North Africa—possibly even enough to bring about a paradigmatic shift in the politics of the region—is a question to which the present volume is addressed. Authoritarian stability does not describe the Maghreb at present, however. Nor does the suppression of Islamist political currents presently seen in Egypt describe the situation in Tunisia, Algeria, or Morocco. On the contrary, particularly in Tunisia and Morocco, mainstream Islamic-tendency movements and political parties that campaign under the banner of Islam not only participate in the country's political life, they have also scored electoral victories and held positions of national authority.

Accordingly, whatever the future may hold with respect to political order, the strength or weakness of popular support for political Islam will play a role in shaping the decisions and actions of the Maghreb's political leaders. It seems most likely that Tunisia, Algeria, and Morocco will each continue on its present course, despite elements of uncertainty in all three countries. But it is also possible that one or more of the three will succumb to the lure of authoritarian stability, however real or illusory, as perceived by its leaders and citizens. But no matter what path is chosen, political Islam, and especially the degree to which the platforms of Islamist movements find support among broader publics, will be among the determinants of the countries' political futures during the third decade of the twenty-first century. Against this background, the present chapter explores the nature and determinants of the attitudes toward political Islam held by ordinary people in Tunisia, Algeria, and Morocco.

Popular Attitudes toward Political Islam

The division of opinion about Islam's political role in Tunisia, Algeria, and Morocco is reflected, in the aggregate, in the response distributions presented in table 2.1. The table shows the level of agreement and disagreement with three statements about the role of religion in political and socioeconomic affairs. Table 2.2 shows the country-specific and time-specific responses to the same three items. Tables 2.1 and 2.2 employ data from the surveys carried out after the Arab Spring events in Tunisia, Algeria, and Morocco as part of the third wave, conducted in 2013, and fourth wave, conducted in 2016, of the Arab Barometer. More information about these surveys, and about the Arab Barometer more generally, is given in the methodology section of this chapter.

Table 2.1 shows that the response distributions vary across the three items, and table 2.2 shows that these distributions also vary across the three countries and two time periods. This variation notwithstanding, a couple of conclusions can be drawn. First, the tables show that most respondents disagree with the two statements that posit a greater role for religion in political affairs and agree with the one statement that posits a separation between religion and socioeconomic life. This is clear in table 2.1, and this response pattern is replicated in fifteen of the eighteen cells shown in table 2.2. Accordingly, it appears to be clear that most people in the Maghreb do not believe that Islam should play a leading role in government and political affairs.

There is a second conclusion to be drawn, however, and this is the takeaway most relevant for the present study. In addition to being skewed toward secularism, or at least toward a less prominent political role for

Table 2.1. Attitudes toward political Islam in Tunisia, Algeria, and Morocco in 2013 and 2016 (pooled)

To what extent do you agree or disagree with the following statements? (figures in table are percentages)		
Your country would be better off if more religious people would hold public positions in the state	Strongly agree / agree	40.2
	Disagree / strongly disagree	59.8
Religious clerics should have influence over the decisions of government	Strongly agree / agree	31.3
	Disagree / strongly disagree	68.7
Religious practice is a private matter and should be separated from socio-economic life	Strongly agree / agree	56.3
	Disagree / strongly disagree	43.7

Table 2.2. Attitudes toward political Islam in Tunisia, Algeria, and Morocco in 2013 and 2016 (by country and year)

	To what extent do you agree or disagree with the following statements? (figures in table are percentages)					
	Your country would be better off if more religious people would hold public positions in the state		Religious clerics should have influence over the decisions of government		Religious practice is a private matter and should be separated from socio-economic life	
	Strongly agree / agree	Disagree / strongly disagree	Strongly agree / agree	Disagree / strongly disagree	Strongly agree / agree	Disagree / strongly disagree
Tunisia 2013	43.1	56.9	26.6	73.4	76.0	24.0
Tunisia 2016	24.0	76.0	22.1	77.9	74.8	25.2
Algeria 2013	52.7	47.3	34.0	66.0	50.5	49.5
Algeria 2016	43.3	56.7	41.7	58.3	35.0	65.0
Morocco 2013	35.1	64.9	32.5	67.5	53.7	47.3
Morocco 2016	44.5	55.5	31.1	68.9	47.2	52.8

Islam, the response distributions show that opinions are far from unanimous. On the contrary, an opinion favorable to political Islam is expressed by a very substantial minority of respondents, ranging from 31.3 percent to 43.7 percent in table 2.1 and from 22.1 percent to 49.5 percent in table 2.2. The median percentage of those favoring an important political role for Islam is 35.0 percent. Thus, in addition to noting the central tendency, it is necessary to recognize that there exists an important division of opinion in matters pertaining to the place that Islam should occupy in a country's political life.

Explaining this variation—identifying some of the factors that predispose individuals toward either greater support or lesser support for political Islam—is the central objective of this inquiry. Additionally, and equally important, the study seeks to determine whether the same or different factors have explanatory power in Tunisia, Algeria, and Morocco and, in each country, in 2013 and 2016. To the extent that findings are similar across the three countries and the two points in time, there will be a basis for suggesting that these findings are of reasonably broad applicability. Alternatively, to the extent that findings differ from one country or point in time to another, it will be clear that findings are not broadly applicable but are rather conditional, and it will be necessary in this case to invite reflection, or at least speculation, about the country-specific and time-specific attributes that play a conditioning role.

Accounting for Variance

Tables 2.1 and 2.2 provide useful information about the distribution of attitudes toward political Islam across the three Maghreb countries over time. But this leaves unanswered questions about the reasons that some people in each country and time period hold positive views about the role that Islam should play in government and political affairs, while others in each case have unfavorable views about political Islam. Accordingly, it is necessary to go beyond these descriptive accounts and identify the factors that account for this variance. Two hypotheses will be introduced and tested in pursuit of this objective.

The information required to account for variance goes beyond specifying the correlations between attitudes toward political Islam and various individual-level attributes, orientations, or circumstances. Rather, accounting for variance requires seeking causal stories, first, by developing hypotheses that give coherence and specificity to the search for factors that have explanatory power; second, by testing these hypothesis through multivariate analyses that hold other factors constant and reduce the likelihood of spuriousness when making causal inferences; and third, by identifying the contextual circumstances, or conditionalities, that define the locus of applicability of whatever significant explanatory relationships have been identified.

Causality can only be inferred in such analyses, and causal inference should not be mistaken for proof that a statistically significant relationship establishes a causal connection. Nevertheless, an analysis that succeeds in identifying factors that are part of a plausible and presumably persuasive causal story, and that then is able to show that the hypothesized relationships have significant and independent predictive power, goes a considerable distance toward discovering not just what people think about Islam's political role but also why they hold certain views. What then remains is to identify the distribution over space and time of these significant explanatory relationships and to both offer and invite informed speculation about the reasons particular hypotheses sometimes do and sometimes do not have explanatory power. An analysis that proceeds in this manner can produce instructive and valuable insights about the determinants of attitudes toward political Islam.

The dependent variable in this analysis is, of course, individual judgments about the role that Islam should play in government and politics—a continuum of individual preferences ranging from strong support for to strong opposition to the proposition that Islam should occupy an important place in a country's political life. The operationalization of this dependent variable is an index based on the three survey items used to construct tables 2.1 and 2.2. Information about the construction of this index, and about its validity and reliability, is provided in the methodology section of this chapter.

Two hypotheses will be tested in an effort to shed light on some of the pathways leading to differing views about Islam's political role. Both hypotheses concern satisfaction-dissatisfaction with the political and economic status quo. More specifically, the independent variables in these hypotheses are, first, political judgments, and in particular an evaluation of the regime and institutions governing the country in which an individual lives; and, second, personal economic well-being, measured by both subjective assessments of economic circumstance and objective reports of personal consumer possessions. Both variables reference a satisfaction-dissatisfaction continuum; the difference is that one variable pertains to the national scene, and to the governing regime in particular, and is thus a political and sociotropic consideration, while the other pertains to the personal economic circumstances of the respondent. A test of propositions in which each is an independent variable will provide information about the explanatory utility of judgments about the government and its institutions and about one's personal economic situation. In addition, a comparison of findings about the two hypotheses will also shed light on the relative explanatory power of political and sociotropic considerations, on the one hand, and personal and economic factors, on the other, in accounting for variance in attitudes toward political Islam.

Many other factors may also be important determinants of the views citizens hold about Islam's political role, and some of these have been explored in my recent book, *Islam and Politics in the Middle East: Explaining the Views of Ordinary Citizens*.[6] Indeed, the present chapter extends some of the analyses presented in that book through a deeper look at the countries of the Maghreb. But this chapter, like the book, makes no claim to being exhaustive, nor even to considering more than an important subset of the factors that may play a role in shaping citizens' attitudes toward political Islam. In the present study, this subset concerns judgments about the political and economic status quo—judgments that may involve grievances that push people in the Maghreb either toward or away from support for political Islam.

Political Judgments and Regime Evaluation

A number of analysts, the present author included,[7] have argued that support for political Islam, and perhaps particularly for Islamist movements, is in part a protest against the political and economic status quo and, more specifically, against the regimes that ordinary citizens hold responsible for the situation about which they complain. The complaints of these people in the Muslim-majority countries of the Middle East and North Africa, especially but not only in those countries with very autocratic regimes, include persistent poverty, a large gap between rich and poor, corruption and favoritism that promote inequality and limit economic and status mobility, and a political system that severely restricts the prospects for meaningful change and rarely tolerates even modest public criticism. Thus, in the eyes of many ordinary citizens, their country is governed for the benefit of a small political and associated consumer class that supports its privileged lifestyle with resources that should be used for national development, while people like themselves continue to live in conditions of distress. Although not equally prominent and intense everywhere, this popular assessment of the prevailing political and economic order is widespread.

These complaints were prominently on display during the massive Arab protests that erupted in Tunisia in December 2010 and shook much of the Arab world in the months that followed. The rallying cry of many of the protesters in Tunisia and elsewhere, and of the populations for which they claimed to speak, was "dignity" (*karama*). Expressed in this context, an insistence on dignity signified a refusal to be led by a regime that did not consider its citizens worthy of attention and consideration. As expressed by Roy, the demonstrators' demand for "dignity" was a call for "elections, democracy, good governance, and human rights"[8]—a call, above all, for leaders who would respect the people they governed, would work on their behalf, and would be concerned about their welfare. These demands were both articulated and translated into action by young people and many others who came into the streets and who, as it is often described, "crossed the barrier of fear" in their determination that there would be no return to business as usual.[9]

Nor are these complaints or the protests to which they gave rise entirely new. On the contrary, this constellation of grievances sparked mass demonstrations and even riots, sometimes on more than one occasion, in Morocco, Algeria, Tunisia, Egypt, Palestine, Jordan, and elsewhere as early as the 1970s, 1980s, and 1990s. In these instances, as well as in some countries where public discontent did not give rise to rioting or even large-scale and sustained demonstrations, large segments of the public have for several decades been alienated from the regimes by which they are governed and sought leaders whose priorities do not center on their own power and privilege. As expressed in the early 1990s by a scholar of Egyptian origin, there is a "severe, multi-dimensional, and protracted crisis faced by many regimes in the Muslim world. This crisis has been evidenced by a decline of state legitimacy and has resulted in 'state exhaustion.'"[10] Similarly, describing the mood in the Arab world during this period, a Jordanian journalist wrote, "[The problem is] autocratic rulers and non-accountable power elites who pursue whimsical, wasteful and regressive policies,"[11] and "[there is] a profound desire for change—for democracy and human rights . . . for accountability of public officials, for morality in public life . . . and for a new regional order characterized by honesty, dignity, justice and stability."[12]

Government officials often contend that these complaints about regime performance are unreasonable and exaggerated. They assert that demands for rapid progress are unrealistic, with many citizens, and especially the young, failing to appreciate that development goals can be achieved only over the long haul. Officials also frequently insist that much has been accomplished, sometimes suggesting that complaints are the result not of government failures but rather of aspirations fostered by successful development efforts, most notably in the field of education. Whatever the accuracy of these rebuttals, however, they rarely strike a responsive chord among the disillusioned and alienated segments of the public, presumably because so many find confirmation in their own lives of the charge that something fundamental is amiss in the nation as a whole. These people reason, logically although perhaps somewhat simplistically, that if the government were allocating its energies and resources wisely, in accordance with the true interests of the populace, they, their families, and so many of their friends would not be confronted with stagnation or even a decline in their modest standards of living.

The desire for an alternative to the political and economic status quo has led some, and most likely many, to believe that a more appropriate and responsive political formula might be found in Islam. Both Arab and foreign analysts have for decades argued that a growing interest in political Islam has been fueled, at least in part, by disaffection with those in power. As reported in studies of Tunisia and Morocco at the end of the 1980s, the growth of the Islamist movement is "a symptom of a deeper malaise within society"[13] and will continue as long as "the problems of social disadvantage and deprivation and of political marginalization" remain unaddressed.[14] Similarly, writing several years later about the Arab world in general, a political scientist from the United Arab Emirates argued that "as long as governments in the Arab world resist political participation and the tolerance of different political opinions, the strength of Islam as a political ideology will continue to be a serious alternative."[15] And more recently still, as noted in a broad overview by a British scholar of Sudanese origin, "the rise of the Islamic movements is a symptom of the dire crises that beset the land of Islam. . . . [They] emerged as a reaction to the crisis they wanted to get out of."[16]

Consistent with these analyses, many Arab and other analysts have long predicted that Islamist parties would be victorious if free and open elections were permitted.[17] And indeed, this has very often been the case, with complaints about the governing regime and its policies reflected in the strength of Islamist parties when competitive elections were permitted, as in Jordan, Tunisia, and Algeria in the late 1980s and early 1990s, and more recently in Turkey, Palestine, Yemen, Morocco, Kuwait, and elsewhere. And, of course, the post–Arab Spring elections in Tunisia, Egypt, and Morocco are the most recent examples of Islamist victories propelled, at least in part, by the desire for an alternative to the pre–Arab Spring status quo.

The dynamic fueling the relationship between political and economic discontent, on the one hand, and the electoral strength of Islamist parties, on the other, is nicely captured in the statement of a young Algerian who explained to an American journalist why he had supported the Islamic Salvation Front (FIS) in the local and regional elections of June 1990: "In this country, if you are a young man . . . you have only four choices: you can remain unemployed and celibate because there are no jobs and no apartments to live in; you can work in the black market and risk being arrested; you can try to emigrate to France to sweep the streets of Paris or Marseilles; or you can join the FIS and vote for Islam."[18]

As this account suggests, the FIS was the only available and viable opposition movement through which it was possible to cast a meaningful vote against the regime. For the most part, this has been the case because authoritarian governments have usually been more successful, and sometimes more motivated, in working to suppress secular opposition movements. As reported in a recent overview of electoral politics and political participation in the Arab world, "The major opposition movements and parties across the region today are Islamist parties and actors [whereas] secular opposition parties seem to have lost the sway and influence they possessed in the 1960s and 1970s."[19]

As the preceding discussion suggests, Islamist movements have been able to capture support, or at least votes, from opponents of the political and economic status quo who may not favor Islamist social and cultural policies. For these individuals, who are not the Islamists' core constituency and may be described as "strategic" voters, support presumably reflects the view that an Islamist political movement is the best available alternative, whatever its drawbacks, to the regime in power. If this is the case, at least some strategic voters lend their support to Islamist movements not because of but in spite of these movements' social and cultural agendas, perhaps also assuming, or at least hoping, that the party will use whatever influence it possesses or acquires to address problems of political economy and put its social and cultural objectives on the back burner.

Strategic voters may not be the whole story, however. Individuals who are discontent with the political and economic status quo may believe not only that Islam is the best available alternative; they may also believe that the solution to their country's problems is to be found in Islam. They believe, in other words, that Islam, as opposed to Islamists, should play a role in government and political affairs. One reason for this may be Islam's emphasis on equality, on protection of the weak and vulnerable, and on help for the needy. Relevant, too, may be a belief that Islam, as a religion of laws, will bring a commitment to justice and the rule of law. There will be disagreement about whether these values and commitments have in practice been any more respected by religious officials and advanced by religious institutions than by their secular counterparts. Nevertheless, to the extent that ordinary citizens who have an unfavorable view of the governing regime find these normative orientations in Islam and believe they will bring a positive and needed correction to their country's political affairs, their discontent is likely to foster support for political Islam anchored in a belief that Islam really is the solution to the problems their society faces.

Whether or not any of these dynamics do indeed shape the judgments of a significant number of ordinary citizens is a question for empirical analysis. Accordingly, the following hypothesis is offered to guide the analysis by which the relevance and explanatory power of these various causal stories can be evaluated.

> H1. Individuals who are more dissatisfied with the performance of their political institutions and officials are more likely than are individuals with higher levels of political satisfaction to favor a political formula that gives Islam an important role.

The causal story posited by H1 assumes that the regime in power is largely secular, or at least that it does not have a strong Islamic connection. The dynamic assumed to be operating is that those who are unhappy with the regime are significantly more likely than those with a positive evaluation of the regime to want Islam to play a significant political role precisely because the government and political leaders of which they disapprove do not draw on the religion for guidance and insight. In other words, Islam is the alternative, either institutionally, ideologically, or both, to what people believe they have and do not like. This has been the case in Tunisia, Algeria, and Morocco during the period on which the present analysis focuses, perhaps with the partial exception of Tunisia at the time of the 2013 survey.

For the application of H1 to countries governed by a regime that does have a strong Islamist connection, which is beyond the scope of the present inquiry, the proposed relationship would have to be modified. It would express the proposition that dissatisfaction with the political and economic status quo predisposes ordinary citizens to oppose a political formula that gives Islam an important role.[20]

The causal story referenced by H1 is not only persuasive on its face; it also involves a political attitude-shaping dynamic to which many accounts of popular support for political Islam have called attention. Accordingly, it might seem that there is no reason to consider the proposition that it is actually positive political judgments and a more favorable assessment of the governing regime and its institutions that push toward support for political Islam. Nevertheless, the possibility that the direction of the relationship posited in H1 is reversed, if not generally then at least in some countries and time periods, is not totally implausible and deserves consideration.

The author's 2015 book, *Islam and Politics in the Middle East: Explaining the Views of Ordinary Citizens*, does not explicitly consider the possibility that positive political judgments push toward support for political Islam, but it does report findings that suggest that H1, however plausible, may not be an entirely satisfactory explanation of the relationship between political judgments and views about the role Islam should play in government and politics. Drawing on thirty-one nationally representative surveys carried out in ten Muslim-majority countries between 1988 and 2011, a test of H1 found no significant relationship in the pooled analysis and only a weak ($p < .05$) relationship in one of four demographic categories when the data were disaggregated.[21]

The study reported in *Islam and Politics in the Middle East* included but did not focus on countries in the Maghreb. Also, the data are from surveys conducted before the events of the Arab Spring, and particularly before the complicated and troubling Tunisian and Egyptian experiences with Islamist governance. So perhaps findings reported in the author's 2015 book are not an appropriate basis for formulating expectations about determinants of attitudes toward political Islam in the Maghreb of 2013 and 2016. Nevertheless, these findings do suggest that something might be gained by thinking about alternatives to the relationship posited in H1.

Toward that end, and focusing specifically on the proposition that more favorable judgments about the government and its institutions push toward support for political Islam, the operating dynamic might involve the following elements. First, in a country with an overwhelming Muslim majority, in which most people are at least somewhat religious, if not very religious, there may be an underlying assumption that Islam should be connected to political life. Second, many of these citizens may think that Islam should only play a meaningful role, not a leading role, in government and political affairs. Indeed, they may want to be sure that Islamic officials do not have too much political power, inclining the country to drift toward theocracy. And therefore, third, they may believe that Islam can play the important but nonetheless contained role they favor only if the county has strong and trusted political institutions that provide checks and balances and ensure that no political formula, political Islam in this case, becomes too dominant.

There is another way that ordinary citizens might connect positive political judgments and confidence in governing institutions with a favorable predisposition toward political Islam. If support for political Islam represents a call for the moralization of public life, which has been described as a moral order that will not only restrain the despot but also provide "basic decency,"[22] then viable and trusted political institutions become a necessary component in the political equation through which this can be realized. In other words, Islamists cannot provide good governance by themselves. As Roy observes, even where they have taken control, as in Iran and Gaza, Islamists have not been able to establish a successful model of an Islamic state. At the same time, he continues, the Islamist electorate is conservative; it wants order; it wants leaders who will kick-start the economy.[23] Political Islam thus needs strong institutions—institutions that inspire and deserve confidence, and this, if understood by ordinary citizens, may be a prerequisite for giving their support to an Islamist program.

This line of reasoning differs from that offered previously, which considered the possibility that supporters of political Islam want religion to exert influence in political life, but not too much influence, and thus see political institutions in which they have confidence as providing necessary checks and balances. Alternatively, this second line of reasoning suggests that strong and viable political institutions are seen as necessary partners in the provision of governance that is both moral and effective. Both of these lines of reasoning stand in opposition to the rationale offered in support of H1. In this case, it is not opposition to the political and economic status quo that pushes toward support for political Islam; rather, assigning to Islam an important role in government and political affairs is most appealing, and perhaps only appealing, if there exist trusted political institutions.

These two alternative causal stories are for the most part original, and they may both prove to be off base given the appeal of the rationale that underlies H1. But they receive some support, or at least some encouragement, from an important recent study of the success of the Muslim Brotherhood in Egypt. The author, Tarek Masoud, first considers two possible explanations. The first is that there is something special about Islam and that Muslims are primed by their religion to desire Islamic government. Masoud quickly rejects this primordial and essentialist explanation. The second is that Islamists are better organized than their secular opponents and thus usually prevail in the competition for supporters and adherents. This explanation, Masoud contends, is partial at best. Thereafter, Masoud offers an alternative theory that emphasizes "broader structural factors that shape both citizens' choices and parties' strategies."[24]

Masoud's thesis does not resemble either of the two dynamics that have been proposed here as alternatives to, or modifications of, H1. But Masoud does provide encouragement by his apparently successful search for explanations that depart from conventional wisdom about the ability of Islamists to gain support and win elections. Further, and perhaps more important, Masoud calls attention to the importance of structural factors and institutional considerations—factors central to the causal stories being proposed here as alternatives to H1—in shaping the way that citizens think about the place they want Islam to occupy in the political affairs of their country.

With all of these considerations in mind, and particularly the original and alternative causal stories presented above, the following alternative hypothesis, H1a, can be offered.

> H1a. Individuals who are more satisfied with the performance of their political institutions and officials are more likely than are individuals with higher levels of political dissatisfaction to favor a political formula that gives Islam an important role.

Personal Economic Circumstances and Personal Economic Satisfaction

The various and alternative causal stories that inform H1, a hypothesis in which the independent variable is political judgment and regime evaluation, may have an equal or even greater measure of explanatory power when satisfaction-dissatisfaction pertains to individual-level economic circumstances. At the country level, economic and political concerns often reinforce one another, coming together under the rubric of political economy. As the discussion in the previous section makes clear, complaints about a country's political rulers and the regime and institutions through which they govern may be fueled by discontent about the economic situation, as well as by discontent about the absence of political freedoms or the violation of human rights. At the individual level, the importance of economic considerations, relative to political considerations, would seem to have an even greater degree of explanatory power. Accordingly, guided by the logic presented in the preceding section—that discontent fosters support for political Islam in a country governed by a regime that is essentially secular in character, or that at least does not have a clear and explicit Islamist connection—the following hypothesis, H2, may also be offered.

> H2. Individuals with lower levels of economic satisfaction are more likely than are individuals with higher levels of economic satisfaction to favor a political formula that gives Islam an important role.

It might once again be argued, however, that the direction of the relationship proposed in H2 should be reversed—that support for political Islam is actually greater among more affluent individuals, among citizens with higher levels of economic satisfaction. Although perhaps less persuasive, as in the discussion of H1 and H1a, the causal story that informs this alternative proposition is at least plausible. The logic here is, first, that support for political Islam, whatever its origins, reflects a view about country-level governance, which is a sociotropic consideration, and that more affluent individuals, who tend to be better educated and more politically conscious, are disproportionately likely to be thinking about the path the country should follow.

Thereafter, second, it is possible that the greater political awareness of these individuals brings recognition and, despite their relative affluence, concern about the fact that they live in a country where many do not share their own well-being. If this is the case, they may believe that it is in their interest to be governed in accordance with a political formula that will address and correct the inadequacies of the political and economic status quo.

This alternative causal story, which is expressed in Hypothesis 2a below, is not entirely implausible, and an analysis using Arab Barometer data from Tunisia, Algeria, and Morocco will determine whether there is evidence to support it. More probable, however, is the proposition, derived from the logic from which H1 is also derived, that individuals with greater grievances, based on less favorable economic circumstances in this case, are disproportionately likely to seek an alternative to the political and economic status quo. And in countries governed by an essentially secular regime, this desire for an alternative is disproportionately likely to involve support for a political formula that assigns an important role to Islam.

> H2a. Individuals with higher levels of economic satisfaction are more likely than are individuals with lower levels of economic satisfaction to favor a political formula that gives Islam an important role.

Data and Method

Data from the Arab Barometer will be used to test these hypotheses about the explanatory power of country-level and individual-level political and economic grievances. More specifically, data from third-wave and fourth-wave Arab Barometer surveys in Tunisia, Algeria, and Morocco will be used. All of the surveys are based on nationally representative probability-based samples, with the survey instrument administered in face-to-face interviews conducted by trained enumerators. The dates and sample sizes of the surveys are given in table 2.3. Additional information about sampling and other methodological considerations, including quality control measures, are available on the Arab Barometer website (arabbarometer.org). The full survey instruments used in each wave are also given on the website. Third- and fourth-wave data, as well as data from the first and second waves, may be downloaded in either SPSS or Stata format.

The dependent variable, attitude toward political Islam, is measured by the three items to which responses are shown in tables 2.1 and 2.2. Factor analysis has been used to determine whether these items load strongly on a common factor, indicating unidimensionality, and since this is the case, as shown in table 2.4, the three items have been combined to form a scale by generating factor scores. The same procedure has been used to generate a scale measuring political judgments and regime evaluation, which is the independent variable in H1 and H1a. The scale is based on an item that asks respondents to indicate the extent of their trust in a number of government institutions, and specifically in the government (the cabinet), the elected council of representatives (the parliament), and the forces of public security (the police). Factor analysis has again been used to form a scale by

Table 2.3. Survey dates and sample sizes

Country	Barometer wave	Date	N
Tunisia	3	February–March 2013	1199
Algeria	3	March–April 2013	1220
Morocco	3	April–May 2013	1116
Tunisia	4	January–February 2016	1200
Algeria	4	May 2016	1200
Morocco	4	May–June 2016	1200

Table 2.4. Results of factor analyses used to create a scale measuring attitudes toward political Islam

	Factor loadings					
	Tunisia 2013	Algeria 2013	Morocco 2013	Tunisia 2016	Algeria 2016	Morocco 2016
Your country would be better off if more religious people would hold public positions in the state	.840	.873	.854	.805	.820	.826
Religious clerics should have influence over the decisions of government	.792	.844	.871	.812	.911	.776
Religious practice is a private matter and should be separated from socio-economic life	−.505	−.669	−.577	−.643	−.477	−.700

Note: Response options are *strongly agree, somewhat agree, somewhat disagree,* and *strongly disagree.*

generating factor scores, and the results are shown in table 2.5. Finally, the same procedure has been used to operationalize personal religiosity, which will be a control variable in the regression analysis by which hypotheses are tested. The individual items used to construct the personal religiosity scale ask about the extent to which respondents would describe themselves as religious, the frequency with which they pray, and the frequency with which they read or listen to the Quran or other religious materials. These results are shown in table 2.6.

It may be noted in connection with these procedures that factor analysis is useful not only for generating a scale by selecting and combining individual items; it also provides a basis for assessing reliability and validity.

Table 2.5. Results of factor analyses used to create a scale measuring political judgment and regime evaluation

I would like you to tell me to what extent you trust each of the following institutions:	Factor loadings					
	Tunisia 2013	Algeria 2013	Morocco 2013	Tunisia 2016	Algeria 2016	Morocco 2016
The government (cabinet)	.896	.893	.906	.692	.850	.600
The elected council of representatives (parliament)	.897	.791	.900	.707	.703	.799
The forces of public security (police)	.729	.751	.848	.659	.815	.629

Note: Response options are *to a great extent, to a medium extent, to a limited extent,* and *absolutely do not trust.*

Table 2.6. Results of factor analyses used to create a scale measuring personal religiosity

	Factor loadings					
	Tunisia 2013	Algeria 2013	Morocco 2013	Tunisia 2016	Algeria 2016	Morocco 2016
Generally speaking, would you describe yourself as religious, somewhat religious, or not religious?	.787	.658	.704	.775	.832	.817
Do you pray daily always, most of the time, sometimes, rarely, or never?	.816	.827	.759	.800	.793	849
Do you listen to or read the Quran (or the Bible) always, most of the time, sometimes, rarely, or never?	.764	.689	.767	.711	.850	.733

Strong loadings on a single factor demonstrate unidimensionality, which means that the items measure the same underlying concept and thus are reliable. Validity can only be inferred, not demonstrated, but if each item in a battery of items measuring the same underlying concept possesses face validity, it is reasonable to infer that the measure is also valid—that it actually measures what it purports to measure.

The remaining independent variable is economic circumstance and economic satisfaction, and this is measured by an index composed of two highly intercorrelated items. The first item asks respondents, "Generally speaking, how would you compare your living conditions to those of the rest of your fellow citizens?" Response options are *much worse, worse, similar,* and *better.* The second item asks respondents whether they have a computer, a car, both, or neither.

Drawing on these measures, support for political Islam will be regressed against the independent variables in our two hypotheses: political judgment and regime evaluation, and personal economic circumstance. In addition to personal religiosity, other variables included as controls are age, sex, and level of education. It is particularly important to include personal religiosity as a control variable since it is very strongly correlated with attitudes toward political Islam.

Findings and Discussion

Do political and economic grievances foster support for political Islam in the post–Arab Spring Maghreb? This question, posed in the title of this chapter, can now be addressed directly. The evidence to consider when offering an answer, or several answers, is presented in table 2.7. The table presents the results of an ordinary least squares (OLS) regression carried out to test H1, H1a, H2, and H2a. The dependent variable, attitudes toward political Islam, is regressed against measures of the two independent variables, political judgment / regime evaluation and personal economic circumstance. As discussed, and as indicated in tables 2.4 and 2.5, the measures of attitude toward political Islam and of regime evaluation are based on factor scores. The measure of personal economic circumstance is based on a subjective assessment of economic well-being and whether or not the respondent possesses a personal computer or a car. Included in the regression analysis reported in table 2.7 are four control variables: personal religiosity, again based on factor scores, as shown in table 2.6, and age, sex, and education.

Table 2.7 presents results based on a pooled analysis of data from the three countries and two time periods and then, separately, for each country and time period. In the pooled analysis, the data reveal a strong and statistically significant relationship between support for political Islam and positive evaluations of the governing regime and its institutions. This provides evidence in support of H1a, a pattern that was considered earlier but was thought to be less likely than the inverse relationship posited by H1.

Table 2.7 also shows that there is no statistically significant relationship between attitudes toward political Islam and personal economic circumstance. Thus, neither H2 nor H2a is confirmed in the pooled analysis.

Table 2.7. OLS regression coefficients showing the influence on attitudes toward political Islam of political judgments and regime evaluation and of personal economic circumstance among all respondents and among respondents grouped by country and year

	All	Tunisia 2013	Tunisia 2016	Algeria 2013	Algeria 2016	Morocco 2013	Morocco 2016
More positive regime evaluation	.100*** (.013)	.246*** (.031)	−.040 (.031)	.218*** (.047)	−.037 (.028)	.146*** (.034)	.153*** (.030)
More positive economic circumstance	.016 (.014)	−.004 (.034)	.030 (.033)	−.021 (.039)	−.007 (.029)	−.143*** (.041)	−.094** (.032)
Control	–	–	–	–	–	–	–
More personally religious	.238*** (.014)	.098*** (.028)	.268*** (.032)	.279*** (.039)	.120*** (.028)	.243*** (.041)	.372*** (.030)
Older age	−.100*** (.013)	−.017 (.033)	−.195*** (.033)	−.008 (.039)	−.048 (.027)	−.046 (.034)	−.084** (.030)
Female gender	−.086*** (.027)	−.046 (.065)	−.225*** (.067)	−.138* (.065)	.003 (.052)	−.052 (.070)	−.045 (.054)
Higher level of education	−.045*** (.008)	.051* (.022)	−.073*** ((.020)	−.008 (.028)	−.047** (.016)	−.026 (.022)	−.068*** (.016)
Constant	.575*** (.068)	.326 (.186)	.619*** (.176)	.362* (.188)	.697*** (.134)	.280 (.159)	.673*** (.144)

Note: Higher values of the dependent variable indicate higher support for political Islam; the table presents unstandardized coefficients; standard errors are in parentheses.
*Significant at .05 level.
**Significant at .01 level.
***Significant at .001 level.

Two possible causal stories associated with H1a were discussed in the previous section. In one, it was speculated that positive political judgments might push toward support for political Islam because citizens who favored an important political role for Islam also wanted checks and balances to ensure that Islam did not crowd out other equally necessary components of the country's political formula. In the other story, it was speculated that supporters of political Islam might regard strong and trusted political institutions as necessary partners, without which leadership under the banner of Islam would be unlikely to bring tangible benefits. Both of these causal stories are largely original and essentially speculative, as stated. Accordingly, it is possible that neither accurately describes the dynamic that is at work. Nor do they exhaust the possible pathways leading from positive judgments about the governing regime and its institutions to support for political Islam. Nonetheless, having found that negative judgments of an essentially secular regime do not push toward support for political Islam, as expected and as expressed in H1, these causal stories lay a foundation for additional reflection, and hopefully additional research, on how and why positive political judgments increase the likelihood of favoring political arrangements in which Islam plays an important role.

Some interesting relationships involving the control variable may also be briefly noted, even though these are not central to the questions about grievance that are the primary concern of the present study. As expected, there is a strong, positive, and statistically significant relationship between personal religiosity and support for political Islam. Beyond this, persons with a favorable attitude toward political Islam are disproportionately likely to be younger, male, and less well educated in the pooled analysis.

Turning to the country-specific and time-specific results presented in table 2.7, the patterns reported from the pooled analysis hold in some instances but not in others. More specifically, support for H1a is found in Tunisia in 2013, in Algeria in 2013, and in Morocco in both 2013 and 2016. In Tunisia in 2016 and in Algeria in 2016, there is no statistically significant relationship between political judgments and attitudes toward political Islam. Further, there is no statistically significant relationship between personal economic circumstance and attitudes toward political Islam in either Tunisia or Algeria in either 2013 or 2016, but there is a strong and inverse statistically significant relationship between the two variables, as posited in H2, in Morocco in both 2013 and 2016.

With respect to relationships between the dependent variable and the control variables, greater personal religiosity is, as expected, strongly associated with greater support for political Islam in all six of the country-specific and year-specific categories. Otherwise, the pattern of relationships involving age, sex, and education varies across the six country and time categories, indicating that conclusions about the predictive and explanatory power of these demographic variables based on the pooled analysis do not apply across the six cases included in the pool. Only in Tunisia in 2016 is support for political Islam significantly more likely, as in the pooled analysis, among individuals who are younger, male, and less educated.

There is a unique pattern of significant relationships in each of the other five country-year categories. Only in Morocco in 2016 is age significantly and inversely related to support for political Islam, only in Algeria in 2013 are those who support political Islam disproportionately likely to be male, and level of education is positively related to support for political

Islam in Tunisia in 2013 and inversely related to support for political Islam in all three countries in 2016. That the demographics of support for political Islam should vary so dramatically across the three countries and two time points is an unexpected finding that, although beyond the scope the present study, deserves attention in future empirical investigations.

Conclusion

Three takeaways may be offered as we return to the paper's primary concern: whether, and if so where and when, judgments about a country's political leaders and institutions and one's personal economic circumstance push toward support for political Islam. First, somewhat surprisingly, discontent with the political and economic status quo does not lead to support for political Islam in the countries and during the period that are the focus of the present study. Perhaps this was the case earlier, or perhaps not; but it was not the case in Tunisia, Algeria, or Morocco in 2013 or 2016. Accordingly, attitudes toward political Islam do not appear to be shaped by political grievances and antiregime sentiments in the post–Arab Spring Maghreb.

Second, a favorable judgment about the political and economic status quo pushed toward support for political Islam across the Maghreb in 2013, in part, perhaps, because of problems associated with unpopular Islamist governments in Tunisia and Egypt at the time of the 2013 surveys. Conversely, the basis for this pattern in Morocco in 2016, and perhaps also in 2013, may lie at least partly in the stability that has accompanied participation in the government of Morocco's Islamist Justice and Development Party.

Third, personal economic circumstance had no impact on attitudes toward political Islam in either Tunisia or Algeria in 2013 or 2016. In Morocco, by contrast, an unfavorable personal economic situation increased the likelihood of a favorable attitude toward political Islam in both 2013 and 2016. The reason, possibly, lies in the interaction between Morocco's overall relative and absolute poverty, being one of the poorest countries in the Arab world, and its experience with the Justice and Development Party.

These three takeaways merely provide another description of the findings presented in table 2.7. Causal stories that connect the specifics of place and time to the statistically significant relationships that have been identified for the most part remain to be discovered. Nevertheless, pursuit of these analytical insights, whether conditional or more broadly generalizable, must begin, as has been done here, with the testing of propositions about factors that push either toward or away from support for political

Islam. Thereafter, drawing on the results of these tests and considering the rationale offered for each hypothesis, and then including information about the circumstances of each country in the post–Arab Spring Maghreb, the incremental quest to understand why some North Africans support political Islam while others do not can go forward. The present investigation provides a foundation for this continuing effort.

The introduction to this chapter called attention to the importance of popular attitudes toward political Islam for governance in the Maghreb, offering the presumably not-very-controversial proposition that these popular predispositions play a role in shaping the political calculations and strategies of incumbent regimes, and, for this reason, they will be a factor in determining the political futures of Tunisia, Algeria, and Morocco. Although the extent and drivers of popular support for the agenda of political Islam, at least those drivers concerned with political and economic grievances, vary considerably across the countries and time span of the post–Arab Spring Maghreb, the present analysis and the three concluding takeaways do not diminish the salience of this proposition. Other factors are important, of course, and some may be more important in particular settings. But there is significant public support for assigning to Islam an important place in government and political affairs in at least some respects, and there are also important divisions of public opinion on this issue. These are considerations to which the leaders of Tunisia, Algeria, and Morocco are required to pay close attention.

This chapter's introductory discussion also raised questions about the potential appeal of authoritarian stability, possibly as it is perceived to exist in Egypt and several Arab countries further to the east, and about what this might mean for regime policies toward political Islam and popular judgments of such policies. The concluding takeaways from the present chapter's data-based analysis do not provide a single unifying insight addressed to these questions. But, at least based on evidence from the 2011–13 period, these takeaways do suggest that grievance-related drivers of popular attitudes toward political Islam are unlikely to push either leaders or ordinary citizens toward an embrace of authoritarianism in pursuit of stability. Support for political Islam is not associated with antiregime attitudes, thus removing whatever motivation political leaders might have, as apparently was the case in Egypt, to suppress public discourse and dissent in the name of stability. Similarly, the data suggest that Maghrebi leaders do not have to worry that personal economic discontent is driving support for political

Islam; thus, again, they will have little reason to suppress dissent to prevent any possible Islamist challenge. The Moroccan case is an exception to the latter observation since economic grievances are a determinant of support for political Islam in that country. But since an Islamist party has been part of the government in Morocco, and since support for political Islam is associated with positive attitudes toward the governing regime, it seems very unlikely that an Islamist challenge, or at least a challenge from mainstream political Islam, would reinforce any possible impetus toward greater authoritarianism in the name of stability.

In sum, the following two propositions, which admittedly remain unavoidably general and point to a need for further reflection and research, set forth what this analysis of Arab Barometer survey data suggests about the connection between popular attitudes toward Islamist agendas and the political future of the Maghreb in the years immediately ahead. First, public attitudes and a division of opinion relating to Islam's place in government and political life are an important factor in present-day Maghrebi politics and will play a role in shaping the political future of Tunisia, Algeria, and Morocco. Second, the relationship between political and economic grievances and public attitudes toward political Islam does not push toward the embrace of authoritarian stability. Whether a push in this direction will come from other sources remains to be seen. But should this be the case in one or more of the North African countries, it is unlikely that the views about political Islam held by ordinary citizens will be an important part of the story.

MARK TESSLER is Samuel J. Eldersveld Collegiate Professor of Politics at the University of Michigan. His books include *Public Opinion in the Middle East: Survey Research and the Political Orientations of Ordinary Citizens* (Bloomington: Indiana University Press, 2011); and *Islam and Politics in the Middle East: Explaining the Views of Ordinary Citizens* (Bloomington: Indiana University Press, 2015). Tessler is also codirector of the Arab Barometer Survey Project.

Notes

1. Lecture at the Henry L. Stimson Center, May 9, 2011. Similarly, Ali Gomaa, at the time the grand mufti of Egypt, stated that Egypt's Arab Spring uprisings had swept away decades of authoritarian rule but had also "highlighted an issue that Egyptians will grapple with as they consolidate their democracy: the role of religion in political life." See Ali Gomaa, "In Egypt's Democracy, Room for Islam," *New York Times*, April 2, 2011.

2. Olivier Roy, "The Transformation of the Arab World," in *Democratization and Authoritarianism in the Arab World*, ed. Larry Diamond and Marc Plattner (Baltimore: Johns Hopkins University Press, 2014), 26–7.

3. Ellen Lust-Okar, *Structuring Conflict in the Arab World: Incumbents, Opponents and Institutions* (Cambridge: Cambridge University Press, 2005).

4. Michael Robbins and Mark Tessler, "The Effect of Elections on Public Opinion toward Democracy: Evidence from Longitudinal Survey Research in Algeria," *Comparative Political Studies* 45 (October 2012): 1255–76.

5. Michael Robbins and Lawrence Rubin, "How States Can Wield 'Official Islam' to Limit Radical Extremism," *Washington Post Monkey Cage*, November 3, 2017, https://www.washingtonpost.com/news/monkey-cage/wp/2017/11/03/four-ways-states-can-wield-official-islam-and-what-that-means-for-extremism/?utm_term=.dcc448afc527.

6. Mark Tessler, *Islam and Politics in the Middle East: Explaining the Views of Ordinary Citizens* (Bloomington: Indiana University Press, 2015).

7. Mark Tessler, "The Origins of Popular Support for Islamist Movements: A Political Economy Analysis," in *Islam, Democracy, and the State in North Africa*, ed. John Entelis (Bloomington: Indiana University Press, 1997), 93–126. For evidence from the Tunisian and Egyptian elections of 2011, see also Mark Tessler, "Change and Continuity in Arab Attitudes toward Political Islam: The Impact of Political Transitions in Tunisia and Egypt, 2011–2013," in *Visions and Perspectives in the Study of Human Values in the Middle East*, ed. Mansoor Moaddel and Michele Gelfand (London: Oxford University Press, 2016).

8. Roy, "Transformation of the Arab World," 15.

9. With respect to the meaning of dignity in this context, Fukuyama writes, "Authoritarian regimes have many failings. . . . But their greatest weakness is moral: They do not recognize the *basic dignity* [emphasis in original] of their citizens and therefore can and do treat ordinary people with at best indifference and at worst with contempt" (Francis Fukuyama, "The Drive for Dignity," *Foreign Policy Online*, January 12, 2012). More generally, as expressed by Lynch, "The Arab uprising unfolded as a single, unified narrative of protest with shared heroes and villains, common stakes, and a deeply felt sense of shared destiny" (Marc Lynch, *The Arab Uprisings: The Unfinished Revolutions in the New Middle East* [New York: Public Affairs, 2012], 8).

10. Ibrahim Karawan, "'ReIslamization Movements' According to Kepel: On Striking Back and Striking Out," *Contention* 2 (Fall 1992): 162.

11. Rami Khouri, "A Lesson in Middle East History and Humanity," *Jordan Times*, May 28, 1991.

12. Rami Khouri, "The Arab Dream Won't Be Denied," *New York Times*, December 15, 1990.

13. Dirk Vandewalle, "From the New State to the New Era: Toward a Second Republic in Tunisia," *Middle East Journal* 42 (1988): 617.

14. David Seddon, "The Politics of 'Adjustment' in Morocco," in *Structural Adjustment in Africa*, ed. Bonnie K. Campbell and John Loxley (New York: St. Martin's, 1989) 263.

15. Jamal Al-Suwaidi, "Arab and Western Conceptions of Democracy: Evidence from a UAE Opinion Survey," in *Democracy, War and Peace in the Middle East*, ed. David Garnham and Mark Tessler (Bloomington: Indiana University Press, 1995), 13.

16. Abdulwahhab El-Affendi, "Islamic Movements: Establishments, Significance and Contextual Realities," in *Islamic Movements: Impact on Political Stability in the Arab World*, (Abu Dhabi: Emirates Center for Strategic Studies and Research, 2003), 23, 46.

17. Brief citations from many analysts making this argument are given in Tarek Masoud, *Counting Islam: Religion, Class, and Elections in Egypt* (New York: Cambridge University Press, 2014), 2–3.

18. Youssef Ibrahim, "Militant Muslims Grow Stronger as Algeria's Economy Grows Weaker," *New York Times*, June 25, 1990.

19. Amaney Jamal, "Actors, Public Opinion and Participation," in *The Middle East*, ed. Ellen Lust (Washington, DC: CQ Press, 2011), 204–5.

20. For additional discussion and a test of this alternative hypothesis, see Tessler, *Islam and Politics in the Middle East*, especially pp. 125–6.

21. Tessler, *Islam and Politics in the Middle East* (see ch. 3 and especially p. 143).

22. Abdou Filali-Ansari, "The Languages of the Arab Revolution," in *Democratization and Authoritarianism in the Arab World*, ed. Larry Diamond and Marc Plattner (Baltimore: Johns Hopkins University Press, 2014), 9–10.

23. Roy, "Transformation of the Arab World," 19–26.

24. Masoud, *Counting Islam*, 3–5.

3

DEMOGRAPHIC PRESSURE, SOCIAL DEMANDS, AND INSTABILITY IN THE MAGHREB

Wai Mun Hong

IN TUNISIA IN DECEMBER 2010, PROTESTS SWIFTLY SENT waves across the Arab region and, within months, overthrew two of the longest-serving leaders in the world.[1] The cause of these protests was thought to have been social injustice. This conjecture is not without basis. Before the Arab Spring, the economic prospects of North Africa[2] were optimistic, as the region was experiencing an annual average growth of 7 percent. On average, income per capita across the region was also growing steadily. But underneath these bullish economic figures was a region marred by protracted socioeconomic inequities that North African citizens struggled with every day.

Unemployment is one such chronic socioeconomic inequity that North Africa faces. According to the International Labour Organization (ILO), unemployment is a situation in which a person who is economically active is actively looking for work and yet finds himself or herself jobless. A protracted period of unemployment brings hopelessness and frustration. Some North African countries found themselves in this situation in 2010, and the perception of poor institutional enforcement and governance in North Africa only intensified the sense of helplessness, which fed into a buildup of dissatisfaction against those in power. When society's frustration finally burst out, a social uprising erupted in Tunisia and spread across the Arab world within a few weeks.

Despite a promising economic outlook, North Africa remains a region that has been strained, for a long time, by rampant unemployment. Unemployment rates hit double digits on the eve of the Arab Spring, revealing the reality that economic benefits did not actually trickle down to the population. Pre–Arab Spring economic policies had failed to translate into real growth and development that people at the bottom of the economic ladder could feel. Instead, these policies had created more and wider socioeconomic inequity in North African society.

Interestingly, though there had been a high rate of unemployment for a decade, and the rate was still high, the unemployment situation in North Africa actually improved in the period preceding the 2010–11 social uprisings. The rates fell to one of the lowest points in the past decade, and new jobs were created at a rate faster than the rate of growth of the labor force. Clearly, the supposed positive impact of these improvements was hardly felt by the people, especially in Egypt and Tunisia, where the Arab Spring began.

At the onset of the Arab Spring, the attention was directed at young people, who constituted the bulk of the protesters and were clearly frustrated with their socioeconomic situation, most likely related to unemployment. In fact, the unemployment rate among youth aged fifteen to twenty-four in some North African countries peaked at 30 percent on the eve of the Arab Spring, indicating that youth were more likely to find themselves jobless or vulnerable to unemployment than were other working age groups of the population. Indeed, job searching was increasingly daunting in North Africa during the period before the Arab Spring, when a poll showed that more than half of the youth in the region felt it was not a good time to find a job.[3]

Many observers associated the grim socioeconomic situation in North Africa with the region's demographics. Despite falling population growth rates since the early 1990s, the North African population remains youthful, with 41–53 percent of the population aged twenty-four and under in 2010, and without much variation since. The impact of any demographic change on society will take at least a generation to appear. For now, North Africa's youthful population will continue to put pressure on the job market's capacity to absorb new members, with multiple entrants for each person who retires from the labor force, a trend expected to last for some time to come.

Policy makers could, in fact, turn the youth demographic into an asset with coordinated human development efforts and market reforms. The socioeconomic quandary haunting North Africa today resulted in part from outdated, equity-oriented policies made during the postcolonial period in the process of nation building. The North African policy makers at that time focused heavily on public investment in education to modernize their economies. Generous spending to expand the public sector aimed to provide job and social security for the population. In many cases, these postcolonial policies were an attempt to consolidate power and strengthen the legitimacy of leadership of the North African states after gaining independence. It was not until the 1970s that the impact of the postcolonial policies became unsustainable. The governments found themselves grappling with depleting public funds, and the public sector was forced to shrink to reduce the pressure on the public budget. These policies had and still have a long-lasting impact on the population's attitude and perception, which have been slow to react and adjust to the new economic reality. This impact became visible as highly educated persons in North Africa, hoping to secure a life-long job in the public sector, suddenly found themselves excluded. They also faced difficulties in entering the job market as they were not equipped with the skills the private sector demanded.

The popular protests in 2011 pressured the regimes to undertake political reform, but the socioeconomic situation has not necessarily improved. In Egypt, the problems that existed before the Arab Spring, which are thought to have provoked the protests, have remained unaddressed, and instability has ensued, making daily life more difficult for ordinary people. The statist regimes in Algeria and Morocco for decades pursued welfare policies to insure political stability, with varying degrees of success. In fact, there were protests in these countries but on a smaller scale than those in Egypt and Tunisia. The governments in Algeria and Morocco were quick to react and managed to normalize the situations by giving in to the demands of the people while still maintaining a firm grip. The fallouts of the Arab Spring uprisings and the risks and uncertainty of democratic reforms have revived interest in the old-style authoritarianism, usually with a single dominant actor, whether a king or an army general.

Against this background, this chapter will explore the intricacies of and interactions between the demographic and human development dynamics affecting the socioeconomic landscape in North Africa, particularly unemployment among the youth, in an attempt to explain what might have caused the Arab Spring. More than five years have passed since the Arab Spring first erupted in Tunisia in December 2010, yet the same socioeconomic worries continue to haunt policy makers in North Africa. To provide a more updated perspective, this chapter will examine if and how the demographic structure has changed and the impact of human development on the employment situation since the Arab Spring, and will compare this situation with the situation before the Arab Spring. The aim is to learn if the role of demographics in the Arab Spring has been overestimated, and thus to learn if and how the situation is heading toward stability.

Unlike the many qualitatively oriented papers on this topic, this chapter uses straightforward statistical analysis methods, as a complement to the existing work, to identify the differences in socioeconomic dynamics across the North African countries. This analysis seeks to illustrate and explain how the nuanced differences provoked sociopolitical upheavals in the North African countries. More than five years on, are those North African countries heading toward some kind of stability? Are the North African countries that were not affected by the 2010–11 sociopolitical disruptions at risk of disruption, or will stability prevail?

These questions will be addressed in five sections. From a perspective comparing the situation before and after the Arab Spring, the first four sections focus on the following four areas: demographics, unemployment and youth, the youth labor force and job market trends, and human development. The first section presents an overview of the demographics of the North African countries and analyzes the impact of the demographics on the socioeconomic structure. The second section focuses on the unemployment situation and structure, and how demographic transitions influenced unemployment among the youth before the Arab Spring between 2001 and 2010 and after between 2010 and 2014. The third section explores the labor force and job market trends with a focus on the youth. The fourth section identifies aspects of human development that might have hindered socioeconomic progress in North Africa and indirectly contributed to the root cause of the Arab Spring. Despite the shortcomings of statistical analysis in capturing the intricate interactions between demographic, socioeconomic, and human developments, the last section provides plausible explanations of the results from the analyses in the four sections, and goes beyond the existing narratives on the impact of demographics on the socioeconomic landscape in North Africa.

Demographics in North Africa

It is important to highlight at the outset if and how demographics have played and will continue to play a role in the sociopolitical prospects in North Africa. Banal as it may sound, understanding demographic dynamics

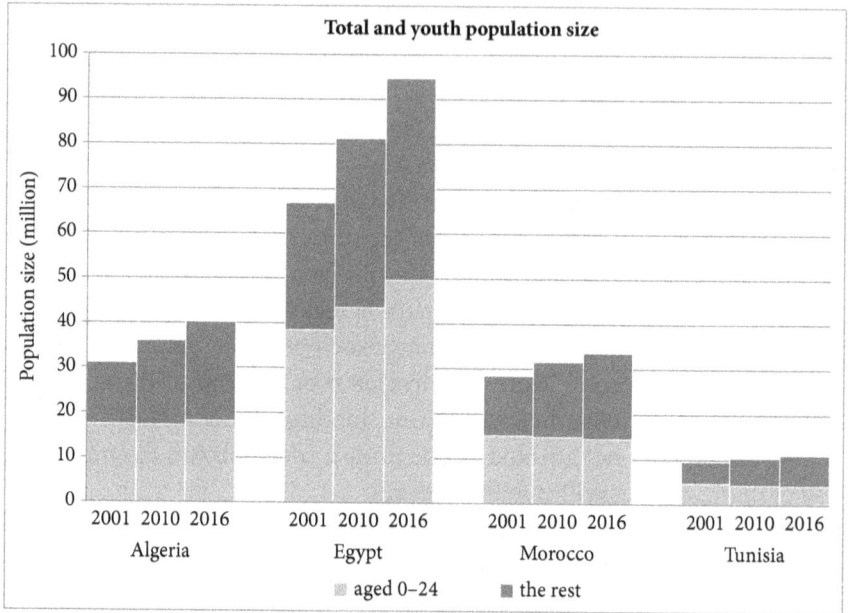

Chart 3.1. Population size and growth rate in North Africa. *Source*: Author's own calculations based on data from the US Census Bureau's International Data Base, including population by five-year age groups for the years 2001, 2010, and 2016.

helps policy makers make long-term plans, devising strategies to reap economic gains as the population expands and to minimize negative effects as the population contracts. The youth should be given particular attention as they are typically more energetic, more aspiring, and easily inspired, and they are becoming increasingly educated and well informed due to their greater access to the internet and social media. More importantly, the youth are characterized as the driving force of economies as they reach the working age.

Although the population growth rate has fallen, the population of North Africa continues to expand. The population of North Africa was approximately 160 million on the eve of the Arab Spring, in 2010, and today it has reached almost 180 million, an increase of 20 million. Between 2010 and 2016, the population of the region has grown by approximately 13 percent, compared to 17 percent the decade before between 2001 and 2010 (see chart 3.1). All North African countries experienced a drop in population growth between the two periods (pre- and post–Arab Spring) by between 3.5 and

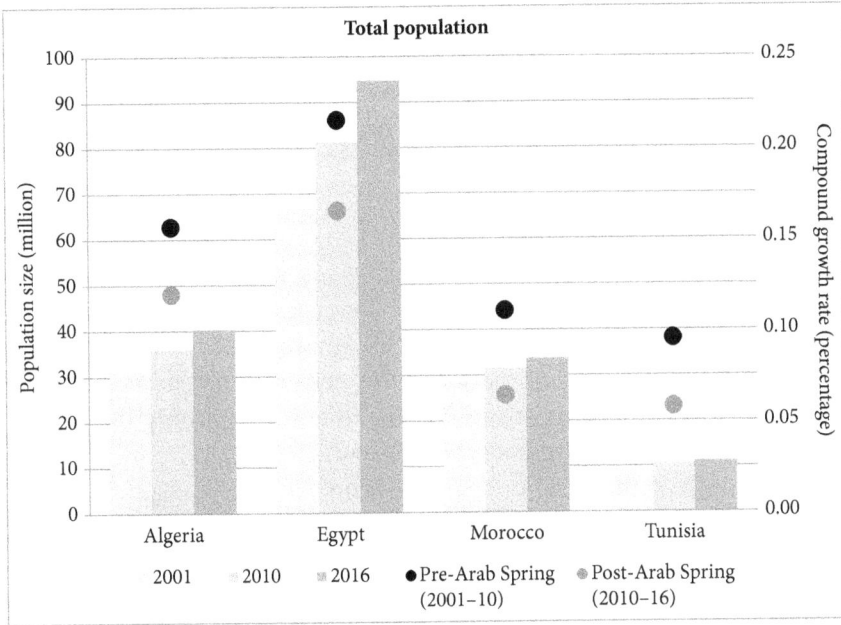

Chart 3.2. Youth population size and growth rate in North Africa. *Source:* Author's own calculations based on data from the US Census Bureau's International Data Base, including population by five-year age groups for the years 2001, 2010, and 2016. "Youth" is defined as ages twenty-four and below.

5 percent. From an optimistic perspective, these countries' economies would grow as their populations continued to expand, driving up demand for goods and services, provided the demand could be met by domestic production. If the demand could not be met with domestic production, the population of North Africa would be at risk of growing in an unsustainable manner, as the economy would become dependent on imports, prompting a negative balance of payments and putting pressure on the public budget.

In regard to the youth, despite the youth population growing at a slower rate than the total population both before and after the Arab Spring, the demographic structure of North Africa remains marked by a relatively young population. Today, between 38 and 52 percent of the region's total population is age twenty-four or below; in comparison, in more developed countries, the youth population is typically less than 30 percent.

In the decade before the Arab Spring, the population aged twenty-four and below declined in all North African countries except Egypt. After the Arab Spring, Algeria's youth population began to expand, and that of

Egypt continued to grow. Morocco's youth population declined by 2–2.5 percent, and Tunisia's youth population growth rate declined by 3 percent (see chart 3.2). As a result, the youth population in North Africa expanded by only 4.2 million in the decade before the Arab Spring and has expanded by 6.5 million since.

Demographic trends in North Africa did not change significantly from before to after the Arab Spring; however, some countries in the region are experiencing difficulties. The labor participation rate has remained largely unchanged, and to reap the benefits of the expanding youth population, the domestic economy would need to create more economic opportunities to absorb them in the labor market. The employment situation confronting North African countries will thus be to absorb not only the current pool of unemployed persons, but also the new members. The growing youth population will continue to pressure the economy to create sufficient jobs, whether to employ the entire labor force or to maintain the unemployment rate, to ensure sustainable socioeconomic stability.

Unemployment in North Africa

Among other factors, unemployment and poor employment opportunities are thought to be two of the causes that led to the Arab Spring. The social injustice of the unemployment situation of working-age youth became fertile ground for developing the sentiments that led to the uprisings.

By 2010, the average unemployment rate in North Africa was slightly more than 10 percent, or 5.12 million unemployed persons. Although this was one of the lowest points in the previous decade, in both rate and absolute number (see chart 3.3), it was still a high rate, and there had been consistently high rates for a decade. Tunisia had the worst unemployment of the region in 2010 and had had an unemployment rate fluctuating between 12 and 15 percent for a decade. Egypt had a better situation than Tunisia, yet this did not prevent the sociopolitical unrest. It could be that the stable unemployment rate throughout the decade 2001–10 failed to create a sense of socioeconomic improvement and heightened the population's frustrations. Unemployment in Algeria, on the other hand, fell steadily from above 25 percent in 2001 to 10 percent by 2010, showing the greatest improvement among the North African countries. Morocco's unemployment rate, although similar to that of Egypt, fell by 3 percent from 2001 to 2010.

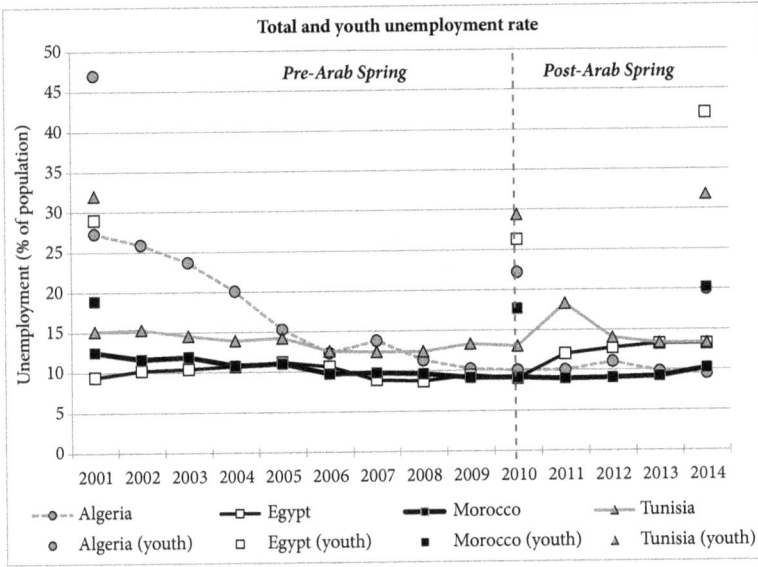

Chart 3.3. Trends of the unemployment rate in North Africa. *Source*: Author's own elaboration based on data from the World Bank's World Development Indicators and Global Financial Development Database on total unemployment (% of total labor force) and total youth unemployment (% of total labor force ages fifteen to twenty-four).

The immediate period after the Arab Spring saw unemployment situations deteriorate further. Sociopolitical instability in Egypt and Tunisia almost halted economic activities, and unemployment in Egypt and Tunisia surged by 36 percent (or 895,539 persons) and 43 percent (214,303 persons), respectively, between 2010 and 2011. Subsequently, the situation in Tunisia improved quickly as the number of unemployed persons declined by 22 percent in 2012. The situation in Egypt, however, worsened, as the number of unemployed persons continued to increase to 3.6 million in 2012. During this period, unemployment in Morocco increased by 21 percent (or 224,117 persons). By 2014, unemployment in North Africa had increased by 34.6 percent (or 1.77 million persons) since 2010.

In a region with a significant share of young people, it is easy to assume that working-age youth are most vulnerable when unemployment rises. Indeed, the statistics show that the unemployment rate of those aged between fifteen and twenty-four was higher than the rate of the total labor force, both before and after the Arab Spring, supporting this assumption (see chart 3.3). This trend was common across North Africa and was in part a result of slower job growth in the public sector.

The difference between the unemployment rates of the total labor force and the youth labor force across North African countries has shown some improvement overall, but the gaps have widened in most countries. Algeria's gap decreased steadily from before to after the Arab Spring. The gaps in Egypt, Morocco, and Tunisia widened. Data show that Egypt faces the highest risk of a continuously widening gap, more than any other country in the region.

The above statistical evidence on the gap between the unemployment rates of the total labor force and the youth labor force supports the hypothesis that discontent among the youth gave rise to more violent social uprisings in Egypt and Tunisia, while Algeria and Morocco experienced lesser unrest. High youth unemployment rates persisted in the decade preceding the Arab Spring in Egypt and Tunisia, as shown by the dots on chart 3.3, and were at 26–29 and 30–32 percent, respectively. Although the unemployment situation for youth had improved since 2001, the effects were insignificant, and the youth hardly felt the benefits. Since the Arab Spring, the economic uncertainties brought on by the sociopolitical instability have worsened the unemployment situation of youth in Egypt and Tunisia, with Egypt the worse of the two.

Youth unemployment trends before and after the Arab Spring were a mirror of the overall unemployment patterns in North Africa. The improving trends preceding the Arab Spring turned out to be a mistaken indication of better socioeconomic prospects for young North Africans, particularly in Egypt and Tunisia. With free time to socialize and lament, unemployed youth grew restless, and frustrations built until they manifested as the Arab Spring. This explanation is not the only possibility, but it is plausible. A similar situation could occur with groups of any age.

This analysis shows that the unemployment rates in North African countries since the Arab Spring have worsened, without showing signs of stabilizing. The hope that sociopolitical transformation could improve the socioeconomic lives of the population increasingly pressures policy makers to meet the expectations not only of the youth but of the entire population. Because the job market has not improved and the economic situation has become less stable under the pluralistic order, the lure back to the statist system that existed before the Arab Spring will become more attractive.

Labor Force and Job Market Trends and Prospects in North Africa

The North African countries experienced steady economic growth in the decade before the Arab Spring at between 7.5 and 12 percent per annum on average.[4] With the sociopolitical and economic reforms following the social unrest, however, economic growth slowed as the affected North African countries adjusted to the new realities.

The unemployment rate indicates how well the labor and job markets are doing in a given economy. In a working economy, more new jobs are created as the economy grows. The job market expanded in North Africa before and after the Arab Spring. Whether the number of new jobs is enough to absorb the additional persons in the labor force, however, is a different narrative. Given the high unemployment rate that still persists in some North African countries, the economies are clearly not generating enough new jobs.

On the eve of the Arab Spring, the labor force in North Africa was approximately 53.8 million. It had grown by 25 percent from 2001 to 2010, which was equivalent to 10.8 million entrants into the labor force. The region had generally succeeded in stabilizing the unemployment rate by stimulating a job creation growth of 32 percent between 2001 and 2010, or 11.8 million new jobs added to the job market, more than sufficient to absorb the 10.8 million labor force entrants. Despite these promising figures, the sociopolitical uprising across North Africa occurred, presenting further evidence that unemployment statistics were an inaccurate indication that might have led to miscalculations in policy making, provoking the uprisings and their negative socioeconomic outcomes.

Job creation and labor force expansion patterns remained unbalanced among the North African countries before and after the Arab Spring, although the countries shared a similar characteristic. From 2001 to 2010, the number of new jobs created overall in North Africa grew at a faster rate than the number of new labor force members. If one ignored the details, this pattern could be seen as an encouraging sign of the labor and job market in North Africa.

In fact, this promising growth in new jobs overall disguised problems in some countries. Before the Arab Spring, Algeria and Morocco had created more new jobs than the number of new labor force members, whereas Egypt and Tunisia had failed to do so. Between 2001 and 2010, Egypt was experiencing a deficit of 522,846 jobs, and Tunisia 3,670 (see chart 3.4).

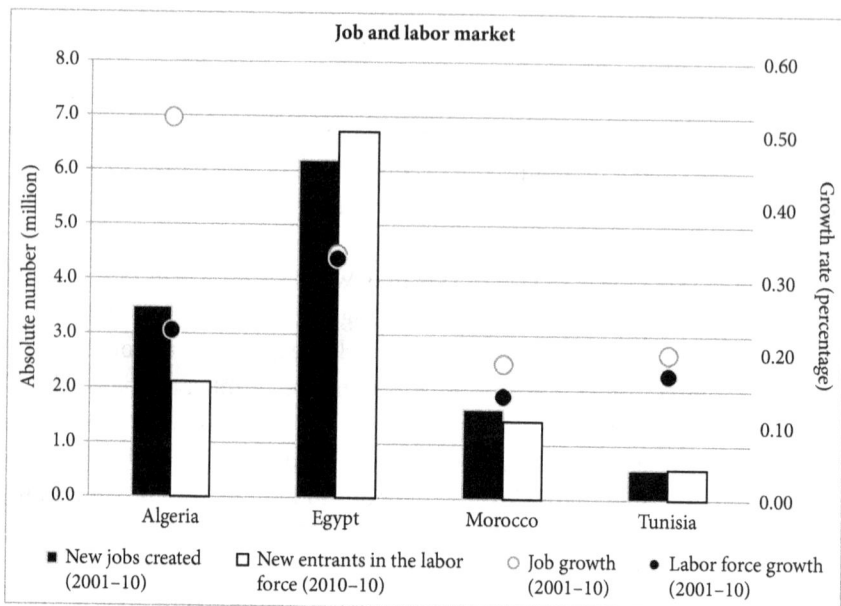

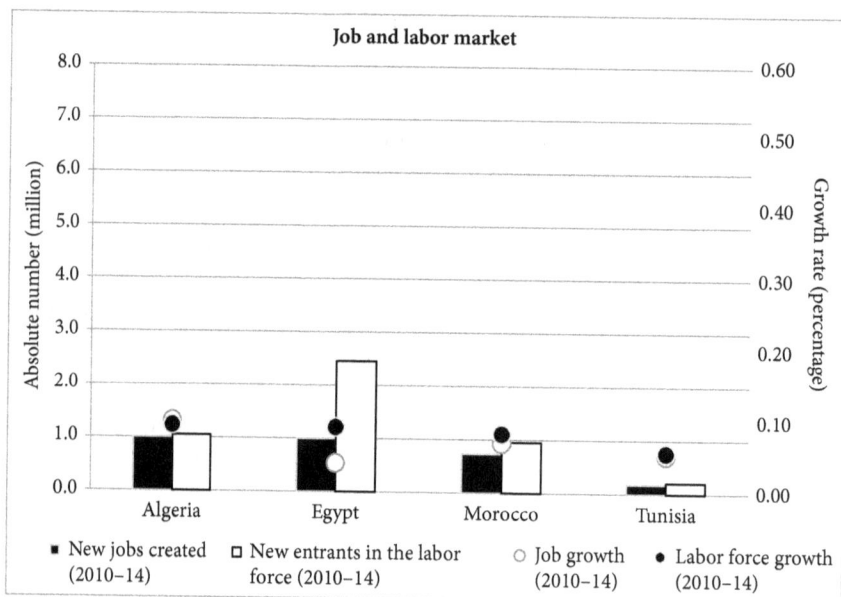

Chart 3.4. Job market and labor force trends before and after the Arab Spring. *Source*: Author's own calculations based on data from the World Bank's World Development Indicators and Global Financial Development Database on total unemployment (% of total labor force) and total labor force.

Labor and job market trends in North Africa after the Arab Spring were only grimmer. Between 2010 and 2014, all four North African countries failed to create enough new jobs to absorb the labor force entrants. On the regional level, North Africa experienced a deficit of 1.77 million new jobs, the number needed to employ the entire labor force of 58.47 million persons.

Nonetheless, the diverse performance of the labor and job markets across the North African countries before the Arab Spring influenced how the overall landscape was perceived, even as the situation headed to the decline of the post–Arab Spring period. The ability of Algeria and Morocco to create 1.38 million and 214,061 new jobs, respectively, in the period before the Arab Spring more than offset those countries' deficits of 42,893 and 224,117 jobs in the period after the Arab Spring. In Egypt and Tunisia, however, already in dire job deficits, the worsening labor and job markets only increased the burden on the economies.

Regarding the youth in the North African labor force, those aged fifteen to twenty-four were 20–35 percent of the total labor force. The share decreased from before to after the Arab Spring as the size of the youth labor force continued to shrink. All countries except Egypt experienced a shrinking youth labor force as a result of the shrinking youth population (aged fifteen to twenty-four) and its falling labor force participation rate (see chart 3.5).

The shrinking youth labor force and falling participation rate, however, did not alleviate the pressure to create enough jobs to employ the young people. The young job hunters continued to face more difficulties when looking for jobs. By the eve of the Arab Spring, 74 percent of the unemployed in North Africa were youth. The rate was highest in Egypt, where more than 90 percent of the unemployed were youth. At some point, all the North African countries except Egypt did experience improved youth unemployment, as the share of unemployed youth decreased. This progress was particularly marked in Algeria and Tunisia. In Algeria, the share of unemployed youth relative to the total number of unemployed persons decreased from 61.24 percent in 2010 to 48.72 percent in 2014. On the eve of the Arab Spring, the youth in Tunisia had a lower share of unemployment than their peers in the region, with youth making up only 53 percent of the total number of unemployed persons; compared to their peers in other North African countries, the youth in Tunisia were less vulnerable to joblessness (see chart 3.5).

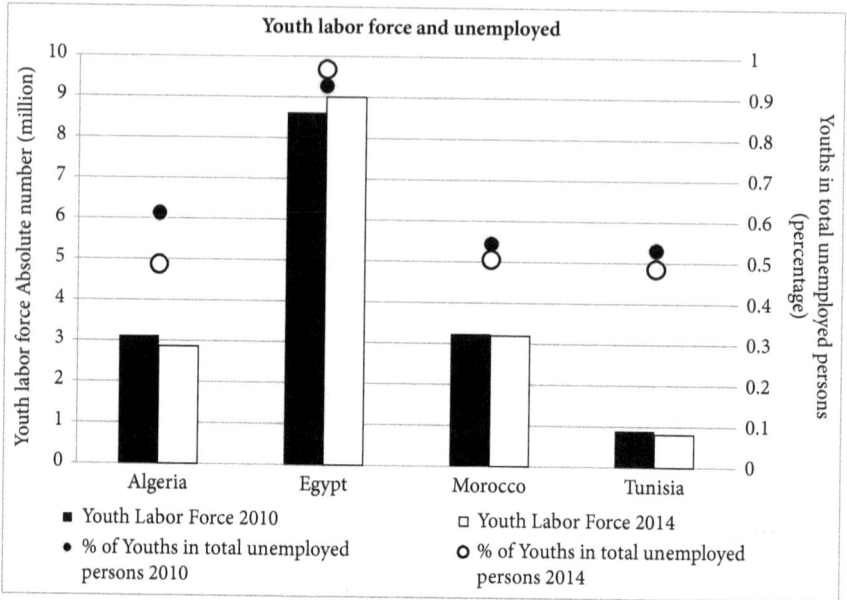

Chart 3.5. Size of youth labor force and youth share of total unemployed persons.
Source: Author's own calculations based on data from the World Bank's World Development Indicators and Global Financial Development Database on labor force participation rate for ages fifteen to twenty-four and total (%), and the US Census Bureau's International Data Base data on population by youth age groups.

The low employment rate of young people in North Africa before the Arab Spring demonstrates the seriousness of the situation: only 13.23 percent of the 11.87 million new jobs created were occupied by youth (see chart 3.6). The situation and dynamics, however, differed from one country to another across the region. Unlike in Morocco and Tunisia, the youth in Algeria and Egypt were more likely to benefit from the expansion of the job market; 11.96 percent and 28 percent of the new jobs added to the job market in Algeria and Egypt went to young people. But this situation did not persist. By the end of the Arab Spring, youth in all North African countries were being excluded from the benefits of job market expansion, as the number of employed youth shrank. The age segment of the labor force outside the range of fifteen to twenty-four years old benefited the most from the expansion of the job market.

Comparing the shares of employed and unemployed youth with the number in new jobs and the total number of new jobs reinforces the evidence that the benefits of job market expansion were disproportionately

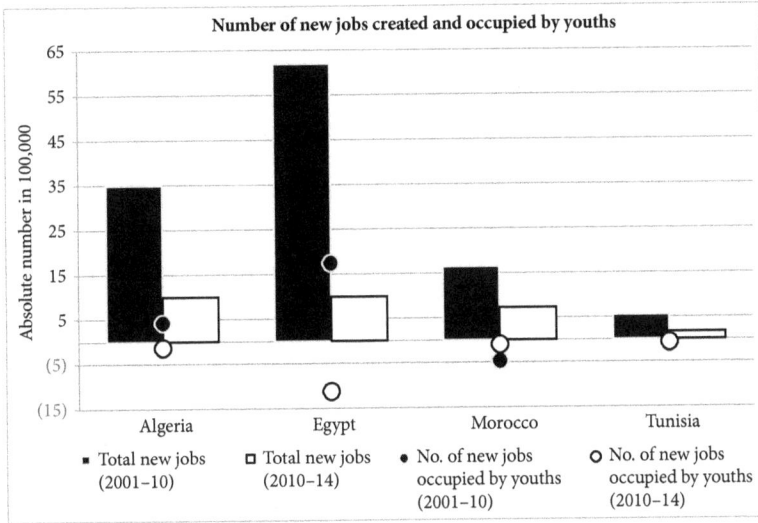

Chart 3.6. Job market prospects for youth. *Source*: Author's own calculations based on data from the World Bank's World Development Indicators and Global Financial Development Database on total youth unemployment (% of total labor force ages fifteen to twenty-four), total labor force participation rate for ages fifteen to twenty-four (%), the population aged between fifteen and twenty-four, total unemployment (% of total labor force), and total labor force; and the US Census Bureau's International Data Base data on population by youth age groups.

unavailable to youth. In addition, young people in North Africa had a higher risk of marginalization after the Arab Spring than before it. Nevertheless, in the presence of demographic change, it becomes increasingly unclear if the low employment rate of young people is an outcome of the shrinking youth population and their falling labor force participation rate, factors the region will continue to face; or if it is due to the youth's weaker job market prospects or the economy simply not generating the types of jobs that the youth are trained for.

One possible explanation of the weaker job market prospects the youth face is the time-lag effect of the equity-oriented socioeconomic policies North African governments lavishly spent on to expand the public sector. The expansion of the public sector provided lifelong job security and a social safety net to the people during the postindependence period. Many workers in the public sector, employed during the postindependence period, will not vacate their jobs until they reach retirement age. Shrinking the size of the public sector in the face of the depleting public budget would probably exacerbate the youth unemployment situation.

Regardless, the imbalance between entrants into the labor market and the number of new jobs created would no doubt produce discontentment in any age group that was negatively affected by it. If it were not the youth, then it would be the older job seekers suffering unemployment.

Human Development and the Socioeconomic Landscape in North Africa

Pure quantitative statistics provide an overarching view of the demographics, unemployment, and labor force and job market situation in North Africa. However, this approach does not explain the possible factors that gave rise to the conditions in North Africa in the periods before and after the Arab Spring. As suggested in the introduction of this chapter, human development is closely linked to demographic, labor force, and job market trends and could be an area for investigation to address the question.

Education is a significant part of human development. In education, unsurprisingly for a social equity–oriented region, North African countries performed better than other regions at a similar level of economic development, or even above global standards. Public education is free in some North African countries, and in a few countries is free even up to the tertiary level. Therefore, North African countries' investment in education as a share of government expenditure is significantly high. This investment is a reflection of the importance of education in North African countries' national socioeconomic policies, which focus on equal opportunity. As an example, Tunisia led its North African peers in public investment in education. Expenditure on education represented 25 percent of Tunisia's total government expenditure, compared to Morocco's share of 17.38 percent, 12.29 percent in Egypt, and 11.43 percent in Algeria (see table 3.1).

Although spending on education is important to the government, it may not translate into socioeconomic benefits that are hoped for. With higher public expenditure in education, the government has greater control over education, particularly on what is taught. Besides, as the public sector tends to be less responsive, with greater government control, the education system and curriculum are rarely quick enough to react to the changes in skills and knowledge demanded by the market.

Considering the government's investment in education as a share of the gross domestic product (GDP), instead of as a share of total government expenditure, could be a rough gauge to assess the efficiency and

Table 3.1. Public investment in education, average between 2001 and 2010

	Share of government expenditure (%)	Share of GDP (%)
Algeria	11.43	4.24
Egypt	12.29	4.31
Morocco	17.38	5.30
Tunisia	25.96	6.39
North Africa	16.77	5.08

Source: Author's own calculations based on data from the World Bank's World Development Indicators and Global Financial Development Database on expenditure on education as a percentage of total government expenditure, and total government expenditure on education as a percentage of the GDP. (For the post–Arab Spring period, there is no data from 2010 to 2014 for any North African country except Tunisia, which has data available from 2010 and 2012.)

effectiveness of public expenditure on education. The logic is that education is one of the variables that contribute to economic growth, and that greater investment in education will produce more educated persons to take up economically productive occupations. Among the North African countries, Egypt's investment in education is the most efficient and effective; government expenditure on education represented 4.31 percent of Egypt's GDP, followed by Algeria (4.38%), Morocco (5.3%), and Tunisia (6.39%; see table 3.1). However, this situation, in which policy makers in North Africa have done well, is only part of the story.

As a first step into the details, consider that more public investment in education should lead to a positive outcome, such as greater accessibility to education. All North African countries except Morocco maintained an enrollment of more than 95 percent for primary school education, although the rates fell from the period 2009–10 to the period 2014–15 (see chart 3.7). For secondary education, enrollment rates increased in all North African countries from 2009–10 to 2014–15 and ranged from 68 percent to 97 percent after the Arab Spring. Similarly, tertiary education enrollment rates improved in all North African countries except Egypt. These results show that North African citizens are more likely to receive an education than their peers in other countries that are at a similar level of economic development. Despite falling in primary enrollment rates, the improvement in overall enrollment rates for secondary and tertiary education from before

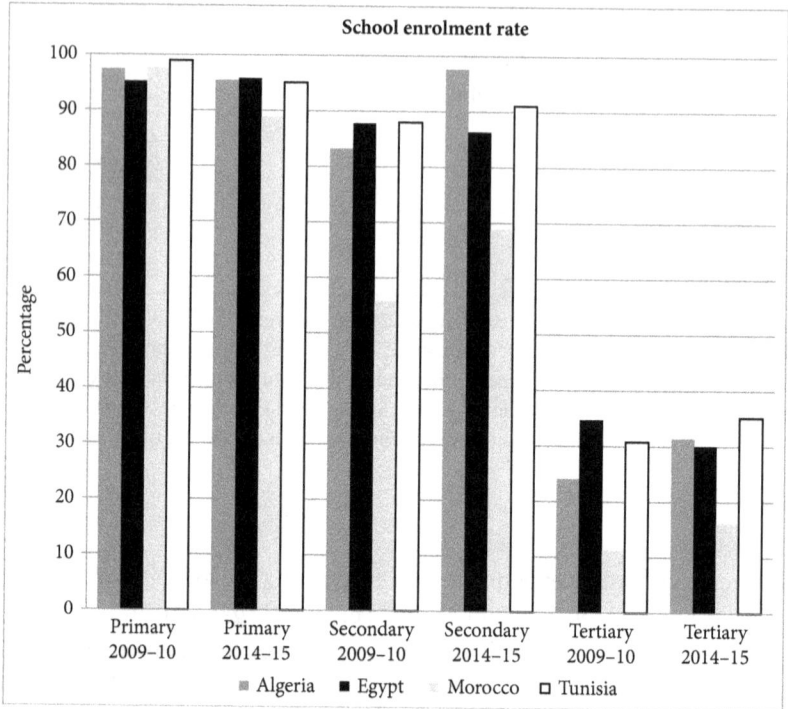

Chart 3.7. School enrollment rates for children ages five to eighteen. *Source*: Author's own elaborations based on the World Economic Forum's Global Competitive Index's series on primary education enrollment (net, %), secondary education enrollment (gross, %), and tertiary education enrollment (gross, %).

to after the Arab Spring could be a sign of the population's reviving confidence in their socioeconomic prospects.

Considering only enrollment, however, is a strategy policy makers adopt to acquire an immediate, quantitative outcome. To ensure a sustainable outcome, policy makers in North Africa would have to improve the quality of the education system, which more directly impacts the socioeconomic outcome. Sizable investment in education in North Africa has not necessarily translated into better education systems, despite evidence of improvement, even compared with other regions at a similar level of economic development. Two specific areas that are closely related to the overall quality of the education system are math and science education and management skills; these areas are considered below.

The overall perceived quality of the education system across North Africa remains below the median mark (3.5 on a scale of 1 to 7). This is

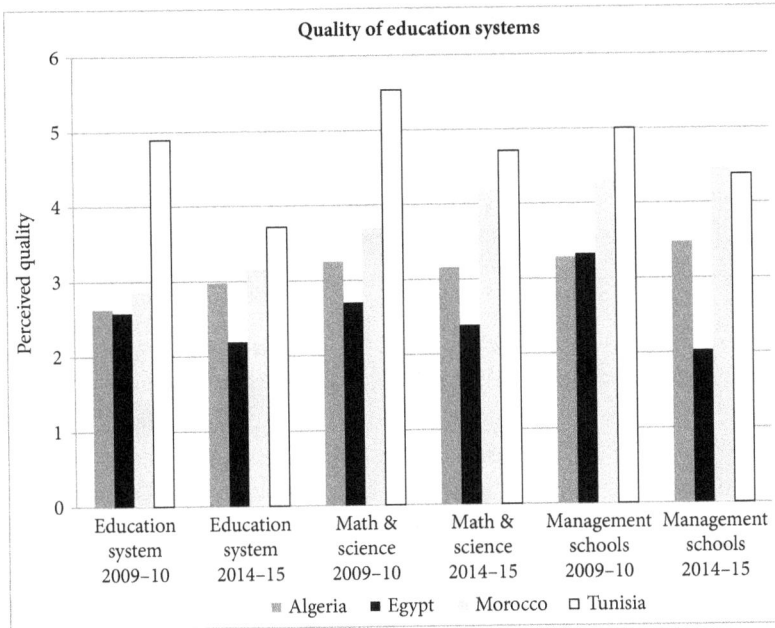

Chart 3.8. Perceived quality of education systems and schools in North Africa.
Source: Author's own elaborations based on the World Economic Forum's Global Competitive Index's series on the quality of the education system (scale of 1–7, 7 is best), quality of math and science education (scale of 1–7, 7 is best), and quality of management schools (scale of 1–7, 7 is best).

true for all North African countries both before and after the Arab Spring, except Tunisia (see chart 3.8). Only in Algeria and Morocco did the perceived quality of education system improve.

Underpinning the entire education system, and keeping it relevant to the fast-changing socioeconomic environment, is math and science education. In today's economic system, mathematical and scientific knowledge is increasingly important to technological development and advancement. The ubiquitous use of technology is driving up the productivity and efficiency of the economic system at a breakneck speed. The assumption is that high-quality math and science education will better prepare the labor force to adopt and create new technologies. Some North African countries have not performed well in this area. The higher-than-median score for the region's perceived quality of math and science education is owed mostly to Morocco (3.69 in 2009–10 and 4.19 in 2014–15) and Tunisia (5.53 in 2009–10 and 4.71 in 2014–15).

Management skills are another crucial area used to gauge the ability of the students to manage resources efficiently, effectively, and strategically. Although the perceived quality of management schools may not give the most accurate reflection of the quality of education in general, as a proxy, it provides a rough gauge. As with math and science education, the perceived quality of management schools in North Africa overall dropped from before the Arab Spring to after, although perceived quality improved in Algeria (from 3.28 in 2009–10 to 3.48 in 2014–15) and Morocco (from 4.32 to 4.46).

These findings shed light on the problem of a skills mismatch between the labor force and the job market in North Africa, which has led to structural unemployment in the region. North African countries faced difficulties in attracting businesses in increasingly knowledge- and technology-intensive sectors because their labor force was inadequately qualified. In an increasingly interdependent global economic environment, North African countries have displayed little compatibility between the supply structure of their economies and the global demand, thus making them more vulnerable to external competition and more likely to lose out than to benefit from globalization. The quality of their education systems could threaten the skills adequacy of the labor force.

The Executive Opinion Survey conducted by the World Economic Forum (WEF) provided evidence of a skills mismatch in North Africa, although after the Arab Spring, the mismatch became less problematic in all North African countries except Morocco. The percentage of respondents in Morocco who chose an inadequately educated workforce as the most problematic factor when doing business increased from 8.3 percent in 2009–10 to 11.3 percent in 2014–15 (see chart 3.9). Egypt and Tunisia improved the most; the percentage of respondents indicating an inadequately educated workforce as the most problematic factor dropped from 10.4 percent in 2009–10 to 5.4 percent in 2014–15 for Egypt, and from 8.7 percent to 4.6 percent for Tunisia. Despite the progress, a skills mismatch remains one of the top problem areas in doing business in North Africa.

In addition, the background qualification profile of the labor force provides evidence of a skills mismatch as North African countries are beginning to promote knowledge- and technology-intensive sectors, such as the renewable energy sector in Morocco. Using the share of tertiary graduates by program as a rough estimate, more than half of the labor force in North

Inadequate educated workforce as most problematic in doing business

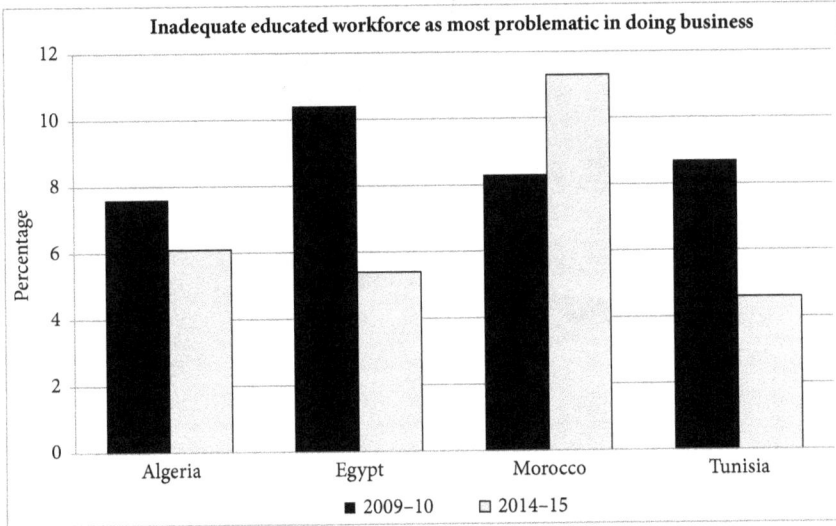

Chart 3.9. Percentage of respondents who chose an inadequately educated workforce as the most problematic factor in doing business. *Source*: World Economic Forum Global Competitive Report, 2009–10 and 2014–15.

Africa has a nonmathematical or nonscientific background (see chart 3.10). The numbers vary across the North African countries: 44.37 percent of tertiary graduates in Tunisia are trained in the sciences, engineering, and information technology (IT); 35.25 percent in Morocco; and 31.2 percent in Algeria. To catch up with global trends and thus meet the demands of and benefit from economic globalization, North African countries need a larger part of the labor force to be well trained in mathematics and science. This labor force would absorb knowledge in the fast-changing technological environment, not only to improve technologies but also to create new technologies to increase productivity and efficiency.

Although the reason many students in North Africa choose the humanities, arts, and social sciences is hard to determine, survey results measuring the attitudes of Arab youth revealed some plausible explanations. In 2010, more than 50 percent of those interviewed expressed a preference to work for the government, where salaries are higher and job and social security benefits are better compared to the private sector (typically, a bureaucratic system does not require mathematics and science training). This attitude originated with the postcolonial policies in which education

Algeria, 2015

- Science, engineering and information technology
- Not specified
- Services
- Forestry, Fisheries and Veterinary
- Education
- Health and Welfare
- Arts, Humanities and social sciences

Morocco, 2010

- Science, engineering and information technology
- Not specified
- Services
- Forestry, Fisheries and Veterinary
- Education
- Health and Welfare
- Arts, Humanities and social sciences

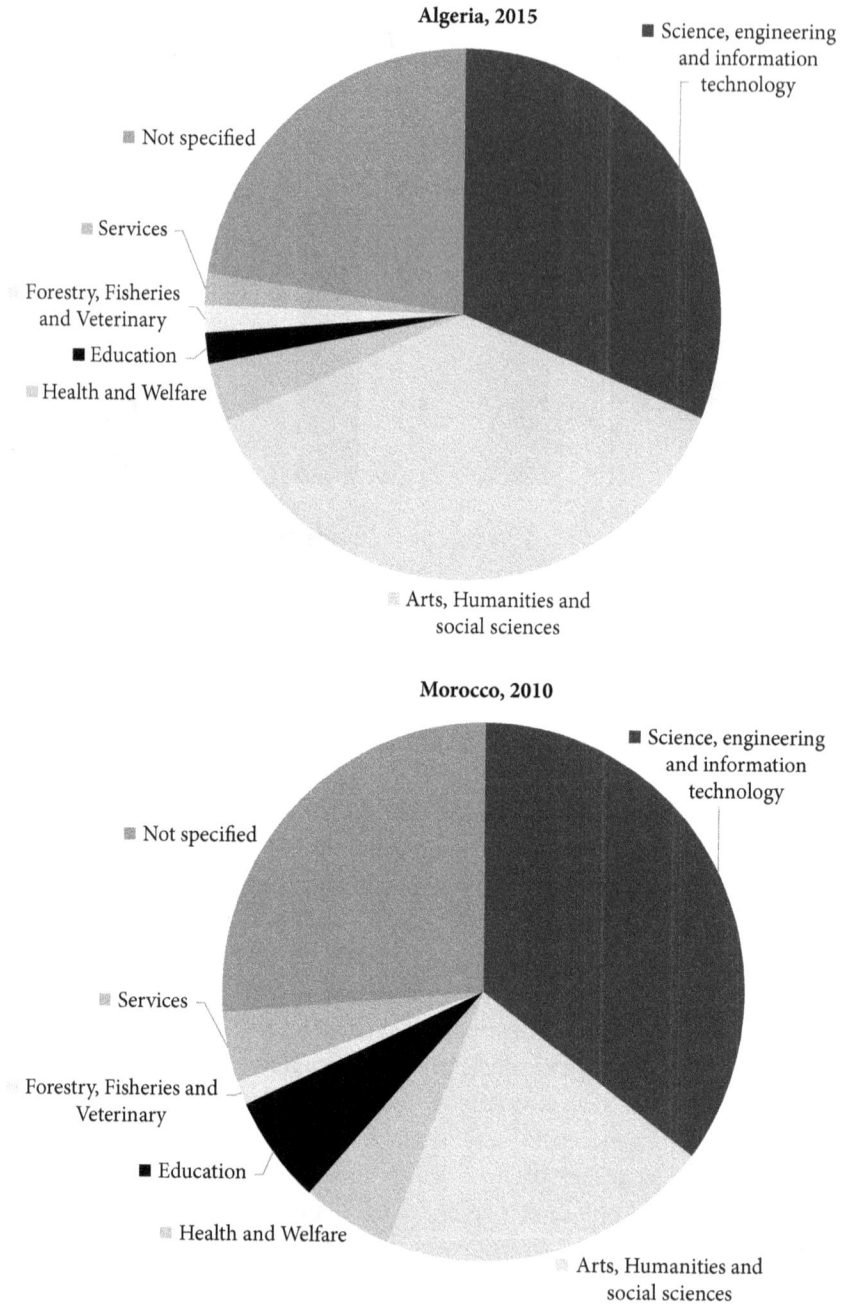

Chart 3.10. Share of tertiary graduates by program. *Source*: UNESCO Institute for Statistics' Data Centre's series on the distribution of tertiary graduates by program from 1999 to 2016. Note: Data shown is the latest for each country. No data for Egypt.

Tunisia, 2015

Science, engineering and information technology

Not specified

Services

Forestry, Fisheries and Veterinary

Education

Health and Welfare

Arts, Humanities and social sciences

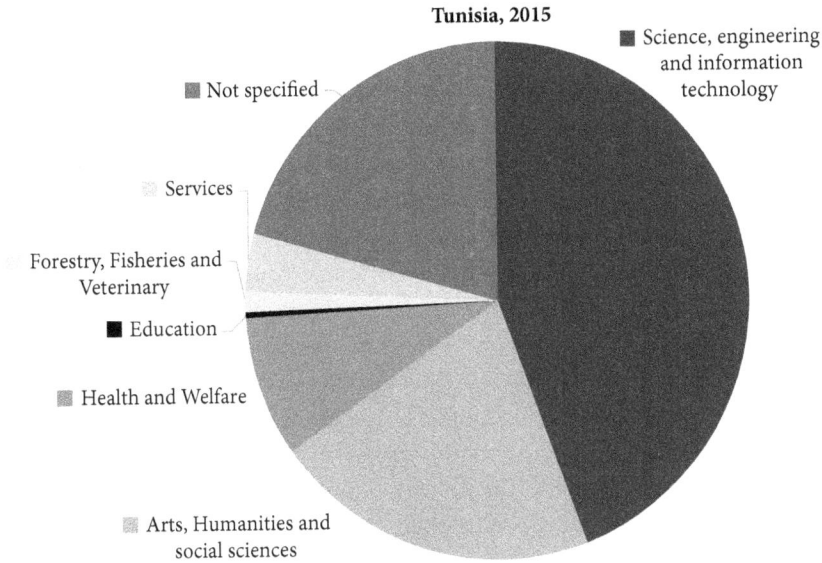

Chart 3.10. (*continued*)

was free, including higher-level education, and university graduates were guaranteed jobs in the public sector.[5]

Supporting the persisting mind-set of the youth's preference to work in the public sector in North Africa, the latest edition of the Executive Opinion Survey, published in 2013, revealed that a declining percentage of youth feel satisfied with the availability of good jobs. In Algeria, the percentage fell from 46 percent in 2010 to 28 percent in 2012; in Egypt, from 13 percent to 8 percent; in Morocco, from 34 percent to 18 percent; and in Tunisia, from 35 percent to 16 percent.[6] This lower perception of the availability of good jobs will result in a stronger preference to join the public sector. The statistics showed that the unemployment in North Africa was in part a structural problem, where workers' skills did not match the demands of the job market, despite much public investment in education.

Discussion and Conclusions

The sheer magnitude of the participation of young people in the 2010–11 social uprising across North Africa has directed the attention of policy makers in North Africa to the young people's mind-set, attitude, and socioeconomic situation. Before the Arab Spring, socioeconomic data gave a false signal of better prospects that led to higher hopes, rather than capturing the reality of the social injustice that the majority of the North African population was subjected to.

Although unemployment rates were falling before the Arab Spring uprisings, the number of unemployed persons remained high, particularly among youth. Although they represented less than a third of the labor force, the youth remained more vulnerable to joblessness than other age segments of the labor force in North Africa. Their unemployment was blamed on demographics, namely, the large population of young people. However, as the youth labor force continued to shrink, in some cases faster than the total labor force, the employment situation for youth did not improve.

The role of demographics in the situation could have been overestimated. That is, demographics might only partially explain the unemployment problem. In fact, demographic factors interact with and respond to policies, the effects of which are hard to quantify.

Given the history of North Africa, it is logical to relate the postcolonial equity-oriented policies that shaped the mind-set of the population to the socioeconomic realities. Policy makers in North Africa performed well, and in some cases better than the global standard, in creating access to education. This education, however, did not match the global economic environment, which has become increasingly dynamic. The North African postcolonial policies produced a young labor force among which a majority hoped to work in the public sector, with its higher salaries and better social security.

By the early 1970s, North African governments found themselves with tremendous public debts that forced them to adopt neoliberal reforms. These neoliberal reforms led to high economic growth in the 1970s and 1980s, but the unemployment situation did not improve because the benefits went mostly to the natural resource sectors. Employment elasticity in the natural resource industry is typically low, and therefore the economic growth had a limited influence on job market expansion. Policy makers were not quick enough to respond to the dire situation and to promote the private sector outside of the natural resource industry, to make up the shortfall in jobs.

Mind-set is hard to change. Despite the fact that the public sector has ceased to expand, hopeful students still covet a place in it. Because of this hopefulness, the students prefer to be trained in the humanities and social sciences, areas that fit better in the public sector. Many graduates plan to wait until a job in the public sector becomes available. As the reality of protracted unemployment finally hits them, however, the graduates turn to the private sector as an alternative, only to realize their skills do not match the demands of the job market. Some continue waiting for a job, if they can afford to do so, whereas some return to school to gain new skills to increase their employability.

Regardless, the youth feel frustration, disappointment, and hopelessness. A common Franco-Arab slang word, "hittistes," aptly describes the phenomenon in North Africa where young people literally lean against a wall on the street, watching the day go by, without doing anything out of hopelessness. Possessing more free time and greater internet access, in the years leading to the Arab Spring, the young people interacted, socialized, and mobilized with an ever-larger pool of young people facing similar predicaments. This only aggravated the frustration with and displeasure at those in power, causing the young people to demand change.

The findings from the statistical analyses and narratives, although not conclusive, provide some explanations and understanding of the cause of the social uprising in 2010–11. The findings support what many observers of North Africa have maintained: social injustice caused the uprising. What exactly contributed to the social inequity could come from many fronts. In the context of demographics, the labor force, and human development, social injustice resulted from the compound effect of the demographic pressure imposed by the youthful population and the failure of policy makers to design strategies that take advantage of the demographic transition and improve the job market environment, by promoting the private sector and adjusting the training programs to match the job market's demand in the face of a contracting public sector. In other words, policy makers have failed to prepare a labor force with adequate skills and accurate expectations.

More than five years after the Arab Spring swept across North Africa, socioeconomic situations have improved little and in some cases have worsened. Although a sociopolitical transformation toward a more pluralistic order has taken place in Tunisia, socioeconomic stability remains fluid, which makes it more challenging for policy makers to implement new strategies. Algeria and Morocco may have narrowly escaped the disruptive social unrest experienced by Egypt and Tunisia, but it would be wise for Algeria and Morocco to remain vigilant of the nuanced dynamics and interactions between the labor force and job market, as well as pay more attention to the different geographic segments of the society as discontent is not confined to urban youth. Discontent can occur in any demographic and geographic segment, among middle-aged salaried persons as much as among rural dwellers.

In all cases, stability in labor force and job market dynamics is not necessarily desirable, as more North African citizens become more educated and expect opportunities for upward social mobility. Hence, policy makers face not only the challenge to address the present problems in North Africa, but also the challenge to develop future strategies to improve and thrive in a sustainable manner.

After all, stability on the state level is no longer limited to the political will of the concerned country. In an increasingly interdependent global economy, North African policy makers face constant challenges from external competition. If they cannot keep up, they will lose out, and the consequence could be another wave of social disruptions. In Egypt, residents have been increasingly lured back to a more statist regime. The patience of the Egyptian people wore thin as the socioeconomic situation only worsened with the political change toward pluralism. In Algeria and Morocco, although the socioeconomic environment is not improving as fast as desired, there is at least some stability.

WAI MUN HONG is a research associate with a master's degree in international relations and security from the Geoeconomics and Geopolitics program at the Universidad Autónoma de Madrid.

Notes

1. An earlier version of this chapter was published as Wai Mun Hong, "Youth Unemployment in the Southern Mediterranean: Demography Pressure, Human Development and Policies," in *Youth, Revolt, Recognition. The Young Generation during and after the "Arab Spring,"* edited by Isabel Schäfer (Berlin: MIB/HU, 2015), 86–106, doi:10.18452/3120.

2. North Africa in this chapter refers to Algeria, Egypt, Morocco, and Tunisia.

3. Silatech and Gallup, "The Silatech Index, Series: Mindset Score," Silatech, 2010, https://www.wamda.com/2011/04/the-silatech-index-voices-of-young-arabs-20111.

4. Economic growth here refers to gross domestic product (GDP). The figures are the author's calculations based on data from the World Bank's World Development Indicators and Global Financial Development Database on GDP (in current US dollars).

5. See Lisa Anderson, "The State in the Middle East and North Africa," *Comparative Politics* 20 (1987): 1–18; Pedro Teixeira, "Mass Higher Education and Private Institute," in *Higher Education to 2030: Globalization*, vol. 2 (Paris: Center for Educational Research and

Innovation, OECD, 2009), 231–58; Elizabeth Buckner, "The Role of Higher Education in the Arab State Society: Historical Legacies and Recent Reform Patterns," *Comparative & International Higher Education* 3, no. 1 (2011): 21, http://higheredsig.org/cihe/Number03-06 .pdf.

6. Silatech and Gallup, "Silatech Index Brief," Silatech, 2013, http://www.silatech.org/en /publication/publication-details/docs/default-source/publications-documents/silatech-index -brief-july-2013-ar.

4

SHIFTING COURSES

Economies of the Maghreb after 2011

Karen Pfeifer

Contradictions of the Arab Spring Movements and Their Aftermath

The Arab Spring movements were the first wave of an ongoing tsunami of popular movements around the globe expressing resentment of ruling regimes that facilitated the neoliberal form of globalization. Neoliberal globalization had benefited mainly the wealthy and politically connected and left many ordinary people behind. Despite running critiques by economic experts that North African economies did not undertake liberalizing structural reforms fast enough or thoroughly enough, these economies were sufficiently integrated into the globalization process to roll with its growth and crisis in the 2000s and to suffer from the aftermath of the Great Recession and subsequent stagnation. In this larger context, the problems and limitations the Maghreb economies faced internally as of 2016 were framed by inexorable external factors that impeded their growth and development, from the least politically stable and economically successful of the group, Libya, to the most stable and successful, Morocco. It was inaccurate and unfair to blame continuing slow growth in North Africa solely on the Arab Spring uprisings, especially in the case of Tunisia, either explicitly or implicitly.[1]

The Arab Spring movements demanded both economic and political change, to adjust growth and development trajectories to benefit the middle and working classes. However, with the partial exception of Tunisia, these demands were not met. Indeed, in some cases, such as Libya, the movements resulted in civil war and economic anarchy that had yet to be brought under control as of 2017. In other cases, including Algeria, Mauritania, and Morocco, political regimes made minor concessions, but governance and economic structures remained fundamentally the same. Indeed, as the editors of this volume argue, authoritarianism was rejuvenated in the years after the Arab Spring. Even in Tunisia, where economic transformation was stalled by the inability of the newly reformed competitive parliamentary system to produce a viable program, a fragile democratic governance was steadily threatened by restraints on citizens' rights under the state emergency law (renewed again in November of 2017), which gave the executive branch power to constrict freedom of the press, labor actions, and civic assemblies, and by newly drafted laws granting amnesty to corrupt officials from the Ben Ali era and increased power and impunity to state security forces. Economic malaise and the rejuvenation of authoritarianism seemed to reinforce each other.

The Maghreb in Global Economic Context

International agencies and researchers reported in 2016 that the world economy seemed to be in a period of prolonged stagnation, with contributing factors on both the demand and the supply sides.[2] In October 2016, the International Monetary Fund (IMF) forecast only a modest rise in growth over the next five years, if conditions improved and major risks were avoided. Even at their best, these rates would be significantly lower than the average 4.2 percent per year during the 1998–2007 boom years. The pattern was strongly influenced by very low growth in the "advanced" economies, especially the Euro area and Japan, and by the "rebalancing" of China's economic strategy to focus more on its domestic market and on services.[3] Chart 4.1 offers a comparison of average rates of growth by country group, including the Middle East and North Africa (MENA).

The consequence of reduced demand by the biggest trading partners was an unexpected reduction in the rate of growth in the volume of world trade and a reduced share of foreign trade in global GDP.[4] Fifteen economies, including the "advanced" and China, accounted for about 63 percent of the value of world trade in 2015, so their decreased demand for imports from "emerging and developing economies" (EMDEs), which include all

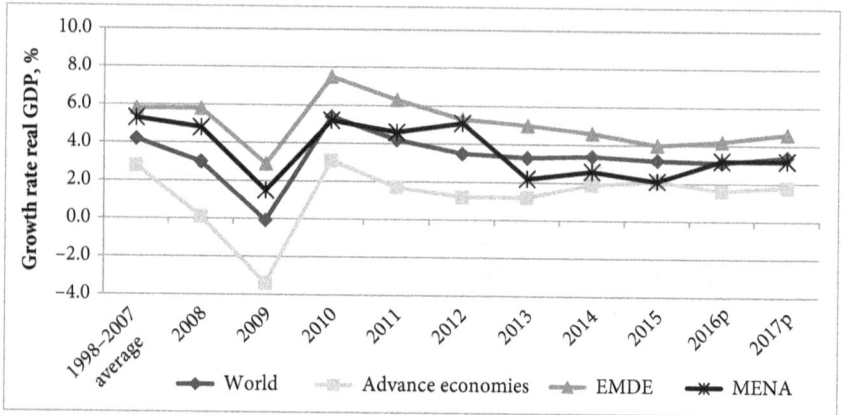

Chart 4.1. Real GDP growth, world and regions. Note: Advanced economies include the United States, Europe, Japan, and others at a similar level of development. EMDEs are emerging and developing economies and include all regions of the world outside of the advanced economies. Algeria, Libya, Mauritania, Morocco, and Tunisia are included among MENA countries, and all are classed as EMDEs and as upper or lower middle-income by the World Bank as of 2016. *Source*: IMF, *Global Economic Prospects*. June 2016, Washington DC: World Bank. http://pubdocs.worldbank.org/en/842861463605615468/Global-Economic -Prospects-June-2016-Divergences-and-risks.pdf, table A1, p. 228 (accessed 12/6/16).

five North African economies (Morocco, Tunisia, Algeria, Mauritania, and Libya), dragged down growth in those regions.[5] Reduced demand for primary commodity exports caused prices to fall and the terms of trade to turn against the exporters.[6] Gross oil revenues fell by more than 50 percent for North African economies in 2015 from their previous peak in 2012, Libya's drop being the worst due to supply disruptions, while weak global demand and a steep fall in phosphate and iron ore prices from 2012 to 2016 similarly affected export revenues for Morocco, Tunisia, and Mauritania.[7] Among the four Maghreb economies, leaving Libya aside, the biggest drop in demand was from the European Union and the second biggest from the Asia-Pacific region, although imports from those regions remained stable. The consequent decline in net exports contributed to current account deficits and the drawdown of foreign reserves.[8] All five currencies depreciated vis-à-vis the US dollar in 2015, and further devaluation continued in the following years. By 2018, Algeria's Dinar for example lost 48 percent of its value.[9]

While the average rate of growth of output had slowed in all three major groups of economies in the world (advanced, EMDEs, and low-income developing or LIDs) from 2008 to 2016, the EMDE and LID rates remained significantly higher than the advanced-economy rate, as shown in chart 4.1.[10] Since the EMDEs as a group accounted for three-fourths of world output in 2016, the international financial institutions (IFIs) expected the EMDEs, led especially by India and other "emerging" Asian economies (not including China), to be the driving force in restoring global growth over the following five years.[11] The North African economies would be particularly useful in this project as stepping-stones in a chain of advanced capitalist penetration of sub-Saharan Africa with its vast but as yet underdeveloped potential.[12] However, this "solution" to global stagnation faced three daunting obstacles.

One obstacle was that fiscal deficits tended to depress public spending on the infrastructure investment and human development needed for these "emerging" economies to diversify away from commodity-export dependence and to introduce new technology to raise productivity. This slowed the pace of "convergence" of income per capita in EMDEs and LIDs with that of the advanced economies,[13] further dampening demand for advanced-economy exports and feeding back into slow growth overall.

A second obstacle was a slowing of investment in the advanced economies, as measured by gross fixed capital formation (GFCF), which actually shrank in 2008 and 2009 and then remained weak from 2010 to 2016.[14] This helps explain slow productivity growth in the advanced economies in the post-2008 period, which fed back into a cycle of slow overall growth.[15] The flow of capital from the advanced economies for investment to the EMDEs and LIDs also slowed after 2012.[16] The partial exceptions were parts of East and South Asia and, in the Maghreb, Morocco. International capital flows were the equivalent of 16 percent of world GDP in 2007, but just 2 percent in 2015.[17] This decline in capital flows was a second factor in rising current account deficits in EMDEs and LIDs, including the Maghreb, and slowed the cross-border technology transfer, productivity growth, and job creation that could be gleaned from well-managed foreign direct investment.[18]

A third obstacle to the EMDE-led solution was growing uncertainty regarding changes in the advanced countries' economic policy and immigration, as well as political conflict in the Middle East and North Africa and other regions. Some leading economies seemed to be retreating from their commitment to globalization, as indicated by new restrictions on trade since 2008, including by the United States; the failure of World Trade Organization negotiations in 2015; the foundering of the Trans-Pacific Partnership

Table 4.1. Maghreb economies—basic economic indicators

	Algeria	Libya	Mauritania	Morocco	Tunisia
Population in millions 2015	39.7	6.3	4.1	34.4	11.3
GDP per capita, $US PPP, 2015	14,386.0	14,793.0	4,039.0	7,986.0	11,304.0
Economic diversity index, 2014	4.5	1.6	4.7	47.3	44.4
Export growth, average annual %, 2010–2014	0.0	–14.7	6.6	9.4	–0.6
% of population below the national poverty line	N/A	N/A	(2008) 42.0	(2007) 8.9	(2010) 15.5
GINI index	(1995) 35.3	N/A	(2008) 37.5	(2007) 40.7	(2010) 35.8
Labor force participation rate, 2013	43.6	53.8	47.1	49.0	47.8
Unemployment rate, 2013	9.8	20.6	30.8	9.2	15.9

Source: African Development Bank 2016, tables 1, 8, 14, and 20.

Table 4.2. Maghreb economies—human development indicators

	Algeria	Libya	Mauritania	Morocco	Tunisia
Life expectancy at birth, 2015	75.0	71.8	63.2	74.3	75.0
Adult literacy, % pop. age > 15, 2010–15	80.2	91.0	52.1	72.4	81.8
Prim school, net enrollment, 2010–15 (1)	97.3	N/A	74.4	98.4	98.6
Gender inequality index, 2014 (2)	41.0	13.0	61.0	53.0	24.0
Gender development index, 2014 (3)	84.0	95.0	82.0	83.0	89.0
Access to water supply, % pop., 2013	84.0	N/A	58.0	85.0	98.0
Access to sanitation, % pop., 2013	88.0	97.0	40.0	77.0	92.0
Internet users per 100 inhab., 2014	18.1	17.8	10.7	56.8	46.2

Source: African Development Bank 2016a, Tables 15, 16, 18, 19, 26.
Notes:
(1) The percentage of children of primary school age enrolled in school.
(2) Lower is better: Lower score = fewer socio-ecconomic-political disparities between male and female.
(3) Higher is better: Higher score = closer to parity in human development between female and male.

in the United States; and the Brexit decision in the United Kingdom.[19] In the view of the IFIs, this trend is counterproductive, impeding the movement of goods, services, capital, and, in particular, labor that could serve to overcome global stagnation.[20] Indeed, the global net flow of migrants from poor to rich countries had already begun to decline, from sixteen million from 2006 to 2010 to twelve million from 2011 to 2015.[21] Examples are the return to Tunisia of expatriate workers from Libya during its civil conflict and the growing difficulties for would-be migrants from the Maghreb, and Africans transiting through the Maghreb, to make their way to Europe.

Comparative View of the Maghreb Economies, 2010–2016

In the 2000s, aggregate GDP growth in the Maghreb economies had averaged 4–4.5 percent, high enough to raise per capita incomes and to fund increases in human development, but not high enough to absorb the unemployed as well as new labor force entrants. These economies would need real GDP growth of 6 to 7 percent over the course of five years to do that. As indicated in table 4.1, all had low labor force participation rates, as compared to their peers around the globe, and unemployment averaged 11 percent as of 2010. Youth unemployment was about twice as high, and all economies were judged to have large informal sectors. Chart 4.2 shows per capita growth, that is, output per person, for the four economies (excluding Libya because of extreme volatility), which indicates changes in the standard of living over time. Aggregate growth, along with growth in investment and inflation, is shown for each country separately below.

Human Development

Table 4.2 provides snapshot data on human development indicators, and chart 4.3 shows the evolution of the human development index (HDI) for the Maghreb countries from 1980 to 2014. The overall pattern was for significant improvement from 1980 to 2005, then a slowing of the pace from 2005 to 2010, and minor improvements thereafter (with an actual decline in Libya). The average value for the Arab states in 2014 was 0.686. Algeria, Libya, and Tunisia, in that order, were above the Arab average, while Morocco was slightly under. Mauritania's HDI was significantly below the Arab average and also below the average of 0.518 for sub-Saharan Africa.[22]

In the global context, one of the weakest dimensions of economic and human development in the region was the relatively poor record on gender parity, considered by economists to be one to the main factors holding these countries back from vigorous sustainable growth. On the Gender Inequality Index (GII) in 2014, the Arab region as a whole ranked fifth out of six world regions, with an average score 53.7. As shown in table 4.2, four Maghreb countries scored better than the Arab average (lower is better on this index), and two scored better than the Europe / Central Asia regional

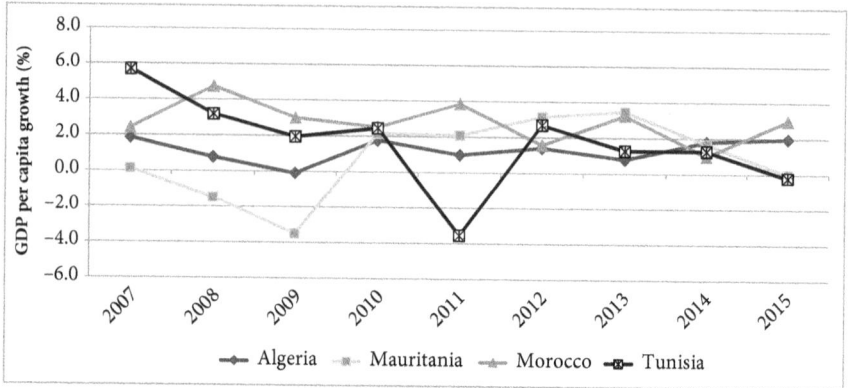

Chart 4.2. Real GDP per capita, annual percentage growth. *Source*: World Bank: World Development Indicators Databank, http://data.worldbank.org/data-catalog/world -development-indicators, (accessed January 17, 2017).

average of 30.0.[23] Libya's score was the best in the region, followed by Tunisia, Algeria, Morocco, and Mauritania. On the Gender Development Index (GDI) in 2014 (higher is better on this index), Libya again scored the best, followed by Tunisia, Algeria, Morocco, and Mauritania.

On a different measure, the Gender Gap Index, which takes account of other dimensions of female participation in the labor force and political institutions, the MENA region scored worst of all global regions, although there had been some significant changes in the North African countries. After 2011, Algeria, Morocco, and Tunisia made legal changes to increase female political participation and protect against violence, and all five had reduced the male-female disparity in education and health care, although Morocco and Mauritania lagged behind in adult literacy.[24]

Economic Status as of 2014

At the approximate midpoint of the post–Arab Spring era, the economies of what the IFIs called the "Arab Countries in Transition" (ACTs) were stable, but growth had been constricted by the decline of European demand for their exports, foreign direct investment, and tourism, slowing the inflow of the foreign exchange needed to purchase imports. The best growth as of early 2014 was for commodity exporters, except in Libya, which had descended into anarchy, and Tunisia, which was transiting out of political crisis but was economically rudderless. Thanks to higher prices for oil,

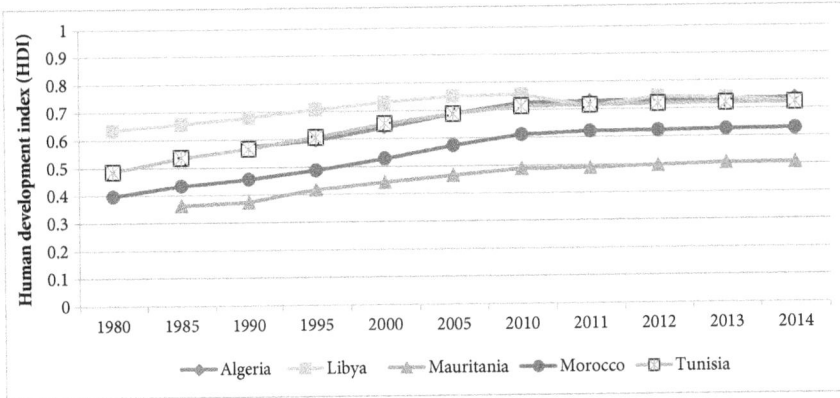

Chart 4.3. Human development index (HDI) in Maghreb countries. Note: 2014 human development ranges are "very high," 0.896–0.944; "high," 0.744–0.895; "medium," 0.630–0.743; and "low," 0.505–0.629. *Source*: Human Development Report 2015, http://hdr.undp.org /en/data (accessed January 13, 2017).

gas, iron ore, and phosphates, Algeria and Morocco were able to maintain rates of growth from 2010 to 2014 of close to 4 percent, while Mauritania's growth rate rose to 6 percent.[25] However, spillover from the conflict in Libya affected all its neighbors, as well as intersecting with radical Islamist movements and terrorism passing through porous borders. The spillover hit Tunisia and Algeria the hardest. Morocco and Mauritania were more distant but not immune.

Development aid and personal remittances remained important sources of national income in the Maghreb. Chart 4.4 shows overseas development aid (ODA) per capita from 1990 to 2014. Algeria's had been consistently low, as was Libya's until 2011, when it received a burst of aid, and then smaller amounts from 2012 to 2014, in response to humanitarian needs in a collapsing economy. Aid to both Morocco and Tunisia declined somewhat in the late 1990s–2000s as their economies were relatively stable, but aid rose again from 2008 to 2014 in response to the economic crisis and new needs after the Arab Spring. Aid to Mauritania fluctuated wildly, rising after elections and being withheld after coups d'états, but it was always the highest until 2014, when it was surpassed by Tunisia. As indicated in chart 4.5, remittances from émigré labor have long been important to Morocco and Tunisia, averaging 7.1 percent of GDP for Morocco and 4.5 percent of GDP for Tunisia in the 2000s. Expatriate Moroccans lived mostly in France and Spain, while Tunisians lived mostly in France and

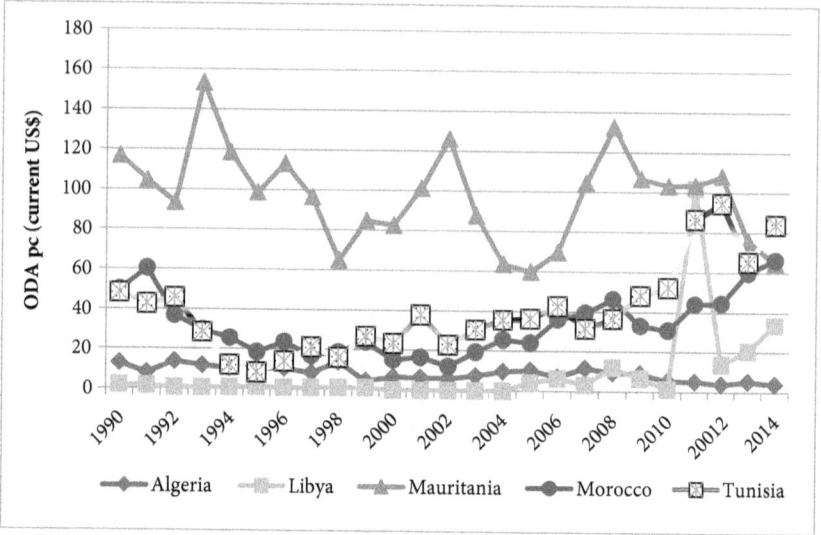

Chart 4.4. Overseas developmental aid (ODA) per capita. *Source*: World Bank: World Development Indicators Databank, http://data.worldbank.org/data-catalog/world-development-indicators (accessed January 17, 2017).

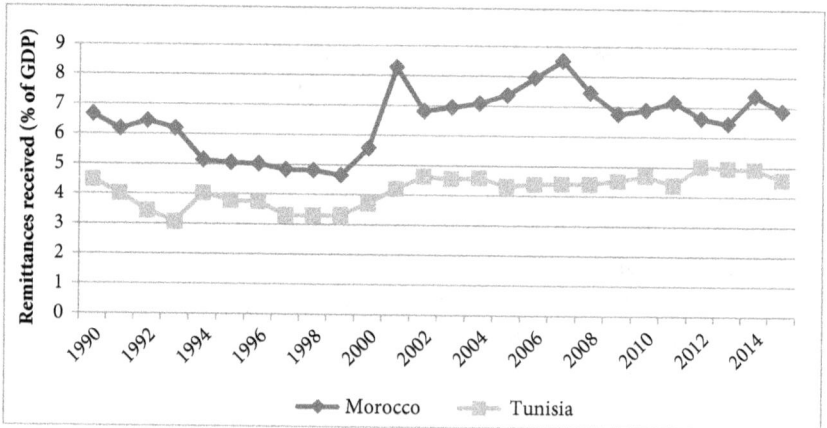

Chart 4.5. Remittances received, percent of GDP. *Source*: World Bank: World Development Indicators Databank, http://data.worldbank.org/data-catalog/world-development-indicators (accessed January 17, 2017).

Italy, some as temporary workers who return home (also typical of Tunisians in Libya) and others as permanent residents in the host countries.

By 2016, global economic conditions had changed and the paths of the five economies diverged. Due to prolonged civil conflict, Libya's growth was negative from 2013 to 2016. Algeria managed to maintain growth, despite the collapse of hydrocarbon revenues in the second half of 2014, by drawing on its foreign reserves to keep up public spending, and by bringing a greater volume of oil and gas to market. Mauritania suffered a sharp drop in growth due to the collapse of iron ore prices, but, with generous development aid, the country supported growth with increased public spending and bringing a new mine into operation. Morocco had a high rate of growth of exports, but still aggregate growth varied from year to year depending on how the weather affected agriculture. Tunisia's growth remained low but positive from 2012 to 2016, as the political system stabilized and the economy muddled through without clear direction. Inflation remained low or moderate in most economies, except in Libya, where it reached more than 10 percent.[26]

Financial System

Morocco had the most complex and sizable financial sector among the five Maghreb economies and even compared favorably to Egypt. As of 2013, with a population and GDP about 40 percent the size of Egypt's, Moroccan banks were relatively the largest, with assets equal to 145 percent of GDP, compared to Egypt's 70 percent, Tunisia's 63 percent and Algeria's 40 percent.[27] For the period from 2010 to 2013, Morocco's banks issued the highest level of credit at 100 percent or more of GDP, while Tunisia and Egypt issued 75–80 percent, Mauritania less than 50 percent, Algeria 0 percent, and Libya less than 0 percent.[28] Moroccans also had the highest rate of participation in the banking system and the lowest rate of nonperforming loans.[29]

The five Maghreb economies had about the same number of commercial banks each, between fifteen and twenty-one, of which five or six were publicly owned. All had some privately owned banks, a significant presence of foreign privately owned banks, and some nonbank institutions such as investment companies and international funds-transfer intermediaries, providing diverse functions, such as Islamic finance and microfinance.[30] Morocco's equities market was comparatively strong. The Casablanca bourse had 81 companies listed in 2013, seemingly fewer relative to its size than Egypt with 212 and Tunisia with 76. But the Moroccan companies were relatively richer as a group, with a bourse capitalization in 2012 worth 50 percent of GDP, compared to Egypt's 21 percent and Tunisia's 19 percent. In contrast, Algeria's stock market had just five members and miniscule capitalization, Mauritania did not yet have a stock market, and Libya's stock market was defunct during the civil conflict.[31]

Financial Policy Dilemmas

As economic growth remained sluggish in 2015–16 and deficits and debt built up (see individual country figures below), each government faced financial and fiscal policy dilemmas. For example, to encourage domestic investment, stimulatory monetary policy dictates lowering interest rates and expanding credit to the private sector. However, higher interest rates are needed to keep current account deficits and inflation under control. Financing budget deficits became more difficult with tighter funds and higher interest rates in international markets. At the same time, borrowing on the domestic market and changing the taxation system to raise more revenue could have a dampening effect on domestic growth.[32] Allowing the currency to depreciate could make exports more competitive but raise the costs of imported food and industrial inputs, thus feeding inflation. One tempting solution to these dilemmas was to turn to the IFIs for support, but that came with conditions, such as austerity budgeting and liberalization requirements, that were politically unpopular.

The IFIs had long criticized the Maghrebi governments for their remaining statist policies and their slowness, albeit at varying paces, to fully adopt liberalizing reforms. Although they followed a stable monetary policy and inflation rates were relatively low, governments continued to impose price controls on many consumer items and provided subsidies on fuel and food. The Maghreb countries were considered to have unfriendly business environments and to lack competitiveness in global export markets. Other deficiencies were inadequate investment in physical and social infrastructure, especially in more remote regions, and inequalities in wealth and income distribution related to corruption and cronyism, despite the Arab Spring protests.[33]

In exchange for financial backing, then, IFI advisors continued to urge more structural reforms "to strengthen fiscal and external buffers" and to get "coordinated support from the international community for finance, trade and capacity building" in order to reduce uncertainty and win back private investor confidence. [34] These reforms included reducing and gradually eliminating energy and other subsidies, changing the taxation structure, and reforming governance and budget management, so as to free up funds for approved public investment and for directing welfare payments only to the deserving poor. The IFIs also pushed for opening banking and finance to market forces, improving the business climate (e.g., simplifying regulations, protecting private property), and reducing protections in the labor market to make it simpler for employers to hire and fire and presumably create more jobs. [35] Of key importance was the IFIs' insistence on the virtues of improving "competitiveness" and opening to foreign direct investment.

Contradictions of Foreign Direct Investment

An integral part of the neoliberal agenda and the programs promoted by the IFIs in the EMDEs and LIDs, openness to foreign direct investment (FDI) had long been touted as the gateway to industrialization and catching up to the advanced economies. However, the experience of the Maghreb countries with FDI was not always positive. [36] For one thing, without tightly negotiated contractual arrangements, FDI could be withdrawn or withheld, sometimes on short notice. As indicated in chart 4.6, Algeria, Morocco, and Tunisia, like many other EMDEs, were recipients of higher levels of FDI inflow during the boom years of the mid-2000s, only to suffer sharp declines during the recession years after the 2008 financial crisis. Libya experienced a temporary surge of FDI from 2005 to 2009 after the lifting of sanctions, and Mauritania, with the most volatile record of the group, experienced peaks around the time hydrocarbons were discovered off the coast (2005) and when (under IFI conditionality) it opened more mining and fishing projects to nonnational investors (2012).

As for the argument that FDI helps industrialize the host country and transfers up-to-date technology and knowledge for dissemination into other parts of the economy, there are two major limitations. One limitation is the foreign investors' motivation and ability to invest in only the sectors that profit them, as illustrated by the sectors in which FDI was active in the Maghreb from 2011 to 2015. [37] In Algeria, the largest shares went into metals, real estate, and construction. In Libya, it was real estate, with hydrocarbons a distant second. In Mauritania, the vast bulk was in metals. Morocco's FDI was somewhat more diversified and job creating as it went into

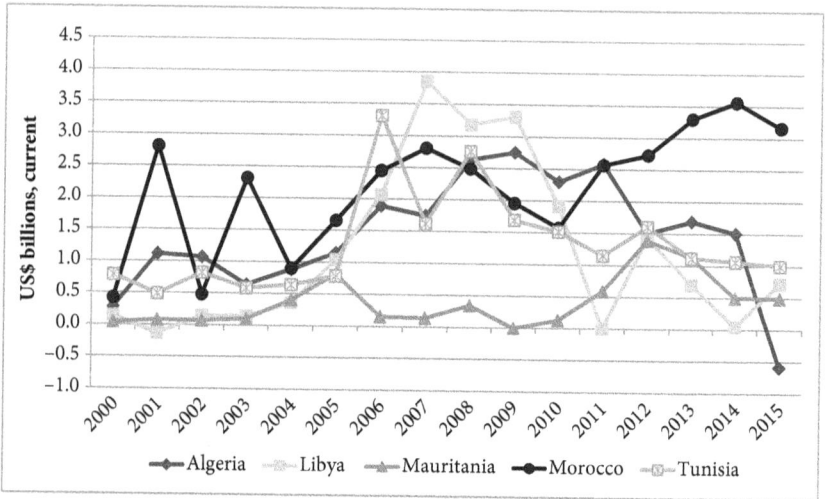

Chart 4.6. Foreign direct investment (FDI) inflow. Note: Morocco on an asset/liability basis. *Source*: United Nations Commission on Trade and Development (UNCTAD) 2017. UNCTADStat. http://unctadstat.unctad.org/wds/ReportFolders/reportFolders.aspx?sCS _ChosenLang=en (accessed January 15, 2017).

automotive manufacturing, alternative/renewable energy, real estate, and business services. Tunisia's FDI was the most diversified, including food and tobacco processing, hotels and tourism, communications, alternative/ renewable energy, and automotive components, although 33 percent still went into hydrocarbons. Given Morocco as the partial exception, FDI did not go mainly into manufacturing, and agriculture/forestry/fishing was not even listed as a category for any of the five economies, not even Mauritania, in which fishing was still a major source of livelihood.

The second limitation is that much of FDI, especially in manufacturing, is done in special economic zones (SEZs), enclaves insulated from the domestic economy either to protect intellectual property rights (such as patents on technology) or to produce intermediate or final goods in a global production chain that requires efficient free-zone imports and exports. Under the Ben Ali regime, Tunisia's SEZs were almost hermetically sealed and transferred virtually no new technology or knowledge into the domestic economy.[38] Morocco's Tangier SEZ hosted assembly plants for French automobiles, mostly for export back to Europe, along with multinational automotive parts suppliers. The positive caveat was that in 2014 the government added "a suite of incentives to encourage the emergence of local players . . . with sector specific training programs" for workers.[39]

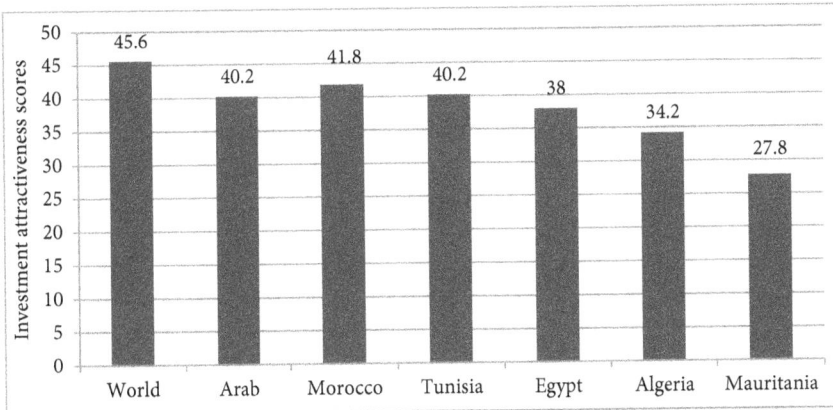

Chart 4.7. Investment attractiveness scores, 2015. Note: The higher the score, the more attractive is the country to foreign investors. The Arab World as a whole and the Maghreb countries are below the global average. *Source*: Dhaman, the InterArab Investment and Export Guarantee Corporation, 2016. Investment Climate in Arab Countries. Shuwaikh, Kuwait: www.Dhaman.org, Dhaman iaigc.net/Climate-2016-ENG-ALL-C.pdf: 121, 125, 177, 181, 185 (accessed October 25, 2016).

The IFIs put consistent and intense pressure on EMDEs and LIDs all over the world to become more "competitive" with each other in the scramble to attract FDI. The World Bank and World Economic Forum put out annual scorecards on all countries in the world, with "competitiveness" measured on the degree to which the many features of "structural reform" were realized by the competing countries. Dhaman, a pan-Arab institution in Kuwait, published its own annual index of "investment attractiveness" tailored to the Arab world. The report scored and ranked the Arab economies using this index, comparing individual countries to one another, sub-regions to one another, and both of those to regional and world averages.[40]

In the global scores, the Arab region ranked below average in 2015. It came in fourth out of seven regions, below the OECD countries, East Asia and Pacific, and Eastern Europe and Central Asian regions, but above Latin America and the Caribbean, South Asia, and sub-Saharan Africa. Within the Arab region, the Gulf Cooperation Council (GCC) sub-region ranked as "good," the Levant (which includes Egypt) and Maghreb were both considered "poor" but close to average, and the low-FDI group, which includes Mauritania, Iraq, Sudan, and Yemen, ranked as "very poor."[41]

Chart 4.7 shows the scores and ranks for the North African countries, excluding Libya due to the political crisis there, but including Egypt for comparative purposes.[42] While there was significant variation among countries on dimensions such as access to electricity, trade performance, and financial mediation, Morocco got the highest overall score, above the Arab average but below the world average. Tunisia scored at the Arab average, while Egypt, Algeria, and Mauritania, in descending order, scored below the Arab average. A summary of the deficiencies in the Arab region that account for these scores included features such as the quality of education, the institutional environment (e.g., corruption, lack of transparency, weak rule of law), and the low level of technological advancement.[43]

The Interaction of Economic Malaise and Authoritarianism

The rejuvenation of authoritarianism in the Maghreb in the years after the Arab Spring matched the slowing of human development, weak improvement in the economic lives of ordinary citizens, and the failure to address governance defects such as corruption and lack of accountability. The tendency of Maghrebi governments to repress freedoms of the press and association, to control civil society organizations from the center, to constrain labor actions, and to neglect their poor interior regions seemed necessary to the ruling regimes in order to restore their power. This combination of actions undermines citizens' trust in government, restricts the opportunities of citizens to be creative and undertake new economic projects, and shrinks the social capital needed to renew the sense of community and common purpose that the Arab Spring demanded. Although worldwide stagnation imposed external constraints on the Maghrebi economies in these years, their own internal contradictions made adapting to a challenging global economy more difficult.

Algeria

During the boom years of the 2000s, Western energy analysts had considered Europe to be "fortunate to have gas rich North Africa lying off its southern shores" and enthusiastically published charts, maps, and detailed descriptions of existing and planned export facilities. In "partnership" with Algeria, Egypt, and Libya, they expected the total level of North African natural gas exports to Europe to be sustained through 2020 and, along with expanding sources in Africa, to provide the diversification of energy suppliers needed to reduce dependence on Russia and replace diminishing domestic European production.[44]

This approach was formally endorsed by the European Commission in 2008 in its "Energy Security and Solidarity Action Plan" and directed specifically toward Algeria, Egypt, and Libya through the "Barcelona Process: Union for the Mediterranean" signed that same year, with those southern-shore "partners" promising expanded openings for the international oil/energy corporations, still referred to as IOCs due to their oil-dominant heritage.[45] In addition to liquefied natural gas (LNG) export terminals in Algeria and Egypt, as of 2011 there were four working gas pipelines under the Mediterranean to southern Europe, all sharing sponsorship by the Italian energy corporation ENI: the Trans-Mediterranean from Algeria via Tunisia to Sicily and the Italian mainland, the Maghreb-Europe from Algeria via Morocco to Spain, the Medgaz from Algeria directly to Spain, and the Green Stream from Libya to Sicily, where it joined up with the Trans-Med. These pipelines supplied 30 percent of Italian and 20 percent of Spanish gas consumption,[46] and two more were planned, the GALSI from Algeria via Sardinia to Italy and the Trans-Saharan from Nigeria to Algeria and beyond.[47]

However, by 2013 circumstances had changed, and Europe's passion waned. The Arab Spring in 2011, the continuing political uncertainties in Tunisia and Egypt, the civil conflict in Libya, and anxiety about spillover to Tunisia and Algeria undermined the "partnership" approach. Algeria and Libya had failed to offer the better deals to IOCs for foreign direct investment, and the IOCs found themselves underbid by competitors from Asia. Algeria was slow to improve its own investment management, while Europeans turned toward more green energy and to importing coal from the United States.[48] Accordingly, "most North African countries have seen their hydrocarbon sectors stagnate and are viewed [in Europe] as unreliable suppliers of energy. Similarly, European demand has stagnated . . . due to the economic crisis. . . . As the major thrust of the world hydrocarbon markets shifts east in terms of demand and west in terms of supply, the Mediterranean and North Africa will be seen as less important for energy security in the coming decade [2013–23]."[49]

Mainstream analysts and the IFIs had long fretted over Algeria's still-state-dominated economy and relatively "closed" and "opaque" political system with a strong internal security apparatus, while piling their compliments on Morocco and Mauritania, and now to a lesser extent on Tunisia, for their encouragement of private business and foreign direct investment.[50]

Yet Algeria still managed to pull off a viable economy over its independent history, resisting the heavy hand of foreign financial intrusion and using its comparative advantage as a global hydrocarbon supplier to lubricate the social system. Hydrocarbons accounted for 95 percent of exports and about 65 percent of government revenues; seven out of the ten largest companies, including hydrocarbon producers, were state owned; and six state-owned banks served 80 percent of the domestic market. In the global context of 2016, there were some signs that the ruling elite might have to adjust its strategy, but the extent of such adjustment was negotiable.

The government had responded to the Arab Spring demonstrations by amending the constitution in ways that validated the protestors' demands for political reform, including restructuring the internal security system and making it more transparent, requiring greater female participation in political and civil institutions, and protecting females from sexual harassment. Furthermore, in order to stimulate higher growth and greater job creation, the government launched a five-year public investment and spending program to be financed out of then-surplus export revenues.[51] As shown in chart 4.8a, growth approached a high point of 4 percent in 2015 but created too few jobs, leaving unemployment to rise from 9.8 percent in 2013 to 11.3 percent in 2015. Women's unemployment rose to 16.6 percent, and, worse yet, the youth rate was 29.9 percent, while the rural poor still relied on low-productivity subsistence agriculture and the urban poor remained stuck in the informal sector.[52]

As hydrocarbon revenues declined from mid-2014 to the end of 2016, current account deficits and fiscal deficits worsened (chart 4.8b), leading the state to draw down on its foreign reserves and sell off some of its sovereign wealth fund assets. The dinar was devalued by 20 percent, raising the cost of essential imports and contributing to an increase in the rate of inflation (chart 4.8a). While private consumption and investment declined, despite the monetary authorities making more credit available to the private sector, the government sustained public consumption at the expense of public investment, causing gross fixed capital formation to plunge (chart 4.8a). It paid for the deficit spending by borrowing on the domestic market, causing debt to rise relative to GDP (chart 4.8b).[53]

Although nonhydrocarbon growth remained sluggish, the state was able to stave off recession in 2016 by restoring a critical source of natural gas[54] to feed into the pipelines to Europe, the higher quantity of gas sold in part compensating for the fall in prices.[55] However, Algeria's ability to

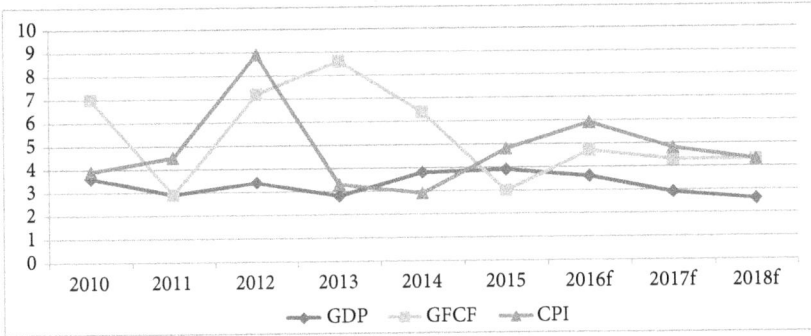

Chart 4.8a. Percent change in GDP, gross fixed capital formation (GFCF), and consumer price index (CPI) in Algeria. *Source*: World Bank, Economic Outlook, October 2016. Washington DC: World Bank: Algeria, http://pubdocs.worldbank.org/en/267701475460651472/Algeria -MEM-Fall-2016-ENG.pdf (accessed January 18, 2017).

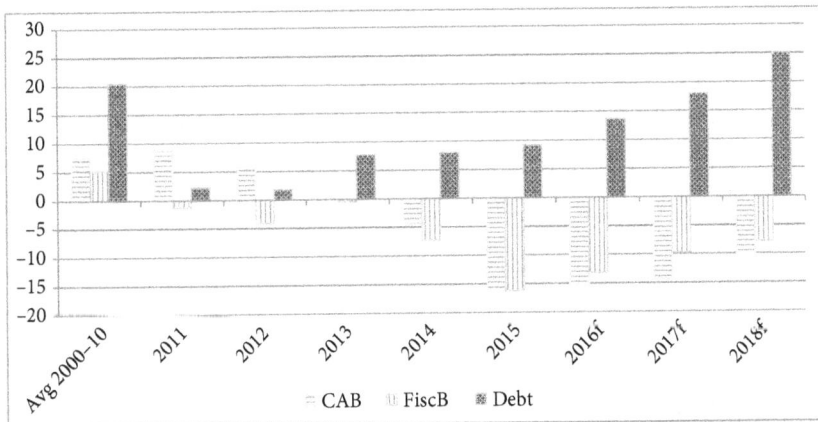

Chart 4.8b. Current account balance (CAB), fiscal balance (FiscB), and debt as percentage of GDP in Algeria. *Source*: World Bank, Economic Outlook, October 2016. Washington DC: World Bank, Algeria, http://pubdocs.worldbank.org/en/267701475460651472/Algeria-MEM -Fall-2016-ENG.pdf (accessed January 18, 2017).

increase the volume of hydrocarbon exports might be limited in subsequent years, despite the start of production in new fields, because of increases in its own domestic demand, especially for gas-fueled electricity; the long-term glut of oil and gas in the global market; and the need for massive new investment to revive aging facilities and bring new ones online.[56] The investment might better be spent on other sectors to reduce dependency on a volatile market and on demand from Europe.

The IFIs continued to push for reforms, such as reducing the wage bill and freezing public sector employment, cutting subsidies and letting domestic energy prices rise, increasing other sources of government revenues, investing more in infrastructure to support nonhydrocarbon activity, and diversifying the economy.[57] As of May 2016, the IMF was pleased that the 2016 budget recognized the need for "consolidation" and that some changes, such as to tax administration and bank regulation, seemed to be underway. However, its report expressed dissatisfaction with the national authorities' limited response to the IMF's recommendations, saying "insufficient action was taken in 2015 in response to the oil price shock" and the Algerian government did not enact "reforms that would increase economic openness and reduce the state's control over the economy."[58] Of the seventeen recommendations the IMF staff made for structural reforms, they judged that only partial progress had been made on eight items, such as simplifying consumer lending and stock market modernization, while no progress had been made on the other nine items, such as lifting foreign exchange controls and lending to small or medium enterprises (SMEs).[59]

Nevertheless, private foreign capital had long had a partnership role in Algeria, for example in building and operating public transportation, and was expecting more from the government's 2016 announcements of greater "openness." Indeed, Sonatrach, the national energy company, negotiated a partnership with ENI, the Italy-based energy corporation, for a major solar photovoltaic project. The private foreign capital viewpoint is illustrated by the Oxford Business Group (OBG), which cultivated a warm relationship with the Algerian government, for example, cosponsoring the 2016 African Investment and Business Forum and the international trade show for global agricultural and livestock suppliers in Algiers. In 2016, OBG enthusiastically reported on new plans to open more state enterprises to public-private partnerships and list them on the stock exchange, to award 4G licenses to contractors to expand mobile phone services, and to promote investment in high value-added sectors such as agribusiness, renewable energy, the digital economy, the automotive sector, and even tourism.[60]

The government promulgated a new investment code in July 2016, simplifying business procedures for private investors and entrepreneurs, and in December broadened the definition of SMEs to make it easier to obtain credit and tax exemptions and other incentives. These programs may have been responding to the IMF's critique, but they exemplified the kind of

controlled and guided foreign direct investment that defied the IFIs' promotion of unfettered "free market" relations between international capital
and developing countries, an alternative strategy used successfully by more
statist economies such as China during the neoliberal era.

Libya

As of 2010, Libya's economy was even more hydrocarbon dominated and less
diverse than Algeria's, although similar in income per capita, infrastructure
development (e.g., water and sanitation access), and human development, as
indicated in tables 4.1 and 4.2. The private sector was very small and limited
mainly to trade and personal services.[61] International oil companies, usually of the maverick stripe like Occidental Petroleum, had served as exploration and production partners and service contractors to the Libyan national
oil and gas company, but, as in Algeria and in other MENA hydrocarbon-
exporting countries, international companies were prohibited from owning
the resources under the ground. However, when sanctions were lifted in
2004–05, Libya experienced a surge of FDI similar to the other Maghreb
economies (chart 4.6), and a stock market was created in 2007.

The lifting of international sanctions on Libya also provided a relative opening to trade, tourism, and cultural exchange, but the Qaddafi
regime still maintained very tight internal security and kept national political institutions small and feeble. As of 2010, there was a weak sense of
national identity among the populace and no defined political opposition.
When the Arab spring protests began in 2011 and the state responded with
violence, the opposition quickly fragmented into competing social forces,
and the struggle devolved into a complex multisided civil war. Elections
in 2012 produced a government that was able to claim national authority
only briefly, temporarily restoring oil exports and reducing economic anarchy enough to have positive growth. However, when the country became
polarized into two competing spheres, oil facilities were again blockaded.
Meanwhile, international firms and expatriate workers fled the country,
investment collapsed completely, and, when production resumed in 2014, it
was on a much smaller scale.[62]

As indicated in chart 4.9a, GDP fell dramatically in 2011, rose again
in 2012, and then decreased each year from 2013 through 2016, while the
annual inflation rate accelerated and formal sector unemployment rose to

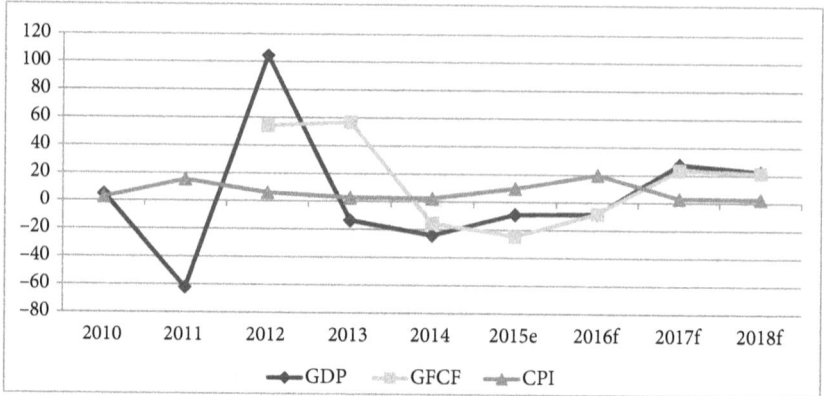

Chart 4.9a. Percent change in GDP, gross fixed capital formation (GFCF), and consumer price index (CPI) in Libya. *Source*: World Bank, Economic Outlook, October 2016. Washington DC: World Bank, Libya, http://pubdocs.worldbank.org/en/282581475460786200 /Libya-MEM-Fall-2016-ENG.pdf (accessed January 18, 2017).

20 percent.[63] As of 2016, hydrocarbon production and export was one-fifth of potential output, with revenues equal to just 7 percent of their 2012 value, causing the current account deficit to soar (chart 4.9b). With net foreign reserves depleted, the dinar lost 73 percent of its value relative to the dollar in the parallel market. Food prices rose as imports became scarcer and more expensive, contributing further to inflationary pressures and placing the population in danger of a widespread humanitarian crisis. Despite sharp cuts in subsidies and wages and capital expenditure, public budget deficits widened (chart 4.9b), and, due to domestic borrowing to finance the deficit, debt soared to an estimated 110 percent of GDP in 2016.[64]

The one functioning public institution, the central bank, had become the agent for managing the budget and negotiating export contracts, in addition to exercising foreign exchange controls to try to bring the parallel markets and inflation under control.[65] If the civil conflict were to end and a national unity government formed that included representatives of all groups in the country, and if facilities and infrastructure were rebuilt, hydrocarbon production and export could resume at close to full capacity by 2020. However, sustainable growth and development would require restructuring and diversifying the economy and restoring now-depleted human capacities. Whether that process will be in the form the IFIs prefer[66] or something more like the course that Algeria seemed to be following[67]

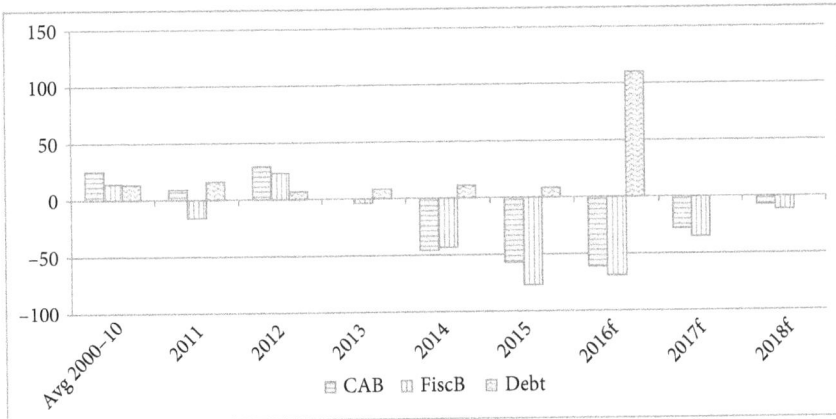

Chart 4.9b. Current account balance (CAB), fiscal balance (FiscB), and debt as percentage of GDP in Libya. *Source*: World Bank, Economic Outlook, October 2016. Washington DC: World Bank, Libya, http://pubdocs.worldbank.org/en/282581475460786200/Libya-MEM-Fall-2016-ENG.pdf (accessed January 18, 2017).

would have to be determined through a nonviolent political process, and might best be done in the context of regional integration.[68]

Mauritania

Despite its relatively small population of four million in 2015 (table 4.1) and lack of attention in Western media, Mauritania is an economically, socially, and religiously complex society with a vibrant politically active population. Arab Spring–like protests set off by a self-immolation in January of 2011 continued into 2012 and involved thousands of people at a time. The central demands were for democratic reform of a clientelist government that reeled between alternating coups d'états and managed elections; for economic reform that would tackle unemployment, inequality and poverty; and for the final eradication of slavery.[69] As of 2016, the president had been a general who helped lead at least two coups but who was formally elected in 2014 in the face of an opposition boycott protesting its exclusion from the process. Lively and prolonged political activism did not supersede authoritarian tendencies.

Mauritania became a member of the Economic and Social Commission for Western Asia (ESCWA) in 2015, "marking an important step towards realizing the dream espoused by ESCWA of Arab integration," in the words of Executive Secretary Rima Khalaf.[70] Indeed, Mauritania was already an experienced regional integrator. It was a founding member of the Arab Maghreb Union (AMU), a project that had yet as of 2016 to fulfill its promise. It was also a founding member of a more active project, the Senegal River Basin Development Organization, with its neighbors to the east and south, Mali, Senegal, and Guinea. The project succeeded in building dams and other works to control flooding during the wet season and provide water for consumption and irrigation and other economic uses during the dry season. But it also displaced part of the population, sending young people into the cities to seek a livelihood, and caused environmental problems such as the growth of invasive weeds and waterborne diseases, processes that were difficult to reverse.[71]

Advised by the IFIs, which were dissatisfied with the slow pace and inconsistency of change, the government had been pursuing a liberalization and structural reform program since 2011 to encourage the private sector and bring in more foreign investment.[72] Mauritania did indeed get the desired foreign investment (chart 4.6), mainly in oil and mining, but, as shown in tables 4.1 and 4.2, the country had a low economic diversity score, high rates of unemployment and poverty, and lagging human development, in spite of having long been the recipient of development aid and concessional loans. As shown in chart 4.4, it had the highest official development aid (ODA) per capita among the Maghreb countries from 1990 until 2014, when it was surpassed by Tunisia. One wonders what was done with all that aid.

ESCWA grouped Mauritania with its "least developed" member countries, including Comoros, Djibouti, Sudan, and Yemen. Based on income per capita, however, the World Bank put Mauritania just over the lower boundary of "lower-middle income" countries in 2016, a category that also includes Morocco and Tunisia higher up in the range, while Algeria and Libya were classified as "upper middle." Mauritania's economic growth fluctuated widely, as shown in chart 4.10a, but was intermittently high enough during the booming 2000s and again from 2010 to 2014 to pull up its income per capita (chart 4.2). As indicated in chart 4.10a, this growth was associated with a big boost of investment in Mauritania's natural resource sectors and the surge of demand for and high prices of its iron ore exports.[73]

Mauritania experienced both the blessing and curse of primary commodity export dependence, with iron ore contributing almost 50 percent of exports, until the collapse of iron ore prices from 2014 to 2016. The boom in the capital-intensive extractive industries had not created many jobs

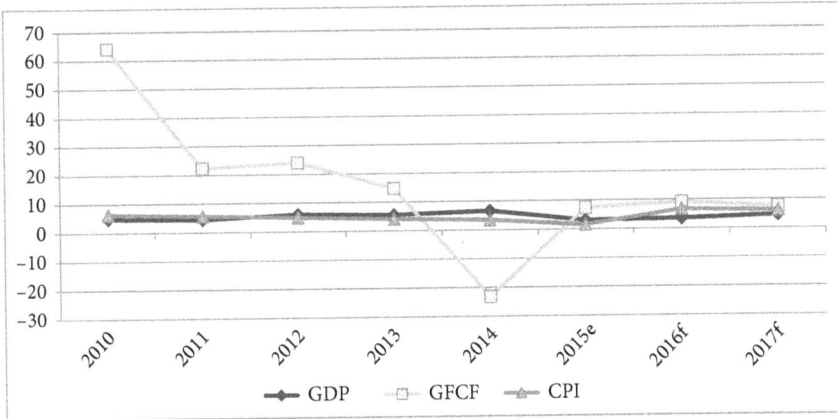

Chart 4.10a. Percent change in GDP, gross fixed capital formation (GFCF), and consumer price index (CPI) in Mauritania. *Sources*: African Development Bank, Africa Economic Outlook. Abidjan, Côte d'Ivoire: African Development Bank Group. https://www.afdb.org /en/knowledge/publications/african-economic-outlook/ (accessed January 18, 2017). African Development Bank, Mauritania Economic Outlook. https://www.afdb.org/en/countries /north-africa/mauritania/mauritania-economic-outlook/ (accessed January 17, 2017). World Bank, World Development Indicators Databank http://data.worldbank.org/data-catalog /world-development-indicators (accessed January 18, 2017). Moody's Analytics, 2017. https:// www.economy.com/mauritania/real-fixed-investment-gross-fixed-capital-formation (accessed January 18, 2017).

outside the precarious informal sector, and the benefits had not been widely distributed, leaving the economy in 2016 with widespread rural poverty, a growing set of social problems from chaotic urbanization, too little investment in infrastructure and human development, and dependence on foreign aid.[74]

The IFIs continued to offer their standard programmatic recommendations for "fiscal consolidation" to reduce the resulting twin deficits and debt at 60 percent of GDP or more, as shown in chart 4.10b. The Mauritanian government was advised to open more opportunities to foreign capital investment in its mining sector (gold) and natural gas production in its coastal waters, and to encourage the private sector, including the fishing and agricultural sectors, which employed between one-third and one-half of the labor force, to increase capital-intensive technology and productivity.[75] Whether Mauritania, like Algeria and Libya, could overcome the resource blessing-and-curse cycle and achieve such diversification with adequate job creation and rising incomes for its citizenry remained an open question.[76]

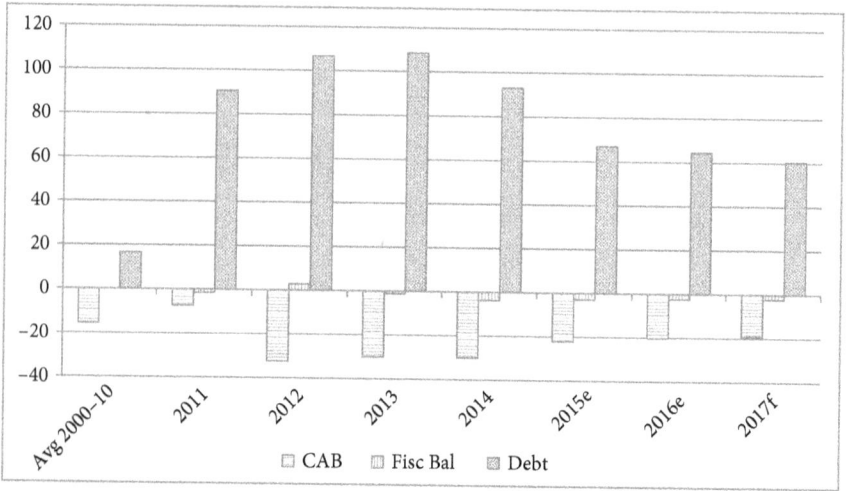

Chart 4.10b. Current account balance (CAB), fiscal balance (FiscB), and debt as percentage of GDP in Mauritania. *Sources*: African Development Bank, Mauritania Economic Outlook. 2016. https://www.afdb.org/en/countries/north-africa/mauritania/mauritania-economic -outlook/ (accessed January 17, 2017).
International Monetary Fund: IMF Data Bank (accessed January 17, 2017):
    Table 11. General Government Fiscal Balance, as Percent GDP
    http://data.imf.org/regular.aspx?key=60600903
    Table 21. Current Account Balance, as Percent GDP
    http://data.imf.org/regular.aspx?key=60600900
    Table 23. Total Gross External Debt, as Percent GDP
    http://data.imf.org/regular.aspx?key=60600915.

Morocco

The kingdom of Morocco was a favorite of the IFIs among MENA countries for its close integration with Europe and alliance with the United States on both the economic and security dimensions. It was credited with hav- ing taken structural adjustment and liberalizing reforms seriously.[77] For example, as of 2010, state-owned banks accounted for just 20 percent of the financial system. It had a more diverse economy than the other four Maghreb states (see table 4.1), with a still significant agricultural sector; a well-developed tourism sector; mining, mostly of phosphates; and manu- facturing. Although it had to import energy, inputs for industry, and part of its food supply, Morocco's foreign exchange income from exports, tourism, remittances, aid, foreign direct investment, and profits from its own firms' investments abroad generally made up for the costs of imports.[78]

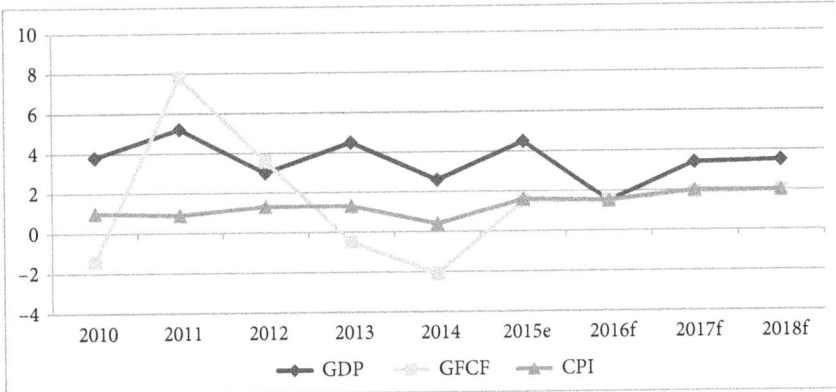

Chart 4.11a. Percent change in GDP, gross fixed capital formation (GFCF), and consumer price index (CPI) in Morocco. *Source*: World Bank, Economic Outlook, October 2016. Washington DC: World Bank, Morocco, http://pubdocs.worldbank.org /en/828061475460788728/Morocco-MEM-Fall-2016-ENG.pdf (accessed January 18, 2017).

Although some significant changes were made to the political system in response to the Arab Spring protests of 2011,[79] the new political configuration of a working alliance between the king and the Islamist party that dominated parliament entailed no change of economic program. Instead, the government pursued the IFI agenda of improving the business climate, such as simplifying customs and property registration, and promoting manufactured exports in conjunction with foreign capital.[80] When growth slowed in 2012, and capital investment plunged, as shown in chart 4.11a, the government used restrictive monetary policy to control inflation and turned once again to the IMF for support. In exchange for a "precautionary liquidity line" of potential credit of $6.2 billion from 2012 to 2014, the government decreased subsidies on energy and other commodities in order to reduce its fiscal and current account deficits, shown in chart 4.11b, while debt soared to over 60 percent of GDP. However, unlike the other four Maghreb economies, Morocco also received a surge of FDI, worth more than $10 billion, from 2012 to 2015 (chart 4.6).

New investment restored the rate of capital formation, as shown in chart 4.11a. The rate of GDP growth returned to an average of about 4 percent through 2015, second only to Mauritania's average, but was still not enough to bring the unemployment rate below 10 percent.[81] In comparison to Algeria, Libya, and Tunisia, Morocco had a higher rate of growth of exports and a lower rate of formal unemployment, but also a higher level of

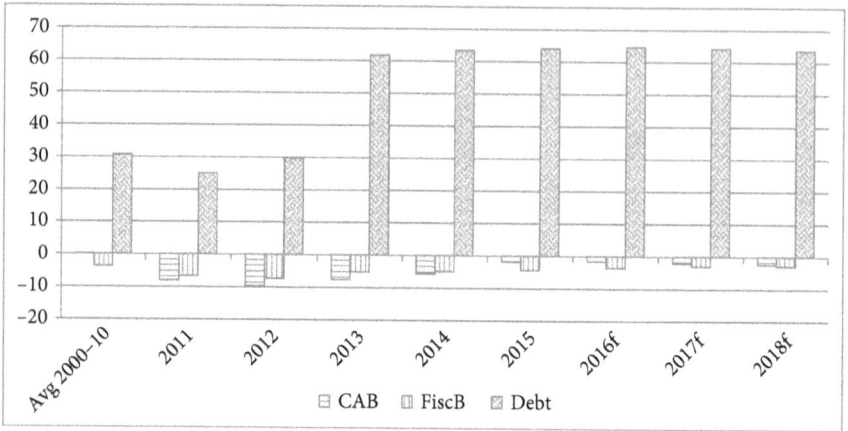

Chart 4.11b. Current account balance (CAB), fiscal balance (FiscB), and debt as percentage of GDP in Morocco. *Source*: World Bank, Economic Outlook, October 2016. Washington DC: World Bank, Morocco, http://pubdocs.worldbank.org/en/828061475460788728/Morocco -MEM-Fall-2016-ENG.pdf (accessed January 19, 2017).

inequality and a weaker showing on adult literacy, gender equity, and access to modern sanitation (tables 4.1 and 4.2). Despite the positive public reviews Morocco received from the World Bank, these seeming contradictions were explained in two internal World Bank research papers, which found that neoliberal restructuring tended to induce greater labor mobility in a situation of "jobless growth," and that, in Morocco, these changes were much less accommodating to women jobseekers than to men.[82]

Economic power continued to be centrally concentrated in Morocco, and this may have contributed to the higher level of income inequality and lags in human development, particularly in the rural areas, in comparison to its peers in the region and elsewhere. The two largest companies were the state-owned Office Chérifien des Phosphates (OCP), the revenues from which accounted for about 5 percent of GDP, and the Société Nationale d'Investissement (SNI), which is 60 percent owned by the royal family and holds a large share in the biggest private bank, the Attijarawafa Bank.[83]

The Attijarawafa Bank was the sixth largest bank in Africa and, with branches in twelve African countries, was credited as a successful example of an Africa-based multinational corporation.[84] In concert with SNI, it had led other Moroccan firms to expand their businesses into the economies of western and central Africa.[85] Morocco was cited as a successful model for Africa in developing an industrial policy that, in cooperation with foreign capital, balanced production for the domestic market with export promotion.[86]

Morocco is a major producer of phosphates and by 2015 was the world's leading exporter of unprocessed phosphates. In the decade before 2015, the OCP had put extensive investment into not only raw phosphate production but also new facilities for transporting the raw material to the Atlantic coast for processing into higher-value-added exportable products such as fertilizer. The integrated facility at Jorf Lasfar was considered a major accomplishment, and, although this commodity export suffered from the decline in global demand and a 50 percent plunge in prices from 2014 to 2016, its future prospects were considered strong.[87] The caveat was that such capital-intensive investment would make only a small contribution to new job creation.

Another aspect of investment in the phosphate industry that tended to be overlooked by IFI and other reports was the cultivation of an integrated mining, processing, and exporting facility in the Western Sahara, with a major port in the city of Laajoune.[88] The Saharawi people living in the territory and those living in exile in Algeria protested what they considered to be the usurpation of the right to exploit this resource in a territory still recognized as "occupied" by pan-African organizations and the United Nations. Morocco had claimed this "province" as an integral part of its nation since 1976, and refused to allow a referendum among Saharawis on the territory's fate. Although the European Court invalidated the agricultural component of Morocco's free trade agreement with the EU in 2016 because it involved the Western Sahara, the OCP pursued development of the phosphate complex unhindered.

Morocco had success in reducing poverty from 8.9 percent in 2007 to 4.2 percent in 2014, but 19 percent of the rural population was still considered vulnerable to poverty (table 4.1).[89] As in Tunisia, Moroccan families depended on remittances, which were the equivalent of 7 percent of GDP from 2011 to 2015 (chart 4.5). Like Mauritania, Morocco had long been a recipient of development aid, and ODA per capita actually increased after 2010 (chart 4.4), even as FDI increased and economic growth rose. Like Mauritania, Morocco's economy was criticized for preserving large precapitalist sectors alleged to hold back the growth needed to reduce unemployment and raise incomes. For example, as shown in chart 4.11a, good weather boosted agriculture's contribution to the 4.5 percent growth rate in 2015, but bad weather helped drag the growth rate down to 1.5 percent in 2016.[90] The World Bank overview of Morocco in October 2016 stated that the economy remained "structurally oriented toward non-tradable activities (such as construction, public works, and low value-added services) and a volatile, weakly productive rain-fed agriculture. Given this orientation, Morocco has made little productivity gains over the past two decades despite high levels of investment. Investment efforts—dominated by publicly funded large infrastructure projects—have not yet triggered a growth takeoff. Morocco has yet to secure the productivity and competitiveness gains needed to further integrate into world markets."[91]

This statement contradicts the World Bank's enthusiastic support for Morocco's grand agricultural program, the Plan Maroc Vert, initiated in 2010. The "first pillar" of the plan attracted FDI into the high-productivity, high-profit production of specialty crops such as fruit, flowers, and olive oil for export to the EU. Most of that investment went to the most fertile and best-irrigated farmland near the coasts with convenient transport to Europe. The Plan Vert's "second pillar" was supposed to promote the adoption of new techniques by small farmers producing essential crops for food security in the domestic market.[92]

As the achievements of the first pillar mainly benefited wealthier Moroccan investors, foreign capital, and European consumers, independent researchers did not find much benefit for ordinary farmers from this "second pillar."[93] Citing a Moroccan economist, one source concludes that "the vast majority of the country's water goes to a few crops with export potential. There is no taking into account of natural resource preservation or of food security."[94] As with Mauritania, one wonders what was done with all the ODA.

Tunisia

As of 2010, Tunisia had been considered a "good student" of the neoliberal reform program that the IFIs had been promoting since the 1990s, although the IFIs still criticized the remaining statist elements for being a drag on reform and growth.[95] Tunisia was relatively attractive to foreign investment (chart 4.7), and FDI had come in at a record pace in the boom years of the mid-2000s (chart 4.6). Both GDP per capita (chart 4.2) and human development (chart 4.3) improved over the 2000s. As shown in tables 4.1 and 4.2, Tunisia's GDP per capita placed it in the middle rungs of the "emerging" economies, and its human development and infrastructure accomplishments were among the best in the Arab region. The economy was more diversified than many other MENA economies, including agriculture, mining, manufacturing, and services such as tourism. The remnants of "statism" in the economy were five public banks that held about 40 percent of financial assets at that time, and state-owned enterprises (SOEs) in industry, utilities, transportation, water, and agriculture, with employees organized into a strong trade union federation, the Union Générale des Travailleurs Tunisiens (UGTT).[96]

While the IFIs complained that liberalizing reforms had not gone far enough and had ignored the human and civil rights violations perpetrated by the Ben Ali regime, they did not recognize the many negative aspects of Tunisia's structural transformation that were known to firsthand researchers outside of IFI circles. These aspects included corruption, cronyism, and growing inequality from slow job creation and stagnant incomes for the middle and working classes, as well as severe disparities between the coastal and inland provinces. Families increasingly depended on precarious employment in the growing informal sector and remittances from members working abroad, mostly in Libya and Europe.[97] As shown in chart 4.5, remittances averaged close to 5 percent of GDP in the 2000s.

The inflow of FDI in the 2000s helped increase the diversity of Tunisia's economy (table 4.1) and growth of manufactured exports. However, the most dynamic investment was concentrated in insular export-processing enclaves in the coastal provinces that profited international capital and a set of privileged Tunisian partners connected to the ruling family. Very little knowledge transfer or modern technology bled into the domestic economy, and much of the raw material and intermediate inputs needed for manufacturing were imported rather than supplied by domestic producers.[98] Furthermore, a significant portion of FDI went into the hydrocarbon sector, and when FDI did penetrate the domestic economy, it took the form of financial and telecom acquisitions, construction of luxury shopping malls and apartment buildings for the wealthy, and construction of grand resorts, hotels, and transportation facilities to meet the needs of foreign tourists and businesses.[99]

The demands of the protestors in the Arab Spring movement reflected the populace's real and pressing needs for responsive and fair government and for an economy that would generate decent jobs and income for ordinary people. In response to the uprisings, a series of key reforms in the legal and political structures made the system more pluralistic and inclusive and opened elections to genuine competition among political parties for the first time. This entailed a prolonged and contentious dialogue over how to restructure the polity, with frequent turnovers of top government officials. The population was frustrated to find that all of the postuprising governments were slow to enact reforms to the security and judicial systems and that none had come up with a comprehensive economic program to tackle

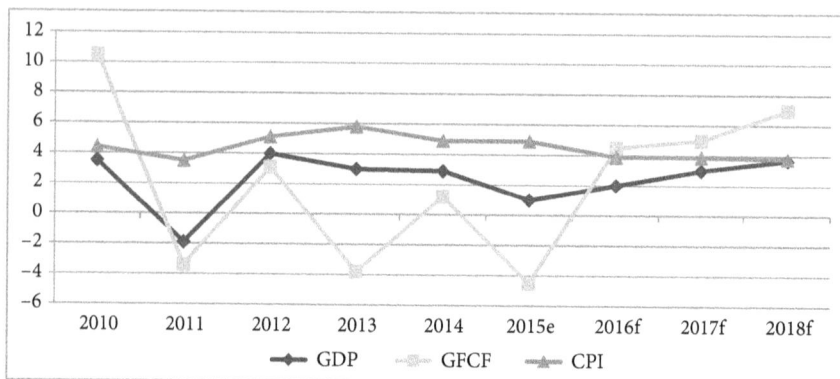

Chart 4.12a. Percent change in GDP, gross fixed capital formation (GFCF), and consumer price index (CPI) in Tunisia. *Source*: World Bank, Economic Outlook, October 2016: Washington DC: World Bank, Tunisia, http://pubdocs.worldbank.org/en/831791475460801718/Tunisia-MEM-Fall-2016-ENG.pdf (accessed January 18, 2017).

the many problems that had led to the uprising.[100] The continuing protests, strikes, and demonstrations, including against austerity budgets, and the lack of forward momentum in the economy fed into a cycle of decreasing investment, declining tourism, and stalled job creation and income generation, except to the extent that government could create jobs in temporary programs and raise public sector wages.[101]

During the same period, civil strife was raging in Libya and spilling over into Tunisia, sometimes in the form of terrorism, with a costly impact on all aspects of the Tunisian economy, especially tourism. Compared to IMF projections in 2010, ESCWA estimated that private investment in 2015 was 25 percent lower than expected and that Tunisia had missed out on 3.86 percentage points of growth per year between 2011 and 2015.[102] In addition, ebbing global demand for phosphates led to a fall in their export price by 50 percent from 2012 to 2016, but Tunisia could not make up in quantity what it lost in price (as Algeria had done with natural gas) as long as labor/ management disputes at Gafsa limited supply.[103]

As shown in chart 4.12a, economic growth and investment were low through 2015, while inflation and the current account and budget deficits grew (chart 4.12b) and unemployment rose to over 15 percent. To cover the deficit, the government drew down on foreign reserves and turned to borrowing, pushing up the projected debt to over 50 percent of GDP by 2016, a situation that seemed unsustainable without a restoration of growth.

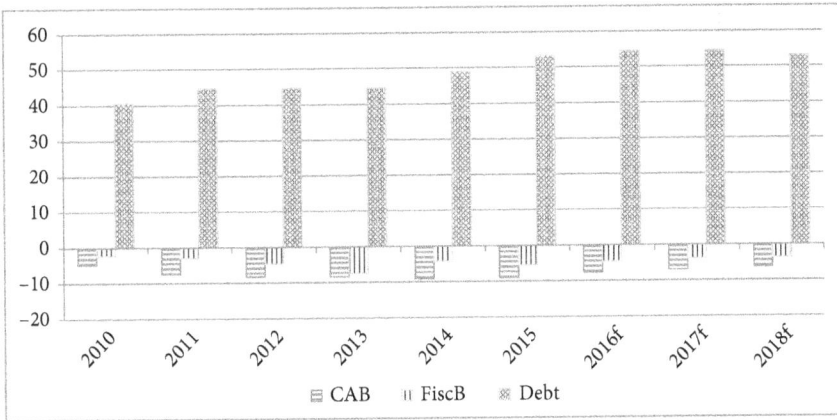

Chart 4.12b. Current account balance (CAB), fiscal balance (FiscB), and debt as percentage of GDP in Tunisia. Note: Fiscal balance for 2010 is the average for 2000–10 (IMF Databank). *Sources:* World Bank, Economic Outlook, October 2016. Washington DC: World Bank, Tunisia, http://pubdocs.worldbank.org/en/831791475460801718/Tunisia-MEM-Fall-2016 -ENG.pdf (accessed January 18, 2017). International Monetary Fund: IMF Data Bank (accessed January 17, 2017): Table 11. General Government Fiscal Balance, as Percent GDP http://data.imf.org/regular.aspx?key=60600903.

Without a program of its own, the desperate Tunisian government turned to the IMF in 2013. The deal was for a Stand-By Arrangement (SBA) in which the IMF would provide up to $1.74 million in concessional lending to be disbursed as needed over two years, from June 2013 to May 2015 (later extended to May 2016).

This form of assurance led to increased inflows from the World Bank and other donors and enabled Tunisia to sell its government bonds on the international market with guarantees from the United States.[104] Chart 4.4 shows the resulting rise in development aid. The external financial support was conditioned on the government's reducing the budget deficit by cutting spending, especially for subsidies; improving revenue collection; and reducing the current account deficit by allowing the dinar to depreciate. Beyond that, the government was to deepen structural reforms that, the IFIs argued, would eventually restore investor confidence, economic growth, and job creation.[105]

The IMF compared Tunisia unfavorably to Morocco, ignoring Tunisia's much greater vulnerability to spillover of conflict from Libya and the strain on its resources from caring for refugees. Its "competitiveness" was weaker, so currency depreciation was not followed by an increase in share of global exports as it had been in Morocco. Tunisia's scores on the "competitiveness" indexes for infrastructure, education, finance, and trade had all worsened by 2015, and its score on regulatory reform had not improved. Raising public sector wages to help workers had increased Tunisia's budget deficit, whereas Morocco had imposed "cost-saving reforms" on its workers and reduced its deficit. Tunisia had made some progress on reforms such as phasing out subsidies on energy, electricity, and water; increasing central bank independence; and improving taxation to reduce exemptions and loopholes and raise thresholds, but Morocco's progress was judged broader and deeper.[106]

As of 2016, Tunisia still faced the risk of "worsening of fragile domestic security or political instability" due to the "absence of material improvement in living and business environment conditions in the five years since the Arab Spring."[107] To try to find a fresh approach, the government organized a national dialogue in March 2016, which resulted in the "Carthage Document." The document was signed by top representatives of government, leaders of the trade union federation UGTT and the employers' association UTICA, and representatives of civil society organizations and NGOs. The document was broad enough that it left room for differing interpretations.

From the point of view of workers, civil society, and, to a lesser extent, UTICA, the document committed the country to a development plan aimed at creating the highest number of decent jobs, in particular in neglected regions of the country and for women.[108] Government would provide support for the start of new businesses and the formalization of informal business, by reducing barriers to finance and registration and counterproductive bureaucratic interference (including corruption on the local level). This would be done in conjunction with active labor market policies that put the unemployed to work as quickly as possible in building the infrastructure and providing the services needed to improve the quality of life in the hinterlands. Organized training or retraining of workers plus matching workers to jobs would be critical to the success of the program, with incentives to local business to train workers on the job as well. This sounded very much like what the ILO and UNDP had proposed for Tunisia during the year after the uprising.[109]

From the point of view of the IFIs, in contrast, the meaning of the Carthage Document became clear with the formation of a new "national unity" government in August 2016. With public backing from the IFIs and other donors, the government proclaimed a "Five Year Vision" with five pillars aiming to address all the unresolved demands raised during the Arab Spring: (1) transparent and effective government, (2) diversification of the economy, (3) human development and social inclusion, (4) reduction of regional disparities, and (5) economic growth.[110]

However, this vision was not a program. The program to which the government soon committed itself was actually the vigorous pursuit of the same structural-reform package required by the IFIs in exchange for their continued "significant and flexible" financial and technical support. These reforms included unpopular policies such as tightening the public wage bill, restructuring management of the civil service and SOEs, and expanding the private sector through public-private partnerships (PPPs) in, for example, managing utilities.[111]

The success of this program, in the IFIs' eyes, rested on several assumptions. First, they assumed that for-profit operations were more efficient and effective, a tenet that was not empirically well established and was mistrusted by many Tunisians. Second, they assumed that SMEs were the best-sized firms to promote because they were more innovative and would create more jobs. However, research had shown that "SMEs" were very diverse and that optimal firm size for productivity growth, export performance, and employment creation varied greatly by type of product, available technology, and ability to capture economies of scale. Even within the broad grouping of SMEs, the larger ones, with twenty to fifty employees each, provided significantly more jobs and more stable employment than those with fewer than twenty employees,[112] so an active labor market policy would have a bigger and quicker impact if it targeted the medium-sized firms first.

Third, the IFIs assumed that attracting FDI was the most efficient way to transfer knowledge, advance technical change, and become more integrated in the global economy, but Tunisia's previous experience had shown that this was not necessarily true. This transfer is not automatic but has to be negotiated with potential foreign investors by a savvy and clear-eyed government, as even researchers at the World Bank had come to realize.[113] The IFIs also assumed that global capital flows to, and demand for the exports of, Tunisia and other "emerging" economies would soon revive, and so Tunisia should prepare by improving its business climate and increasing its ability to compete with other EMDEs. However, the IFIs themselves were predicting that global capital flows and demand would remain sluggish in the forecastable future.

Furthermore, the IFIs seemed to assume that the public would not notice if the government gradually restored various pre–Arab Spring authoritarian features of governance. As of mid-2017, these features included using the state of emergency (renewed again in November 2017) to restrict freedom of the press, assembly, and association (such as in labor unions and civil society organizations); granting amnesty to corrupt officials from the Ben Ali regime; and providing impunity for the security services and police from public scrutiny or criticism of their behavior.[114] Ongoing strikes, protests, and demonstrations, however, indicated that the public noticed not only the slippage away from democratic governance but also the failure to implement a meaningful economic program to meet the goals of the Carthage Document.

Prospects for the Maghreb: IFI-Led Marshall Plans versus Regional Integration

The IFIs' expressed preference in late 2016 was to return to the principles of globalization and free trade as the proven ticket to global economic growth.[115] Fearing that continued financial stagnation and rising protectionism "could result in a loss of world output by about 3 percent through 2021,"[116] they urged the EMDEs, including the Maghrebi countries, more desperately than ever to press ahead with liberalizing reforms.[117] However, they had also come to realize that much more might be needed, even to the point of abandoning austerity and adopting planning. They proposed, first, something like a Marshall Plan for the world, including fiscal stimulation in all country groups; second, coordination of cross-border financing of investment in infrastructure and human development; and, last, provision of "a stronger global safety net . . . to protect [EMDE and LID] economies with robust fundamentals that may nevertheless be vulnerable to cross-border contagion and spillovers, including strains that are not economic."[118]

Region-based organizations, most affiliated with the United Nations, offered an alternative vision, in which the ruling concept was that human well-being, in contrast to economic growth, was the ultimate goal of development.[119] This approach also has three pillars. First, given the global phenomenon of "jobless growth," the prevailing tendency toward precarious employment, and the rise in unemployment globally in 2015, "full and productive employment and decent work for all" should be at the core of new development programming. Indeed, a key element of the Sustainable

Development Goals (SDGs) agenda, which 190 countries endorsed in 2015, would be to achieve this goal worldwide by 2030.[120] It would be the core mechanism for poverty eradication and the reduction of inequality around the world.

Second, this approach proposed restoration of the developmental state, with democratically elected leaders who could pursue a clearly defined and nationally agreed-upon vision for sustainable and inclusive development.[121] As ESCWA put it, for example, in explaining the drop in FDI from advanced countries to EMDEs since 2008, potentially investable surpluses were sitting idle in advanced country corporate coffers in what was effectively a "savings glut": "Markets have failed to act as an intermediary to direct funds from developed to developing economies, and so an alternative framework is necessary to solve this serious global imbalance."[122]

Third, the necessary programs could be carried out most effectively in the context of regional integration, involving not only trade but also investment finance and labor mobility. This interstate engagement could facilitate development (for example, jointly constructing an integrated electricity grid in the Maghreb fueled not by hydrocarbons but by solar and wind power) and reduce the likelihood of violent conflict and dependence on volatile international commerce and financial markets.[123] Proposals for and reports on existing dimensions of financial integration validated this idea.[124] Another positive sign was the effort undertaken by Algeria and Egypt in 2016 to reconcile the main factions in Libya to peacefully negotiating a more inclusive national unity government.

Perhaps Tunisia's announced economic program at the end of 2016 had elements of this second approach, assuming it had strong democratic leadership with a "developmental state" vision. The IFIs were willing to compromise with skeptical workers in Tunisia by including active labor market programs in their financial support packages for the program.[125] However, Tunisia's program would be more likely to succeed if the war in Libya ended and the threat of terrorism receded, outcomes that can be achieved only in a regional framework. The two alternative approaches diverged on the question of what overarching structure should shape the future trajectory of Tunisia and its neighbors: the IFI-led global orientation or the locally-led regional orientation. Whether the two approaches are substitutes or complements for sustainable development in the Maghreb was still unresolved, as was the troubled interface between the rejuvenation of authoritarianism and the democratic aspirations of the Arab Spring movement.

KAREN PFEIFER is Professor Emerita of Economics at Smith College. Her most recent research appears in *Political and Socio-Economic Change in the Middle East and North Africa: Gender Perspectives and Survival Strategies.*

Notes

1. See for example Egyptian Center for Economic Studies (ECES), "The Arab Spring Protest Movement Has Cost the Region $614 Billion in Lost Growth," *Our Economy and the World*, no. 37 (November 27, 2016), accessed November 28, 2016, http://eces.org.eg /MediaFiles/ViewOnNews/7e41ba19.pdf, which misinterprets United Nations Economic and Social Commission for Western Asia (ESCWA), *Survey of Economic and Social Developments in the Arab Region, 2015–2016* (Beirut, Lebanon: United Nations, 2016), accessed November 14, 2016, https://www.unescwa.org/sites/www.unescwa.org/files/publications/files/survey -economic-social-development-arab-region-2015-2016-english.pdf, as citing the uprisings as the cause of subsequent GDP foregone in both the countries in conflict (e.g., Libya) and neighboring countries affected by spillovers from conflict (e.g., Tunisia). Other examples are Mohsin Khan and Karim Mezran, "Aftermath of the Arab Spring in North Africa," in *Issue Brief* (Washington, DC: Atlantic Council, Rafik Hariri Center, October 2016), accessed November 7, 2016, http://www.atlanticcouncil.org/images/publications/Aftermath_of _the_Arab_Spring_in_North_Africa_web_1031.pdf; and McKinsey Global Institute, *Lions on the Move II: Realizing the Potential of Africa's Economies* (Brussels, Belgium: McKinsey and Company, September 2016), accessed September 15, 2016, http://www.mckinsey.com /global-themes/middle-east-and-africa/lions-on-the-move-realizing-the-potential-of -africas-economies, which describe each country's evolution since 2011 (Algeria, Libya, Morocco, and Tunisia) in terms of its own internal dynamics while giving little notice to external forces.

2. International Monetary Fund (IMF), *World Economic Outlook, October 2016* (Washington, DC: IMF, 2016), accessed November 7, 2016, http://www.imf.org/external /pubs/ft/weo/2016/02/pdf/text.pdf; IMF, *Global Financial Stability Report: Fostering Stability in a Low-Growth, Low-Rate Era* (Washington, DC: IMF, 2016), accessed November 7, 2016, http://www.imf.org/external/pubs/ft/gfsr/2016/02/pdf/text.pdf; World Bank, *Global Economic Prospects, June 2016* (Washington, DC: World Bank, 2016), accessed December 6, 2016, http:// pubdocs.worldbank.org/en/842861463605615468/Global-Economic-Prospects-June-2016 -Divergences-and-risks.pdf; ESCWA, *Survey Arab Region* and *Annual Report 2015* (Beirut, Lebanon: United Nations, 2016), accessed November 15, 2016, https://www.unescwa.org /sites/www.unescwa.org/files/publications/files/annual-report-2015-english.pdf; Binyamin Appelbaum, "A Little-Noticed Fact about Trade: It's No Longer Rising," *New York Times*, October 30, 2016, accessed November 1, 2016, http://www.nytimes.com/2016/10/31/upshot /a-little-noticed-fact-about-trade-its-no-longer-rising.html; Ruchir Sharma, "When Borders Close," *New York Times*, November 12, 2016, accessed November 15, 2016, http://www .nytimes.com/2016/11/13/opinion/sunday/when-borders-close.html?_r=0.

3. IMF, *World Economic Outlook*, 1–5.

4. Sharma, "When Borders Close"; IMF, *World Economic Outlook*, table A9, 241.

5. Appelbaum, "Fact about Trade."

6. IMF, *World Economic Outlook*, table A9, 241.

7. ESCWA, *Survey Arab Region*, 24–6, 45, 48.

8. ESCWA, *Survey Arab Region*, 41.

9. "Tough Days Ahead for Algeria's Currency," *North Africa Post*, August 8, 2018.

10. IMF, *World Economic Outlook*, table A1, 228.

11. IMF, *World Economic Outlook*, 19–20; IMF, *Regional Economic Outlook: MENAP and CCA, October 2016* (Washington, DC: IMF, 2016), xi, accessed December 12, 2016, http://www.imf.org/external/pubs/ft/reo/2016/mcd/eng/pdf/mreo1016.pdf.

12. McKinsey, *Lions on the Move*. Most of McKinsey's report is about sub-Saharan Africa, but the North African economies are mentioned several times, usually in a positive light (e.g., 11–6, 24, 56–7, 63–7, 76, 88, and 93).

13. IMF, *World Economic Outlook*, 16–8.

14. IMF, *World Economic Outlook*, table A3, 230–1.

15. IMF, *World Economic Outlook*, 27.

16. IMF, *World Economic Outlook*, 7–8; Appelbaum, "Fact about Trade."

17. Sharma, "When Borders Close."

18. ESCWA, *Survey Arab Region*, 16, 19.

19. Appelbaum, "Fact about Trade"; Sharma, "When Borders Close."

20. IMF, *World Economic Outlook*, 11–3; IMF, *Global Financial Stability*, foreword and xiii–xviii. Immigration of younger generations had previously been demonstrated to transfer a demographic dividend to advanced economies, reducing the labor force dependency ratio and, in the medium to long run, raising income per capita and productivity growth overall without a significant negative impact on employment or wages of native workers.

21. Sharma, "When Borders Close."

22. United Nations Development Program (UNDP), *Human Development Report 2015* (New York: UNDP, 2015), table 1, 222–5, accessed January 13, 2017, http://hdr.undp.org/sites/default/files/2015_human_development_report.pdf.

23. ESCWA, *Survey Arab Region*, 51–2.

24. ESCWA, *Survey Arab Region*, 52–4.

25. IMF, *Arab Countries in Transition: Economic Outlook and Key Challenges* (Washington, DC: IMF, October 2014), 3–5, accessed December 23, 2015, https://www.imf.org/external/np/pp/eng/2014/100914.pdf; Karim Mezran, "North African Transitions in 2014," in *MENA Source* (Washington, DC: Atlantic Council, Rafik Hariri Center, 2014), accessed November 7, 2016, http://www.atlanticcouncil.org/blogs/menasource/north-african-transitions-in-2014.

26. ESCWA, *Survey Arab Region*, 31–2.

27. Nabil Jedlane and Dhafer Saïdane, "Les Systèmes Financiers d'Afrique du Nord: Mutation Contrastée et Intégration Hésitante," *Revue d'Economie Financière* 4, no. 116 (2014): 99.

28. Libya's banks were calling in loans as they were running out of capital during the conflict.

29. Jedlane and Saïdane, "Systèmes Financiers," 103–5.

30. Jedlane and Saïdane, "Systèmes Financiers," 113–8.

31. Jedlane and Saïdane, "Systèmes Financiers," 100–1.

32. ESCWA, *Survey Arab Region*, 49–50.

33. Khan and Mezran, "Aftermath of the Arab Spring."

34. IMF, *Arab Countries in Transition*, 3.

35. IMF, *Arab Countries in Transition*, 4–5.

36. Karen Pfeifer, "Gulf Arab Financial Flows and Investment, 2000–2010: Promises, Process and Prospects in the MENA Region," *Review of Middle East Economics and Finance* 8, no. 2 (2012): 17–24.

37. Dhaman, *Investment Climate in Arab Countries* (Shuwaikh, Kuwait: Dhaman, 2016), accessed October 25, 2016, http://dhaman.net/en/wp-content/uploads/sites/3/2016/09/Climate-2016-ENG-ALL-D.pdf.

38. Mounir Belloumi, "The Relationship between Trade, FDI and Economic Growth in Tunisia: An Application of the Autoregressive Distributed Lag Model," *Economic Systems* 38 (2014): 269–87; Assaad Ghazouani and Hedia Teraoui, "Technology Transfer and FDI: Some Lessons for Tunisia," *Asian Economic and Financial Review* 4, no. 1 (2014): 90–104; Karen Pfeifer, "Neoliberal Transformation and the Uprisings in Tunisia and Egypt," in *Political and Socio-Economic Change in the Middle East and North Africa: Gender Perspectives and Survival Strategies*, ed. Roksana Bahramitash and Hadi Salehi Isfahani (New York: Palgrave-Macmillan, 2016), 34–40.

39. McKinsey, *Lions on the Move*, 76.

40. Dhaman, *Investment Climate*, 8–10. Dhaman, meaning "guarantee" or "surety," was the appealing nickname for the Arab Investment and Export Guarantee Corporation, headquartered in Kuwait and funded by subscriptions from the member countries of the Arab League. Founded in 1974, its original formal name was "the Inter-Arab Investment and Export Guarantee Corporation," and its orientation was to encourage investment and trade within the Arab region. Although it was never opposed to investment from elsewhere coming into the region, it gradually shifted to focus on FDI from outside the region in the neoliberal era, especially in the 2000s, as it adopted the ideology of FDI as the savior for developing countries and the need for Arab economies to become more business friendly and "competitive" in the fierce global struggle to attract FDI (Dhaman, *Investment Climate*, 10, 105).

41. Dhaman, *Investment Climate*, 36–43.

42. The details on all index components for all groups are in Dhaman, *Investment Climate*, 44–65, and the details for each country are on the "Country Profile" pages, 106–90.

43. Dhaman, *Investment Climate*, 61–2; Tidiane Kinda, Patrick Plane, and Marie-Ange Véganzonès-Varoudakis, "Firm Productivity and Investment Climate in Developing Countries: How Does Middle East and North Africa Manufacturing Perform?," *The Developing Economies* 49, no. 4 (2011): 429–62.

44. Euan Mearns, "The European Gas Market," December 13, 2007, accessed January 6, 2017, www.theoildrum.com/user/Euan+Mearns, via 321Energy.com, http://www.321energy.com/editorials/mearns/mearns121307.html.

45. Gawdat Bahgat, "North Africa and Europe: Energy Partnership," *OPEC Energy Review* (September–December 2009): 155–69 (Malden, MA: Blackwell Publishing).

46. Stefan Lochner and Caroline Dieckhöner, "European Gas Imports from North Africa: Reassessing Security of Supply in the Light of Political Turmoil," *Intereconomics* 3 (2011): 143–7.

47. Theodora.com, "North Africa Pipelines," May 6, 2008, accessed January 7, 2017, http://www.theodora.com/pipelines/north_africa_pipelines_map.jpg.

48. Fareed Mohamedi, "North Africa and the Mediterranean," in *Energy and Security: Strategies for a World in Transition*, 2nd ed., ed. Jan H. Kalicki and David L. Goldwyn (Washington, DC: Woodrow Wilson Center Press, and Baltimore: Johns Hopkins University Press, 2013), 245–7.

49. Mohamedi, "North Africa," 244–5.

50. Mezran, "North African Transitions."

51. Khan and Mezran, "Aftermath of the Arab Spring."

52. World Bank, "Algeria," *Economic Outlook 2016*, accessed October 18, 2018, http://pubdocs.worldbank.org/en/267701475460651472/Algeria-MEM-Fall-2016-ENG.pdf.

53. World Bank, "Algeria"; ESCWA, *Survey Arab Region*, 42–5.

54. The restarted facility was the In Amenas plant in the southwest, which had been damaged in an al-Qaeda-linked attack and hostage taking in 2013 in which many people were killed.

55. Lamine Chikhi, "Algeria's Gas Exports to EU Set to Rise 15 Percent in 2016: Official," Reuters.com, May 4, 2016, accessed January 10, 2017, http://www.reuters.com/article/us-algeria-energy-idUSKCN0XV0UG; Mark Smedley, "Algeria Increases Gas Exports by Pipe," NaturalGasWorld.com, September 5, 2016, accessed January 10, 2017, http://www.naturalgasworld.com/algeria-increases-gas-exports-by-pipe-31427; IMF, *Regional Economic Outlook*, 17–9.

56. Jude Clemente, "Will Algeria Be Able to Export More Natural Gas and LNG?," Forbes.com, May 4, 2016, accessed January 10, 2017, http://www.forbes.com/sites/judeclemente/2016/05/04/will-algeria-be-able-to-export-more-natural-gas-and-lng/#470bc4ec6147; Ali Aissaoui, *Algerian Gas: Troubling Trends, Troubled Policies*, OIES Paper NG 108 (Oxford, UK: Oxford Institute for Energy Studies, May 2016), accessed January 8, 2017, https://www.oxfordenergy.org/wpcms/wp-content/uploads/2016/05/Algerian-Gas-Troubling-Trends-Troubled-Policies-NG-108.pdf; ESCWA, *Survey Arab Region*, 25–6.

57. IMF, *Regional Economic Outlook*, 17; World Bank, *Global Economic Prospects*, 135–8; ESCWA, *Survey Arab Region*, 44–5.

58. IMF, *Algeria: Staff Report for the 2016 Article IV Consultation* (Washington, DC: IMF, 2016), 48, accessed May 26, 2016, http://www.imf.org/external/pubs/ft/scr/2016/cr16127.pdf.

59. IMF, *Algeria Staff Report*, 49–50.

60. See http://www.oxfordbusinessgroup.com/country/Algeria for links to OBG reports and articles.

61. Khan and Mezran, "Aftermath of the Arab Spring."

62. Khan and Mezran, "Aftermath of the Arab Spring."

63. Khan and Mezran, "Aftermath of the Arab Spring."

64. World Bank, "Libya," *Economic Outlook 2016*, accessed October 18, 2018, http://pubdocs.worldbank.org/en/282581475460786200/Libya-MEM-Fall-2016-ENG.pdf.

65. IMF, *Regional Economic Outlook*, 41.

66. World Bank, *Labor Market Dynamics in Libya: Reintegration for Recovery* (Washington, DC: World Bank, 2015), accessed June 3, 2016, https://elibrary.worldbank.org/doi/abs/10.1596/978-1-4648-0566-0 (accessed 6/3/2016); IMF, *Libya: 2013 Article IV Consultation* (Washington, DC: IMF, May 2013), accessed December 23, 2015, https://www.imf.org/external/pubs/ft/scr/2013/cr13150.pdf.

67. For example, Issa Ali and Charles Harvie, "Oil and Economic Development: Libya in the Post-Gaddafi Era," *Economic Modelling* 32 (2013): 273–85.

68. ESCWA, *Survey Arab Region*, 99–101.

69. Sumedh Rao, *Conflict Analysis of Mauritania* (Birmingham, UK: GSDRC, University of Birmingham, 2014), accessed January 21, 2017, http://www.gsdrc.org/wp-content/uploads/2015/07/GSDRC_ConflAnal_Mauritania.pdf; Sharif Nashashibi, "Mauritania's 'Overlooked' Arab Spring," *Guardian*, May 26, 2012, accessed January 20, 2017, www.theguardian.com/commentisfree/2012/may/26/mauritania-overlooked-arab-spring.

70. ESCWA, *Annual Report 2015*, 3.

71. Undala Alam and Ousmane Dione, "Fueling Cooperation: A Regional Approach to Reducing Poverty in the Senegal River Basin," in *Attacking Africa's Poverty: Experience from the Ground*, ed. Louise Fox and Robert Liebenthal (Washington, DC: World Bank, 2006), 95–115; United Nations Economic, Social and Cultural Organization (UNESCO), "Senegal River Basin (Guinea, Mali, Mauritania, Senegal)," in *UN World Water Development Report 1: Water for People, Water for Life* (Paris: World Water Assessment Programme Paris, UNESCO; and New York, Berghahn Books, 2003), 447–61, accessed January 20, 2017, http://www.unesco.org/new/fileadmin/MULTIMEDIA/HQ/SC/pdf/wwap_Senegal%20river%20 Basin_case%20studies1_EN.pdf.

72. Ozgur Demirkol, Luc Moers, and Dragana Ostojic, "Case Studies from the Middle East and North Africa," in *Energy Subsidy Reform: Lessons and Implications*, ed. Benedict J. Clements, David Coady, and Stefania Fabrizio (Washington, DC: IMF, 2013), 90–6; IMF, *Islamic Republic of Mauritania: Staff Report for the 2016 Article IV Consultation* (Washington, DC: IMF, 2016), 22–3, accessed May 26, 2016, https://www.imf.org/external/pubs/ft/scr/2016 /cr16115.pdf.

73. ESCWA, *Survey Arab Region*, 45.

74. African Development Bank, "Mauritania Economic Outlook," 2016, accessed January 17, 2017, https://www.afdb.org/en/countries/north-africa/mauritania/mauritania-economic -outlook/.

75. World Bank, "Mauritania Overview," April 2016, accessed January 17, 2017, http://www.worldbank.org/en/country/mauritania/overview; IMF, *Mauritania Staff Report*, 1–3.

76. Adeel Malik, "De la Malédiction des Ressources à la Malédiction de la Rente dans la Région MENA," in *Document de Travail: Série sur les Notes de Politiques en Afrique du Nord*, African Development Bank, 2015, www.afdb.org.

77. As with Algeria, the Oxford Business Group is an informative source for reports and articles on the most recent policy decisions and the outcomes of previous programs in Morocco and Tunisia (https://www.oxfordbusinessgroup.com/country/morocco).

78. Khan and Mezran, "Aftermath of the Arab Spring."

79. Background explanation on the roots of the Arab Spring protests specifically in Morocco can be found in two articles by Koenrad Bogaert, one written before and one written after the Spring: "The Problem of Slums: Shifting Methods of Neoliberal Urban Government in Morocco," *Development and Change* 42, no. 3 (2011): 709–31; and "The Revolt of Small Towns: The Meaning of Morocco's History and Geography of Social Protests," *Review of African Political Economy* 42, no. 143 (2015): 124–40.

80. IMF, *Arab Countries in Transition*, 15–6; Khan and Mezran, "Aftermath of the Arab Spring."

81. Khan and Mezran, "Aftermath of the Arab Spring."

82. Paolo Verme, Abdoul Gadiry Barry, and Jamal Guennouni, "Female Labor Participation in the Arab World: Some Evidence from Panel Data in Morocco," Policy Research Working Paper 7031 (Washington, DC: World Bank, September 2014); Paolo Verme, Abdoul Gadiry Barry, Jamal Guennouni, and Mohamed Taamouti, "Labor Mobility, Economic Shocks, and Jobless Growth: Evidence from Panel Data in Morocco," Policy Research Working Paper 6795 (Washington, DC: World Bank, March 2014).

83. Khan and Mezran, "Aftermath of the Arab Spring."

84. McKinsey, *Lions on the Move*, 95.

85. World Bank, "Economic Outlook," Morocco, accessed January 17, 2017, http://pubdocs .worldbank.org/en/828061475460788728/Morocco-MEM-Fall-2016-ENG.pdf; Mezran, "North African Transitions"; McKinsey, *Lions on the Move*, 88.

86. McKinsey, *Lions on the Move*, 56–7, 63, 67, 76.

87. ESCWA, *Survey Arab Region*, 26.

88. Reuters, "Morocco Launches $1.8 Billion West Sahara Investment Plan," Reuters.com, February 5, 2016, accessed December 19, 2016, http://af.reuters.com/article/moroccoNews /idAFL8N15K3T1.

89. World Bank, "Economic Outlook," Morocco.

90. ESCWA, *Survey Arab Region*, 44.

91. World Bank, "Five Things Morocco Is Doing about Climate Change," November 17, 2016, accessed January 22, 2017, http://www.worldbank.org/en/news/feature/2016/11/17/5 -things-morocco-is-doing-about-climate-change.

92. Gabriella Izzi, "Supporting Small Farmers in Morocco Adapt to Climate Change & Boost Yields," World Bank, April 1, 2013, accessed January 22, 2017, http://blogs.worldbank .org/arabvoices/supporting-small-farmers-morocco-adapt-climate-change-boost-yields; World Bank, "Morocco's Farmers to Benefit from Opening Markets and Agricultural Modernization," March 27, 2013, accessed January 22, 2017, http://www.worldbank.org/en /news/press-release/2013/03/27/morocco-farmers-benefit-opening-markets-agricultural -modernization; World Bank, "Five Things Morocco Is Doing."

93. Ursula Lindsey, "Morocco Plans for Less Reliance on Volatile Farming: Efforts Are Being Made to Limit the Disruptiveness of Chronic Droughts," *Financial Times*, March 23, 2016, accessed January 21, 2017, https://www.ft.com/content/0b145cac-cb48-11e5-a8ef -ea66e967dd44; Celeste Hicks, "Morocco's Progress on Food Security Acknowledged by UN but Work Remains," *Guardian*, October 27, 2015, p. 15, accessed January 22, 2017, https:// www.theguardian.com/global-development/2015/oct/27/morocco-food-security-un-special -rapporteur-hilal-elver-plan-maroc-vert.

94. Lindsey, "Morocco Volatile Farming."

95. Pfeifer, "Neoliberal Transformation."

96. Khan and Mezran, "Aftermath of the Arab Spring."

97. Pfeifer, "Neoliberal Transformation," 27–30, 42–60.

98. Belloumi, "Trade, FDI and Growth in Tunisia"; Ghazouani and Teraoui, "Technology Transfer and FDI."

99. Pfeifer, "Neoliberal Transformation," 34–40; Pfeifer, "Gulf Arab Financial Flows,"19–24.

100. Khan and Mezran, "Aftermath of the Arab Spring."

101. Pfeifer, Karen, "Rebels, Reformers and Empire: Alternative Economic Programs for Egypt and Tunisia," *Middle East Report* 274, 45, no. 1 (2015): 2–3, accessed April 17, 2015, http://www.merip.org/mer/mer274/rebels-reformers-empire.

102. ESCWA, *Survey Arab Region*, 89–91.

103. ESCWA, *Survey Arab Region*, 26–7.

104. Khan and Mezran, "Aftermath of the Arab Spring"; Mezran, "North African Transitions"; IMF, *Arab Countries in Transition*, 16–7.

105. IMF, *Arab Countries in Transition*, 16–7.

106. IMF, *Regional Economic Outlook*, 34–5, 38–9.

107. World Bank, *Global Economic Prospects*, 137.

108. Egyptian Center for Economic Studies (ECES), "Employment—North Africa Governments' Objective," *Our Economy and the World*, no. 24 (August 14, 2016), accessed December 16, 2016, http://www.eces.org.eg/MediaFiles/ViewOnNews/f5e605b.pdf.

109. Pfeifer, "Alternative Economic Programs," 6–7.

110. Khan and Mezran, "Aftermath of the Arab Spring."

111. IMF, *Regional Economic Outlook*, 39; IMF, *Tunisia: Staff Report for the 2015 Article IV Consultation* (Washington, DC: IMF, 2014), 15–30; World Bank, "Economic Outlook," Tunisia, accessed January 17, 2017, http://pubdocs.worldbank.org/en/831791475460801718 /Tunisia-MEM-Fall-2016-ENG.pdf; World Bank, *Country Partnership Framework for the Republic of Tunisia for the Period FY 2016–2020*, Report No. 104123-TN (Washington, DC: World Bank, 2016), v–vii, 1–3.

112. Mongi Boughzala, "Youth Employment and Economic Transition in Tunisia," *Global Economy and Development*, Working Paper 57 (Washington, DC: Brookings Institution, January 2013).

113. Roberto Echandi, Jana Krajcovicova, and Christine Zhenwei Qiang, "The Impact of Investment Policy in a Changing Global Economy: A Review of the Literature," Policy Research Working Paper WPS7437 (Washington, DC: World Bank Group, 2015).

114. Human Rights Watch, "Draft Law Could Return Tunisia to a Police State," July 24, 2017, accessed November 10, 2017, https://www.hrw.org/news/2017/07/24/draft-law -could-return-tunisia-police-state; Human Rights Watch, "One Step Forward, One Step Back in Tunisia," September 15, 2017, accessed November 10, 2017, https://www.hrw.org /news/2017/09/15/one-step-forward-one-step-back-tunisia; France 24, "Tunisia Extends State of Emergency," November 10, 2017, accessed November 10, 2017, http://www.france24.com /en/20171110-tunisia-extends-2015-state-emergency; Reuters, "Tunisia Tightens Restrictions on Journalists, Press Freedom at Risk—Union," April 11, 2017, accessed November 10, 2017, http://www.reuters.com/article/us-tunisia-politics-censorship/tunisia-tightens-restrictions -on-journalists-press-freedom-at-risk-union-idUSKBN17D1RQ?il=0.

115. IMF, *Global Financial Stability*, foreword and xiii–xviii.

116. IMF, *Global Financial Stability*, x.

117. IMF, *World Economic Outlook*, 32–3; IMF, *Arab Countries in Transition*, 3–6; IMF, *Regional Economic Outlook*, xii, 3, 6.

118. IMF, *Global Financial Stability*, xviii; IMF, *World Economic Outlook*, 35–6.

119. ESCWA, Arab Development Outlook: Vison 2030 (Beirut, Lebanon: United Nations, 2015), 7, accessed December 18, 2016, https://www.unescwa.org/sites/www.unescwa.org /files/publications/files/arab-development-outlook-vision-2030-english_0.pdf. Region-based organizations include the Economic and Social Commission for Western Asia (ESCWA), with affiliations to the United Nations Development Program (UNDP), the International Labor Organization (ILO), the United Nations Commission on Trade and Development (UNCTAD), and the African Development Bank. Even Dhaman, despite its infatuation with FDI and earnest pursuit of a business-friendly investment climate in the Arab world, posited a model such as this incorporating FDI only as appropriate into the program (Dhaman, *Investment Climate*, 105–10).

120. ESCWA, *Survey Arab Region*, 19.

121. Pfeifer, "Alternative Economic Programs," 6–7.

122. ESCWA, *Survey Arab Region*, 16, 19.

123. ESCWA, *Arab Development Outlook*, 10–5; ESCWA, *Annual Report 2015*, 26, 28, 41.

124. Mehdi Ben Guirat and Corinne Pastoret, "Financial Constraints on Economic Growth in the Maghreb Countries," *International Journal of Political Economy* 38, no. 4 (2010): 66–85; Mezui Mbeng and Cèdric Achille, "Approfondir les Marchés Africains des Capitaux pour le Financement des Infrastructures," *Revue d'Economie Financière* 4, no. 116 (2014): 165–76; McKinsey, *Lions on the Move*; Jedlane and Saïdane, "Systèmes Financiers," 105–7, 111.

125. IMF, *Regional Economic Outlook*, 42–3.

5

GEOPOLITICAL EVOLUTIONS IN NORTH AFRICA AFTER THE ARAB SPRING

Pierre Razoux

IN THE AFTERMATH OF THE ARAB SPRING UPRISINGS in 2011, the regional geopolitical evolution of the Maghreb has developed a pattern that resembles domestic old-style authoritarianism.[1] The proliferation of jihadist fronts, particularly in Libya, has prompted governments in North Africa to restrict cross-sectoral cooperation and close east-west borders, while tolerating the porosity of the north-south borders. The new regional postures, illustrated by a new arms race, have amplified existing rivalries, especially between Morocco and Algeria. Indeed, three vertical stripes coexist in a quasi-hermetic way, allowing Morocco, Algeria, and Egypt to project their soft power toward sub-Saharan Africa, while they worry about the black hole that threatens to absorb Libya, menaced with fragmentation.

In North Africa, rivalries between the regional powers of the Middle East (Turkey, the Gulf monarchies, and Iran) manifest themselves. Rivalries are also evident between global players such as the United States, Russia, and China. The discovery of important gas fields in the eastern Mediterranean has accelerated international restructuring for the benefit of coastal states and Russia, but to the detriment of NATO and the European Union (EU). Both NATO and the EU seem to have difficulty adapting to the new situation, especially after the vote in favor of Brexit (UK exit from the EU) and the election of Donald Trump in the United States, leaving room for tailor-made partnerships such as the 5 + 5 toward the west of North Africa (Mauritania-Morocco-Algeria-Tunisia-Libya + Portugal-Spain-France-Italy-Malta) and the 2 + 2 to the east (Egypt-Israel + Greece-Cyprus). This development could encourage Turkey to look more toward Russia and Iran than to the United States and the Maghreb countries. In the end, North Africa remains an important partner for southern European countries. However, if they want to break the impasse that hinders their economic development and development potential, Maghrebi elites will have to change mentalities and promote intra-Maghreb cooperation.

Twenty years ago, a few years after the collapse of the Soviet Union, Europeans could rejoice in the refounding of a homogeneous Eastern Europe, united around common values, with democratic political regimes and a geopolitical environment dominated by NATO and the EU, both guarantors of their security and material comfort. The transition was positive, despite the conflicts arising from the breakup of the former Yugoslavia. European and Atlantic solidarities help explain the successes that have not been fundamentally challenged by the Ukrainian crisis and the renewed tensions between Russia and Eastern Europe. Since 1991, NATO and the EU have almost doubled the number of their member states, with Brexit representing an outlier.

Seven years after the outbreak of the Arab revolutions in 2011, North Africans live in an uncertain space, reinforcing authoritarian instincts and tendencies within an unstable geopolitical context, characterized by tensions, rivalries, and threats. This situation should induce maximum cooperation and synergy between the countries of North Africa.[2] Mustapha Benchenane explains this state of affairs as the failure of the nation-state in this region, aggravated by the failure of development strategies.[3] Without such an effort of cooperation, historical links between the northern and southern Mediterranean may not be enough to restore meaning to a compartmentalized Maghrebi space that no longer has minimal unity, or to counterbalance the risks inherent in geopolitical evolutions affecting North Africa and the Saharan area. This chapter proposes to analyze these multiple geopolitical evolutions by considering their consequences. It will particularly scrutinize Smail Kuttroub's hypothesis, which estimated that although the Arab Spring undoubtedly upset previous balances, it did not lead to a major geopolitical reversal in the region, even though it accelerated the withdrawal of traditional powers and the emergence of new actors.[4] On his own, Pierre Berthelot carried out a first geopolitical assessment of the Arab Spring, concluding that a zero-sum game situation was prevailing, which brought about a new form of nonalignment in the region.

The Proliferation of Jihadist Fronts and Its Consequences
on the Borders

At the end of 2011, after the fall of the Tunisian, Egyptian, and Libyan regimes, the jihadist groups likely to threaten the Maghrebi countries were confined to Iraq and to a limited portion of the Sahel-Saharan stripe. Since then, jihadist fronts have multiplied, thriving on anarchy and chaos caused by the absence of the state in some areas, the violent reactions of some regimes, the worsening of the socioeconomic situation, the absence of political solutions, the disproportionate ambition of some individuals lacking defined points of reference and values, and unscrupulous mafia groups, as well as the ambiguous agenda of some regional actors.

By autumn of 2016, four main fronts could be identified. The first covers a significant portion of Iraq and Syria under the control of the Islamic State (ISIS), led by its self-proclaimed caliph, Abu Bakr Al-Baghdadi, and jihadist groups affiliated with the al-Qaeda movement. Initially, the jihadist groups active on this broad front sought to gain a foothold along the Syrian and Lebanese coasts to gain access to the eastern Mediterranean, and thus to solve some of their logistical problems, while at the same time being able to launch new terrorist attacks on maritime traffic and the tourist industry and to exploit offshore gas. However, they have not succeeded and have experienced several stinging setbacks, forcing them to retreat to their sanctuaries in Raqqa and Mosul, where crucial battles involving an imposing international coalition are now taking place. Once they are expelled from these two cities, it is very likely that the surviving jihadists will join other fronts.

The second front is located in the Sinai Peninsula. There, jihadist groups are targeting the Egyptian military government and its Israeli, Jordanian, and Saudi neighbors.[5] Supported by the radical wing of Hamas entrenched in the Gaza Strip, they could eventually threaten the Suez Canal as well as maritime traffic and offshore gas in the eastern Mediterranean and the Red Sea.

The third front, arguably the most dangerous in the short term, includes Libya, the far south of Tunisia, and the most eastern part of the Algerian desert. Extremely active, this front accelerates the process of "Somalization" of Libya as well as the illegal emigration of desperate refugees. It poses multiple risks to the stability and security of Egypt, Tunisia, Algeria, Chad, and Niger, as well as southern European countries in the center of the Mediterranean, such as Italy, Malta, and Greece. Jihadist groups affiliated with ISIS or al-Qaeda are fighting each other[6] while allowing piracy to prosper, threatening maritime traffic off the Libyan coast. These groups could pose a serious ecological threat if their leaders decide to open the valves of oil wells, allowing oil spillages in coastal areas, as Saddam Hussein did during the 1991 Gulf War. Finally, the last jihadist front continues to spread along the huge Sahel-Saharan stripe, threatening the countries of the Sahel, especially Mali and Niger.[7]

The existence of these four jihadist fronts transformed the vision that the Europeans had of the Maghreb. Although for decades Europeans favored an approach based on building bridges and on north-south cooperation, they are now worried, viewing North Africa only through a security lens. This makes them ask a crucial question: where to place the border of European security interests in the face of threats from the Maghreb? Should this new line of defense be shifted to the middle of the Mediterranean, as many populist parties and European leaders with little awareness of the real issues regarding the Mediterranean basin desire? Or is it necessary to place this line of defense against jihadism much further south so as to push the threats back as far as possible? To do this would imply cooperating closely with the Maghrebi governments to help them fight a scourge that threatens them as much as the Europeans.

The North African and southern European states have a vital interest in preventing the unification of these four jihadist fronts, because if this were to happen, the stability of the entire Maghreb and southern Europe would be threatened. Egypt, at the intersection of three of them, is particularly targeted, especially because it controls access to the Suez Canal. This is one of the reasons that many Western countries, including France, but also Russia, Saudi Arabia, and the United Arab Emirates, unconditionally support the military regime of Egyptian president, Abdel Fattah el-Sisi.

The Maghreb has not experienced any continental drift in the geological sense, but its geostrategic dimension and external influences have considerably amplified over the last six years. The leaders of the countries of North Africa rediscovered the Sahel as the natural extension of the Maghreb to the south. All of them now maintain close relations with their neighbors in the Sahel-Saharan strip, knowing that their security and stability, as well as their economic prosperity, depend on it. They all have understood that their country no longer necessarily constitutes a transit territory between Africa and Europe, but that it is more and more akin to a terminus where immigrants of all kinds settle in search of a better future. In fact, the Maghrebi states no longer consider the Sahara and the Sahel as impassable spaces that provide them with a buffer zone in relation to sub-Saharan Africa. On the contrary, they look more and more toward the south. Not only do they refrain from looking sideways, toward the west and the east, because of their incessant rivalries, but they are increasingly disappointed by the north, whose populist and inward-looking trend they deplore, a trend accentuated by the economic crisis and the terrorist attacks of 2015 and 2016.

Three consequences flow from this geopolitical expansion. First, there are clearly three vertical strips of influence conveying toward the south the geopolitical interests of Morocco (to Mauritania, Senegal, Guinea, and Côte d'Ivoire), Algeria (to Mali, Niger, Burkina Faso, and Nigeria), and Egypt (to Sudan and Southern Sudan). Only Tunisia continues to look primarily at Europe, from which it expects a lot to defend its democratic experience. Libya, on the other hand, is a "black hole" that threatens to engulf local actors.

The second consequence is that the Maghrebi governments increasingly court the African Union and the African regional organization-representing countries in their vicinity, such as the Economic Community of West African States (ECOWAS) and the Economic Community of Central African States (ECOCAS). Finally, one can only take note of the clinical death of the political unification of the Maghreb through the Arab Maghreb Union (UMA, according to its French acronym). The UMA was created in 1989, and its council of Foreign Affairs Ministers has not met since May 2013, except that in view of the security emergency, the UMA Council of Interior Ministers managed to meet in April 2016, without achieving tangible results.

As a third consequence, the geopolitical dimension of North Africa expanded eastward toward Turkey. As early as the beginning of the Arab Spring, Turkey, the regional riparian power on the Mediterranean, projected its soft power in the direction of Tunisia, Libya, and above all, Egypt, led by President Morsi. These three countries were initially governed by the Muslim Brotherhood. The freezing of the Arab Spring and the counterrevolution led by Saudi Arabia led to a decrease of Turkish influence in Tunisia and Libya and its total loss in Egypt. The Egyptian marshal Abdel Fattah el-Sisi has inimical relations with Turkish president Recep Tayyip Erdoğan, vehemently opposing his Turkish rival with some success, if we consider the loss of Turkish positions in Tunisia, in Libya, and among the Palestinians.

The authoritarian drift of the regime and the migrant crisis with refugees pushed on the European coasts by violence ravaging Iraq and Syria (such as the bombing of the Kurdish population) have not improved the image of the Turkish government, which has been accused of "instrumentalizing" the refugees' wandering, and taking advantage of the fight against ISIS to get rid of the Kurdish issue. Everyone now understands that the outcome of the Syrian and Iraqi crises affects the security of the Mediterranean and, therefore, of the Maghreb.

The multiplication of jihadist fronts, combined with the traditional Maghrebi rivalries and the geopolitical expansion of North Africa both eastward and southward, is affecting the borders of Maghrebi states. There are three main developments, discussed in the following sections.

Closing of East-West Borders

Closed since 1994, the border between Morocco and Algeria is not about to reopen, with both countries invoking the pretext of increased terrorism risk. It is all the more paradoxical that this does not prevent Moroccan and Algerian citizens from traveling to each other's countries, or the frontier populations from developing an important parallel economy across this same border.[8] Further east, since 2011 Tunisia has regularly closed its border with Libya for security reasons. On March 7, 2016, the Tunisian defense minister announced the indefinite closing of the border with Libya and acceleration of construction of a hermetic border fence between the two countries, this being a result of the March 2016 jihadist attacks against the Tunisian border town of Ben Guerdane and threats by ISIS to expand its "caliphate" in southern Tunisia.[9] The border between Libya and Egypt has been closed since October 2013 for security reasons, even if the Egyptian government is willing to open it occasionally to manage the flow of Egyptian workers traveling to Libya, and to facilitate the support Libya provides to the militia of General Khalifa Haftar, whose influence is exercised in the eastern half of Libya and along the Egyptian border. In the autumn of 2016, part of the Egyptian army remained amassed on the Libyan border to prevent any jihadist incursion from Libya, and to increase political and military pressure on Libyan authorities, who have difficulty agreeing on a coalition government. To increase this pressure, Marshal el-Sisi carried out strikes inside Libya and did not rule out the possibility of an Egyptian military intervention, on the condition that it be asked for by one of the two Libyan governments, with a mandate from the UN or the Arab League.[10]

As of this writing, only the border between Algeria and Tunisia remains open. Since an agreement between the two governments was initialed, this border of 965 kilometers has been patrolled jointly by Tunisian and Algerian military forces. The security services of the two countries, very concerned by the increase of jihadist attacks in the area, cooperate closely, to the point that the Algerian military would have a "droit de suite" on Tunisian territory.[11] This agreement could, however, be called into question if Islamists were to win elections in Tunisia.

Porosity of North-South Borders

All the experts agree that over the past six years, the southern borders of Morocco, Algeria, and Libya have remained porous in relation to neighboring countries in the Sahel-Saharan strip (Mauritania, Mali, Niger, Chad, and Sudan), allowing the development of a parallel economy boosted by the multiplication of jihadist groups looking to raise money to finance their activities.[12] Whether it is smuggling gasoline or cigarettes, trafficking in arms or drugs, or operating clandestine immigration routes, it is clear that there is an upsurge of illegal activities in the southern region and desert confines of the Maghreb countries. During the 2011–16 period, the priority of these countries was to secure the Mediterranean coastal strip or the outskirts of the capitals to protect the powers in place. In fact, only Algeria has sealed its southern border with Mali, Niger, and Libya during the weeks after the al-Qaeda in the Islamic Maghreb (AQIM) attack on its oil fields of In Amenas in January 2013. However, Algeria rapidly reopened this border under pressure from the local population. For similar reasons, even Egypt reopened its border with Sudan on April 29, 2015, and inaugurated the new Ashkit-Qostol road crossing between the two countries. In fact, both traffickers and combatants can easily travel from the Atlantic coast to the Red Sea, which gives France a justification to continue the Barkhane military operation against jihadist groups scattered between Mauritania, Mali, Niger, Burkina Faso, and Chad,[13] despite the irritation of the Algerian authorities, still very nervous about the presence of Western troops at their borders.

Questioning Libyan Borders

Although the dictatorial regime of Colonel Qaddafi maintained the unity of Libya under duress for forty-two years, his fall revived emancipation dynamics linked to ancestral tribal, ethnic, and local rivalries. As noted by

Karine Bennafla, the Libyan revolution resulted in the resurgence of former precolonial territorial divisions (Tripolitania, Cyrenaica, and Fezzan), the falling back on local and tribal identities (Tripoli, Misurata, Barqa, Djebel Nefusa, Zouwara, Zentan, Darna, and Benghazi), and the multiplication of militias, with de facto creation of myriad microterritories proclaiming themselves independent.[14] This chaos, described by the experts as the "new Libyan civil war,"[15] calls into question the borders of Libya, particularly with the potential fragmentation of the country into several distinct entities. Despite the conclusion of a national unity agreement on February 14, 2016, two authorities were still fighting for power at the end of 2016, namely the government recognized by the international community in Tobruk near the Egyptian border under the protection of General Khalifa Haftar, and a government based in Tripoli, dominated by the Muslim Brotherhood and supported by Qatar and Turkey.

Taking advantage of the chaos, jihadist groups, especially those affiliated with ISIS, initially reinforced their positions around the oil regions of Sirte on the Mediterranean coast, before being chased away in the autumn of 2016 by the troops of General Haftar. These jihadist groups remain firmly entrenched in the south of the country in areas difficult to reach. Some hoped that the de jure fragmentation of Libya would set a precedent and open a Pandora's box for all those hoping for a remodeling of the borders of the Middle East, including Palestinians, Kurds, and Iraqi and Syrian Sunnis. No one knows what further violence such a redrawing of borders could cause, and which other North African countries would be affected.

New Regional Postures and Their Consequences

The states of North Africa have responded differently to ongoing developments, each one seeking to preserve its interests and improve its positions. All of them, at one stage or another, were tempted to boost authoritarian tendencies to strengthen internal security and to contain what they perceived as external threats or challenges. Let us examine these countries one by one. Morocco is becoming more and more detached from the Maghreb, turning toward West Africa and the Atlantic Ocean, while maintaining excellent relations with France, Spain, and Portugal and increasing its access to Brazil. It wants to be an indispensable partner to the EU and the United States, both in the fight against terrorism and in terms of economic cooperation. Morocco is now looking to Brazil, the United States, and India, three buyers of its phosphates used for intensive agriculture in these countries. Morocco knows that its status as a guardian of the Straits of Gibraltar, along with the United Kingdom and Spain, translates into an unwavering support on the part of the United States and European countries eager to preserve at all costs the security of this strategic strait, which controls the vital sea route from the Atlantic Ocean to the Indian Ocean via the Mediterranean. Convinced that it will take time to ease tensions with Algeria, linked to the issue of the sovereignty of Western Sahara, which would restore the free movement between the two countries, the Moroccan government has decided to speed the development of the Tangier Med port terminal inaugurated in 2007, allowing for faster communication between Moroccan and European ports.

The Moroccan authorities are hoping that this hub will become a growth pole for the region when the border between Morocco and Algeria reopens. Sidelined by the African Union under pressure from both Algeria and South Africa, but also in reaction to statements by former UN secretary-general Ban Ki-Moon on Western Sahara, Morocco seems to have abandoned its claims for Maghrebi leadership. On the other hand, it is moving closer to ECOWAS and projects its soft power in West African Francophone countries, forging several joint ventures with them in banking, services, and trade. This strategy, called the "new frontier," is about renewing ties with states that were historically within its sphere of influence, and preventing Algeria from reaching the Atlantic Ocean.[16] It is no coincidence that King Mohammed VI delivered his annual Green March speech in Dakar during his state visit to Senegal, during which he signed important economic cooperation agreements. In keeping with this logic, the king hosted the World Climate Conference (COP 22) in Marrakesh in November 2016.

Algeria, for its part, seeks to ostracize Morocco and show its neighbors and partners on both sides of the Mediterranean that it remains the regional heavyweight, without which nothing is possible, despite the many challenges it faces with the postponement of reforms, the opacity of a gerontocratic governance, the excessive weight of the military, the rivalries between various profiteers, and the collapse of oil and gas revenues. In fact, the Algerian government has multiplied regional multilateral initiatives with the Sahel countries, particularly in the security area. It has established a Joint Operational Military Staff Committee (CEMOC-JCC) in Tamanrasset, with the armed forces of Mali, Mauritania, and Niger, to fight more effectively against the jihadist groups present in the south of Algeria.

This committee voluntarily excludes Morocco and Tunisia. Its intelligence appendage (the Fusion and Liaison Unit) has been extended to Libya, Nigeria, Burkina Faso, and Chad. To reaffirm its central role, Algeria did not hesitate to authorize the French Air Force to fly over its territory during the first phase of Operation Serval in Mali in January 2013.[17]

Algeria is also seeking to diversify its partnerships by opening up even more to China, Russia, and Turkey. However, as Aomar Baghzouz reminds us, Algeria is now at a crossroads.[18] The government is quite shaken, as was the case at the end of the 1980s when oil prices decreased over a long period. This is particularly true after Donald Trump has declared that he will maintain hydrocarbon prices at low levels, causing more concern and alarm for the Algerian authorities, who realize that the days they could buy social peace through subsidies are counted.[19] The Algerian authorities decided hastily to split the powerful Intelligence and Security Department (DRS) into three distinct divisions. The DRS is the only government entity to recognize the urgency of major structural reforms. The Algerian military, on the other hand, is adopting a prudent posture, observing the situation and acting as the good student of its Western partners (NATO and the 5 + 5 Defense Initiative), biding its time, and perhaps hoping for developments that would bring the military to power, such as in Egypt.[20] Such developments placing the Algerian army on the throne would not improve democratization of the Maghreb and could encourage other regional states to follow this path.

To further strengthen their position, the military convinced the Algerian government to acquire large quantities of advanced weapons from Russia (see below). One point that seems clear is that the generation of officers currently waiting for promotion is not opposed to possible changes in foreign policy. Contrary to the current official position against conducting military operations outside the national borders under the principle of noninterference,[21] a rejuvenated team could accept the idea of engaging armed forces in Algeria's neighborhood to assert its authority and fight more effectively against jihadist and other mafia-like groups active on the borders of the country.[22]

Concerned primarily with the defense of its very young democratic institutions, and threatened by active jihadist groups in Libya, as well as by the radical Salafist movement present on its soil, Tunisia has little time to worry about geopolitics. The current Tunisian government has distanced itself from Turkey and Qatar, which had used the appointment of a Tunisian government close to the Muslim Brotherhood in 2012 to strengthen their influence in the country. In 2017, the new coalition government's energy has been devoted to increasing internal security by working closely with the Algerian authorities, but also with its Western partners that consider Tunisia a "democratic laboratory for the Arab world which should not be allowed to fail." That is why French, Germans, Americans, and Britons are very active in protecting it. For the first time since World War II, British special forces have even been deployed in southern Tunisia to help local authorities fight jihadist groups more effectively.[23]

Plagued with chaos, Libya is not in a position to frame its actions within any geopolitical thinking.[24] At most, it is putting up with the events and trying to restructure its institutions, while fighting against rebel and jihadist groups that proliferate on its territory. In this respect, General Khalifa Haftar seems to have been able to impose himself as a kingmaker because he controls the armed forces and the largest part of the Libyan territory. Pending a political solution, the fragmentation of the country into two or even three entities (Tripolitania in the west, Cyrenaica in the east, and Fezzan in the south) reinforces the vertical division of competing influences in North Africa to the detriment of horizontal cooperation between all the governments of the southern shore of the Mediterranean.

This cooperation is not really Cairo's priority either. The events linked to the Arab Spring convinced the Egyptian military to develop a new geopolitical approach to deal with a regional strategy that remains unchanged. This strategy consists of restoring Egypt as a beacon of the Arab world and strengthening its aura, its economy, and its military, while fighting terrorism, autonomist demands, and political Islam originating from Turkey, the Gaza Strip, Qatar, or Iran.[25] Democratic evolution is no longer on the top of the Egyptian leadership's agenda; restoring security is the new long-term paradigm. Troubled by the ambiguous attitude of the US administration during the 2011 revolution, and the positions taken by then–secretary of state Hillary Clinton in favor of the Muslim Brotherhood government, President el-Sisi distanced himself from the United States. Unlike his predecessors, who relied on a strategic alliance with Washington, the new president wishes to diversify the partnerships by establishing special ties with Saudi Arabia and the United Arab Emirates, which can help him fight against the Muslim Brotherhood movement and support him in the Arab world, and with France, Russia, and China, which can provide him with the weapons and investments he needs. These countries indeed seem reliable, and they enjoy the privilege of veto power at the UN Security Council.[26] According to President el-Sisi's advisors, these partnerships must allow for adaptation to all configurations, including the occasional opposition or the loss of one of these five privileged partners. Egyptian strategists do not discount the possibility of profound changes in Saudi Arabia when the royal family, faced with a lasting decrease in oil prices, will no longer be able to buy social peace. Indeed, Egypt is looking to its northern coasts to protect its offshore gas fields, to the south to secure the Red Sea and to fight the jihadists firmly established in the Sinai Peninsula, to the Strait of Bab-el-Mandeb and the sources of the Nile, and to Israel, with which Cairo maintains close security cooperation. The Egyptian authorities do not look very much at the Maghreb; they consider that region a source of problems and rivalries with which Egypt does not wish to interfere, as long as its western border is not threatened.

Saudi Arabia, Qatar, and Iran are now considered real players in the geopolitics of the Mediterranean Sea. The first fights the other two by supporting the Egyptian counterrevolution, spreading its vision of a Salafist Islam throughout the region, and fighting the Muslim Brotherhood, which is accused of conveying a political Islam seeking to establish Islamic republics, considered existential threats by the ultraconservative monarchies unwilling to limit their absolute power. The United Arab Emirates, with an ideological agenda similar to that of Saudi Arabia, also projects its influence in the Mediterranean, particularly in Egypt and Libya, but in a subtler and less visible way, even if their aviation has intervened on several occasions against jihadist groups in Libya.[27]

For its part, Qatar, Saudi Arabia's main rival within the Gulf Cooperation Council, supports the Muslim Brotherhood with all the power of its diplomacy and its finances, with several investment projects in Tunisia, Libya, and even Turkey. The strategic rapprochement between Turkey and Qatar is demonstrated by an agreement between the two countries, allowing Qatar to deploy fighter jets in Turkey, and allowing Turkey to build a military base in Qatar.[28]

The Iranian authorities are working hard to counter Saudi influence in the Mediterranean, especially in Lebanon and Syria, but also in Morocco, where the royal family has ties with the Saudi royal family. In addition, Saudi investments in Morocco are significant. The Iranian approaches seem to bear fruit. In Lebanon, Tehran has succeeded in restoring the influence of the Hezbollah Shiite militia, as evidenced by the election of President

Michel Aoun in October 2016. In Morocco, the Iranian government successfully convinced the king of Morocco to renew diplomatic relations with Tehran, which were reestablished in January 2015, after having been broken in 2008 under strong Saudi pressure on Morocco. This is also proof of the influence of Shiite communities in Mauritania, Senegal, and Guinea, at a time when Morocco is seeking financial support to project its influence in West Africa.[29] The Saudi authorities were quick to retaliate in Lebanon by canceling the financing of French armament acquisition by the Lebanese military. On the other hand, they remain cautious vis-à-vis Morocco, continuing their annual investment of US\$1 billion to strengthen the ties between the two monarchies. To fortify its positions, Saudi Arabia announced an agreement with the Egyptian government for the return of the Red Sea islands of Tiran and Snapir, in order to build a bridge linking Egypt and the Wahhabi kingdom.[30]

What are the consequences of these new regional postures? Three can easily be identified.

1. *A new arms race in North Africa.* In five years (2011–16), Algeria, Morocco, and especially Egypt acquired large quantities of sophisticated weapons, added to already-imposing arsenals. These three countries alone bought (or were offered) 4 observation satellites, 770 tanks, 1,910 light armored vehicles, 222 helicopters, 169 combat aircraft and 63 warships, including 10 frigates and 2 large amphibious landing craft (Mistral class BPC delivered by France to Egypt after the cancellation of their sale to Russia), not to mention several tens of thousands of missiles (see table 5.1). During this period, North Africa emerged as the third largest arms-importing region after the Arabian Peninsula and Southeast Asia. As emphasized by Djallil Lounnas, the quantity and quality of the armament bought reveals a double concern. The first concern is related to the fight against terrorism, and the second to an external threat accentuated by NATO intervention in Libya.[31]

2. *Renewed tensions between Morocco and Algeria.* The wariness of the Algerian regime fighting for its survival, the crystallization of the Western Sahara issue, the strategic interests of Morocco, the acquisition of sophisticated weapons whose cost needs to be justified, and the proliferation of cross-border trafficking are factors suggesting that neither Rabat nor Algiers will make the slightest concession to one another in the event of sudden crisis, whatever its nature. On the contrary, each government might be tempted to ostracize the other by using it as a scapegoat to unite its own population behind it, diverting attention away from socioeconomic difficulties that all indicators show will increase in the upcoming years.

Table 5.1. Weapons purchase in Northern Africa during 2011–2016

	Morocco	Algeria	Tunisia	Libya	Egypt
Defense budget as a percentage of GDP	3.7%	5.4%	1.8%	6.2%	2.0%*
Satellites	2	—	—	—	2
Land weaponry					
Tanks	**200** (M-1A1, T-90)	320 (T-90S)	—	—	250 (M-1A1)
Light armored	280	1 180	100	870	450
SP guns	72	68	—	—	—
Antitank missiles	100	8,500	—	1,150	9,000
Aircraft					
Combat aircraft	24 (F-16C)**	46 (30 Su-30K, 16 Yak-130)	—	5 (MiG-21)	94 (24 Rafale, 50 MiG-29M, 20 F-16C)
Helicopters (attack)	3	97 (42)	22	18 (4)	82 (56)
UAVs	3	—	—	4	18
Transport	4	—	2	—	24
Warships					
Frigates	4 (1 FREMM)	5	—	—	1 (FREMM)
Corvettes	—	2	—	—	8
Amphibious	1	—	—	—	2 (BPC)
Submarines	—	2 (Kilo)	—	—	4 (Type 209)***
Patrol crafts	—	21	—	—	13

* Egyptian military weaponry is largely funded by the United States, Saudi Arabia, UAE, and Kuwait.
** Morocco also continues to upgrade its 27 Mirage F-1s.
*** The second of four submarines was received in 2017.

Source: SIPRI Arms Transfers Database, March 2016, [https://www.sipri.org/sites/default/files/Trends-in-international-arms-transfers-2016.pdf].

3) *A risk of "Somalization" of Libya that increases the possibility of military interventions in this country.* Despite the existence of a supposed national unity government led by Fayez el-Sarraj, Libya remains basically divided into three zones of distinct influence around Tripolitania, Cyrenaica, and Fezzan.[32] Clannish and tribal rivalries remain very strong, as are the struggles to gain control of oil and gas resources and their transport. For their

part, the jihadists belonging to the Islamic state or al-Qaeda still control pockets of resistance between Syrte and Ras Lanouf, and thus several oil terminals. They are trapped between the two main factions established in Tripoli and Tobruk. General Khalifa Haftar announced after his successes of the summer of 2016 that he would not pledge allegiance to any central power, under the condition of being appointed head of the future Libyan national army. This chaotic situation is reminiscent of that of Somalia, and several experts anticipate a "Somalization" of Libya.[33] That is why ad hoc external military interventions are more likely every day, to prevent jihadist groups from becoming stronger and threatening both maritime traffic in the Mediterranean and the stability of neighboring countries. Egypt and the UAE have already struck jihadist camps several times and seem ready to start again if necessary. Former British foreign secretary Philip Hammond is on record as saying, before leaving his position after Brexit, that the United Kingdom would not rule out sending troops to Libya to help secure the country if the legitimate government requested it.[34] At the same time, Jean-Yves Le Drian, the French minister of defense, announced the creation of a Franco-British Joint Force that could intervene in Libya, if an official request was made to that effect by the Libyan legitimate authorities. In order to avoid this intervention, one can imagine that the main Libyan factions would be able to agree on the fight against the jihadist groups plaguing their country, putting off the most difficult political and institutional choices.

International Restructuring

The discovery of large offshore gas deposits in the eastern Mediterranean in the early 2000s, some of which are now in operation (notably Tamar, Dalit, and Leviathan, off the Israeli coast), has sharpened the appetite of neighboring countries (Egypt, Israel, Lebanon, Syria, and Cyprus). This renewed appetite for gas has revived rivalries between Israel and Cyprus on the one hand, and Turkey, Syria, and Lebanon on the other, especially on the delicate issue of the delineation of maritime borders. Egypt, which has significant undisputed offshore deposits, remains outside these rivalries for the time being, deploying efforts to quickly put these deposits into operation.[35] Russia, which would like to limit as much as possible the channels—other than its own—of supplying natural gas to Europe, is keenly aware that Europeans are seeking to diversify their sources of energy, looking toward Norway, North America, and the Mediterranean, in order to reduce their reliance on Moscow.[36]

This is one of the reasons for the renewal of Russian activism in the eastern Mediterranean, especially since Vladimir Putin decided to intervene militarily in Syria in September 2015. In doing so, the Russian president neutralized the two projects of competing pipelines from Iran and from Qatar and Saudi Arabia. Both had to go through the Syrian coast to feed the countries of southern Europe. But more so than the power plays revolving around energy, the desire to contain the jihadist thrust northward toward the Caucasus and Russia explains the new Russian strategy in the Middle East and the Mediterranean.[37] The Kremlin has set up an advanced line of defense based on its main allies and partners: Iran, the Kurdish Autonomous Province of Iraq, the Syrian regime, Israel, and the Greek Cypriot government with which Moscow has negotiated naval facilities and enhanced economic and military cooperation. This advanced line of defense has the advantage of isolating Turkey at a time when relations between Moscow and Ankara are extremely tense. Finally, by defending his Syrian ally and pointing out his role as the privileged interlocutor of Washington, Vladimir Putin seeks to convince Arab leaders of the undeniable and reliable character of Russia on the regional chessboard. His aim is to advance his pawns and win new contracts of armament, particularly in Egypt, where Marshal el-Sisi seems fascinated by Vladimir Putin, but also in Algeria, whose worried authorities look for reassurance and purchase arms from Russia.

For its part, the new Trump administration will probably continue the changes in policy started by President Obama. Contrary to what some journalists suggested at the time of the Arab Spring, when they mentioned a shift toward Asia, the United States did not withdraw from North Africa and the Middle East but rather revised its strategy, adopting a much more cautious attitude on the military level, but more offensive on the oil level. Unlike the Clinton and Bush eras, the US administration is no longer as ready to intervene militarily in this region. It would do so only if the five major interests of the United States in the region were threatened. These interests are (1) to ensure maritime freedom from the Strait of Gibraltar to the Indian Ocean, especially with regard to the Suez Canal and the Straits of Bab el-Mandeb; (2) to protect the safety of American citizens along this vital axis of maritime communication, intervening where necessary to evacuate them; (3) to ensure the security of Israel in the event of external aggression, while at the same time making the Israeli government understand that it would now assume any consequences of aggression on its part against states in the region; (4) to remain present in the region to control, directly or indirectly, oil flows to Asia;[38] and (5) to maintain a certain level of geopolitical uncertainty in the region so that Washington's allies continue to buy sophisticated US weapons. As President Clinton pointed out, the economic interests of the United States ultimately prevail, an analysis that Donald Trump seems to endorse as well.

Today, the United States sees itself as the referee, rather than one of the players, in the chess game taking place in the vast region covering North Africa and the Middle East. Their aim is no longer to have one side win over the other, but to ensure that none of the factions will gain a decisive advantage and upset the fragile regional balance. In many respects, the "realistic" geopolitical vision of American elites is reminiscent of the one that prevailed in the late 1970s, when the White House agreed with the Kremlin to resolve major crises, relying on non-Arab actors in the region (Turkey, Israel, and Iran) to deal with minor crises. This is why one can clearly see the reluctance of the Trump team to interfere in the Russian-Iranian zone of influence that now encompasses Iraq and Syria. However, the United States could decide to adopt a more intrusive strategy in North Africa, especially to defend Tunisia and Morocco, but also to regain lost positions in Egypt. Marshal el-Sisi did not fail to emphasize that he had every reason to agree with an American president uninterested in the defense of human rights but ready to invest economically in his country.

The Chinese remain on the lookout for economic opportunities, targeting primarily raw-materials and energy resources in endowed countries. They formed the first foreign community in Algeria, with forty thousand workers, engineers, and traders, all involved in energy and infrastructure construction (highways, bridges, public buildings, pipelines), via the powerful China Railway Construction Corporation (CRCC).[39] Further to the east, although the Tunisian government has rejected, for the moment, Chinese offers regarding national petroleum and phosphate industries, it has nevertheless opened the doors of its universities to an increasing number of Chinese students who come to learn Arabic and French, to better penetrate the Maghreb and African markets.[40] Tunisia, greatly affected by an economic crisis, has largely opened its supermarkets to the relatively inexpensive Chinese products. Further south, Beijing remains interested in Libyan hydrocarbons and would like to send most of the thirty-six thousand Chinese workers evacuated in 2011 at the beginning of the civil war back to Libya. In Egypt, Chinese companies are active in the construction sector, building friendly relations with the Egyptian authorities, which enable them, in the long term, to guarantee the passage of Chinese commercial ships through the Suez Canal. After the withdrawal of Saudi funding, the Chinese government has said it was ready to finance the construction of the new Egyptian administrative capital, in the middle of the desert, halfway between Cairo and Suez.[41]

Even Morocco, which until 2015 had resisted Chinese economic entryism, seems to have changed its strategy. The Moroccan government saw Beijing as its biggest competitor in the world market for phosphates, while criticizing Chinese companies for using only Chinese workers on North African construction sites. Morocco was also critical of Beijing's international positions, often perceived as contrary to Moroccan interests. In April 2016, a delegation of several hundred Chinese business leaders visited Morocco at the king's invitation, to explore avenues of cooperation in the manufacturing, industrial, renewable energy, and tourism sectors. Beijing has also expressed its desire to see Morocco host several million Chinese tourists, a boon to the Moroccan economy. In May 2016, King Mohammed VI traveled to China for a long official visit and signed many of these contracts.

While major powers benefit from these geopolitical developments in North Africa and the Mediterranean, international organizations may not. The EU and NATO are apprehensive. The Arab League has become inaudible. As Abdennour Benantar points out, Europe faces the dilemma of how to improve the situation by cooperating with regimes that are the main source of the problems.[42] Management of the Syrian and Iraqi refugee crisis is a glaring example of this dilemma, even though on June 22, 2015, the European Council agreed to launch Operation Sophia, to identify, capture, and dispose of vessels used by traffickers. This decision sets a precedent because the UN Security Council adopted Resolution 2240 on October 9, 2015, recognizing the right of concerned states to intercept, inspect, and seize vessels suspected of smuggling migrants. However, the EU is more interested in managing the political consequences of Brexit and the rise of populism in Europe than in defining a concerted strategic vision for the Mediterranean and North Africa.

On its side, NATO is trying to mobilize support through its Mediterranean Dialogue, which includes Mauritanians, Moroccans, Algerians, Tunisians, Egyptians, Israelis, and Jordanians, without much success because of the rivalries and tensions between member countries. In fact, countries on the southern shore of the Mediterranean prefer bilateral relations with NATO to increase the interoperability of their armed forces and improve the training of their cadres without fully responding to the purpose of the partnership. As a result, NATO now favors "à la carte" relations by relying on states willing to contribute militarily to NATO's operations, including "Active Endeavor" (surveillance of the Mediterranean in prevention of international terrorism). Following the EU and the United Nations, the North Atlantic Council reached an agreement on February 11, 2016, to set up a new naval mission to combat migrant smuggling in the Aegean Sea, after the influx of refugees from Libya, Syria, and Iraq.

A major problem within NATO, as well as the EU, is the lack of a common vision—and hence a coherent strategy—for the southern flank (for NATO) and the neighborhood policy (for the EU). These two organizations remain divided among the states with strong interest in Russia, those interested in the Mediterranean and the Middle East, and those who simply do not understand the stakes represented by the countries on the southern shore of the Mediterranean. The latter criticize Turkey's ambiguous position, failing to realize that the priority of President Erdoğan, who understood that Turkey would never be part of the "European club," was to obtain official statements from NATO and the EU formally opposing the creation of a Kurdish independent entity in the region.

Faced with this new geopolitical situation, the governments of Israel, Greece, and Cyprus announced in February 2016 their willingness to create a new geopolitical bloc in the eastern Mediterranean, to better defend their interests, notably in terms of gas, but also to strengthen their security by heightening the isolation of Turkey, with which these three states have difficult relations.[43] In a particularly detailed study, Eran Lerman, inspired by the success of the 5 + 5 initiative in the Western Mediterranean, proposed to create a 2 + 2 partnership in the Eastern Mediterranean between Israel and Egypt for the southern shore, and Greece and Cyprus for the northern shore.[44] Lerman, a former ambassador of Israel to Greece, believes that such an initiative would strengthen economic and energy cooperation between these four states, while strengthening the security of offshore gas fields and increasing the geopolitical isolation of Turkey to pressure the government of President Erdoğan to relax its positions on the regional scene.

Egyptian President el-Sisi, who expressed interest in this partnership, has yet to formally respond to this proposal. However, the proposal is apparently backed by the Israeli government, and the reestablishment of diplomatic relations between Israel and Turkey in the summer of 2016 does not fundamentally call it into question.[45]

North Africa: An Important Partner for Europe

In conclusion, it should be recalled that North Africa remains an important economic and security partner for Europe, even if it is necessary to remain cautious regarding the mollifying discourses showing the Mediterranean as an inland sea, a bridge and a house common to both shores of the Mediterranean.[46] It is tempting to acknowledge, with Jean-François Daguzan, that the three myths surrounding the intellectual construction of the Mediterranean (the unity of the Mediterranean sea, the lost paradise of al-Andalus, and peace through economics), as desired by Fernand Braudel, have vanished.[47] As this researcher points out, neither Europe nor the Maghreb countries seem quite aware today that they are threatened not only by a return of war, but also by marginalization, because the axis of the world has shifted to Asia and the Pacific.

However, the Maghreb area is considered by some counts to have 97 million inhabitants, or 265 million, if extended to Egypt and the Sahel-Sahara strip. This is half the population of the EU. This area has the potential of becoming one of the EU workshops, as well as a captive market, which it is already if we consider the amount of commercial exchanges: in 2013, 70 percent of goods purchased in North Africa originated in the EU, and 66 percent of exported products from North Africa were sent to the EU. Three years later, these ratios have fallen sharply and have not been compensated for by a renewed cooperation among the countries of North Africa. This is a shame, for Europe needs a strong and united Maghreb. Those who reason in terms of a zero-sum game did not realize that the present situation was actually lose-lose. Neither the countries on the southern shore nor those on the northern shore are winners, nor are Turkey, Saudi Arabia, and Qatar, which were hoping to break into the region. The only beneficiaries for the time being are the internal lobbies keen to promote authoritarian regimes and the small groups that have relied on chaos and weak states.

If the Arab revolts created an opportunity for further cooperation in North Africa,[48] the counterrevolutions have swept away this opportunity, which remains the most viable option for Maghreb governments if they want to break their deadlock and if they want to exist economically and politically. Unfortunately, the lure of authoritarianism does not encourage multilateral cooperation, even if Tunisia puts forth all efforts to promote commercial exchanges and political discussions within Maghreb states, as the author of this article realized during a field study tour in Tunisia (October 12–18, 2017). The paradox is that there is today a major route linking the Atlantic Ocean and the Red Sea, but instead of connecting the capitals of North Africa along the coast, it traverses the southern borders of these countries by stealth, benefiting only traffickers and jihadist groups, without generating any tax revenue. Worse, it increases instability. To escape this vicious circle, the Maghrebi elites must tackle the most imperative task, which is to change prevailing mentalities. There would be the true geopolitical revolution.

PIERRE RAZOUX is Research Director in charge of strategic studies at the Institute for Strategic Research / Ecole Militaire (IRSEM) in Paris. His most recent book is *The Iran-Iraq War.*

Notes

1. The author is expressing himself in a personal capacity. He warmly thanks Mohez Ellala, researcher-trainee at IRSEM, for his very valuable assistance.

2. Without even mentioning the economic cost of the "non-Maghreb," assessed at between 2 and 3 percent of GDP, see "Combien coûte la non intégration maghrébine?," *Dernières Info d'Algérie*, April 27, 2016, http://dia-algerie.com/combien-coute-non -integration-maghrebine/.

3. Mustapha Benchenane, "Les incertitudes stratégiques liées aux révolutions arabes," *Revue Défense Nationale*, no. 766 (2014), http://www.defnat.com/bibliotheque/resultats _auteur.php?renvoi=1&cidaut=192&&cauteur=%27Mustapha%20Benchenane%27.

4. Smail Kouttroub, "Printemps arabe et nouvel ordre géopolitique au Maghreb," *L'Année du Maghreb* 9 (2013), http://anneemaghreb.revues.org/1885.

5. See the prescient analysis of Hélène Sallon, "Le Sinaï pris en étau entre les djihadistes et l'armée," *Le Monde*, January 25, 2016, http://www.lemonde.fr/proche -orient/article/2016/01/25/le-sinai-pris-en-etau-entre-les-djihadistes-et-l-armee_4852938 _3218.html.

6. For a comprehensive overview of jihadist opposing forces, we recommend the following excellent article: Hélène Bravin, "La Libye en guerre," *Revue Défense Nationale*, no. 777 (2015), http://www.defnat.com/bibliotheque/resultats.php.

7. Olivier Hanne, "L'impact du Printemps arabe sur le Sahel," *Revue Défense Nationale*, no. 777 (2015), http://www.defnat.com/bibliotheque/resultats.php.

8. Ahmed Belkhodja, "Etude de géographie politique de la frontière algéro-marocaine," *Diploweb*, December 28, 2015, http://www.diploweb.com/La-frontiere-algero-marocaine .html.

9. The Tunisian government is resolved to take this action even if the closing of the border is detrimental to the local Tunisian economy. See "Tunisie : attaque terroriste sans précédent à Ben Guerdane," *AFP*, March 7, 2016, http://www.france24.com/fr/20160307 -tunisie-attaque-armee-ben-guerdane-frontiere-libye-ei-etat-islamique.

10. Mario Calabresi and Gianluca Di Feo, "Al Sisi: 'Libia, l'Italia rischia un'altra Somalia.' Intervista esclusiva a Repubblica," *La Repubblica*, March, 17, 2016, http://www.repubblica.it /esteri/2016/03/17/news/al_sisi_libia_l_italia_rischia_un_altra_somalia_intervista _esclusiva_a_repubblica-135666541/.

11. "Retour de terroristes en Tunisie: l'armée algérienne renforce son niveau d'alerte à la frontière," *HuffPost Maghreb*, January 5, 2017, https://www.huffpostmaghreb.com/2017/01/05 /armee-dz-tunisie_n_13969368.html.

12. Karine Bennafla, "Tournant frontalier au Maghreb et au Moyen-Orient," *Confluences Méditerranée* 3, no. 94 (2015), doi:10.3917/come.094.0133.

13. For an overview of the latest developments in Operation Barkhane, please refer to the website of the French Ministry of Defense: "Opération Barkhane," Ministère des Armées, December 28, 2017, http://www.defense.gouv.fr/operations/sahel/dossier-de-presentation -de-l-operation-barkhane/operation-barkhane.

14. Bennafla, "Tournant frontalier." For an overview of the history of Libya and the evolution of its borders, see André Martel, *La Libye, essai de géopolitique historique* (Paris: Presses Universitaires de France, 2016).

15. Bravin, "La Libye en guerre."

16. "Relations Maroc-Afrique: l'ambition d'une nouvelle frontière marocain," La Direction des études et des prévisions financières du gouvernement, July 2015, http://www .finances.gov.ma/depf/SitePages/publications/en_catalogue/etudes/2015/Relations_Maroc _Afrique.pdf.

17. Thierry Oberlé, "Pourquoi la France a passé la vitesse supérieure au Mali," *Le Figaro*, January 13, 2013, http://www.lefigaro.fr/international/2013/01/13/01003 -20130113ARTFIG00184-pourquoi-la-france-a-passela-vitesse-superieure-au-mali.php.

18. Aomar Baghzouz, "La politique Méditerranéenne de l'Algérie à l'épreuve des mutations géopolitiques régionales: changement ou continuité?," *Maghreb-Machrek* 3, no. 221 (2014), doi:10.3917/machr.221.0023.

19. According to several Maghrebi economists who spoke at the Réalités Magazine International Forum (Hammamet, Tunisia, April 28–29, 2016), Algeria would have spent in two years $80 billion of the $200 billion that it kept in reserve to face a decrease in hydrocarbon prices. At this rate, it would have only two years of financial reserves.

20. Yahia Zoubir highlights the Algerian and Egyptian military powers' common interests and similarities in "Algeria's Roles in the OAU/African Union: From National Liberation Promoter to Leader in the Global War on Terrorism," *Mediterranean Politics* 20, no.1 (2015), doi:10.1080/13629395.2014.921470.

21. In accordance with this principle, Algeria condemned NATO's intervention in Libya in 2011, adopting a neutral attitude and welcoming on its territory part of the family of the former Libyan dictator, which has increased its diplomatic isolation.

22. This information comes from discussions with senior Algerian military and security personnel who requested confidentiality.

23. Colin Freeman, "At Least 30 Killed as militants Attack Tunisia Border Security Mission Mentored by UK Troops," *Telegraph*, March 7, 2016, http://www.telegraph.co.uk /news/worldnews/africaandindianocean/tunisia/12186136/At-least-30-killed-as-militants -attack-Tunisia-border-security-mission-mentored-by-UK-troops.html.

24. But see Barah Mikail, "Les défis de la Libye," *Confluences Méditerranée* 3, no. 94 (2015), doi:10.3917/come.094.0029.

25. Michael Wahid Hanna, "The Sisi Doctrine," *Foreign Policy*, August 13, 2014, http://foreignpolicy.com/2014/08/13/the-sisi-doctrine/.

26. This information comes from discussions with senior Egyptian military and security personnel in Cairo, from November 5 to December 1, 2015.

27. Particularly during spring 2014. Jean-Dominique Merchet, "Les frappes des Emirats en Libye ont été effectuées avec des Mirage 2000-9," *L'Opinion*, August 28, 2014, http://www.lopinion.fr/blog/secret-defense/frappes-emirats-en-libye-ont-ete-effectuees -mirage-2000-9-15748.

28. Olivier Decottignies and Soner Cagaptay, "Turkey's New Base in Qatar," Washington Institute, January 11, 2016, http://www.washingtoninstitute.org/policy-analysis/view/turkeys -new-base-in-qatar.

29. Antony Drugeon, "La très progressive réconciliation du Maroc et de l'Iran," *Tel Quel*, February 27, 2015, http://telquel.ma/2015/02/27/tres-progressive-reconciliation-du-maroc -liran_1436181.

30. Ehud Eiran, "La diplomatie des îles de l'Egypte et de l'Arabie Saoudite," *I24News*, April 13, 2016, https://www.i24news.tv/fr/actu/international/moyen-orient/109561-160413 -analyse-la-diplomatie-des-iles-de-l-egypte-et-de-l-arabie-saoudite.

31. Djallil Lounnas, "Confronting Al-Qa'ida in the Islamic Maghrib in the Sahel: Algeria and the Malian Crisis," *Journal of North African Studies* 19, no. 5 (2014), doi:10.1080/13629387 .2014.974033.

32. Jean-Yves Moisseron and Rafaa Tabib, "Daech (ISIS) dans la Libye fragmentée," *Hérodote* 1, no. 160–1 (2016), doi:10.3917/her.160.0389.

33. Kader Abderrahim, "La Libye, un pays en voie de somalisation?," IRIS, June 27, 2014, http://www.iris-france.org/43886-la-libye-un-pays-en-voie-de-somalisation.

34. Tim Ross, "Philip Hammond: We Can't 'Rule Out' Sending Troops to Libya," *Telegraph*, April 24, 2016, https://www.telegraph.co.uk/news/2016/04/23/philip-hammond -we-cant-rule-out-sending-troops-to-libya/.

35. Especially since the discovery of the huge "Zhor" offshore deposit north of Port-Said will allow Egypt to eventually meet its needs and become an exporter of natural gas, probably starting in 2020.

36. Nicolò Sartori, "The Mediterranean Energy Relations after the Arab Spring: Towards a New Regional Paradigm?," *Cahiers de la Méditerranée* 89 (2014), http://cdlm.revues.org/7762.

37. According to experts, there were at the beginning of 2016 about four thousand jihadist fighters from the Caucasus present in Iraq and Syria; see Joshua Yaffa, "Chechnya's ISIS Problem," *New Yorker*, February 12, 2016, https://www .newyorker.com/news/news-desk/chechnyas-isis-problem.

38. As we discussed in the course of numerous interviews with US diplomats and security officials in North Africa and the Middle East from 2012 to 2015, 75 percent of natural gas and oil exports from the Arabian Peninsula and the Gulf are purchased by Asian countries, especially China and Japan. The United States did not hesitate to use oil as leverage, organizing the collapse of the price of oil, in close consultation with Saudi Arabia, to weaken their geopolitical opponents as they had done successfully in the late 1980s to end the Iran-Iraq war and ruin the Soviet economy.

39. Farid Alilat, "Qui sont les Chinois d'Algérie ?," *Jeune Afrique*, June 2, 2015, http://www .jeuneafrique.com/233388/politique/qui-sont-les-chinois-d-alg-rie/.

40. As explained to us at the Réalités Magazine International Forum (2016) mentioned above.

41. Interview with Hicham Mourad, professor at Cairo University, Paris, November 22, 2016.

42. Abdennour Benantar, "Maghreb, Levant et Golfe: des recompositions à l'œuvre," *Revue Défense Nationale*, no. 772 (2014), http://www.defnat.com/bibliotheque/resultats _auteur.php?cenvoi=1&cidaut=3525&cauteur=%27Abdennour%20Benantar%27.

43. Arye Mekel, "A New Geopolitical Bloc Is Born: Israel, Greece & Cyprus," *Jerusalem Post*, February 21, 2016, http://www.jpost.com/Opinion/A-new-geopolitical-bloc-is-born -Israel-Greece-and-Cyprus-445645.

44. Eran Lerman, "The Mediterranean as a Strategic Environment: Learning a New Geopolitical Language," *Mideast Security and Policy Studies*, no. 117 (2016), https://besacenter .org/mideast-security-and-policy-studies/mediterranean-new-geopolitical-language/.

45. Ibid.

46. As insisted the Tunisian intellectual Hele Beji, on April 29, 2016, during the Réalités Magazine International Forum.

47. Jean-François Daguzan, "La fin de la Méditerranée? Conséquence des révolutions arabes," *Cahiers de la Méditerranée* 89 (2014), http://cdlm.revues.org/7684.

48. Frédéric Volpi, "Reconfiguring Post-Cold War Views of International Order in the Mediterranean: The Arab Uprisings as a Conceptual and Material Turning Point?," *Cahiers de la Méditerranée* 89 (2014), http://journals.openedition.org/cdlm/7698.

6

JIHADISM IN THE POST–ARAB SPRING MAGHREB

Daveed Gartenstein-Ross

IN THE WAKE OF THE ARAB SPRING, JIHADIST groups have flourished in the Arab Maghreb Union countries, capitalizing on state weakness. Libya's descent into civil war has provided these groups with a particularly important boost. Not only has its central government been unable to reestablish a writ since dictator Muammar al-Qaddafi's fall, but there is no agreement within the country on who that "central government" is. The chaos in Libya has, in turn, had a spillover effect on other Maghreb countries.

This chapter explores the current state of Salafi jihadism in the Arab Maghreb Union states. *Salafism* is not a monolithic phenomenon. Salafists can be defined broadly as belonging to a conservative religious movement that strives for a practice of Islam that it believes to be consonant with that of the prophet Muhammad and the first three generations of Muslims. Salafism tends to be textually focused, on the Quran and *ahadith*, and literalist in its interpretation. One division of Salafism is Salafi jihadism. Quintan Wiktorowicz notes that Salafi jihadists "take a more militant position" than other Salafi strains; they argue "that the current context calls for violence and revolution."[1] Similarly, Stefano Torelli, Fabio Merone, and Francesco Cavatorta define this form of practice as "a form of violent opposition to 'unjust rule,' aimed at establishing an Islamic state."[2] Salafi jihadist groups such as al-Qaeda and the Islamic State (ISIS), both of which have a significant presence in the Arab Maghreb Union states, aim to forcibly impose a hard-line version of *sharia* (Islamic law).

In addition to Libya, certain trends involving Salafi jihadism can be discerned in the other Arab Maghreb Union countries. Tunisia has been the most stable postrevolution country and is often regarded as an Arab Spring success story. However, the spillover of jihadist terrorism from Libya into Tunisia has been severe. In 2015, the country saw two significant attacks on tourist targets, which is alarming given tourism's centrality to the Tunisian economy. The attackers in both of these incidents trained in Libya before striking Tunisia. Tunisia remains relatively stable yet alarmingly fragile.

Algeria—once the region's most benighted country, during the bloody civil war of the 1990s—now faces few immediate threats from jihadist groups. Algeria was largely immune to the political turmoil that has swept North Africa and the Middle East. Despite the country's present stability, there are concerns that could diminish Algerian stability in the medium to long term.

Morocco has been generally stable, especially since its government passed a package of reforms in 2011. Although Morocco faces a threat of terrorism, especially from al-Qaeda in the Islamic Maghreb (AQIM), its security forces have managed to prevent significant attacks.

For socioeconomic and political reasons, militancy and the threat of violent conflict have dominated Mauritanian politics for decades. Despite this, the country has experienced a noteworthy downward trend in actual jihadist attacks. While some commentators attribute this to a successful package of counterterrorism policies, evidence suggests that Mauritania may be paying al-Qaeda not to attack within its borders.

The threat of jihadist terrorism, substate violence, and instability in these states has helped reinforce authoritarian tendencies in all of them, except perhaps Tunisia. In some cases, the governments may use jihadist threats as a mere pretext for grabbing power. In others, the authoritarian steps being taken may be more principled and perhaps even pragmatic in a Hobbesian sense, based on the view that a Leviathan state is preferable to a war of all against all.[3] But regardless of the nature of the conviction underlying the steps taken toward authoritarian, the trend is unmistakable, and the lure of authoritarianism can be observed in different dimensions and in varying degrees across the region.

This chapter now provides a granular look at the state of jihadism in these countries.

The Jihadist Movement in Libya

Libya's transition away from Qaddafi's misrule initially looked promising. Transitional authorities held successful elections in mid-2012 that returned a parliament that was broadly representative of the major social and political currents in Libya. The major factions in this transitional parliament worked fairly well together from 2012to 2013, producing reformist legislation. The factions formed coalition governments and quickly restarted oil exports. This progress was unable, however, to overcome deep regional divisions.

The rough governing coalition that had led the transition faltered in late 2013 and early 2014. Long-simmering tensions between rival armed factions erupted into violent conflict in May 2014, when Khalifa Hifter launched Operation Dignity in Benghazi, a military campaign aimed at eliminating Islamist factions (including but not limited to Salafi jihadists) from eastern Libya. Hifter's offensive tapped into the fears and concerns of the Libyan public, which had grown disillusioned with the growing influence of Islamist militias and was alarmed by rising levels of violence. Jihadist groups have been able to entrench themselves during the Libyan civil war.

The Libyan Civil War

Although the country's divisions are often described as primarily Islamist versus nationalist, they in fact reflect several deeper divides, including ethnic, tribal, and regional tensions, as well as a clash between so-called revolutionary and counterrevolutionary forces.

The primary geographic conflict is between Zintan and Misrata. During the Qaddafi era, the Zintanis maintained close ties with two tribes, the Warfalla and the Qadhadhfa, that were closely allied with the regime. As such, Zintan was long perceived as a "regime stronghold."[4] As with most generalizations, this perception wasn't universally accurate: despite the benefits Zintan received, many Zintanis "remained rather critical of Qaddafi and his Jamahiriya state," and some even took part in a 1993 coup attempt.[5] The Misratans and Zintanis put aside their differences during the anti-Qaddafi uprising, and both cities played important roles in bringing down the regime. But after the war, the rivalry between the two cities reemerged, fueled by Misratan accusations that Zintanis had colluded with the Qaddafi regime during the war and failed to bear an equal burden in the conflict.[6] The power vacuum that emerged after Qaddafi's fall further exacerbated the rivalry. Misratan and Zintani forces tried to claim as much territory as possible in Tripoli, carving the capital into rival strongholds. Minor skirmishes frequently occurred between Zintani and Misratan factions the city.

The Zintani militias' practice of recruiting from the ranks of Qaddafi-era security brigades to bolster their capabilities also drew the ire of Misratan revolutionaries. After gaining control of key territories in Tripoli, Zintani militia leaders began recruiting from a variety of defunct forces previously affiliated with Qaddafi, including the Thirty-Second Brigade, which had been considered one of the most capable and well-trained brigades in Qaddafi's forces, and the Maghawir Brigade, a predominantly Tuareg unit. Zintanis also recruited from the population of Bani Walid, which had long been considered a bastion of pro-Qaddafi support.[7]

The conflict between revolutionary and counterrevolutionary factions long centered on whether Libya should pass a "political isolation" law to exclude former Qaddafi officials from positions in government. The Islamist bloc in the General National Congress (GNC), Libya's democratically elected legislative body, aligned itself with actors who considered themselves *thuwwar* (revolutionaries), and upon gaining the upper hand in parliament, that coalition proposed—and passed—a political isolation law. The GNC also established an Integrity and Reform Commission for the armed forces in June 2013 to identify and exclude members of the military who had been involved in Qaddafi's efforts to crush the revolution.[8] Both of these policies were highly exclusionary, as the political isolation law prevented anyone who had held even a midlevel role in the Qaddafi regime between 1969 and 2011 from serving in a wide array of positions in politics, the media, and academia.[9]

Although Hifter characterized his offensive primarily as anti-Islamist, there are obvious echoes of both the Zintan-Misrata rivalry and the revolutionary-counterrevolutionary divide. For some factions who found themselves excluded from postrevolution opportunities, Hifter's campaign offered an opportunity to recover political power, including for a number of military units disillusioned by the GNC's lustration policies and fearful that they would be increasingly excluded. Some tribes aligned with Hifter had also been accused of sympathizing with the Qaddafi regime. The involvement of former Qaddafi allies and officials in the Dignity campaign led the revolutionary bloc to portray Hifter's movement as a counterrevolutionary initiative aimed at reversing the gains of the 2011 uprising.

After Hifter announced the launch of Operation Dignity in Benghazi in May 2014, Dignity-aligned forces soon stormed the parliament building in Tripoli and called for the GNC's dissolution.[10] The GNC's leading political bloc—composed of Islamist political parties, former revolutionaries from Misrata, and members of the Berber ethnic group, among others—viewed Operation Dignity's raid on the GNC as a direct assault on its power.

After its defeat in the June 2014 parliamentary elections, the Islamist-Misrata bloc launched a military campaign of its own, dubbed Operation Dawn, which aimed to seize control of Tripoli and reassert the bloc's political influence. In August 2014, the Dawn coalition drove pro-Dignity forces from Tripoli, leaving the capital's airport, which had been the primary base for pro-Dignity forces, in ruins.[11] Upon removing Dignity forces from Tripoli, political forces aligned with the Dawn coalition reconvened the GNC, which had originally been expected to transfer power to the victorious House of Representatives after the June elections. The GNC's refusal to hand over power left Libya fragmented, with two separate parliaments and two governments, both claiming legitimacy and both fighting each other militarily.

The civil war may have been further complicated by the international community's attempts to resolve it. The Government of National Accord (GNA) was forged out of the desire to create a legitimate coalition government that could serve as Libya's new central authority. But there was little buy-in to the idea of the GNA within Libya's warring factions, so to many observers, the GNA seemingly interjected another armed player into an already complex conflict. Against this backdrop, jihadist groups rose to a position of power quickly—though ISIS in particular overplayed its hand, thus leading to its severe weakening in comparison to early 2016.

ISIS in Libya

ISIS first made its presence in Libya known in Derna, though it ultimately exaggerated its influence there (and convinced the mainstream media to believe its exaggerations in the process). Derna's Islamic Youth Shura Council (IYSC) first announced its support for ISIS in June 2014. In October 2014, IYSC managed to convince a number of major media outlets that Derna had entirely come under ISIS's control.[12] Despite IYSC's hyperbolic claims, Derna remained divided between various armed groups, including a number of factions loyal to al-Qaeda. These other jihadist factions included an umbrella group known as the Derna Mujahedin Shura Council (DMSC) and the Abu Salim Martyrs Brigade (ASMB), which was a major player in DMSC.

These other militant groups would ultimately be ISIS's undoing in Derna. Even before IYSC pledged allegiance to ISIS, the group began launching attacks against fighters from other militant factions.[13] Tensions between IYSC and DMSC escalated early in 2015 and came to a head in May of that year, when an IYSC-affiliated preacher in a Derna mosque said in a sermon that ISIS was the only legitimate force in the city. In response, DMSC issued a "final warning" to IYSC.[14] IYSC answered by killing a key DMSC leader, triggering a bout of intense conflict. But IYSC's bark proved to be more potent than its bite: just two weeks after the clashes erupted, IYSC militants were forced to withdraw from Derna to the suburbs. The fact that DMSC did not need to call in reinforcements to drive out IYSC shows that the media had vastly overestimated the ISIS-affiliated group's control over Derna. In April 2016, the remaining ISIS forces in and around Derna withdrew from the city.[15]

Though ISIS's influence in Derna was always exaggerated, it did manage to capture the city of Sirte for an extended period. But ISIS overplayed its hand in Sirte, adopting such a loud and brutal posture that the various factions in Libya's civil war could at least agree that they wanted to push ISIS from its stronghold. ISIS's capabilities in Libya have deteriorated dramatically since May 2016, when armed factions aligned with the GNA launched a military campaign to drive ISIS from Sirte.

ISIS's losses in Sirte are a blow to the group's prospects in Libya, and in Africa more broadly. Sirte was widely considered a fallback option for ISIS in the event that the group experienced major defeats in Syria and Iraq. Accordingly, ISIS invested significant resources in its Libyan province.[16] Starting in late 2014, ISIS began issuing propaganda statements encouraging militants from across Africa to migrate to Libya, and by early 2016, ISIS had redirected several hundred foreign fighters initially bound for Syria to Libya.[17]

The fall of Sirte will hamper ISIS's efforts to build its African network. As ISIS developed its governorate in Sirte, the city became a major command-and-control hub for operations across North and West Africa. Evidence indicates that ISIS commanders in Sirte provided instructions and guidance to both Wilayat Sinai, ISIS's Sinai Peninsula–based province, and the ISIS-aligned Nigerian jihadist group Boko Haram.[18] Similarly, ISIS officials in Sirte oversaw operations in the western Libyan city of Sebratha, which, until March 2016, served as the central hub of ISIS's Tunisian network. The collapse of the Sirte hub will make it more difficult for ISIS's leadership to maintain its patronage of ISIS factions and supporters in North and West Africa.

Though ISIS no longer controls significant territory along the Libyan coast, the group will continue to pose a challenge to Libya's security. Although GNA forces established a security cordon around Sirte in an effort to prevent ISIS militants from escaping, ISIS will be able to maintain a residual force in the country, at the very least. Libyan and Western officials have expressed concern that dozens to hundreds of militants who were based in Sirte fled south before the military offensive on the city commenced, possibly using trans-Saharan smuggling routes.[19]

In addition to the threat that ISIS fighters will remain in Libya, there is a danger that foreign fighters who based themselves in Sirte will return to their home countries to perpetrate attacks or build local pro-ISIS networks. In May 2016, Moroccan officials detained a Chadian ISIS member who was allegedly planning to carry out attacks on hotels and security forces in the country. Several Moroccans who had returned from Libya were also arrested on the suspicion that they were coordinating with the Chadian.[20] In August 2016, Egyptian forces disrupted a cell based in al-Gharbiyah governorate that was led by an Egyptian who had fought alongside, and remained in contact with, ISIS members in Libya.[21] These incidents and other similar ones raise the possibility that ISIS fighters are deploying back to their home countries.

In addition to ISIS, Libya has its share of other jihadist groups. While ISIS has been the loudest and most brutal, al-Qaeda is likely the greater challenge, given its greater regional strength and the way it has been able to embed itself within the population. The aforementioned DMSC, for example—which militarily expelled ISIS from Derna—is openly affiliated with al-Qaeda.

The Jihadist Movement in Tunisia

Tunisia has experienced far less turmoil than other regional postrevolutionary states since the overthrow of Zine El Abidine Ben Ali, and is often held up as a model of successful transition to democracy in the Arab world.

But the country has also experienced rising levels of jihadist violence, and successful attacks against tourist targets are of particular concern.

The Salafi jihadist movement grew far more quickly in Tunisia after dictator Ben Ali's fall than most analysts expected. Ansar al-Sharia in Tunisia (AST) was initially the most visible of these groups. In post–Ben Ali jihadism's nascent phase, AST managed to foster a social movement around Salafi jihadist beliefs by operating legally and in the open, and by focusing its activities primarily on *dawa* (evangelism). But even during this period, the group also employed violence. Its primary use of violence was *hisba*, a concept denoting "forbidding wrong," which for AST entailed the enforcement of religious norms within—and sometimes beyond—the Tunisian Muslim community.

But soon Salafi jihadists' violence against the state escalated. A key inflection point was December 2012, when militants shot and killed Anis Jelassi, an adjutant in the Tunisian National Guard, in the Kasserine governorate in western Tunisia.[22] This incident prompted Tunisian authorities to publicly identify, for the first time, an al-Qaeda-affiliated militant group known as Katibat Uqbah ibn Nafi (KUIN). The February 2013 assassination of secularist politician Chokri Belaïd was another escalation. Belaïd's assassination prompted great anger domestically but no crackdown against AST.

Thereafter there were several more progressions in the escalating conflict between Salafi jihadists and the Tunisian government. The state stepped up its security operations in western Tunisia, and soldiers patrolling there suffered from frequent landmine attacks. The state also interrupted AST's public lectures and other *dawa* activities and canceled the group's annual conference in the city of Kairouan. But jihadists' escalation hit an apex in late July 2013, when in a single week militants gunned down another prominent secularist politician, Mohammed Brahmi, and KUIN launched an ambush in western Tunisia's Chaambi Mountains that killed eight soldiers, five of whom had their throats slit.[23]

These attacks provoked a crackdown by the Tunisian government. As authorities proscribed groups like Ansar al-Sharia and stepped up their policing activities, jihadists became a less visible sight on Tunisia's streets, many key leaders were arrested, and both the media and citizens largely (with exceptions) rallied behind the government's counterterrorism policies. But the jihadists also succeeded in mounting several devastating attacks against tourist targets. In March 2015, an attack at the Bardo National Museum in Tunis left twenty-one tourists and a Tunisian dead.

That attack was followed just three months later by a horrific attack at a beach resort in Port El Kantaoui that claimed thirty-eight lives, mainly Western tourists. These attacks place the Tunisian tourist industry in jeopardy, and it is no exaggeration to say that terrorism and substate violence pose a fundamental challenge to the future of the country.

The Tunisian Economy

Tunisia's economy is still beset by deep-seated structural economic issues. Restrictive labor policies offer employers little flexibility in their hiring and firing decisions and inhibit job creation. Excessive regulation, including limits on the number of firms allowed to produce goods for the domestic market and high taxes on companies that sell locally, creates high barriers to entry and discourages private investment. Moreover, Tunisia's investment policies, which segregate companies producing for domestic consumption and those focused on exports, have created distortions in the Tunisian economy, limiting productivity.[24]

These structural problems have hindered job creation and resulted in high levels of unemployment and underemployment, which have a disproportionate impact on Tunisian youth. Weak economic growth has left many recent university graduates unemployed or working in jobs that are not commensurate with their level of education: over 30 percent of university graduates were unemployed in 2012, more than double the unemployment rate for the same cohort in 2005.[25]

Although Tunisia's youth unemployment and underemployment is of obvious concern in itself, it also intersects with the danger of jihadism. Young, unemployed Tunisians may be a prime source of discontent and unrest and may be vulnerable to the appeal of jihadist ideology as a brutal utopian solution to their grievances. Many of those who have left Tunisia to join ISIS and other extremist groups in Syria and Iraq—and Tunisia boasts the largest number of "foreign fighters" of any country—have come from the ranks of Tunisia's unemployed and underemployed university graduates.[26]

ISIS in Tunisia

ISIS functions primarily as a clandestine terrorist network in Tunisia. The group maintains sleeper cells, including in and around Tunis, which are connected to senior planners and facilitators. This senior cadre was, for a time, based in the western Libyan city of Sebratha, but after upheaval in Sebratha in early 2016, several leaders left that area.

ISIS's Tunisian leadership has orchestrated several large-scale, mass-casualty attacks against hard and soft targets in Tunisia, and the group continues to plot, although its operational capabilities have diminished since early 2016. ISIS's core Tunisian network is led by former AST members, many of whom fled to Sebratha and other cities in Libya after the Tunisian government banned AST in August 2013. Several individuals who migrated to Sebratha, while nominally affiliated with AST, disagreed with the group's more low-profile post–Arab Spring strategy—one that focused on legal *dawa* while the group slowly ratcheted up its use of violence—and believed that AST should adopt a more confrontational stance.[27] This contingent's approach aligned with ISIS's aggressive growth model, and the Sebratha network eventually broke with AST and joined ISIS instead.

Sebratha subsequently became the operations hub for ISIS's activities in Tunisia. Tunisian jihadists traveled to Sebratha to receive military training. Weapons moved in the other direction, as ISIS-linked smugglers transported guns from Libya to cells in Tunisia. Recruits trained in Sebratha were also sent to Tunisia to perpetrate attacks at home. Indeed, the three major terrorist attacks that occurred in Tunisia in 2015 (including the Bardo and Sousse beach attacks and a November 2015 bombing of a bus carrying members of Tunisia's presidential guard) were linked to training camps in Sebratha.[28]

February 2016 marked an inflection point in ISIS's Tunisia operations, as the group lost its Sebratha safe haven. On February 19, the United States carried out airstrikes against ISIS targets in Sebratha.[29] Shortly after the strikes, which killed forty-three, the remaining ISIS militants in Sebratha clashed with Libyan security forces, who forced ISIS out of the city.

The collapse of ISIS's Sebratha safe haven led to the restructuring of its Tunisian network. With jihadists no longer able to plan and stage operations in western Libya, ISIS's operational hub shifted back to Tunisia. In the months following the fall of Sebratha's ISIS network, Tunisian authorities arrested several people who had received training in Libya.[30] The February 2016 air and ground operations against ISIS in Sebratha also disrupted a budding plot to target the Tunisian border city of Ben Guerdane.[31] For several weeks, if not months, before the airstrikes, Tunisian ISIS members had planned a major operation aimed at seizing Ben Guerdane and imposing *sharia* on the city.[32] A great deal of advance planning went into this operation. The Sebratha network smuggled weapons into Ben Guerdane, where they were collected by clandestine cells in the city.[33] According to one Tunisian arrested in Libya in late February 2016, ISIS planned to deploy two hundred militants to Ben Guerdane to seize the town, highlighting the magnitude of the planned assault.[34]

But the United States' February 2016 operations against ISIS in Sebratha significantly reduced ISIS's manpower, forcing the group to launch its Ben Guerdane attack hastily. Although Tunisian security forces were expecting an attack on Ben Guerdane, the militants who struck the town in March 2016 still managed to establish temporary checkpoints and to kill eight civilians and twelve military and police officials, including the head of Ben Guerdane's counterterrorism brigade.[35] Militants deliberately sought out prominent members of the security apparatus, suggesting that the operatives involved in the attack were locals with intimate knowledge of the town.[36] But Tunisian security forces prevented ISIS from seizing control of the city, dealing a blow to the group's ambitions in Tunisia.

Since the Ben Guerdane attack, Tunisian authorities have disrupted several high-profile plots. In May 2016, Tunisian security forces conducted raids on cells in the southern city of Tataouine and in the northern town of Mnihla, located twelve kilometers from Tunis, killing four militants, arresting over a dozen others, and recovering a major weapons stockpile.[37] The Mnihla cell was reportedly planning a series of attacks on Tunisian military installations and Western targets, including a high-ranking US military official, in the coastal town of Hammamet.[38] The commander of the Mnihla cell was allegedly in contact with ISIS leaders in Libya and had sent pictures of the would-be Hammamet attackers to ISIS in Libya—a move likely intended to provide ISIS propagandists with material for the upcoming operation.[39] This incident highlights the ties between ISIS networks in Tunisia and Libya.

Although Tunisian security forces have experienced considerable success in identifying and disrupting domestic cells, the core ISIS network in Tunisia continues to pose a threat. Tunisian authorities disrupted plots intended to occur during the lunar month of Ramadan in 2016, which would have been a part of ISIS's global Ramadan campaign.[40]

In addition to its clandestine, urban-based network, ISIS maintains a support base among a contingent of militants residing in Tunisia's western and central mountains. The western mountains, including those in Chaambi National Park, have historically been a stronghold for KUIN.

But some of KUIN's fighters defected to ISIS, including a unit based in Jebel Mghila, located in Sidi Bouzid governorate.[41] The ISIS contingent based in the western and central mountains has claimed responsibility for several small-scale attacks, but the Tunisian military has carried out multiple successful strikes on the group's leadership. For instance, in May 2016, the Tunisian military killed Seifeddine Jammali, ISIS's leader in Jebel Mghila.[42]

The Tunisian Tourist Industry as a Continuing Terrorist Target

As previously noted, two of the high-profile terrorist attacks in Tunisia in 2015 struck tourist targets. The reason for this targeting is that tourism is essential to Tunisia's economy. The World Travel and Tourism Council estimates the direct contribution of travel and tourism to Tunisia's GDP as 7.4 percent and calculates tourism and travel's total contribution (including indirect effects) as 15.2 percent of GDP. Similarly, the council estimates that travel and tourism directly support 6.8 percent of Tunisia's employment, and that when indirect effects are considered, their total contribution is 13.9 percent of the country's employment.[43]

Indeed, jihadist targeting of Tunisian tourism preceded the attacks at the Bardo museum and at the Sousse beach. Jihadists attempted a simultaneous bombing in Sousse and Monastir on October 30, 2013.[44] Almost simultaneous with the Sousse bombing, authorities arrested an eighteen-year-old named Aymen Sâadi Berchid outside the mausoleum of Habib Bourguiba, the country's secular-minded first president. His backpack was crammed with explosives.[45] In December of the same year, Tunisian authorities disrupted a plot that was believed to target the island of Djerba, another popular tourist destination.[46]

The impact of the 2015 attacks on the Tunisian economy was significant. Tunisian authorities estimated that the Sousse attack alone could cost the tourism sector $500 million.[47] Jihadists will likely to continue to focus on tourist targets, viewing the country's dependence on tourism as a key vulnerability.

The Jihadist Movement in Algeria

Despite Algeria's apparent stability by comparison to other countries in the region, it is not certain that the country would remain shielded from the aftermaths of the Arab Spring and rising religious extremism in the region.

Succession Concerns

There are growing concerns about Abdelaziz Bouteflika's health and the impact that a leadership succession would have on Algeria's stability. Bouteflika, now in his eighties, has been hospitalized several times since experiencing a "ministroke" in 2013.[48] There are significant questions about whether the government can ensure a smooth transition of power when Bouteflika is finally forced to leave the political scene.

The Algerian Economy

Algeria's tenuous economic situation is also a point of concern. Algeria relies on hydrocarbons for about 98 percent of its export earnings and 60 percent of its budget revenues.[49] The global drop in oil prices has damaged Algeria's economy, resulting in a growing budget deficit.[50]

A worsening economic situation in Algeria also raises political concerns. The government is generous with its subsidies, which helps it buy stability to an extent. In fact, when revolutions struck the region in 2011, Algeria "granted zero-interest loans to thousands of unemployed young people and increased the salaries of thousands of public sector employees in an attempt to prevent social unrest from spreading."[51] The issue of potential political instability due to a president whose future is uncertain goes hand-in-hand with the economic problem of Algeria's reliance on hydrocarbons to fund its domestic programs.

Jihadist Groups

Although Algeria does not experience frequent attacks, jihadism is still a real and growing threat. AQIM is a product of the Algerian civil war, a direct descendent of the Groupe Salafiste pour la Prédication et le Combat (GSPC). The GSPC, in turn, grew out of the Groupe Islamique Armé (GIA), a jihadist group that rose to prominence after the Algerian military's decision to cancel the second round of the 1992 parliamentary elections in order to prevent the Islamic Salvation Front (FIS), an Islamist political party, from gaining control of the parliament. In response, the GIA, which included a significant number of Algerians who had fought in Afghanistan against the Soviets in the 1980s, launched a vicious campaign of violence, attacking military and civilian targets in an effort to dismantle the state and impose *sharia*.[52] The GIA's brutality proved internally divisive, and in

1998 a group of militants, disillusioned by the wanton killing of civilians and concerned that the GIA was alienating local supporters, broke from the group and formed the GSPC.[53]

Shortly after breaking with GIA, the GSPC began to attract support from al-Qaeda, which had soured on the GIA because al-Qaeda regarded its methods as strategically counterproductive.[54] After 9/11, as al-Qaeda leaders in Pakistan searched for a new safe haven, Bin Laden reportedly sent an emissary to Algeria to meet with the GSPC. After the emissary's trip, ties between GSPC and al-Qaeda grew more robust.

Upon taking control of the GSPC in 2003, Abdelmalek Droukdel further strengthened ties with al-Qaeda. In 2005, Droukdel issued a message praising Bin Laden, and in September 2006 al-Qaeda's deputy leader Ayman al-Zawahiri announced that al-Qaeda had officially accepted GSPC as an affiliate.[55] Early the following year, GSPC officially changed its name to al-Qaeda in the Islamic Maghreb. In part due to its Algerian roots, AQIM continues to view Algeria as a primary target.

AQIM has been active in the regions near Algeria's borders, including in Tunisia and northern Mali. After the January 2013 French intervention to dislodge AQIM from northern Mali, al-Murabitun—which was at the time an AQIM offshoot but has since rejoined the organization—retaliated by taking hostages at Algeria's In Amenas gas complex.

ISIS also tried to find a foothold in Algeria, but its efforts have been unsuccessful thus far. In September 2014, a group of fighters from AQIM's Center Zone, led by Gouri Abdelmalek, pledged allegiance to ISIS, accusing AQIM of "deviating from the true path," and announced the establishment of a new group, Jund al-Khilafah, or soldiers of the caliphate.[56] The group attained international notoriety just weeks after declaring its allegiance, when it released a video of the beheading of a French mountain climber whom the group had kidnapped in Algeria's Djudjura National Park.[57] This was the high point of ISIS's activities in Algeria.

In the two years since that beheading, Algerian security forces systematically eliminated the group's leadership and rank and file, rendering the group strategically obsolete. In December 2014, Gouri Abdelmalek was killed in a raid in northern Algeria.[58] In May 2015, Algerian security forces conducted a major operation against Jund al-Khilafah, killing twenty-five militants, including the group's new emir and four other senior commanders, in raids targeting a Jund al-Khilafah meeting site.[59] The assault decimated Jund al-Khilafah, which numbered no more than fifty militants at its peak, although it did not destroy the group entirely.

The final blow against Jund al-Khilafah may have been delivered in the summer of 2016, when Algerian security forces mounted another major operation against ISIS units in and around the western province of Bouira. In mid-June 2016, after a multiweek combing operation, Algerian security forces announced that they had "completely dismantled" Jund al-Khilafah.[60]

With its primary fighting force in Algeria largely defeated, ISIS's outlook in Algeria is dim. In 2015, ISIS persuaded several militant units aligned with AQIM to join its ranks, but the defections primarily served a propaganda purpose and did little to boost ISIS's overall military capabilities.[61] Two of the groups that pledged allegiance to ISIS in 2015 had been inactive for several years, and it is likely that neither group had more than twenty fighters in its ranks.[62] Other groups that defected to ISIS have found themselves in the Algerian military's crosshairs.[63]

ISIS's losses in Algeria proved to be al-Qaeda's gain. AQIM has initiated a program, known as Munasahah (rehabilitation), that aims to bring ISIS fighters back into the al-Qaeda fold. In discussions with ISIS fighters, which sometimes take place through text message, AQIM clerics argue that the jihadist movement needs to unify in order to counteract the Algerian military's operations. According to the Algerian media outlet *El Khabar*, around ten ISIS militants have already rejoined AQIM after communications with ideologues under this program, a sizable number considering ISIS's limited manpower in Algeria. The success of the Munasahah program suggests that, among Algerian militants, the balance of power has shifted decisively in AQIM's favor.

ISIS appears to have fared little better in its efforts to establish foreign fighter recruitment networks in Algeria. According to government and nongovernment estimates, between 170 and 200 Algerians have joined jihadist groups fighting in Syria and Iraq, a small fraction of the number of foreign fighters that came from Algeria's neighbors, Tunisia and Morocco.[64] Algeria's resilience to ISIS recruitment may partly reflect the security services' far-reaching capacity to monitor and disrupt domestic threats. Algerian intelligence has penetrated both online and offline recruitment hubs, using a combination of signals intelligence and human intelligence tools, and has acted decisively to disrupt budding networks.[65] For instance, in June 2016, Algerian authorities arrested 332 people suspected of recruiting for or supporting ISIS.[66] Another raid in April 2016 disrupted a six-person cell composed of Algerians and Tunisians involved in recruiting foreign fighters to join ISIS in Syria and Iraq.[67] These sweeping operations enable Algerian authorities to dismantle networks rapidly.

Though ISIS has struggled to gain a foothold in Algeria, turmoil in neighboring Libya could reorder ISIS's force structure in North Africa and potentially provide ISIS with a new opportunity to infiltrate Algeria. Algeria is a less hospitable place for fleeing jihadists than southern Libya or Tunisia, but militants may seek to exploit the long and difficult-to-police Libya-Algeria border.

The Jihadist Movement in Morocco

Morocco has been generally stable, especially since its government passed a package of reforms in 2011, and Moroccan citizens have been able to see the once-optimistic political change in Libya, Syria, and Egypt take a dark turn. Although Morocco's various political parties often get into disputes, the monarch, King Mohammed VI, functions as a "mediator" among them.[68]

Since 2011, Moroccan political parties have made efforts to integrate the voices of protestors. Some parties have also tried to give greater roles to women and youth. But even with these reforms, the ruling Justice and Development Party (commonly known by its French acronym, PJD), "is increasingly becoming the most powerful political group in the kingdom."[69] The PJD is independent of the king, which brings some balance to the party's influence and power.

Although the king retains the right to dissolve the parliament under the 2011 constitution, the PJD has used the powers provided to political parties under the new constitution to its advantage. For instance, Prime Minister Abdelilah Benkirane, who is the PJD's secretary-general, exercised his authority to preside over local elections in June 2013 despite the fact that the interior ministry, which the king controls, was initially appointed to handle much of the election proceedings.[70] Yet the PJD acknowledges its limitations. For instance, the PJD typically defers to the king's circle of advisors even on religious issues.[71] The PJD has in some ways used this deferential approach to its advantage, emphasizing that the "relationship with the king is not always perfect," so as to maintain distance from unpopular political decisions made by the king.[72]

Morocco faces a threat of terrorism, especially from AQIM. Although the number of Moroccan foreign fighters who joined jihadist groups in the Syrian theater is high, Moroccan security forces have generally managed to keep the overall threat in check. Since the Casablanca attacks in 2003, Morocco has implemented a comprehensive counterterrorism strategy that has included hard and soft power initiatives. As part of the hard power component of this strategy, the Moroccan military has stood up three units focusing exclusively on the threats of terrorism, drug smuggling, and irregular migration.

Morocco's main concern with respect to the threat of terrorism and jihadist groups is the challenge posed by foreign fighters returning from Syria and Iraq. Since the outset of Syria's civil war, around fifteen hundred Moroccans have joined rebel groups in Syria and Iraq, making Morocco the third largest contributor of foreign fighters in the MENA region.[73] In August 2013, three Moroccan militants—all former Guantánamo Bay detainees who had previously trained at al-Qaeda camps in Afghanistan—founded Harakat Sham al-Islam, a largely Moroccan Salafi jihadist rebel faction in Syria that is al-Qaeda aligned.[74] The group is believed to have been involved in a massacre of Alawites in Latakia province in August 2013 and was designated a terrorist organization by the US State Department in September 2014. Harakat Sham al-Islam's goals include establishing a jihadist organization in Morocco and conducting attacks against the country's government.

Morocco has consistently maintained a "zero tolerance" approach toward jihadist movements in its borders, including those that supported the movement of foreign fighters. Morocco maintained this approach even while it openly expressed support for the Syrian opposition, including hosting a Friends of Syria conference in Marrakesh in December 2012. Nasser Bourita, the secretary-general of Morocco's ministry of foreign affairs and cooperation, described his country's strategy toward foreign fighters as a three-pronged approach, consisting of traditional security measures, new legal frameworks for addressing aspiring foreign fighters and returnees, and soft-power policies, including human development and religious dialogue.[75]

The traditional security approach that Bourita spoke of includes such preventive measures as dismantling recruitment cells and interdicting individuals planning to travel abroad to fight with jihadist groups. Morocco has also committed to a multilateral approach in its law-enforcement efforts and has readily accepted Western assistance, including from the European Union.

As for Morocco's soft-power approach, the Moroccan government rolled out numerous initiatives aimed at addressing unemployment, poverty, and other potential drivers of radicalization.[76] One of its primary tools for combating the domestic growth of jihadism has been regulating Morocco's religious sphere. The steps that Morocco has taken include vetting and certifying imams, monitoring Friday sermons, approving all religious curricula, and using radio stations to disseminate moderate Islamic messages. Many of these policies were put in place after the 2007 Casablanca bombings, thus predating the recent surge in foreign fighters.

Morocco has adopted an unforgiving approach to returning foreign fighters, immediately arresting and charging those who return from the battlefields in Syria and Iraq. Morocco also amended its legal framework to make it more suitable for dealing with returnees. In January 2015, the parliament criminalized involvement with militant groups and participation in training camps abroad, and criminalized the recruitment of individuals to join terrorist organizations. The legislation also allows the government to prosecute Moroccan nationals and foreigners living in Morocco who have committed terrorist crimes abroad.

The Jihadist Movement in Mauritania

For socioeconomic and political reasons, militancy and the threat of violent conflict have dominated Mauritanian politics for decades. Until the 1990s, extreme inequality based on Mauritania's racial and ethnic caste system triggered most of the tension. Since then, religious extremism has come to the fore. In a country with fragile borders, domestic religious militancy has been compounded by the deterioration of security in the broader Sahel and Sahara region, where al-Qaeda and ISIS-affiliated militants have taken root.

The lack of major attacks in Mauritania in recent years may thus seem surprising, and some analysts have attributed it to successful policies implemented by Mauritania's strongman, General Mohamed Ould Abdel Aziz. While it is possible that his policies have been successful, there may be a darker side to the absence of attacks in the country: Multiple sources suggest that al-Qaeda extorted significant sums of money from Mauritania. Whether or not Mauritania has been funding al-Qaeda, it is clear that this impoverished country, characterized by rigid social hierarchies, economic injustices, political corruption, and undergoverned frontiers, remains a natural candidate for violent extremism capable of breaking down the country's fragile stability.

Tucked between Arab North Africa and black West Africa, Mauritania's racial and ethnic composition forms a complex and pivotal force shaping its politics, with no immediate parallel in the rest of the Maghreb.[77] Arab-Berber Moors or Bidhan (whites) dominate the country economically and politically. They are 30 percent of Mauritania's population of roughly four million people. The Haratin, descendants of black African slaves who constitute 40 percent of the population, share the language (Arabic) and culture of their former masters. Non-Arabized black Africans make up the other 30 percent of the population and face sharp discrimination.

Mauritania was the last country to officially abolish slavery, doing so in 1981, and only made holding slaves a crime in 2007.[78] (Only a single person has been successfully prosecuted under that law.) The UN's special rapporteur on contemporary forms of slavery estimates that 10 to 20 percent of Mauritania's population remains in "real slavery" through coerced labor.[79]

Afro-Mauritanians and black Arabs are indignant about white Arab political, economic, and cultural dominance.[80] This conflict has come to a head before, including in the late 1980s. In 1987, a failed coup attempt by a number of black African officers against the country's white Arab president led to a wave of state repression.[81] In 1989, a conflict between Mauritanian herders and Afro-Mauritanian farmers over grazing rights in the Senegal River valley ended in hundreds of deaths and massive expropriation.[82]

Until the 1980s, Mauritanian governments had largely been able to use Islam as a bridge. Afro-Mauritanians, white Arabs, and black Arabs were all Muslim. Moktar Ould Daddah, father of the country and president from 1961 to 1978, tried to rule through an inclusive single party. Daddah was removed in a military coup, and the country has experienced multiple coups since then. Islamism emerged in Mauritania in the rocky post-Daddah era.

Beginning in 2005, jihadists became more active in Mauritania. In 2005, the GSPC lured a small group of Mauritanians into its camps in the Sahel and Sahara region.[83] In June 2005, the group attacked Mauritania's Lemgheity army base, killing seventeen soldiers.[84] Then, between 2007 and 2011, multiple terrorist attacks struck the capital, Nouakchott.[85]

But jihadist attacks have declined since. Some observers attribute this to President Abdel Aziz's multipronged approach to containing the spread of violent extremism in Mauritania. For one thing, he has attempted a theological housecleaning by encouraging moderate Islamists to engage in theological debates about violence and rebellion in Islamic law.[86] The state has also implemented deradicalization programs, as well as a hard counterterrorism strategy.

However, as previously noted, there are questions about whether Mauritania has been bribing al-Qaeda to refrain from attacks. Letters uncovered in Osama Bin Laden's compound in Abbottabad, Pakistan, explicitly contemplate a truce with Mauritania.[87] Al-Qaeda strategists had expressly considered the *sharia* permissibility of such a truce and found it acceptable.[88] Further, al-Qaeda senior leadership had drafted a sample truce, which would be implemented in exchange for Mauritania paying "the sum of between 10 to 20 million euros annually."[89] A Mauritanian former al-Qaeda official, Mahfoudh Ould Walid, has said in media interviews that this pact was in fact entered into, expressing his satisfaction "with the attitude of the Mauritanian authorities in their policy of 'non-aggression.'"[90]

If there was indeed a truce between Mauritania and al-Qaeda, it means that Mauritania's counterterrorism success may largely be illusory. Such a pact would bolster Mauritania's security at its neighbors' expense.

Conclusion

Since the Arab Spring protests of 2011, the political environment in the Arab Maghreb Union states has been characterized by volatility. All of this has played to the benefit of jihadist organizations. Libya's descent into civil war has been the pivotal factor bolstering these groups, and there are various ways in which this phenomenon affects each country. In Tunisia, the tourist economy is a clear point of vulnerability for the government. Algeria has been probably the most effective country in clamping down on jihadism within its borders. Morocco has been relatively stable but faces a cognizable challenge in its large number of foreign fighters. And Mauritania may feel enough of a challenge that it decided to pay al-Qaeda's extortion demands.

All of this makes for a regional challenge that appears to be enduring—and this challenge in turn reinforces regional authoritarian tendencies. The threat of jihadism provides a reason for governments to maintain robust and frequently extremely intrusive security regimes. And as jihadist groups' exploitation of the regional revolutions becomes clearer, protesters and outside powers will be hesitant about the potential for protest movements to unintentionally usher in state collapse and substate violence.

DAVEED GARTENSTEIN-ROSS is a senior fellow at the Foundation for Defense of Democracies and Chief Executive Officer of the private firm Valens Global. He is author of *Evolving Terror: The Development of Jihadist Operations Targeting Western Interests in Africa* and *Bin Laden's Legacy: Why We're Still Losing the War on Terror.*

Notes

1. Quintan Wiktorowicz, "Anatomy of the Salafi Movement," *Studies in Conflict & Terrorism* 29 (2006): 208.

2. Stefano M. Torelli, Fabio Merone, and Francesco Cavatorta, "Salafism in Tunisia: Challenges and Opportunities for Democratization," *Middle East Policy* 19, no. 4 (2012): 145.

3. Thomas Hobbes, *Leviathan* (Baltimore: Penguin Books, 1968).

4. Peter Cole and Brian McQuinn, *The Libyan Revolution and Its Aftermath* (Oxford: Oxford University Press, 2015).

5. Dario Cristiani, *The Zintan Militia and the Fragmented Libyan State* (Washington, DC: Jamestown Foundation, 2012), 3.

6. Patrick Markey and Aziz el Yaakoubi, "Town vs. Town, Faction vs. Faction as Libya Descends into 'Hurricane,'" Reuters, August 1, 2014, https://www.reuters.com/article/us -libya-security-insight/town-vs-town-faction-vs-faction-as-libya-descends-into-hurricane -idUSKBN0G021F20140731.

7. Wolfram Lacher and Peter Cole, *Politics by Other Means: Conflicting Interests in Libya's Security Sector* (Geneva: Small Arms Survey, 2014), 85.

8. Ibid., 26.

9. Roman David and Houda Mzioudet, *Personnel Change or Personal Change? Rethinking Libya's Political Isolation Law* (Washington, DC: Brookings Institution, 2014), 5.

10. "Libyan Gunmen Storm Parliament Building," Al Arabiya, May 18, 2014, http://english.alarabiya.net/en/News/middle-east/2014/05/18/Heavy-gunfire-in-Libya-s -capital-target-unclear.html.

11. David Kirkpatrick, "Strife in Libya Could Presage Long Civil War," *New York Times*, August 24, 2014, http://www.nytimes.com/2014/08/25/world/africa/libyan-unrest .html?_r=0.

12. For example, see Maggie Michael, "How a Libyan City Joined the Islamic State Group," Associated Press, November 9, 2014, https://www.dailymail.co.uk/wires/ap/article-2827503 /How-Libyan-city-joined-Islamic-State-group.html.

13. Aaron Zelin, "The Islamic State's First Colony in Libya," *Policywatch* (Washington Institute for Near East Policy), October 10, 2014, https://www.washingtoninstitute.org /policy-analysis/view/the-islamic-states-first-colony-in-libya.

14. Thomas Joscelyn, "Veteran Jihadists Killed by Islamic State's 'Province' in Derna, Libya," *Long War Journal*, June 12, 2015.

15. "Libya's Derna Is Now Free of ISIS," *Libya Observer*, April 20, 2016, http://www .libyaobserver.ly/news/libyas-derna-now-free-isis.

16. For a discussion of ISIS's expansion efforts in Libya, see Nathaniel Barr and David Greenberg, "Libya's Political Turmoil Allows Islamic State to Thrive," *Jamestown Terrorism Monitor* 14, no. 7 (April 2016), http://www.jamestown.org/single/?tx_ttnews%5Btt _news%5D=45269&no_cache=1#.V6rm8rh97IU.

17. Suliman Ali Zway, Kareem Fahim, and Eric Schmitt, "In Libya, U.S. Courts Unreliable Allies to Counter ISIS," *New York Times*, January 18, 2016, http://www.nytimes. com/2016/01/19/world/middleeast/in-libya-us-courts-unreliable-allies-to-counter-isis.html? _r=0.

18. See Muhammad Muqallid and Marwah Abdallah, "Masdar Amni: Rasa'el Sawtiyya Kashafat Qiyadat 'Da'esh Libya' Litanzim Bayt al-Maqis al-Irhabi fi Sina" [Security

Source: Voice Recordings Reveal "ISIS Libya" to the Terrorist Organization of Baytul Maqdis in Sinai], *El Watan*, February 9, 2016, http://www.elwatannews.com/news/details/962680, describing the Libya hub's guidance to Wilayat Sinai; Fulan Nasrullah, "Sitrep," *Fulan's SITREP*, August 5, 2015, https://fulansitrep.com/2015/08/05/august-5th-2015-sitrep/, describing the Libya hub's guidance to Boko Haram).

19. Patrick Markey, "Sirte Battle Risks Widening Libya Political Splits," Reuters, July 11, 2016, http://uk.reuters.com/article/uk-mideast-crisis-libya-idUKKCN0ZR0GX; Maria Abi-Habib, "Islamic State Fighters in Libya Flee South as Stronghold Crumbles," *Wall Street Journal*, August 14, 2016, http://www.wsj.com/articles/islamic-state-fighters-in-libya-flee-south-as-stronghold-falls-1471198644.

20. Mounir Abou al-Maali, "Abu al-Batoul al-Thabbah Dakhal al-Maghrib Tazamunan ma Awdat Thalatat Maghareven min Libya," *Al-Yaoum*, May 15, 2016, http://www.alyaoum24.com/596557.html.

21. Ahmad Rahim, "Tafaseel al-Qabd ala Khalaya na'im li 'Da'esh' fi 3 Muhafathat bil-Delta," *60 Minutes*, August 9, 2016.

22. "Tunisie: Décès de l'adjudant Anis Jelassi dans des affrontements à Feriana," *Global Net*, December 11, 2012, http://www.gnet.tn/revue-de-presse-nationale/tunisie-deces-de-ladjudant-anis-jelassi-dans-des-affrontements-a-feriana/id-menu-958.html.

23. Paul Schemm, "Jihadis Threaten Tunisia's Arab Spring Transition," Associated Press, July 31, 2013, https://www.npr.org/templates/story/story.php?storyId=207271524.

24. World Bank, *The Unfinished Revolution: Bringing Opportunity, Good Jobs and Greater Wealth to All Tunisians* (Washington, DC: World Bank, 2014), 17.

25. Mongi Boughzala, *Youth Employment and Economic Transition in Tunisia* (Washington, DC: Brookings Institution, 2013), 6.

26. David Kirkpatrick, "New Freedoms in Tunisia Drive Support for ISIS," *New York Times*, October 21, 2014.

27. Two individuals who played a critical role in shaping the Sebratha network were Ahmed Rouissi and Abu Bakr al-Hakim. Rouissi and Hakim represented the more assertive wing of AST, and both men were implicated in the 2013 assassination of Chokri Belaïd and Mohamed Brahmi. Pierre Longeray, "Tunisian Officials Detain Eight and Hunt Three Men Allegedly Involved in Sousse Massacre," *Vice News*, July 2, 2015, https://news.vice.com/article/tunisian-officials-detain-eight-and-hunt-three-men-allegedly-involved-in-sousse-massacre.

28. See Carlotta Gall and Steven Erlanger, "Gunman at Tunisian Beach Hotel Trained with Museum Attackers," *New York Times*, June 30, 2015, http://www.nytimes.com/2015/07/01/world/africa/gunman-at-tunisian-beach-hotel-trained-with-museum-attackers.html; "Ilqa' al-Qabd ala Irhabi Khateer Muwarrat fil-Hujoum ala Hafilat al-Amn al-Ri'asi whathihi Hawiyyatuh," *Al-Jomhouria*, June 20, 2016, http://www.jomhouria.com/art54699_%D8%A5%D9%84%D9%82%D8%A7%D8%A1; "Five Arrested in Ben Guerdane for Attack Plot, Ties to Sebratha," *Tunisia Live*, February 21, 2016, http://tunisia-tn.com/five-arrested-in-ben-guerdane-for-attack-plot-ties-to-sabratha/. Although the two Bardo attackers attended a training camp in Sebratha, it is not clear from open-source information that the attack was directed by ISIS. The Tunisian government has claimed that KUIN, al-Qaeda's military wing in Tunisia, planned the Bardo attack. However, ISIS claimed responsibility for it.

29. Ahmed Elumami and Aidan Lewis, "U.S. Air Raid Hits Islamic State in Libya, 43 Dead," Reuters, February 19, 2016, http://www.reuters.com/article/libya-security-idUSKCN0VS1A5.

30. Mona Bouazizi, "Tasked with Smuggling Arms through Sea, Hide It in Capital: Uncovering ISIL Members in Bardo, Hey Ezzouhour, Jebel El Ahmar" (Arabic), *Al-Chorouk*, April 20, 2016.

31. Khamis Ben Brek, "Hal Yakhtariq Tanzim al-Dawla Hudud Tunis?," Al-Jazeera, February 28, 2016.

32. "Wathiqa Sirriya Takshuf inna Fajr Libya wara' Kashf Mukhatat Da'esh fi Ben Qardan," *Achahed*, March 12, 2016.

33. Mouna Missaoui, "In a Secret Operation, Terrorist Ghandri Reconstructs the Burying of Weapons in Ben Gardane" (Arabic), *Assarih*, May 26, 2016; Khadija Yahiaoui, "Makhazen Asliha . . . Khalaya Na'ema . . . Muharriboun . . . Sayarat Mufakhakha: Mukhatat Da'esh Listihdaf Tunis," *Al-Chourouk*, March 9, 2016.

34. Khamis Ben Brek, "Hal Yakhtariq Tanzim al-Dawla Hudud Tunis?," Al-Jazeera, February 28, 2016.

35. Sudarsan Raghavan, "Islamic State, Growing Stronger in Libya, Sets Its Sights on Fragile Neighbor Tunisia," *Washington Post*, May 13, 2016, https://www.washingtonpost .com/world/middle_east/islamic-state-threatens-fragile-tunisia-from-next-door-in -libya/2016/05/13/cd9bd634-f82e-11e5-958d-d038dac6e718_story.html.

36. Samy Ghorbal, "Tunisie: Le Bataille de Ben Guerdane," *Jeune Afrique*, March 22, 2016, http://www.jeuneafrique.com/mag/309387/politique/tunisie-bataille-de-ben-guerdane/.

37. "Tunisia Kills Two 'Suspected Jihadists' in Anti-Terror Raid," Agence France Presse, May 11, 2016, https://www.yahoo.com/news/tunisia-kills-two-jihadists-anti-terror-raid -near-111535691.html.

38. Mona Bouazizi, "Al-Dawa'ish Khatatou li 3 Amaliyat Irhabiyah bil-Hamamat fi Ramadan . . . Ightiyal Jeneraal Amriki, w'Istihdaf nadi al-Dubbat w'Madrassat al-Haras," *Al-Chourouk*, June 5, 2016.

39. Ibid.

40. For more on ISIS's Ramadan campaign, see Daveed Gartenstein-Ross and Nathaniel Barr, "Bloody Ramadan: How the Islamic State Coordinated a Global Terrorist Campaign," *War on the Rocks*, July 20, 2016, http://warontherocks.com/2016/07/bloody-ramadan-how-the -islamic-state-coordinated-a-global-terrorist-campaign/. For an example of a disrupted plot in Tunisia that would have been part of the Ramadan campaign, see "Saheefa: Qabl al-Eid, 8 Irhabiyeen Intihariyeen Kanou Sayoufajiroun Anfusuhum fi Qalb al-Asima," *Akher Khabar*, July 11, 2016. The Mnihla cell was also expected to carry out its attack during Ramadan.

41. In November 2015, the ISIS unit based in Jebel Mghila beheaded a Tunisian shepherd accused of providing intelligence to the Tunisian military on ISIS's movements in the region. See "Tunisia Group Claims Beheading of Teen Shepherd for ISIS," Agence France Presse, November 23, 2015, http://english.alarabiya.net/en/News/middle-east/2015/11/23/Tunisia -group-claims-beheading-of-teen-shepherd-for-ISIS-.html.

42. "Tunisian Forces Say Kill Local Islamic State Commander in Clashes," Reuters, May 19, 2016, http://af.reuters.com/article/commoditiesNews/idAFL5N18G2SA.

43. See World Travel and Tourism Council, "Travel and Tourism Economic Impact 2015," http://www.wttc.org/-/media/files/reports/economic%20impact%20research/countries%20 2015/tunisia2015.pdf.

44. "Selon les premiers éléments de l'enquête, la bombe aurait été déclenchée à distance," *DirectInfo*, November 1, 2013, https://directinfo.webmanagercenter.com/2013/11/01/attentats -sousse-selon-les-premieres-elements-de-lenquete-la-bombe-aurait-ete-declenchee-a -distance/.

45. Noureddine Baltayeb, "Tunisia: Ansar al-Sharia Inaugurates Era of Suicide Bombers," *Al Akhbar*, November 1, 2013.

46. Monica Ghanmi, "Tunisia Thwarts New Suicide Bombing," *All Africa*, December 10, 2013.

47. "Tunisia's President Declares State of Emergency after Hotel Attack," *Zaman al-Wasl*, July 4, 2015. The World Travel and Tourism Council assesses that tourism in Tunisia "is likely to suffer well into 2016 and possibly beyond." World Travel and Tourism Council, "June 2015 Monthly Economic Impact," June 2015, http://www.wttc.org/-/media/files/reports /monthly%20updates/wttc%20monthly%20-%20june%2015.pdf. Tunisia's agriculture sector has also been hit hard, with prices dropping 35 percent due to the lack of tourists buying food. Michael J. Totten, "How to Destroy a City in Five Minutes," *World Affairs*, August 25, 2015.

48. "Algeria's Bouteflika in French Hospital, Reason Unclear: Sources," Reuters, November 14, 2014, https://af.reuters.com/article/worldNews/idAFKCN0IY1R120141114.

49. Azzedine Layachi, "The Deluge: Algeria's Pending Succession Crisis," *World Politics Review*, February 17, 2015, http://www.worldpoliticsreview.com/articles/15094/the-deluge -algeria-s-pending-succession-crisis.

50. See, for example, "Oil Price Slump Threatens to Erode Algeria's Status Quo," Al Jazeera, February 3, 2015, http://www.aljazeera.com/news/2015/02/oil-price-slump-threatens -erode-algeria-status-quo-150203102439772.html.

51. Ibid.

52. Lauren Vriens, "Armed Islamic Group (Algeria, Islamists)," Council on Foreign Relations, May 27, 2009, http://www.cfr.org/algeria/armed-islamic-group-algeria-islamists /p9154.

53. Jonathan Schanzer, "Algeria's GSPC and America's 'War on Terror,'" *Policy Watch* (Washington Institute for Near East Policy), October 2, 2002, https://www .washingtoninstitute.org/policy-analysis/view/algerias-gspc-and-americas-war-on-terror.

54. Ibid.

55. Craig Whitlock, "Al-Qaeda's Far-Reaching New Partner," *Washington Post*, October 4, 2006.

56. "Algeria's al-Qaeda Defectors Join IS Group," Reuters, September 14, 2014, https://www.aljazeera.com/news/middleeast/2014/09/algeria-al-qaeda-defectors-join -group-201491412191159416.html.

57. "French Hostage Herve Gourdel Beheaded in Algeria," BBC, September 24, 2014, https://www.bbc.com/news/world-africa-29352537.

58. "Algeria Army Kills Militant behind Frenchman Murder," Agence France Presse, December 23, 2014, http://english.alarabiya.net/en/News/middle-east/2014/12/23/Algeria -troops-kill-chief-militant-behind-Frenchman-s-murder-.html.

59. "Algerian Troops Kill Three Islamist Gunmen in Second Day of Assault," Reuters, May 20, 2015, http://www.reuters.com/article/algeria-security-idUSL5N0YB4KH20150520.

60. "Al-Jaysh al-Watani Yufakik Aakher Khaliya fi Tanzim Da'esh al-Irhabi bil Jaza'er," *Ennahar*, June 19, 2016.

61. For discussion of AQIM units that defected to ISIS, see Nathaniel Barr, "If at First You Don't Succeed, Try Deception: The Islamic State's Expansion Efforts in Algeria," *Jamestown Terrorism Monitor* 13, no. 22 (2015), https://jamestown.org/program/if-at-first-you-dont -succeed-try-deception-the-islamic-states-expansion-efforts-in-algeria/#.

62. "Majmou'at Da'esh fil-Jaza'er . . . Thahira Sawtiyya," *Al-Araby Al-Jadeed*, July 26, 2015.

63. See, for example, "Fima tam Istirja' Silah min naw Klashinkoff—al Qadaa' 'ala Amir Da'esh bi-Sahel Tibaza," *El-Khabar*, March 14, 2016.

64. By comparison, approximately seven thousand Tunisians and fifteen hundred Moroccans have gone to fight with jihadist groups in Syria and Iraq. *Foreign Fighters: An Updated Assessment of the Flow of Foreign Fighters into Syria and Iraq* (New York: Soufan Group, 2015), http://soufangroup.com/wp-content/uploads/2015/12/TSG _ForeignFightersUpdate3.pdf.

65. Farid Alilat, "Algérie: La Traque des Jihadistes Touche-t-elle Vraiment à Sa Fin," *Jeune Afrique*, July 18, 2016, http://www.jeuneafrique.com/mag/340322/politique/algerie-traque -jihadistes-touche-t-vraiment-a-fin/.

66. Nouara Bachouche, "Tawqif 332 Unsur min Shabakat Tajneed al-Jaza'iriyeen Lisaleh Da'esh," *Echourouk El-Youmi*, June 25, 2016, http://www.echoroukonline.com/ara/articles /489745.html.

67. Nabil Chahti, "Tafkik Akhtar Shabakah li-Tajnid al-Jaza'iriyeen fi Da'esh—Ittasalat 'abr Facebook Bizumala' Sabiqeen fil Dirasa," *El Khabar*, April 19, 2016.

68. Rabobank, *Country Report Morocco*, July 1, 2014, https://economics.rabobank.com /publications/2014/july/country-report-morocco/.

69. Maâti Monjib, "Winners and Losers in a New Political Climate," *Qantara*, September 17, 2014.

70. Ibid.

71. David Pollock, "Rule the Casbah: The Moroccan Monarchy's Delicate Balancing Act," *Policy Watch* (Washington Institute for Near East Policy), March 18, 2013, https://www .washingtoninstitute.org/policy-analysis/view/rule-the-casbah-the-moroccan-monarchys -delicate-balancing-act.

72. Monjib, "Winners and Losers."

73. *Foreign Fighters: An Updated Assessment of the Flow of Foreign Fighters into Syria and Iraq* (New York: Soufan Group, 2015), http://soufangroup.com/wp-content/uploads/2015/12 /TSG_ForeignFightersUpdate3.pdf.

74. Maria Abi-Habib, "After Guantanamo, Freed Detainees Returned to Violence in Syria Battlefields," *Wall Street Journal*, June 3, 2014.

75. Embassy of Kingdom of Morocco in the Kingdom of Saudi Arabia, "Inaugural Meeting of the GCTF Working Group on Foreign Terrorist Fighters," December 15, 2014, https://www.moroccanembassy.sa/index.php?route=information/news&news_id=245.

76. Matthew Chebatoris, "Morocco's Multi-Pronged Counterterrorism Strategy," *Terrorism Monitor* 7, no. 13 (May 18, 2009): 5–8.

77. Michael Willis, *Politics and Power in the Maghreb: Algeria, Tunisia and Morocco from Independence to the Arab Spring* (New York: Oxford University Press, 2012), 5.

78. John D. Sutter, "Slavery's Last Stronghold," CNN, March 2012, http://www.cnn.com /interactive/2012/03/world/mauritania.slaverys.last.stronghold/.

79. Ibid.

80. Anouar Boukhars, "Mauritania's Precarious Stability and Islamist Undercurrent," Working Paper (December 2016), Carnegie Endowment for International Peace, p. 4, http:// carnegieendowment.org/2016/02/11/mauritania-s-precarious-stability-and-islamist -undercurrent-pub-62730.

81. Ibid., 5.

82. Ibid.

83. Ibid., 9.

84. Ibid.

85. Ibid., 18.

86. Ibid., 11.

87. See the relevant letter at https://www.dni.gov/files/documents/ubl2016/english/Letter%20about%20matter%20of%20the%20Islamic%20Maghreb.pdf.

88. Ibid.

89. Ibid.

90. *Abamako* (French), March 22, 2016.

PART II

CASE STUDIES

INTRODUCTION TO PART II:
CASE STUDIES

Stephen J. King

THE CHAOTIC AND VIOLENT AFTERMATH OF THE ARAB Spring fostered the renewed appeal of authoritarian stability in North Africa. Part I of this volume explored the cultural, socioeconomic, and security factors in the region that drove the transitions from democratic hopes to authoritarian yearnings. The case studies in part II will provide a country-by-country analysis of political change in North Africa since the Arab Spring erupted.

Decades before the Arab Spring, North African autocrats promised their citizens democracy and introduced its hallmark—multiparty elections. Of course, their intentions were to upgrade and strengthen authoritarianism by holding elections without true competition. While electoral legitimacy without risk was the main goal of these political reforms, other objectives played a part as well. The multiparty elections also had unintended consequences, including the possibility of creating a stepping-stone to democracy.[1] To set the stage for a country-by-country analysis of political change, part II of this volume begins with a discussion of electoral politics in North Africa before the Arab Spring.

The case studies in part II highlight various reasons for dashed democratic hopes in the Maghreb. Partly due to their own civil war in the 1990s and the horrific violence in neighboring Libya, electoral authoritarianism was never seriously challenged in Algeria during the Arab Spring. Within Libya, the abrupt introduction of competitive elections in a country with steep national unity and state-building challenges contributed to a cycle of violence and bloodshed that has many Libyans willing to turn to a strongman, General Khalifa Haftar, who promises stability and little else. To sustain electoral authoritarianism during the challenges of the Arab Spring, Mauritanian strongman Mohamed Ould Abdel Aziz implemented tepid political reforms, reinforced Mauritania's caste-like social structure, and increased direct repression. Early in the Arab Spring, in 2011, Morocco's king implemented what appeared to be substantive democratic reforms, then utilized successful tactics gleaned from prior episodes of political unrest to sustain monarchical dominance of political power. Finally, by keeping the military out of politics and getting the major political parties to compete according to the rules of political democracy, Tunisia has gone a long way toward consolidating its democratic transition. But even in Tunisia, security and economic challenges remain.

STEPHEN J. KING is Associate Professor of Government at Georgetown University. He is author of *Liberalization Against Democracy: The Local Politics of Economic Reform in Tunisia* (Bloomington: Indiana University Press, 2003) and *The New Authoritarianism in the Middle East and North Africa* (Bloomington: Indiana University Press, 2009).

Note

1. Axel Hadenius and Jan Teorell, "Authoritarian Regimes: Stability, Change, and Pathways to Democracy," Working Paper no. 331 (November 2006), Kellogg Institute, https://kellogg.nd.edu/sites/default/files/old_files/documents/331_0.pdf.

7

ELECTIONS BEFORE AND AFTER
THE ARAB SPRING IN NORTH AFRICA

Stephen J. King

Outside of Libya, before the Arab Spring erupted, nominally democratic constitutions and multiparty elections had long been part of the political landscape in North Africa. Similar to other parts of the world, rulers in the region had realized that autocracies with elections are more durable than those without them.[1] In attempts to gain electoral legitimacy without democratic uncertainty, autocrats in North Africa chose from a "menu of manipulations."[2]

Authoritarian elections raise interesting questions about their function for regime elites, voters, and opposition candidates and political parties.[3] If the elections do not decide the country's most powerful collective decision-makers or fundamental policies, why do opposition candidates participate? Why do voters vote? How do autocratic incumbents utilize elections to bolster their hold on power?

Dictators take advantage of elections in a number of ways.[4] Elections are an expedient way to co-opt elites—giving them limited policy input and shares of the spoils of office. Since regime elites can cajole, buy, and intimidate voters to make them turn out and cast ballots in their favor, the incumbents' overwhelming electoral victories deter opposition by demonstrating the regime's seeming invincibility. Elections may be part of power-sharing deals obliging rulers to promote the rank and file to power positions on a regular basis. Authoritarian elections also serve an informational role. The results of multiparty elections help regime incumbents identify their bases of support and opposition strongholds. In certain circumstances, endangered autocrats may conduct free and fair elections to reduce their risk of violent removal from office. Finally, some argue that elections help autocrats establish legitimacy at home and abroad.

For voters, authoritarian elections are an important component of patronage distribution. They vote in favor of incumbents, sometimes despite their preferences, because they recognize that incumbents monopolize patronage resources and the use of force.

Access to patronage is also the prime motivation for proregime candidates to compete in authoritarian elections.[5] Elected officials use their direct access to government ministries and bureaucrats to gain an advantage in bidding on public contracts and obtaining permits and licenses. Often, they enjoy parliamentary immunity, which allows them to engage in illegal wealth-generating practices, including opportunities to move to higher governmental positions where the dividends of corruption are much greater. Candidates are also encouraged to run by family and friends who stand to benefit from having an elected official in their circle.

Opposition candidates and parties have their reasons to run in authoritarian elections as well.[6] A weakening regime, perhaps enfeebled by poor economic performance, may prompt some candidates to join the opposition. Some, especially members of the middle and upper-middle classes (they have less of a need for state patronage), may run for office in opposition for ideological reasons—they want to change the status quo. Social movements, especially religious social movements in the Arab world, may challenge regime incumbents in rigged elections and ineffectual parliaments if they lack other viable options of political participation.

Still, participating in authoritarian elections may backfire against those who enter elections for the opportunity to gain visibility, express policy positions, and mobilize supporters; their entry may legitimize the authoritarian system.[7] In authoritarian elections, opposition candidates are trying to demonstrate that rulers are losing their grip on power, while incumbents are attempting to demoralize and demobilize opposition forces. To use authoritarian elections to their advantage, at times opposition parties may have to decline to participate. They have to evaluate how "unlevel" the playing field created by incumbents is.

The above functions of authoritarian elections, in the Maghreb and elsewhere, are illuminating. But is it also possible for these elections to inadvertently contribute to democratic transitions, especially during periods like the Arab Spring, when autocrats feel pressured to respond to broad demands for political participation? Authoritarian elections can contribute to regime breakdown in a variety of ways.[8] A succession crisis can generate splits within the ruling elite that opponents can exploit, leading to the downfall of the authoritarian regime. Economic crises and liberalization can weaken incumbents' grips on power and transform electoral politics.

As authoritarian power structures begin to fail, authoritarian elections may also inadvertently facilitate democratic transitions.[9] Stolen elections, through massive electoral fraud, can lead to revolutionary outcomes as an imagined community of robbed voters experiences a shared moral outrage that enables them to unite and take collective action. States and international organizations may be able to pressure some regimes to make their multiparty elections truly competitive.

Some also argue that multiparty elections under authoritarian rule can contribute to democratic transitions by acclimating the population to electoral politics even if the outcomes of the elections are not seriously in doubt. Electoral coalitions among opposition parties increase the chances of incumbents relinquishing power.[10] Axel Hadenius and Jan Teorell point to what they call "limited multi-party regimes" as a prime stepping-stone to democratic transitions.[11] Limited multiparty regimes hold parliamentary or presidential elections in which at least some candidates who are independent of the regime are allowed to participate. While they are authoritarian, elections in limited multiparty regimes involve some competition, with autocratic incumbents winning no more than two-thirds of the vote.

Given these general patterns of authoritarian elections, how has the Arab Spring changed electoral politics in the region? Obviously, Tunisia has become a substantive democracy, and Libya did not hold elections under Qaddafi. What about Morocco, Mauritania, and Algeria?

Morocco

Multiparty elections are a hallmark of the postindependence Moroccan regime. However, they do not decide the country's most powerful collective decision-makers. All legislative, executive, and judicial authority in Morocco is subservient to the powers of King Mohammed VI of the Alawite Dynasty, which has ruled Morocco since 1631. Fundamentally, Moroccan elections are designed to provide the king with a mechanism of elite control and renewal from above through co-optation, reward, and exclusion.[12]

The functions of Moroccan elections have often been obscured by periodic reforms. However, despite their declared intentions, episodic democratic reforms and constitutional changes in this "constitutional monarchy" have never significantly reduced the reserved powers of the Moroccan king. The monarchy has also limited voters' range of choices in elections by preventing the deeply embedded Islamist movement, Justice and Charity, from forming a political party and by fragmenting opposition forces with its decisions to legalize some political parties and ban others. Coercion, voter intimidation, and vote buying have also been a part of the Moroccan ruler's menu of manipulation.[13]

Hassan II ruled over a weak formal political process.[14] The king's powers overwhelmed the decisions made in elections for the nominally independent bicameral legislature. Constitutionally, the king appointed (and could dismiss) the prime minister and the cabinet. He could also dissolve the parliament. There were no sanctions for the abuse of royal power. The king and his closest advisors dominated policy making, and it was a crime to even criticize the king's policies and decisions.

The king maintained sweeping powers of appointment including "all governors, heads of administrative provinces . . . directors of public agencies and enterprises, judges and magistrates, as well as half of the members of the High Constitutional Council, including its president."[15] The system of authoritarian maintenance included the king's right to appoint the heads of the "ministries of sovereignty": Justice, Defense, Foreign Affairs, Religious Affairs, and the Ministry of Interior.[16] The Ministry of Interior played an especially important role in the structure of political power.[17] It was responsible for the security services, the training and appointment of rural administrative officials (*qa'ids*), the allocation of local and regional budgets, the licensing of associations and political parties, and the organization and supervision of elections. For most of Hassan II's rule, the "years of lead," the notorious Ministry of Interior, led by Driss Basri, was responsible for a level of repression that made many Moroccans frightened of the security services and police nominally tasked with their protection. Basri was also notorious for manipulating the results of local and national elections.

In the 1990s, Hassan II amended the Moroccan constitution. He did so in order to revive popular support for the "democratic process" and obviate the need for electoral manipulation in preparation for the transfer of power to his son, Mohammed VI.[18] The most important change gave the political party with the largest numbers of elected representatives in the lower chamber of parliament the right to nominate a prime minister and to select a government. This increase in parliamentary power was partly offset, however, by increasing the powers of the advisory upper chamber:

> The Moroccan constitution, as amended in 1992 and 1996, provides for an electoral cycle every six years to a bicameral parliament. The upper chamber of this parliament, the Majlis al Mustasharin (Chamber of Councillors), is directly elected by the municipalities, trade unions and professional organizations, whilst the lower chamber, the Majlis an-Nawwab (Chamber of Deputies), is elected by universal suffrage on the basis of a first-past-the-post system. Although legislation is originated in the executive lower chamber, the advisory upper chamber can override its decisions and dismiss the government by a two-thirds majority vote. The largest party in the lower chamber has the right to nominate a prime minister and to select a government, although the final decision on this is subject to royal approval (the king presides over the council of ministers). The legislative elections are usually preceded by municipal and professional organization elections.[19]

The constitutional changes established the possibility of alternance of power for the first time—from governments dominated by promonarchical parties to a cabinet led by the opposition. Rather than a hegemonic or absolute monarchy, Hassan II had in mind the creation of political system based on alternance, bipolar democracy (two major blocs would alternate in government on the basis of their electoral support), with the king playing the traditional role of arbiter of the political scene, while accepting constitutional limitations of his powers.[20] Alternance was put in practice after parliamentary elections in 1997. An alliance between the Istiqlal, the party that dominated Morocco's nationalist movement before losing out in a struggle for power against the resurgent monarchy, and its splinter party, the more leftist USFP (Union Socialiste des Forces Populaire), won enough parliamentary seats for the USFP leader, Abderrahmane Youssoufi, to become prime minister and control the new government.

Even though King Hassan II limited his own authority by accepting that the party with the electoral majority would select the government and provide the prime minister, alternance and the 1997 elections did not begin a process of sustained democratic transformation in Morocco. While the 1992 and 1996 constitutional amendments transferred more power to the prime minister, they were only partially applied under the Government of Alternance during Prime Minister Abderrahmane Youssoufi's tenure (1998–2002).[21] The king maintained control of major policy issues, including imposing neoliberal economic policies prescribed by the World Bank and the IMF on a "socialist" government.[22] By participating in and winning elections in which they could not fully exercise power, the Istiqlal and USFP compromised their image as true defenders of democracy and the poor to the many Moroccans who had become cynical and resentful toward their political system.[23] The Youssoufi government also took power during difficult socioeconomic times, which it was not able to improve under its nominal leadership.

In the 2002 elections, King Mohammed VI reverted to the practice of naming a prime minister without consideration of election results.[24] In the 2007 elections, based on the votes, Istiqlal party leader Abbas El Fassi became prime minister. He then promptly announced that he would be implementing the "king's program."[25] The moderate Islamist party, the Party of Justice and Development (PJD), emerged as an electoral force in the 2007 elections. They did well enough to position themselves as a replacement for the USFP-Istiqlal socialist alliance as the main party in opposition. In another poor sign of democratic progress during the 2007 elections, a new administrative or king's party was created from whole cloth, the Party for Authenticity and Modernity (PAM), led by the king's close friend Fouad Ali El Himma. In a return to the menu of manipulations of Hassan II's "years of lead," royal patronage quickly propelled PAM into the role of largest parliamentary group.

In sum, ten years after the experiment in alternance began, Morocco seemed no closer to a true constitutional monarchy. The powers of the king and royal advisors had not been vigorously curtailed or counterbalanced by institutions over which the king had no control: "Today the king has the power to appoint a prime minister and government without taking election results in account, to terminate the government and parliament at will, and to exercise legislative power in the absence of parliament. A veritable shadow government of royal advisors keeps an eye on the operations of ministries and government departments. Not only are important decisions taken by the palace, but their execution is also managed—some argue micro-managed—by the royal entourage."[26]

The threat of the Arab Spring prompted King Mohammed VI to experiment with his own set of democratic and constitutional reforms. Shortly after Morocco's Arab Spring uprising, the February 20 movement, began, Mohammed VI delivered a speech calling for "genuine" constitutional and political reforms, although they turned out to be cosmetic.[27] The 2011 constitution returned to the alternance theme of a prime minister selected by the king from the party with the majority of seats in parliament. The prime minister gained the right to dissolve parliament and to declare a state of emergency with royal consent.[28] The prime minister was granted appointment powers, but the king continued to control the ministries of sovereignty and vast discretionary powers.

The moderate Islamist PJD won the plurality of votes in the 2011 legislative elections. Their leader, Abdelilah Benkirane, became prime minister. In terms of institutionalizing democracy, the PJD alternance government has fared as poorly as the USFP Youssoufi-led alternance government that emerged from the 1997 elections. Without a majority, they had to form a coalition government that included members of the king's parties. The king and his shadow government of advisors intervened in politics at will. Supporters were disappointed by the socioeconomic achievements of the compromised government.[29] With the PJD again winning a plurality of votes in the 2016 legislative elections, Benkirane was again appointed prime minister. However, as if to underline where true executive power resides, five months into Benkirane's second term, Mohammed VI replaced him with a more malleable PJD figure, Saadeddine Othmani.

Overall, authoritarian elections in Morocco have done more to solidify the monarchical authoritarian regime than undermine it. They probably helped the transfer of power from King Hassan II to Mohammed VI. Coalition governments haven't threatened the monarchy. By bringing powerful opposition parties into government in what amounts to a junior role, the monarchy has been able to shift the blame for socioeconomic crises to the opposition. The competitiveness of Morocco's elections means that the Moroccan government fits what Hadenius and Teorell term as a limited multiparty regime. Conceivably, this "electoral practice" could serve as a stepping-stone to democracy in the future.

Mauritania

After independence in 1960, nationalist leader and first president of Mauritania, Moktar Ould Daddah, forged a single-party authoritarian regime. The 1964 Mauritanian constitution consecrated his Mauritanian People's Party (MPP) as the sole legal party. A military coup in 1978 banned political parties and transformed Mauritania into a military authoritarian regime with a succession of military rulers.

Mauritania's experimentation with multiparty elections began in 1991. International factors played an important role. After backing Saddam

Hussein in the 1990–91 Gulf War, President Maaouya Ould Sid'Ahmed Taya, who came to power in a military coup in 1984, needed international financial aid from France and other countries, which was contingent on the initiation of "democratic reforms."[30] The 1989–91 Senegalese-Mauritanian racial conflict and protests against human rights abuses contributed as well.[31]

The July 1991 constitution, which inaugurated Mauritania's "Second Republic," authorized political parties and instituted press freedom.[32] Formally, while the Senate and Parliament were given the legislative prerogative, a powerful president, elected for a six-year renewable term, appointed and dismissed the prime minister.[33]

The nominal democratization process established a hybrid military-dominant party regime and stirred up Mauritanian's troubling communitarian relations. Mauritania is one of the most unequal societies in the world. The Arab-Berber population, the Bidan (the whites), dominate all institutions and monopolize all facets of political and economic power. The Bidan, together with the Haratines—their former and frequently current black-skinned slaves (slavery is still widespread in Mauritania) who are descended from black Africans—are called Moors. They all speak Arabic and identify closely with the Arab world. Non-Arabic-speaking black Mauritanians include the Halpulaars, the Soninkes, the Wolofs, and the Bambaras. Mauritanians are also divided tribally.

Unsurprisingly, Ould Taya won the 1992 presidential elections. His newly created Parti Republicain Democratique et Social (PRDS) dominated elections to the lower and upper houses of parliament.[34] In the run-up to legislative elections, the Union des Forces Democratiques (UFD), an unusual and fragile coalition of black Africans and Moors committed to substantive democratic reforms, emerged as the main opposition party. UFD factions differed on whether or not to recognize the regime and participate in its elections. Its coalition included centrist and progressive Moors; Marxists; members of the Haratin freedom movement, *El Hor*; and black African nationalists.[35] The UFD ultimately boycotted legislative elections. In the Second Republic, Islamist, pan-Arabist, and one black African party emerged as well.

The UFD participated in the second legislative elections in 1996, where a third force emerged. Tension between black African communities and Haratins led Haratine leaders to form a new party, Action pour le Changement (AC).[36] Before the second round of elections, the UFD, the AC, and a Nasserist and a Bathist party joined together to form the Front Uni de l'Opposition (FUO). The FUO demanded democratic measures such as the creation of an independent electoral commission, the adoption of a consensual electoral code, a revision of the electoral registration, the eradication of slavery, the return of refugees from the 1989–90 Senegal-Mauritania conflict, and the establishment of a genuine pluralist democracy.[37] Ultimately, Ould Taya's PRDS won seventy out of seventy-nine seats in the National Assembly. Ould Taya was reelected president in 1997. Senatorial elections in 2000 and lower house elections in 2001 continued the dominance of the ruling PRDS. Ould Taya won the 2003 presidential elections decisively.

To ensure that elections would remain authoritarian, Ould Taya and his PRDS took full advantage of the menu of manipulations, especially vote buying and corruption, electoral fraud, the exclusion of some opposition forces, and the reinvigoration of tribalism as the basis for patronage distribution. Once they gained momentum, the regime dissolved the UFD, banned the AC, and repressed the Islamist OUMMA party.[38] In Mauritania people vote more for a personality than for a party, or rather for desired goods they hope to obtain from the leaders.[39] Using the state's political and economic resources, the ruling party established itself at the pinnacle of a traditional hierarchy. To gain their loyalty, the party gave tribal chiefs top positions, such as ministerial posts.[40] The Arab-Berber business elite and the military brass were also part of the regime's core base of support.[41] President Ould Taya's tribe, the Smassid, a *Maraboutiq* tribe from northern Mauritania, benefited the most from the PRDS's control of public resources.[42] In general, Ould Taya managed elites through co-optation and frequent cabinet reshuffles.[43]

A military coup in 2005 startled close students of Mauritanian politics. It came on the heels of a radicalizing opposition and a series of mistakes by Ould Taya's government in managing its own coalition of support. When the August 3, 2005, military coup took place, it wasn't clear if it was the start of a substantive transition to democracy, as the coup leaders announced, or an intervention to sustain the Arab-Berber, military brass–dominated status quo without Ould Taya.[44]

There were early signs that a real democracy was emerging in the wake of the coup.[45] Coup leaders passed a constitutional ordinance barring the coup's own members and those of the transition government it established from standing for elections to be held at the end of the transitional period. The constitution was revised to curtail presidential powers and limit eligibility to two terms. International assistance was sought to ensure free and transparent elections. An independent electoral commission was set up along with working groups on issues such as good governance and constitutional reform.

But there were ominous early signs as well.[46] The military insisted on control of the transition. The legacies of state-sponsored violence, state-tolerated slavery, and human rights abuses against black Mauritanians were ignored. Members of the military council that took power from Ould Taya and members of the transition government were all committed militants and partners in the former regime. There were no overt efforts to tackle the corruption and inequality from which most members of the military council benefited. The neopatrimonial economic system monopolized by a small Arab-Berber elite remained unchallenged.

In the electoral arena, initially, the military held up its end of the democratic bargain. Sidi Ould Cheikh Abdallahi became president of Mauritania on April 19, 2007. He was the first freely and fairly elected president in Mauritanian history. Ould Abdallahi led an elected civilian government. Less promising, after changing its name to the Republican Party for Democracy and Renewal (PRDR) and adding associated independents, Ould Taya's ruling party, the PRDS, won a slight majority of seats in the new National Assembly.[47] The new president's party, National Party for Democracy and Development (PNDD), was dominated by former members of the PRDS, as well.

Within the tight strictures of military supervision and other features of the Ould Taya status quo that limited his room to maneuver, President Ould Abdallahi and his government at least began to address major challenges to democratic consolidation in Mauritania: "(1) to transform civil-military relations in Mauritania to fit a genuine democracy, with the specific objective of ending the vicious cycle of coups; (2) to address the 'human rights deficit' symbolised by thousands of Mauritanian exiles (and slavery and its legacy) in order to extirpate human rights abuse and impunity as features of Mauritanian politics; (3) to avoid setting up another democracy-stifling 'party-state'; and (4) to address the economic needs of Mauritanians by dismantling the corrupt neo-patrimonial economic system woven over the years."[48]

To end military interference and better address Mauritanian hopes for their new democracy, in 2008 Ould Abdellahi fired four military leaders. Their reaction was to overthrow him in an August 6, 2008, coup. General Ould Abdel Aziz became the new strongman in charge. After the coup, using Ould Taya's PRDS as a base, Ould Abdel Aziz created a new ruling party, the Union for the Republic. His party dominated 2013 legislative elections and he handily won presidential elections in 2009 and 2014. After the Senate rejected a move to amend the constitution in order to permit Abdel Aziz to run for a third term, the president spearheaded a constitutional referendum that abolished the Senate.

The Arab Spring did not prevent General Ould Abdel Aziz from reestablishing the type of military-led authoritarian regime that had held sway for more than two decades under Ould Taya. Still, the electoral politics under Ould Taya's Second Republic can possibly be seen as a limited multiparty stepping-stone to a democratic transition. Certainly, the military allowed a transition to take place when Ould Abdulahi won the presidential elections in 2007. However, in line with Mauritanian political dynamics, a military coup ended hope for democratic consolidation.

Algeria

Arguably, Algeria had its "Arab Spring" from 1988 to 1991. Under the initiative of President Chadli Benjedid, Algeria's 1989 constitution and 1991–92 parliamentary elections were either a sudden embrace of multiparty politics and a democratic transition or a bungled attempt by Benjedid to protect his central role in Algeria's military authoritarian regime. The Islamic Salvation Front (FIS) dominated the ruling National Liberation Front (FLN) in local and regional elections and was poised to win an absolute majority in the National Assembly when a military coup in early January 1992 removed Benjedid from power and prevented the second round of elections from taking place. The next decade was bloody, with a struggle between Islamists and the military that killed up to two hundred thousand Algerians.

For a number of reasons, in the late 1980s, President Benjedid felt vulnerable within Algeria's military-backed single-party authoritarian regime. He promoted controversial plans for economic liberalization and a move to a fully market economy that marked a significant change in the character of a regime long self-identified as socialist.[49] Close observers of Algeria claim that this dramatic political opening was designed to undermine the position of hard-line conservatives who opposed the economic reforms and planned to mount a challenge to his presidency and leadership of the FLN at the end of his second term.[50] Drops in oil prices were causing an unprecedented national economic crisis. Corruption at the highest echelon of the Benjedid government was rampant and resented. Formal association with the increasingly unpopular FLN no longer provided legitimacy for the government's leadership.[51] Human rights, Berber rights, and Islamist organizations had emerged as alternative outlets for political participation.[52] These factors, along with the October 1988 riots, during which security forces killed hundreds of rioting civilians, all contributed to Benjedid's decision to seek legitimacy through multiparty elections.[53]

Probably because they were implemented as part of a strategy to bolster one wing of the regime against another, Benjedid's political reforms did not introduce typical authoritarian elections. At times in the multiparty experiment, the main opposition, the Islamist FIS, was a Benjedid ally against the FLN. Benjedid used the FIS to deny his enemies within the FLN popular support and to strengthen his own position.[54] However, instead of full democratization, the aim was to atomize the polity through a maze of political parties while Chadli Benjedid recalibrated his base of support.[55]

In the early 1990s, electoral victories of the FIS foiled Benjedid's plans to outflank his FLN enemies by fracturing the political field and avoiding a single opposition pole that could become a credible alternative to the regime he was in the process of restructuring.[56] The FIS won elections and took power at local and regional levels. Their imminent take-over of the parliament led to the regaime's termination of their legal existence and Chadli Benjedid's presidency.

In the mid-1990s, as the civil war began to tilt in the military's favor, the regime relaunched multiparty elections. However, this time they were more typical authoritarian elections—a play for electoral legitimacy without the uncertainty of outcomes. Common tactics from autocrats' menu of manipulations were deployed. In addition to electoral legitimacy, the authoritarian elections served other purposes.

In 1995 General Liamine Zeroual was elected president, however, a candidate for a new moderate Islamist party, Mahfoud Nahnah of the Movement of Society for Peace (MSP), won over 25 percent of the vote. In the 1999 presidential elections, Abdelaziz Bouteflika took power with 73 percent of the vote after six candidates withdrew on the eve of the election. Notably, Bouteflika faced a challenge from within the FLN by candidate Ali Benflis. In the machinations of the military clans and camps within the FLN, a second state party emerged, the National Rally for Democracy (RND). Ultimately, Bouteflika won 85 percent of the vote as the RND candidate. Benflis of the FLN was second with 6.4 percent. For Bouteflika to compete in and win the 2009 presidential election, the regime had to orchestrate a constitutional revision allowing a candidate to stand for a third term. Incumbent Bouteflika triumphed again in 2014, though he was very ill and only appeared in public once during the campaign.

In the parliamentary elections, the FLN in 1997 was still disabled by the dynamics that had led former president Chadli Benjedid to inaugurate multiparty politics. As new state party, the surging RND won a plurality of votes (34%), while the moderate Islamist party, the MSP, received 15 percent, and the FLN 14 percent. The RND, FLN, and MSP formed a coalition government. By the 2002 elections for the People's National Assembly, the FLN had been rehabilitated as the regime party. It took 34 percent of the vote with the RND receiving 8 percent. Moving forward, the FLN and RND operated as a coalition. The legalized Islamist vote held steady with the MSP receiving 7 percent and a new moderate Islamist party, the Movement for National Reform, receiving 9 percent. The 2004 elections suffered from violence, low turnout, and boycotts by some opposition parties.

Turnout continued to dip in the 2007 parliamentary elections, with only 35 percent of eligible voters participating. The FLN/RND won 34 percent of the vote. The moderate Islamist opposition continued to fracture into mutating political parties, thus obtaining smaller shares of the vote. The FLN/RND incumbents repeated their performance in the 2012 elections. An Islamist coalition, the Green Alliance, faltered badly, receiving only 6 percent of the vote. The FLN/RND coalition increased their win total to 40 percent in the 2017 parliamentary elections. In both the 2012 and 2017 elections, the opposition complained that Algeria had returned to a single-party system.

Algeria's authoritarian elections are manipulated by the military, the strongest power in the country. The military, not elections, has determined all of the country's postindependence presidents. This reserved power operates in parliamentary elections as well. After the FIS's dominance in local and regional elections and the first round of national elections from 1989 to 1991, the regime outlawed the party and thus excluded its most potent opposition force from electoral competition. The military's 1992 coup also prevented the FIS from taking national office. Since multiparty elections resumed, various forms of vote rigging have been a constant, including electoral fraud to determine the main legal opposition. [57] Vote buying is prevalent. In the 1997 parliamentary elections, the first since the 1992 military coup, the regime engineered what amounted to a return to the pre-1989 status quo with pluralist trimmings.[58] In subsequent elections, including those after the Arab Spring, little has changed.

Overall, Algeria's authoritarian elections have served to prop up the legitimacy of ruling groups, co-opt elites, divide the opposition, and deflect attention from socioeconomic challenges. In addition, in light of the spiral of violence that followed Algeria's Spring in the early 1990s and the recent bloody conflict in neighboring Libya, the regime is currently downplaying electoral politics. Instead, knowing their population is reeling, they brandish two unappealing choices: either chaos and violence through further political openness or stability through sham elections.

Libya

Libya, an outlier under Colonel Muammar al-Qaddafi, barred political parties and conventional elections for ideological reasons. In Qaddafi's political philosophy political parties usurp the power of the people. He replaced political parties with direct democracy. In practice, Qaddafi's *Jamahiriya* (state of the masses) devolved into a personalist authoritarian regime dominated by Qaddafi's family and close allies, who wielded unchecked power under the protection of a brutal security apparatus.

Most of the leadership that replaced Qaddafi after the revolution wholeheartedly embraced competitive elections to choose the country's most powerful decision-makers. Unfortunately, the elections probably contributed to the post-Qaddafi Libyan civil war. Unable to forge a democratic bargain, political parties have turned to violence to alter electoral and policy outcomes.

A number of conflicts contributed to the failure to develop a democratic political pact among Libyan political parties. The votes in the July 2012 founding elections of Libya's stumbling democratic transition were largely cast in line with tribal, regional, and local affinities—cleavages destined to pull the country apart.[59] In addition, moderate and radical Islamist politicians used the armed force of their associated brigades and militias to change policy and electoral results.

The National Forces Alliance (NFA), a relatively secular coalition, took a plurality of votes in the 2012 elections for the General National Congress (GNC), a body tasked with governing and producing a permanent democratic constitution within eighteen months from August 8, 2012, when it took power. Ali Zeidan of the NFA became prime minister. Libya's Muslim Brotherhood party, Justice and Construction (JCP), became the main opposition party.

Unwilling to accept the electoral outcomes, Islamist militias and their supporters in the GNC, including the JCP, forced through a political isolation law (PIL) that effectively disqualified anyone involved in Qaddafi's regime from participating in government, administration, and the armed forces. The law was passed while armed militias held the GNC under a military siege, blocked a number of other ministerial buildings in Tripoli, and actively intimidated individual members of the GNC.[60] The net result and likely intention of the PIL was to impose Islamist domination of the GNC, the exact opposite of the results of the July 2012 elections.

The PIL forced many elected NFA members out of the GNC, including its president, Mohammed al-Magarief, and four ministers. As a result, the Muslim Brotherhood's JCP and its more extreme ally, the Islamist Loyalty to the Blood of the Martyr's bloc, led by Abdel Wahab Qayed (the brother of al-Qaeda second-in-command Abu Yahya al-Libi), increased their relative numbers within the GNC.[61] They were able to vote in as president Nouri Abusahmain, a figure sympathetic to their Islamist agenda. In addition, on March 11, 2014, through a no-confidence vote, Islamists successfully removed Prime Minister Zeidan from power.

After Zeidan's departure, the GNC struggled to identify a replacement capable of attaining the 120 GNC votes necessary to elect a new prime minister. On May 5, 2014, a televised vote took place for a prime minister candidate backed by the Islamist bloc, Ahmed Maetig.[62] Maetig, a businessman relatively unknown to the public, attained 113 votes, at which point television service was interrupted nationwide. When it returned one hour later, Maetig had the 120 necessary votes.[63] There were widespread protests from the NFA and the general public, but GNC president Nouri Abusahmain approved the vote and declared Maetig prime minister.[64]

Rejecting the power move by Islamists, GNC vice-president Ezzeddine Al-Awami and other members of the secular-liberal bloc declared the vote null and void and formally asked Abdallah al-Thinni, who had temporarily taken over the office after Zeidan's vote of no confidence, to stay in power as prime minister until elections for a new parliament could be held.[65] Thus, the vote to replace Zeidan with Maetig as prime minister essentially meant that Libya had two prime ministers, one for the Islamist and one for the non-Islamist bloc in the GNC. Both sides had militia support for their claims.

The GNC set June 2014 as the date for elections to replace itself with a new parliament, the House of Representatives.[66] To reduce tensions, all candidates contested the election as individuals or independents instead of running on party lists, although the results were tied to either secular or Islamist factions. Secular forces won decisively, with Islamists winning only thirty seats.[67] Again, the GNC's Islamist bloc refused to accept the results. Their allied militias forced the newly elected parliament to leave Tripoli and set up government in a five-star hotel in Tobruk in eastern Libya near the Egyptian border.[68] Temporary prime minister Abdullah al-Thinni became the first prime minister of the House of Representatives, although the Tobruk lawmakers and their government can do little to enforce anything outside their limited enclave.[69]

In Tripoli, Islamists and others in their coalition set up their own parliament by reinstating the GNC and naming a cabinet led by Prime Minister Omar al-Hassi.[70] The Tripoli government took de facto control over the ministries, relying on a handful of former members of the nominally defunct GNC to provide a veneer of legitimacy.[71] The Tobruk government is backed by a military coalition called Operation Dignity. The Tripoli government counters with Operation Libya Dawn.

Currently, Libya essentially has three governments. A UN-backed unity government operates from Tripoli as well. Both the Tobruk House of Representatives and the Tripoli GNC have reneged on their promises to support the UN initiative.

Tunisia

In Tunisia before the Arab Spring, strongman Zine El Abidine Ben Ali ran the small country like a police state with a thin facade of multiparty politics. Only the weakest of satellite parties were allowed to participate. In addition to barring the deeply embedded, relatively moderate Islamist party, Ennahda, from the electoral arena, his regime grossly restricted political and civil liberties, along with access to media and money. [72] Electoral fraud, redistributive election management, and electoral rules insured that the ruling party and Ben Ali himself regularly won more than 95 percent of the vote in legislative and presidential elections.

Elections after the removal of Ben Ali have been substantively democratic. A well-known definition of regime change asserts that the consolidation of democracy takes place if "the party that takes power in the initial election at the time of transition loses a subsequent election and turns over power to these election winners."[73] Tunisia has passed this two-turnover test. The Islamist Ennahda dominated the founding elections of the country's post–Arab Spring democratic transition. A secular coalition, Nidaa Tounes, won a subsequent election and took power, with Ennahda pressing to become coalition partners or the loyal opposition. The main remaining electoral concern is that many members of Nidaa Tounes were prominent under former president Ben Ali, opening the possibility of a return to the era of those elites.

STEPHEN J. KING is Associate Professor of Government at Georgetown University. He is author of *Liberalization Against Democracy: The Local Politics of Economic Reform in Tunisia* (Bloomington: Indiana University Press, 2003) and *The New Authoritarianism in the Middle East and North Africa* (Bloomington: Indiana University Press, 2009).

Notes

1. Barbara Geddes, "Authoritarian Breakdown: Empirical Test of a Game Theoretic Argument," paper presented at the annual meeting of the American Political Science Association, Atlanta, September 1999.

2. Andreas Schedler, "Elections without Democracy: The Menu of Manipulations," *Journal of Democracy* 13, no. 2 (April 2002): 36–50.

3. Jennifer Gandhi and Ellen Lust-Okar, "Elections under Authoritarianism," *Annual Review of Political Science* 12 (2009): 403–22.

4. Ibid. for a review of this literature.

5. Ibid.

6. Ibid.

7. Ibid., 411.

8. This literature is summarized in Gandhi and Lust-Okar, "Elections under Authoritarianism."

9. Ibid.

10. Marc Morjé Howard and Philip G. Roessler, "Liberalizing Electoral Outcomes in Competitive Authoritarian Regimes," *American Journal of Political Science* 50, no. 2 (2006): 365–81.

11. Axel Hadenius and Jan Teorell, "Authoritarian Regimes: Stability Change, and Pathways to Democracy," Working Paper no. 331 (November 2006), Kellogg Institute, https://kellogg.nd.edu/sites/default/files/old_files/documents/331_0.pdf.

12. Abdelsam Maghraoui, "Monarchy and Political Reform in Morocco," *Journal of Democracy* 12, no. 1 (January 2001): 80.

13. Schedler, "Elections without Democracy."

14. Maghraoui, "Monarchy and Political Reform," 79.

15. Ibid.

16. The king kept these portfolios as guarantor of the constitution and in accordance with Islamic precepts (referring to his role as caliph above secular law); see George Joffe, "The Moroccan Political System after the Elections," *Mediterranean Politics* 3, no. 3 (1998): 107.

17. Maghraoui, "Monarchy and Political Reform," 80.

18. Joffe, "Moroccan Political System," 106.

19. Ibid.

20. Ibid., 120.

21. Maâti Monjib, "The Democratization Process in Morocco: Progress, Obstacles, and the Impact of the Islamist-Secularist Divide," Working Paper no. 5 (August 2011), Brookings Institute, 6, https://www.brookings.edu/wp-content/uploads/2016/06/08_morocco_monjib .pdf.

22. Marina Ottaway and Meredith Riley, "Morocco: From Top-Down Reform to Democratic Transition?" Carnegie Papers, no. 71 (September 2006), 6, https://carnegieendowment .org/files/cp71_ottaway_final.pdf.

23. Ibid.

24. Ottaway and Riley, "Morocco."

25. James Liddell and Maâti Monjib, "Mohammed VI: 10 Years and Counting," Brookings Op Ed., August 5, 2009, https://www.brookings.edu/opinions/moroccos-king-mohammed -vi-10-years-and-counting/.

26. Ottaway and Riley, "Morocco."

27. Mohamed Daadaoui, "Of Monarchs and Islamists: The 'Refo-lutionary' Promise of the PJD Islamists and Regime Control in Morocco," *Middle East Critique* 26, no.4 (2017): 361.

28. Ibid., 362.

29. Ibid.

30. Marianne Marty, "Mauritania: Political Parties, Neo-patrimonialism and Democracy," *Democratization* 9, no.3 (Autumn 2002): 93.

31. Ibid., 95.

32. Ibid., 93.

33. Ibid.

34. Ibid., 96.

35. Ibid., 97.

36. Ibid., 99.

37. Ibid., 100.

38. Ibid., 94.

39. Ibid., 103.

40. Ibid.

41. Boubacar N'Diaye, "Mauritania, August 2005: Justice and Democracy, or Just Another Coup?," *African Affairs* 105, no. 420 (2006): 428.

42. Marty, "Mauritania," 104.

43. Ibid.

44. N'Diaye, "Mauritania, August 2005."

45. Ibid., 435.

46. Ibid.

47. Boubacar N'Diaye, "To Midwife and Abort—a Democracy: Mauritania's Transition from Military Rule, 2005–2008," *Journal of Modern African Studies* 47, no. 1 (March 2009): 137.

48. Ibid., 143.

49. Hugh Roberts, *The Battlefield Algeria 1988–2002: Studies in a Broken Polity* (London: Verso, 2003), 87.

50. Ibid. See also Youcef Bouandel, "Reforming the Algerian Electoral System," *Journal of Modern African Studies* 43, no. 3 (September 2005): 393–415.

51. Bouandel, "Reforming the Algerian Electoral System," 401.

52. Ibid.

53. Ibid.

54. Ibid., 403.

55. Ibid., 402.

56. Ibid.

57. Hugh Roberts, "Algeria's Contested Elections," *Middle East Report*, no. 209 (Winter 1998): 21–24.

58. Ibid., 23.

59. Jason Pack and Haley Cook, "The July 2012 Libyan Election and the Origin of Post-Qadhafi Appeasement," *Middle East Journal* 69, no. 2 (Spring 2015): 182.

60. Roman David and Houda Mzioudet, *Personnel Change or Personal Change? Rethinking Libya's Political Isolation Law* (Washington, DC: Brookings Institution, 2014), 4, http://www.brookings.edu/~/media/research/files/papers/2014/03/17-libya-lustration-david-mzioudet/lustration-in-libya-english.pdf.

61. Sasha Toperich, "Libya: The Muslim Brotherhood's Last Stand," Huffpost, 2017. Accessed February 7, 2019, https://www.huffingtonpost.com/sasha-toperich/libya-the-muslim-brotherhoods-last-stand_b_5618001.html.

62. "Ahmed Maetig: The Youngest Prime Minister in Libya since the Revolution," Al Jazeera, June 5, 2014.

63. "Libya: Two Ministers," *HuffPost Maghreb*, May 5, 2014.

64. Ibid.

65. Ibid.

66. "Libya Proposes June Election as Crisis Escalates," Reuters, May 20, 2014, https://www.reuters.com/article/us-libya-politics-idUSBREA4J0T520140520.

67. Ibid.

68. Ulf Laessing, "Libya's Runaway Parliament Seeks Refuge in Tobruk Bubble," Reuters, October 2, 2014, https://www.reuters.com/article/us-libya-security-insight/libyas-runaway-parliament-seeks-refuge-in-tobruk-bubble-idUSKCN0HR1GO20141002.

69. Ibid.

70. "Omar Al-Hassi Appointed as the New Prime Minister," Al-Arabiya, April 2, 2014.

71. Frederic Wehrey and Wolfram Lacher, "Libya After ISIS," *Foreign Affairs*, February 22, 2017.

72. The Tunisian media was as state controlled as any in the Arab world.

73. Samuel P. Huntington, *The Third Wave: Democratization in the Late Twentieth Century* (Norman: University of Oklahoma, 1991), 267.

8

TUNISIA TRIGGERS THE ARAB SPRING

Stephen J. King

TUNISIA IS GROUND ZERO FOR THE ARAB SPRING. It is where popular uprisings in the region began that toppled several autocrats and struck fear in others. In terms of the academic literature, the situation in Tunisia brought fresh attention to regime transition processes by obliging scholars to pay attention to political change in countries widely viewed as stubbornly authoritarian or exceptional in their resistance to democracy and human rights. For the comparative literature, the Tunisian case points to new variables to explain authoritarian breakdown and, because it is the only relative success story from the region's popular uprisings, new avenues to track democratic consolidation.

Before the Arab Spring, the transitions paradigm was the leading approach to explaining the breakdown of authoritarian regimes.[1] In that approach, questions about how to increase regime legitimacy lead to internal splits among authoritarian incumbents into hard-liners and soft-liners. When soft-liners get the upper hand, the regime cautiously opens political space to increase legitimacy, though without any intention of inaugurating a real transition to democracy. However, once some guarantees of individual rights and some political contestation are extended, "a generalized mobilization is likely to occur, which [the literature] chooses to describe as the resurrection of civil society."[2] This "popular upsurge" breaks down the authoritarian regime completely and begins a substantive transition to democracy. This approach did not reflect the Tunisian experience at all. Authoritarian breakdown in Tunisia was instigated by a martyr, made successful by a popular uprising that did not begin with divisions among regime incumbents and was sustained by social media. It also spurred region-wide revolts, making regional contagion an important component of the Arab Spring and steps toward democracy.

Removing autocrats and holding free and fair elections do not insure the successful consolidation of political democracy. In addition, efforts at national consensus must take place to address conflicts that can derail long-term democratic transformation. These negotiated compromises or pacts may be necessary in several areas. In an important study of democratic consolidation, Guillermo O'Donnell and Philippe Schmitter highlight military (extrication from politics) pacts, political pacts, and socioeconomic pacts.[3] Other authors point to the need for nation-state pacts.[4] The Tunisian case suggests the need for a national effort or pact to transform its *mukhabarat* (intelligence, police) state to one that respects human rights. Called here a security sector pact, it includes transitional justice and changes in both the ministry of interior and the judicial system. Tunisia entered the Arab Spring with broad national unity and an effective national administration compared to other countries in the region, limiting the need for a nation-state pact. Success at military and political pacts have ensured significant regime change in Tunisia, though democratic consolidation is still endangered by challenges to socioeconomic and security sector pacts.

Authoritarian Breakdown in Tunisia

Challenges to former president Zine El Abidine Ben Ali's autocratic rule (1987–2011) followed a general pattern. Protests typically began in the poorer southern and central parts of the country but were usually shut down by security forces before they could spread to the capital and coastal cities.[5] The pattern is evident in what most Tunisians regard as the real start of their Arab Spring revolution: the 2008 revolts in the southern phosphate-mining region of Gafsa near the Sahara.[6] Those protests focused on corruption and working conditions. They were organized by the radical wing of the General Union of Tunisian workers.[7] Six months of sporadic demonstrations led to hundreds of arrests, several deaths, and many injuries at the hands of security forces.[8] However, in a common strategy of authoritarian maintenance, the Tunisian government imposed a successful information blackout during the Gafsa revolt—journalists were not allowed in the region, the state-controlled media ignored it, and little information and images to inspire similar protests filtered out.[9]

The stifling of revolts and dissent in the south before they could reach the coastal population centers in northern Tunisia finally failed during the Arab Spring. Two factors seemed to have enabled countrywide mass protests in late 2010 and early 2011 that finally overcame the regime's southern strategy and brought an end to Ben Ali's dictatorship.[10] First, in despair, Mohamed Bouazizi, a struggling fruit and vegetable vendor, poured paint thinner over his body and lit himself on fire to protest the arbitrary confiscation of his produce and further humiliations by local officials. That act inspired a sense of solidarity and focused anger against the regime that led to mass protests in his hometown and in surrounding areas. Second, a virtual civil society through social media and cell phone technology, which had spread throughout Tunisia by 2010, helped protestors overcome the regime's media bans after protests broke out in the impoverished central region of Sidi Bouzid where Mohamed Bouazizi worked and self-immolated.[11] Bouzizi's martyrdom and social media were crucial factors in the success of the Tunisian Revolution.

Ben Ali's regime used every tool in the police-state tool kit to prevent the type of countrywide information flow and civil society strength that contributed to the regime's ouster in early 2011. But despite regime efforts, social media made a powerful contribution to the Tunisian Revolution by constructing a parallel cyber civil society, out of the reach and understanding of the regime.

The process that led to the successful circumvention of a police state at the end of 2010 can be traced back to 1998 when two Tunisians known as "Foetus" and "Waterman" (names used to guard their anonymity) began what they called a cyber think tank called Takriz (Arabic street slang for "frustrated anger").[12] Takriz's goals included freedom of speech and affordable internet access. Foetus, Takriz's chief technology officer, is a skilled hacker who began hacking because he could not afford Tunisia's then-exorbitant phone and internet costs.[13] The founders recognized that the internet was the only form of media in Tunisia not completely controlled by Ben Ali. The internet also provided relative safety for dissidents through anonymity.

By 2000 Takriz had grown to a loose network of thousands, and their criticisms of the Tunisian regime led to their website being blocked in 2000. Takriz used various tactics from serious political analysis to leaked documents and fierce polemic to reach multiple audiences.[14] Its leaders turned to Arabic slang, obscenities, and street culture to stir up street youth.[15] They also organized protests at football stadiums, one of the few arenas with lax political control. Its members were hunted and exiled for years under Ben Ali. Their cyber activism increased dramatically after 2009, when Ben Ali orchestrated yet another five-year term in office. Takriz's founders saw this as the last straw as they could imagine another decade of Ben Ali and his rapacious family mafia looming, with the formal opposition and general public afraid to act.[16]

Zouhair Yahyaoui, one of the members of Takriz, deserves special note. Yahyaoui, known online as "Ettounsi" (the Tunisian), started TUNeZine, a political webzine and forum that inspired many with humor such as in the following:

> TUNeZine is launching a competition for jokes, reserved for young people, about Ben Ali and his party:
>
> First prize: 13 years in prison.
> Second prize: 20 years in prison.
> Third prize: 26 years in prison.[17]

TUNeZine made Ettounsi famous in Tunisia but also led to his arrest and torture. He was jailed in 2000 after inviting readers to vote on whether Tunisia was " a republic, a kingdom, a zoo, or a prison."[18] According to his family, he was sent to one of the worst prisons in the country—with 120 people in one room, just one bathroom, and hardly any water.[19] He became ill and was beaten when he asked for a doctor. He went on several hunger strikes.[20] Reporters Without Borders (RWB) gave Zouhair Yahyaoui its first Cyber-Freedom Prize in 2003. The Pen American Center gave him its Freedom to Write Award that same year. He was released that year in extremely poor physical condition and died shortly afterward.[21]

The life of Zouhair Yahyaoui was the primary catalyst for the emergence of Nawaat (Arabic for the nucleus or core) in 2004. Its four founders were affected by Yahaoui's articles and committed to his tradition of cyber activism. Nawaat began as a webzine and Nawaat Forums. Later it became a collection of bloggers.[22] In time members of Nawaat became adept at all the social media tools: blogs, forums, Facebook, Twitter, YouTube, and various live-streaming applications. They learned quickly, for example, that Facebook provided an empty space to fill with information in a superior manner to older platforms like WebZine where all users read the comments of one editor. They understood that the power of Facebook and some blogs was in the interaction between writers and readers. Along with blogs and Twitter, Nawaat utilized Facebook to create a cyber civil society: activist platforms with followers, citizen journalism, and social interaction that could partially replace the civil society confiscated by Ben Ali's regime. The social media platforms provided a public space, and between 2007 and 2010 there was an explosion in the number of Tunisians regularly using social media, which provided the public for this new public space.

Ironically, Ben Ali, himself a computer geek who was an electronics technician in the army, may have contributed to the creation of this dissident public sphere. In his fifteenth development plan in 2001, he announced a policy of extending internet connection to 100 percent of the country.[23] Under his rule the number of cyber cafés increased dramatically due to government credits and grants to the unemployed that funded these ventures. The Tunisian version of the internet that became available to many Tunisians was heavily censured, but Ben Ali's technology push did get large numbers of Tunisians online. In addition, his daughter, Cyrine Ben Ali Mabrouk, brought third-generation developments in wireless technology to Tunisia in 2010.[24] Her company, Orange, spread mobile internet services throughout the country. The 3G technology she introduced vastly improved live-streaming capabilities in Tunisia.

Technology to evade internet censorship also rapidly became widespread in Tunisia. Hot-spotting technology that evaded censorship spread to the masses, and when the regime broke down in 2011, thousands posted on their Facebook pages, "hot spotting we won't forget you." Well-trained cyber activists associated with Nawaat were technically able to avoid detection by the secret police for the most part using VPNs (virtual private networks). The bloggers utilized the news feed function on Facebook to share information and develop and maintain thousands if not tens of thousands of followers. These bloggers frequently adapted a revolutionary tone toward the Ben Ali regime.[25]

In sum, between 1998 and the 2010–11 Tunisian Revolution, social media tools were utilized in a manner that gradually created an alternative public sphere, a civil society online in a country that did not allow street demonstrations, associational life, free speech, or independent political parties. This civil society had become committed to political power based on free and fair multiparty elections.

Through its organizational capabilities, Tunisia's cyber civil society contributed to the nationwide mass revolt between December 17, 2010, and January 14, 2011, that ended a dictatorship in Tunisia and inspired the Arab Spring. The catalyst for this revolt was the emergence of a martyr who united and focused the public's anger.

On December 17, 2010, Mohamed Bouazizi, a fruit and vegetable vendor in the impoverished central Tunisian region of Sidi Bouzid, set himself on fire to protest the confiscation of his goods and his constant harassment and humiliation by municipal officials and police officers. As a symbol of exasperation with arbitrary rule, Bouazizi's actions led to immediate protests, beginning first with members of his extended family or "tribe," or with his fellow fruit vendors.[26] Bolstered by a second suicide in Sidi Bouzid a few days later (another young man committed suicide, this time by electrocuting himself on a utility pole—his mother wailed and cried in the streets for hours), protests accelerated.

Unlike in 2008, due to social media the local protests in 2010–11 spread throughout the country. In one of the first videos of the protests from Sidi Bouzid in December 2010, you can hear someone saying, "I'm going to post this on Facebook tonight."[27] Anonymous bloggers organized the December 25, 2010, demonstration in Tunis. To gather critical mass, they hacked into Tunisia's National Trade Union Federation's website to announce the date and time of the demonstration. Doing so allowed them to reach the rank and file of an organization whose leadership had been long co-opted by Ben Ali's regime.

A member of Nawaat, Slim Amamou, filmed the protest, which was broadcast by Al Jazeera. This was the first time that people from Sidi Bouzid realized that their protests had reached Tunis, the capital. In early January 2011, a group of cyber activists called "Anonymous" hacked official government websites, including the president's and prime minister's, to demonstrate the vulnerability of the regime. Between December 17 and January 14, over five hundred videos of Tunisian protests were posted on Facebook. Blogs, Twitter, and YouTube also played a role. Due to social media, social interaction across the country had become too supple for the Tunisian police state. "Like, Comment, Share, Tweet" became tools adapted to Tunisian circumstances, circumstances characterized by anger and a powerful desire to end an unpopular dictatorship.

The Ben Ali regime tried a last-ditch effort to stop cyber activism, but they were largely unsuccessful, with protestors mocking their efforts with slogans such as "Free from 404" (internet language for "file not found").[28] Bloggers posted videos of events in Sidi Bouzid as they occurred—violent images of state murder, the photos of martyrs, the executions by Ben Ali's thugs. They also provided the names of arrested militants.

Despite the banning of YouTube, videos of Tunisian demonstrations appeared on the platform. Tweets were issued under the hashtag #Sidibouzid.[29] Activists filmed confrontations between protestors and Tunisian riot police all over the country and successfully posted them online or had them broadcast on Al Jazeera. By the time that mass demonstrations were taking place in the major Tunisian cities in early 2011, few Tunisians were unaware of the events that had begun in Sidi Bouzid, and many were participating in them.

On January 13, 2011, Ben Ali delivered a televised speech promising democracy, freedom, and lower prices for all staples. The speech was anchored by the repetition of the phrase, "I've understood you." The next day he acknowledged the end and fled to Saudi Arabia.

Once Arabs in other countries of the region witnessed the removal of a despised dictator in Tunisia through popular uprisings, they followed suit. Some found their own martyrs, like the "we are all Khalid Said" campaign in Egypt. There were copycat self-immolations. Social media was leveraged in similar ways to get around the police states. Although the success of the uprisings varied depending on multiple factors unique to each country, the salience of regional dynamics could not be clearer.

Democratic Consolidation: Political and Military Pacts

To successfully consolidate a democracy, political party leaders must strike a democratic bargain or political pact. The political pact involves a package deal among the leaders of a spectrum of electorally competitive parties, which represent all the major factions in the country. The parties agree to compete according to the rules of political democracy and to forego appeals to mass mobilization, violence, and military intervention to alter electoral outcomes.[30] By accommodating vital interests, political pacts enable warring elite factions to deliberately reorganize their relations through negotiated compromises on their most basic disagreements.[31]

During the Arab Spring, party elites had to seek compromises over class, region, tribe, ethnicity, sect, and other conflicts. Conflicts over the role of religion (Islam and Islam's religious law, *sharia*) in politics have posed the most frequent challenge to democratic bargains. A compromise between Islamists and secularists in support of democracy was certainly the main challenge to a political pact in the Tunisian case.

Alfred Stepan has called the successful striking of a democratic political bargain between secularist and religious-based political parties the "twin tolerations."[32] In the first toleration, religious citizens must accord democratically elected officials freedom to legislate and govern, within the bounds of the constitution and human rights, without having to confront denials of their authority based on religious claims—such as the claim that "only God, not man, can make laws." In the second, as long as they follow democratic norms, secular-oriented citizens must tolerate the participation of religious political parties in elections to choose the country's most powerful collective decision-makers. Thus, secularists must accept the legitimacy of elected Islamist governments and the policies they generate as long as their actions do not impinge negatively on the liberties of other citizens or violate democracy and the law.[33]

Implied in the twin tolerations is the need for moderate Islamists to coax Islamic extremists toward moderation and democracy through dialogue and persuasion. The same is true on the other side in terms of moderate and authoritarian secularists. All the state's coercive capacities have to be brought to bear against the recalcitrant jihadi Salafis and Takfiri jihadis, who have far too often turned Arab hopes for the Arab Spring into bloody nightmares.

Although there were setbacks, Tunisian elites built on dialogues between Islamists and secularists during the Ben Ali era to construct a political pact once the transition began.[34] After Ben Ali fled to Saudi Arabia, Tunisia's National Constituent Assembly (NCA) elections took place on October 23, 2011. The NCA was charged with producing a constitution within one year. Parties representing all four of Tunisia's dominant ideological orientations—Islamist, leftist, liberal, and nationalist (with either a leftist or liberal bent)—organized to contest the founding elections of the country's democratic transition.[35] Despite progress toward the twin tolerations, it quickly became clear that political competition in postrevolutionary Tunisia would be dominated by battles between Islamists and secularists, with each fearing the other's political and social projects for the country's future.[36]

Ennahda, a moderate Islamist political party, emerged as the dominant political force in the NCA elections, winning 89 of 217 seats. However, their margin of victory was not large enough to form a government on their own. Notably, to form a government, Ennahda added two secular partners, the Congress for the Republic (CPR), which won 29 seats in the NCA, and the Democratic Forum for Labor and Liberties (Ettakatol), which won 20 seats. The ruling alliance became known by the name Troika. Ennahda's Hamdi Jebali became the prime minister, the most powerful role in the government, although the movement's spiritual leader, Rachid Ghannouchi, remained closely involved in the politics of the transition.[37] The CPR's leader, Moncef Marzouki, became president, and Ettakatol's leader, Mustafa Ben Jaafar, became speaker of the house (president of the NCA).[38]

The Troika created Tunisia's first elected government, a government intended to stay in power until a new one could be elected under the new constitution. From the start, Ghannouchi and Marzouki asserted that the Troika alliance should serve as a model during transitions across the region because it helped overcome the secular-Islamist divide that threatened democratic progress everywhere in the Arab Middle East.[39] While forming the Troika was a deliberate act to bolster the twin tolerations, mutual suspicions between Islamists and secularists remained a challenge to the Tunisian democratic transition:

> In this second phase of the Tunisian uprisings [after the exceptional and ephemeral moment of national unity and shared goals among all participants and sympathizers] anxious interrogations about the place and role of Islam and secularism in Tunisia took over the newly opened and variegated field of political competition... Tunisians who referred to Islam as a normative element of social life and politics demanded the liberation of the discourses and institutions of Islam from state control [Under Ben Ali's and his predecessor, Habib Bourguiba's the public interpretations of Islam and secularism were essentially defined and authorized by the state]. They also wanted to impose limits on what they considered to be non-Islamic behaviors [alcohol consumption, gender mixing in public, dress, artistic portrayal of religious figures, blasphemy, etc.]. Tunisians [with a more secular orientation] demanded the liberation of expression in almost all its forms, but often wanted to impose limits on some expressions of Islam they deemed dangerous or incorrect.[40]

Empowered by electoral success, Ennahda's commitment to democracy was put to the test in how they handled more extreme interpretations of Islam that were hostile to democracy. With some influence from abroad, scripturalist and jihadi Salafis, previously rare in Tunisia, had made their presence known in the more open political environment. Many Tunisians suspected that Ennahda, despite public proclamations supporting democracy, was sympathetic to both scripturalist and jihadi Salafism. As leader of the elected governing coalition and as an Islamist movement, Ennahda was held responsible for the actions of both groups when they threatened lives and rejected individual freedoms and democracy. The two secular members of the Troika ruling coalition were also put on the defensive due to the behavior of some Salafis.

The Troika tended to emphasize the small number of jihadi Salafis in Tunisia and pointed out that there were extremists in every country, especially during the tense times shortly after the end of a dictatorship.[41] The Troika preferred dialogue and persuasion to repression in dealing with Salafis. In their view, they were capable of socializing radical Salafis and extremists of every stripe toward moderation and democracy.[42] Repression, they argued, closed the door on evolution in Salafi thought toward the legitimacy of democracy. It would be a repeat of Ben Ali's police state and antithetical to the atmosphere of freedom and inclusion promised by the revolution.[43] Ennahda leaders declared that the state would not violently battle any religious current, stressing that the era of exclusion and security campaigns in Tunisia had ended.[44]

In an interview, discussing for the first time in public the rise of both the scripturalist and jihadi Salafi currents in Tunisia, Ennahda's spiritual leader, Rachid Ghannouchi, urged Salafis to operate within the emerging legal democratic framework and stated that dialogue with them would lead them in that direction:

> The government has begun consultations with the *Salafists*. I have spoken personally with many [*Salafi*] elders and encouraged them to work within the [Tunisian] legal framework pertaining to associations and political parties. It is not a problem if they receive some votes in elections [he has estimated their total numbers to be no more than five thousand]. The important thing is to avoid confrontation. I do not think *Salafists* pose a terrorist threat. There are extremists of course, but they know that terrorism would be a suicidal path. And you must know that not all *Salafists* are the same. Most reject violence and do not accuse *Ennahda* of disbelief. Dialogue is possible with these people.[45]

Four events changed Ennahda's tolerant stance toward Tunisian Salafism. First, on September 14, 2012, hundreds of protestors, furious about a film produced in the United States denigrating the prophet Muhammad, ransacked the US embassy in Tunisia. This was days after US ambassador to Libya, Chris Stevens, had been killed during an attack on the US embassy compound in Benghazi, Libya. The protestors in Tunisia started fires, broke windows, destroyed property, and raised a black flag indicative of a connection to al-Qaeda that read, "No God but God and Muhammed is his Prophet." They also set fire to the nearby American school. No Americans were hurt, but in restoring order, security forces killed four protestors and injured dozens. Both President Marzouki, a secular member of the ruling Troika, and Rachid Ghannouchi expressed shock at the incident.[46]

Second, on February 6, 2012, Chokri Belaid, secretary-general of the Nationalist Party and leader of the left-wing secular coalition, Alliance of the Popular Front, was assassinated in front of his home.[47] Third, on July 25, 2012, a second secular opposition leader, Mohammed Brahmi, was assassinated. He was also killed outside his home; shot fourteen times in front of his wife and children by two assassins on a motorbike.[48] Mass protests followed both assassinations.

Fourth, jihadi Salafis waged battles against the security forces and the military along the western border of Algeria and in isolated other areas. Salafis, on occasion, also used violence against fellow Tunisians for violating what they considered to be Islamic norms in terms of dress, the consumption of alcohol, mixed dancing, and other matters. In a related vein, groups calling themselves the Leagues for the Protection of the Revolution cropped up in many neighborhoods. Some Tunisians accused them of being Ennahda's private militias.[49]

The violence by radical Islamists, led by the group Ansar al-Sharia and its leader, Abu Ayyad, led to a crackdown by the Troika and a new willingness to confront both jihadi and scripturalist Salafis who acted against the emerging democracy.[50] In the spirit of the twin tolerations, once challenged, Ennahda also backed down on changing Tunisia's liberal personal status law and removed language from a draft constitution that identified women as complementary, rather than equal to men.

While religious extremists tested Ennahda's commitment to a democratic bargain with secularists, secular political parties wavered on the twin tolerations as well. By the end of 2012, secular political parties (those outside the Troika alliance with Ennahda) had regrouped from their poor showing in the NCA elections. They had formed a big-tent secularist political party, Nidaa Tounes (Call for Tunisia), led by elder statesman Caid Essebsi. Nidaa Tounes became the Troika's primary opposition. Witnessing a military coup against an elected Islamist political party in Egypt in July 2013, supporters of Nidaa Tounes and other secularists mobilized in the streets to urge the Tunisian military to do the same. However, they were never able to engage enough Tunisians to push a reluctant military in that direction.

Still, as the one-year deadline to produce and ratify a new constitution passed, the Troika was under increasing pressure to dissolve the NCA and step down in favor of a technocratic government. Witnessing growing instability and the impasse between Ennahda and Nidaa Tounes dragging on, the powerful Tunisian General Labour Union (UGTT) and three civil society partners began holding informal talks with both sides about proposals to end the political deadlock.

In early October 2013, the National Dialogue Quartet, as these four organizations called their group, drafted their own proposal to resolve the political crisis.[51] The mediators produced a triphased road map agreement signed by Ennahda and major opposition parties.[52] In the first phase, negotiators agreed to form a nonpartisan government including a new prime minister, after which the Ennahda coalition would formally step down. In the second phase, the negotiators were required to form a commission of experts to finalize the draft of a new constitution. The 2011 NCA was required to adopt the new charter by a two-thirds majority. In the third phase, the negotiators and NCA members agreed to form an independent electoral body tasked with organizing new legislative and presidential elections by drafting and adopting a new electoral law and setting the dates for the new elections.

There were bumps in the road, but the National Dialogue Quartet's plan resolved the crisis. It took nearly two months to appoint a new prime minister. The minister of industry, Mehdi Jomaa, took over that role. The deadline for a new constitution was pushed back to January 14, 2014. The constitution was finally passed on January 26, relieving the nationwide political tensions caused by the prolonged stalemate.[53] For its efforts, the National Dialogue Quartet won the 2015 Nobel Peace Prize.

Under the new constitution, Tunisia has successfully conducted free and fair elections for parliament and president. In the October 26, 2014, parliamentary elections, the secular coalition party, Nidaa Tounes, gained a plurality of votes, winning 85 seats in the 217-seat chamber. Ennahda won 69 seats. The next most successful party, the Free Patriotic Union, won 16 seats. Nidaa Tounes selected Habib Essid as prime minister. After pressure from Ennahda for a unity government, Essid composed a government of Nidaa Tounes, the liberals of Afek Tounes, and several independents, along with the token participation of Ennahda. Among the twenty-four government ministers and fifteen state secretaries, nine were women.[54] Ennahda was accorded two secretaries of state as well as the Ministry of Women, Family, and Children.[55] Prime Minister Essid promised "work and nothing but work on the country's economic and security problems."[56]

When the government took power in 2015, it marked an important point in Tunisia's transition as it represented two changeovers in power through elections (from the Ennahda-led, Islamist-dominated Troika to the secular Nidaa Tounes). For some analysts, two turnovers in power alone represent a consolidated democracy.[57] Caid Essebsi of Nidaa Tounes won the presidential elections held one month after the parliamentary elections, carrying 55 percent of the vote in a runoff against the Troika's former president, Moncef Marzouki (44%).

Military coups pose the greatest threat to democratic transitions. However, the history of military-civilian relations in Tunisia makes that a relatively remote possibility. The state of civilian control over the military in Tunisia can be evaluated for the Bourguiba era (1956–87), the Ben Ali era (1987–2011), and the transitional period to date. Under President Habib Bourguiba, civilians had more control over the military than perhaps in any other Arab state.[58] During the nationalist movement to end French colonialism, the military followed the policies of Bourguiba and other civilian leaders within the Neo-Destour party. As president, Bourguiba conscientiously created a military establishment supportive of his secular, republican, civilian-led nationalist ideals.[59]

Under Bourguiba's leadership, the Tunisian military also developed into a nonpraetorian, highly professional body of officers and men.[60] During that era the military was described as an establishment "dedicated single-mindedly to defense of the national territory from all enemies foreign and domestic."[61] Even in terms of national defense, Bourguiba kept the military small and relied on former colonial power France for military advice and national defense.[62]

Bourguiba used the constitution of 1959 and his leverage as nationalist hero and leader of the state party to institutionalize civilian control over leadership selection and policy making. The military answered to the authority of civilians controlling the state through the intermediary of a civilian minister of defense.[63] Bourguiba disenfranchised the officer and enlisted corps by denying their right of political association, even within the ruling party.[64] The military never took part in making political decisions under Bourguiba until the crisis-laden period at the end of his rule.[65]

Involvement in internal security can indicate the politicization of the military. However, Bourguiba denied the military a primary role in the suppression of internal dissent, relying instead on the separate forces of a gendarmerie, a national guard, and a special paramilitary Brigade of Public

Order.[66] In 1978 and 1984, Bourguiba did command the army to restore order after nationwide civil disturbances, but they did so under his orders. Both times, the generals were said to have resented assuming police functions and were happy to have their men return to barracks as soon as the crises passed.[67]

In sum, for most of the period when Habib Bourguiba led Tunisia, civilian dominance of the military was manifest in all important decision-making areas. However, Tunisia went through a protracted and in-depth crisis in the mid-1980s, which threatened the stability of the country and opened the door for greater military intervention in politics. The economy stagnated for most of the early 1980s. The powerful UGTT organized a destabilizing national strike.[68] Qaddafi tried to foment a revolution in the southern mining town of Gafsa.[69] An Islamist movement became explicitly political and attacked the regime on multiple levels.[70] To control growing social chaos, Bourguiba relied heavily on his head of internal security, minister of interior at the time, General Zine El Abidine Ben Ali. In particular, Bourguiba ordered the harsh repression of Islamists. By 1986, the conflict between Islamists and the state appeared to be moving toward civil war. In early 1987, Bourguiba named Ben Ali prime minister. On November 7, 1987, Ben Ali overthrew Bourguiba in a bloodless coup.[71]

During the 1980s, some speculated that the Tunisian military as an institution might be on a path from military coup to taking over the Tunisian state.[72] "There was a risk that senior officers would begin to exercise surveillance over important civilian posts and then simply ease the civilians from authority."[73] However, Ben Ali's coup did not lead to the military as an institution taking over the state. He turned out to be a military officer with political ambition who attained presidential power, acted as a civilian in power, and continued Bourguiba's policy of keeping the armed forces on the political sidelines.[74] Moreover, the military played an important political role in Ben Ali's ouster. Army chief of staff, General Rachid Ammar, used his troops to prevent Ben Ali's security forces from violently suppressing the Arab Spring's mass uprising.[75]

The new era of democratic transition, which began on January 14, 2011, has provided many opportunities for the Tunisian military to play an important role in politics, but so far it has maintained the tradition of civilian control of political decision-making. After the revolution, it moved back to the sidelines as soon as an interim civilian government took over the state. The initial interim government was composed of many members from the Ben Ali regime. Mass protests returned to force a change. A second interim government with more popular support took power without the resort to military intervention. The military also returned to barracks as quickly as possible when transition governments ordered it to deal with internal security threats. Finally, it resisted calls for a coup when the Troika failed to produce a constitution within its mandated deadline and when a military coup took place in Egypt during that country's transition.

Democratic Consolidation: Socioeconomic Pacts

While striking political and military pacts insured significant regime change in Tunisia, there remain challenges to socioeconomic and security sector pacts that can reverse progress. As much as it was a call for democracy and human rights, the Arab Spring in Tunisia and elsewhere reflected an intense and widespread desire for better economic opportunities and socioeconomic justice. Socioeconomic pacts entail inclusive policy making to legitimize democratic transitions.[76] To succeed, socioeconomic pacts also have to be based on policies that respond to the demands of mobilized citizens without compromising the viability of the economy:

> Chances for consolidating [political democracies] may be raised or damaged by the quality of their economic policies. If they are to have any chance of success, such policies must meet two requirements which pull in contradictory directions. One is that they have the consistency necessary for a viable economy, able to function without constant crises and to achieve some economic growth. That requirement implies restraints: the ability to limit claims that would seriously damage efficiency or outrun productive capacity. The other is the ability to answer enough of the expectations of the politically aware groups in society to gain and hold their acceptance.[77]

Inclusive policy making offers the best chance to forge economic policies during a democratic transition that to some degree meet demands while maintaining economic viability. Typically, this takes place in corporatist bargaining among labor, employers, and the government.[78] Without it, during transitions, which are usually periods of economic crises, a cycle of strikes and demands followed by government capitulation takes hold. This extends the economic crisis period and stymies economic growth.

A socioeconomic pact between labor, employers, and the government in Tunisia was signed in January 2013.[79] Unfortunately, the political stalemate at the time between Islamist and secular parties suspended its implementation. The early 2014 democratic pact among Tunisia's political parties that was engineered by the National Dialogue Quartet can serve as a model for a National Socioeconomic Pact that brings representatives of all major socioeconomic groups into the economic policy–making process.[80] In fact, this is currently under discussion within Tunisian policy circles.[81]

In the meantime, five years after the beginning of the Arab Spring, severe episodes of social unrest continue in Tunisia, and the country remains in an economic downturn. Strikes, demonstrations, a steep rise in crime, and the state's inability to provide adequate security have caused significant disruption in economic activity. It will likely take four to five years for GDP and employment to reach precrisis levels.[82] In the meantime, shortages of basic products have become widespread. In addition to frequent electricity and water outages, inflation is very high (officially around 6.4%), and infrastructure is deteriorating.[83] The country has become practically dependent on large external loans and foreign aid to support its transition, without which parts of the population could face starvation.[84]

In May 2012, the interim government proposed the "year of white" or year of no wage increases.[85] The secretary-general of the UGTT, Hussein bin Haj Nasr, categorically rejected the proposal on the behalf of organized working people and expressed UGTT commitment to social negotiations and increases in wages.[86] He added that the government should recover the money looted from the country under Ben Ali instead of asking the poor and vulnerable to bear all the sacrifices.[87]

Instead of a year of white, unions under the control of the UGTT used strikes to obtain wage increases in many sectors—from garbage collectors to most of the private sector workforce.[88] In 2011, the Tunisian government reached an agreement with trade unions and employers to boost wages for public and private sector employees by 4.7 percent.[89] These wage increases have been decried by some Tunisian economists, who argue that the government has responded to the demands of strikers by granting huge salary increases, leading to widening fiscal deficits and overseas borrowing to finance its wage bill.[90] In another measure negotiated by the UGTT and decried by some economists, 350, 000 temporary workers secured permanent contracts.[91] Critics claim that these policies made UGTT unskilled workers too expensive and inefficient to hire. In addition, they argue that the government has prioritized social spending at a level that some view as ruinous to economic growth.[92]

Reflecting tension in economic policy making, the governor of the Central Bank in Tunisia, Mustapha Kamel Nabli, was fired for rejecting interference in the making of monetary policy.[93] The government desired more progrowth policies to create much-needed jobs, while the former World Bank head economist for the Middle East insisted on pursuing a strict monetary policy.[94] In July 2012, Tunisia's finance minister, Houcine Dimassi, resigned over disagreements with the government led by Islamist Prime Minister Hamadi Jebali on its economic, monetary, and social policies.[95] Upon his resignation, he stated that while he was attempting to maintain a balance in public finances, most members of the government were following an electoralist policy that was ballooning government spending.[96] Most stridently, he criticized proposals to compensate partisans of the ruling Ennahda party who had suffered under the Ben Ali regime and martyrs of the revolution who had died in the uprising that unseated him in January 2011.[97]

In January 2016, the reactive cycle of demand and commitment reached absurd proportions. Job protests in Kasserine led to protests in several other towns.[98] In response, the finance minister, Slim Shaker, promised five thousand new government jobs in Kasserine.[99] After other towns demanded the same, the promise was retracted.[100]

The sustained economic crisis in Tunisia may yet bring labor, employers, and the government together to forge an economic policy that provides enough benefits to maintain the support of the politically mobilized, while limiting claims that seriously damage economic efficiency or outrun productive capacity. Policy makers involved in discussions along these lines view the employers' association, UTICA, as vulnerable enough to collaborate with government and labor in this regard, but they feel less able to convince labor to commit to compromises, especially at a time when the UGTT is powerful.[101]

Democratic Consolidation: Security Sector Pact

In Tunisia, judicial and security sector reforms are necessary for transitional justice to succeed and to establish the rule of law and protection from human rights abuses that are hallmarks of consolidated democracies. Under Ben Ali, there was no separation of powers. The executive dominated the judicial branch. The constitutional courts conferred misleading constitutional legitimacy to regime projects that limited electoral competition and made Ben Ali de facto president for life. The courts also enabled vast corruption and, instead of delivering justice, facilitated unlawful detentions and other human rights violations that sustained authoritarian rule.

Reform in the judiciary system has been slow, and high levels of corruption persist. The judiciary still employs many old regime figures—some of whom are resistant to change—and it is still commonly viewed as an instrument of repression. The 2014 constitution paved the way for reform by calling for the establishment of a new Supreme Judicial Council and Constitutional Court by the end of 2015.[102] As an independent body, the Supreme Judicial Council (SJC) was designed to decide on judicial appointments and promotions and to advise lawmakers on any reforms that concern the judicial framework.[103]

According to the draft law, to support the independence of the judiciary, a majority of the members of the council would be elected by the judges themselves, rather than by the head of state.[104] The SJC, the president, and the parliament would each name a third of the new Constitutional Court's members.[105] Critics claim that the SJC still gives the executive branch too much power to be considered independent.[106]

Once formed, the Constitutional Court will face many difficult tasks. The constitution contains a number of conflicting articles, and the court will have to harmonize existing Tunisian law with the principles of the new constitution.[107] It will also have to determine the legal role of a number of international treaties that Tunisia has ratified but has not, or has only partly, applied in practice, such as the Convention on the Elimination of all Forms of Discrimination Against Women.[108]

The court will have to address an antiterrorism law that affects the balance between freedoms and security. The constitution guarantees gender equality, but the existing Personal Status Law does not.[109] Finally, it has been difficult to establish a professional and independent judiciary outside the capital as judges and lawyers prefer not to work in the hinterland.[110]

Under Ben Ali, the security services, like the judiciary, protected an authoritarian order dominated by a ruling clique and narrow patronage network that controlled the state and divided its resources. To consolidate democracy, the mission of the security sector has to be redefined from a brutal instrument of internal repression to a professional and neutral public authority that protects citizens' rights and safety. To date, progress has been slow, raising the specter of an avenue for the return to dictatorial rule.

The last five years of transition have been characterized by a head-on fight between the Internal Security Forces (ISF) and the political class.[111]

Many Tunisians portray prospects for security sector reform as a struggle between political forces with democratic ambitions and a domestic security apparatus with authoritarian tendencies.[112] The military, on the other hand, is widely viewed as supportive of the people and democracy since it was perceived to have refused to shoot on the crowds during the 2010–11 revolution.[113]

Early in the transition, on March 7, 2011, the Ministry of Interior announced plans for changes that would begin the process of reorienting the mission of the security services. It pledged to end political police functions whether at the level of structure, mission, or practice. It abolished the State Security Department, whose "political police" spied on and harassed citizens under Ben Ali; and it publicly committed to enforcing the rule of law and respecting freedoms and civil rights.

However, the security forces want to undertake their transformation to a "republican police," independent of oversight by political institutions.[114] They tend to view politicians as incompetent on security matters and tend to deny the right and obligation of government to assert its control or to hold recalcitrant officers accountable.[115] Many security service members believe they are the only ones qualified to handle security matters, all the more so as they consider themselves the primary targets of jihadi Salafis and social protests.[116] In contrast, many self-proclaimed democratic forces dismiss the security forces as supporters of dictatorship and of counterrevolution.[117]

Notably, Tunisia's parliament, whose sessions began in late 2014, includes two committees that in theory have oversight over the internal security forces: the (permanent) Organization of the Armed Forces Committee and the (special) Security and Defense Committee.[118] Still, many people were alarmed by the recent submission of a draft law granting impunity to the internal security apparatus and mandating five years in prison for those who insult its morale.[119]

Rather than fighting for democratic accountability and the rule of law, the political class has been accused of politicizing the security sector. Some members of the security forces and secular politicians accused Ennahda, during its time in power, of facilitating the penetration of the Interior Ministry by jihadi Salafis.[120] The current, more secular government, with its members' ties to Ben Ali's regime, has been accused of facilitating the return of the Ministry of Interior of old. Some claim that the Ministry of Interior is becoming a fiefdom that the main political parties—Ennahda,

Nidaa Tounes, the Front Populaire, and the CPR—hope to conquer and not reform.[121] In the eyes of the security forces, the language of revolution and democratic transition came to symbolize destabilizing, partisan power struggles.[122]

Under Ben Ali, the Ministry of Interior also preserved authoritarian rule at the local level by exercising its legal authority over regional administration. The twenty-four Tunisian governorates and their further subdivided municipalities applied their policies under the ministry's supervision.[123] The 2014 constitution requires direct elections for local representatives. These elections are viewed as essential for entrenching democracy at the local level and for improving the quality and equity of public services through local-level decision-making.[124] The Ministry of Interior is involved in drafting the new law for municipal and regional elections. Through this process, some stakeholders claim that the ministry is attempting to maintain its prerogatives in local areas.[125]

The security sector has issues beyond convincing security personnel and the political class to jointly undertake security sector reforms that support citizens' safety, democratic accountability, and a neutral role for public authorities. The management and capacities of the internal security services are worse than they were under Ben Ali's dictatorship.[126] The dysfunction and inadequacies of the security apparatus have been laid bare by ever more devastating jihadi attacks.[127] Between March and June 2015, the Bardo Museum attack in Tunis and the slaughter on the beach of Port el Kantaoui in the heart of the Sousse touristic zone caused the deaths of sixty-two people, including fifty-nine foreign tourists, making Tunisia's security a matter of national and international concern.[128] Regional turmoil and Tunisia's porous borders with Algeria and Libya have facilitated the flow of arms and religious extremists in both directions.[129]

Tunisia's economy is heavily dependent on tourism, and the jihadi violence has pushed the government toward favoring security over establishing civil rights and democratic accountability. Parliament passed a bill to bolster security that includes provisions that broadly defines terrorism and authorize the death penalty for acts of terrorism.[130] In the bill, detention policy is identical to that in the Ben Ali period.[131] Mosques are being heavily monitored. These measures may contribute to the religious extremism that they are trying to address. They may also bolster the power of the members of the security sector inclined toward maintaining old dictatorial ways.

Conclusion

Tunisia has earned its place as the only Arab Spring success story. It has achieved significant regime change toward democracy. Its greatest achievement is forging a political pact to support democracy between secularist and Islamist forces that can be a model for the region. It also has kept its military out of politics. Still, socioeconomic challenges and a need to remake Ben Ali's police state through security sector reforms remain as vulnerabilities to authoritarian regression.

STEPHEN J. KING is Associate Professor of Government at Georgetown University. He is author of *Liberalization Against Democracy: The Local Politics of Economic Reform in Tunisia* (Bloomington: Indiana University Press, 2003) and *The New Authoritarianism in the Middle East and North Africa* (Bloomington: Indiana University Press, 2009).

Notes

1. The core source and wellspring of the transition paradigm is Guillermo O'Donnell and Philippe C. Schmitter, *Transitions from Authoritarian Rule: Tentative Conclusions about Uncertain Democracies* (Baltimore: Johns Hopkins University Press, 1986).

2. Ibid.

3. Ibid.

4. Juan Linz and Alfred Stepan, *Problems of Democratic Transition and Consolidation: Southern Europe, South America, and Post-Communist Europe* (Baltimore: Johns Hopkins University Press, 1996).

5. Interview with author, March 2011.

6. This was the most common answer given to questions about the genesis of the revolution in interviews conducted in Tunis and Sidi Bouzid, the cradle of the Tunisian Revolution.

7. Tunisian journalist in interview with author, March 2011.

8. Al Wasat Al Tunisiya, "Al Sijn 10 Sanawāt Li Qādat 'Al Tamarrod Al Mosallah Wa Al Shaghab' Fī Qafsa," accessed December 26, 2014, http://www.turess.com/alwasat/12619.

9. Tunisian journalist in interview with author, March 2011.

10. No literature that I am aware of asserts the causal role of galvanizing, solidaristic martyrdom. The power of social media and the internet received some attention before the Arab Spring.

11. Tunisian activist in interview with author, March 2011.

12. John Pollock, "Streetbook: How Egyptian and Tunisian Youth Hacked the Arab Spring," *Technology Review*, September/October 2011.

13. Ibid.

14. Ibid.

15. Ibid.

16. Ibid.

17. Ibid.

18. Ibid

19. Ibid

20. Ibid.

21. Al Shourouk, "Al Faqīd Zouhair Al Yahyaoui: Sāhib Mawqi' Tunezine Az'aja Ben 'Ali Shakhsiyan Wa Kāna Awwal Dahiyyah Li Shurtat Al Ma'lūmātiyah," 2011, accessed December 26, 2014, http://www.turess.com/alchourouk/193288.

22. Much of the following comes from an interview with the author of an early member of Nawaat.

23. Nawaat, "Tūnus Fī Al Taqrīr Al Thānī 'An Hurriyat Al Internet Fī Al 'Ālam Al 'Arabī," December 13, 2006, accessed December 26, 2014, http://nawaat.org/portail/2006/12/13 /rapport-tunisie-libertes-internet-monde-arabe/.

24. "Orange Aurait Monnayé Sa Présence En Tunisie Avec Le Clan Ben Ali," *Le Monde*, March 3, 2011, accessed December 26, 2014, http://www.lemonde.fr/afrique/article/2011/03/03 /orange-aurait-monnaye-sa-presence-en-tunisie-avec-le-clan-ben-ali_1488118_3212.html.

25. Among the most prominent were Fatima Arabica, Slim Amamou, Yassine Ayari, Malek Kadhraoui, and Riadh Guerfali. Fatima Arabica's blog was mainly literary; however, she was arrested in 2009, possibly to send a message to other bloggers.

26. Citizens in Sidi Bouzid, interviewed by the author in April 2012, offered both accounts.

27. The author was unable to verify that degree of intentionality to Mohamed Bouazizi's act of self-immolation.

28. Tunisian activist in interview with author, March 2011.

29. Yasmine Ryan, "How Tunisia's Revolution Began," Al Jazeera, 2011, accessed December 26, 2014, http://www.aljazeera.com/indepth/features/2011/01/2011126121815985483 .html.

30. Guillermo O'Donnell and Philippe C. Schmitter, *Transitions from Authoritarian Rule: Tentative Conclusions about Uncertain Democracies* (Baltimore: Johns Hopkins University Press, 1986), 40–45.

31. Michael Burton, Richard Gunther, and John Higley, eds., *Elites and Democratic Consolidation in Latin America and Southern Europe* (Cambridge: Cambridge University Press, 1992), 13.

32. Ibid.

33. Ibid., 39–40.

34. Ibid.

35. "Al Majlis Al Watanī Al Ta'sīsī Fī Tūnus" [The Founding National Council in Tunisia], Al Jazeera, 2011, accessed December 26, 2014, http://www.aljazeera.net/news/reportsandinter views/2013/9/17/%D8%A7%D9%84%D9%85%D8%AC%D9%84%D8%B3-%D8%A7%D9%84% D9%88%D8%B7%D9%86%D9%8A-%D8%A7%D9%84%D8%AA%D8%A3%D8%B3%D9%8A% D8%B3%D9%8A-%D9%81%D9%8A-%D8%AA%D9%88%D9%86%D8%B3.

36. Al Mogaz, "Istithna' Dīmoqrātī Tahtha Wat'at 'Istiqtāb 'Ilmānī 'Islāmī" [Democratic exception under secular-Islamist recruitment pressure], 2013, accessed December 26, 2014, http://almogaz.com/news/politics/2014/11/25/1744146.

37. "Al Nahdha Turachihu Al Jebali Ra'isan Lil Hukūmah" [Al Nahdha nominates Al Jebali to head the government], Al Jazeera, 2011, accessed December 27, 2014, http://www

.aljazeera.net/news/arabic/2011/10/27/%D8%A7%D9%84%D9%86%D9%87%D8%B6%D8%A9
-%D8%AA%D8%B1%D8%B4%D8%AD-%D8%A7%D9%84%D8%AC%D8%A8%D8%A7%D9%8
4%D9%8A-%D8%B1%D8%A6%D9%8A%D8%B3%D8%A7-%D9%84%D9%84%D8%AD%D9%8
3%D9%88%D9%85%D8%A9.

38. Ibid.

39. Yasmine Ryan, "Building a Tunisian Model for Arab Democracy," Al Jazeera, 2012,
http://www.aljazeera.com/indepth/features/2012/11/2012112714384598012.html.

40. Ibid.

41. Ibid.

42. Ibid.

43. Ibid.

44. "Ghannouchi Retracts Previous Statements on Salafi Militants," *Arab News*,
September 27, 2012.

45. "Ennahda Calls Salafis to Work Within the Country's Legal Framework," *Arab News*,
April 3, 2012.

46. Moncef Marzouki, "Renaissance Unable to Rule Tunisia?," *Arab News*, January 24,
2013.

47. "Man Qatala Chouki Belaid," Al Jazeera, accessed December 27, 2014, http://www
.aljazeera.net/programs/black-box/2014/10/20/%D8%A7%D9%84%D8%B5%D9%86%
D8%AF%D9%88%D9%82-%D8%A7%D9%84%D8%A3%D8%B3%D9%88%D8%AF-%D9%
8A%D9%81%D8%AA%D8%AD-%D9%85%D9%84%D9%81-%D8%A7%D8%BA%D8%
AA%D9%8A%D8%A7%D9%84-%D8%A7%D9%84%D9%85%D8%B9%D8%A7%D8%B1%
D8%B6-%D8%A7%D9%84%D8%AA%D9%88%D9%86%D8%B3%D9%8A-%D8%B4%
D9%83%D8%B1%D9%8A-%D8%A8%D9%84%D8%B9%D9%8A%D8%AF.

48. Al Shourouk, "Man Huwa Al Shahīd Mohammed Brahmi," 2013, accessed December
27, 2014, http://www.alchourouk.com/13612/566/1/12/%D9%85%D9%86-%D9%87%D9%88
-%D8%A7%D9%84%D8%B4%D9%87%D9%8A%D8%AF-%D9%85%D8%AD%D9%85%D8%
AF-%D8%A7%D9%84%D8%A8%D8%B1%D8%A7%D9%87%D9%85%D9%8A-%D8%9F.html.

49. Safa Belghith and Ian Patel, "League for the Protection of the Revolution," accessed
September 2, 2013, http://www.opendemocracy.net/safa-belghith-ian-patel/leagues-for
-protection-of-tunisian-revolution.

50. "Ansar al-Shari'a Terrorist Group," *Herald Sun*, accessed September 2, 2013, http://
www.heraldsun.com.au/news/breaking-news/ansar-al-sharia-terrorist-group-tunisia/story
-fnioxqll-1226705379025.

51. The proposal is available at https://www.facebook.com/notes/ugtt-%D8%A7%D9%
84%D8%A7%D8%AA%D8%AD%D8%A7%D8%AF-%D8%A7%D9%84%D8%B9%D8%
A7%D9%85-%D8%A7%D9%84%D8%AA%D9%88%D9%86%D8%B3%D9%8A-%D9%84%D9%
84%D8%B4%D8%BA%D9%84-page-officielle/initiative-des-organisations-de-la-soci%C3%
A9t%C3%A9-civile-pour-la-r%C3%A9solution-de-la-crise/530662090341554.

52. "Facts on Tunisia Roadmap to End Crisis," *News24*, October 5, 2013, http://www
.news24.com/Africa/News/Facts-on-Tunisia-roadmap-to-end-crisis-20131005.

53. Assabah, "Mabrūk Li Tūnus: Al Musādaqa 'Ala Al Dustūr Fī Qirā'atin 'Ūlā"
[Congratulations Tunisia: A first take on the constitution's approval], 2014, accessed
December 30, 2014, http://www.assabahnews.tn/article/80547/%D9%85%D8%A8%D8%
B1%D9%88%D9%83-%D9%84%D8%AA%D9%88%D9%86%D8%B3-%D8%A7%D9%84%
D9%85%D8%B5%D8%A7%D8%AF%D9%82%D8%A9-%D8%B9%D9%84%D9%89-%D8

%A7%D9%84%D8%AF%D8%B3%D8%AA%D9%88%D8%B1-%D9%81%D9%8A
-%D9%82%D8%B1%D8%A7%D8%A1%D8%A9-%D8%A7%D9%88%D9%84%D9%89.

54. "Ennahda Shut Out of New Tunisian Government," Al Jazeera, January 23, 2015, http://www.aljazeera.com/news/middleeast/2015/01/ennahda-shut-tunisian-government-150123140936298.html.

55. "The Tunisian Government Approved by Parliament," *New Arab*, February 5, 2015, https://www.alaraby.co.uk/english/news/2015/2/5/new-tunisian-government-approved-by-parliament.

56. Ibid.

57. Samuel Huntington, "Democracy's Third Wave," *Journal of Democracy* 2, no. 2 (1991), 348–51.

58. Ibid.

59. Colonel Boubaker Ben Kraiem, "Bourguiba Et L'Armée Tunisienne: Les Raisons D'Une Méfiance," Moncefelmateri.com, accessed December 30, 2014, http://www.moncefelmateri.com/bourguiba-et-larmee-tunisienne-les-raisons-dune-mefiance/.

60. L. B. Ware, "The Role of the Tunisian Military in the Post-Bourguiba Era," *Middle East Journal* 39, no. 1 (Winter 1985): 37.

61. Ibid.

62. Boubacar N'Diaye, "Ivory Coast's Civilian Control Strategies 1961–1968: A Critical Assessment," *Journal of Political Military Sociology* 28 (Winter 2000): 247.

63. Ware, "Role of the Tunisian Military," 37.

64. Ibid.

65. Zoltan Barany, "Comparing the Arab Revolts: The Role of the Military," Journal of Democracy 22, no. 4 (2011), 24–35.

66. Ware, "Role of the Tunisian Military," 37

67. Barany, "Comparing the Arab Revolts," 27.

68. Echaab, "Min Tārīkh Al 'Ittihād Al 'Aām Al Tūnusī Lil Shughl 'Azmat Sanat 1978," 2010, accessed December 30, 2014, http://www.turess.com/echaab/12224.

69. Attounissia, "Al Yawm Dhikrā 'Ahdāth Qafsa," 2013, accessed December 30, 2014, http://www.attounissia.com.tn/details_article.php?t=41&a=80471.

70. Elbaki Hermassi, *L'etat Tunisien Et Le Mouvement Islamiste*, 1st ed. (Annuaire de l'Afrique du Nord, 1989), accessed December 30, 2014, http://aan.mmsh.univ-aix.fr/Pdf/AAN-1989-28_19.pdf.

71. Al Hiwar, "Asrār 'Inqilāb Ben Ali Alā Bourqiba," 2011, accessed December 30, 2014, http://www.turess.com/alhiwar/16646.

72. Ware, "Role of the Tunisian Military," 27–47.

73. Ibid., 41.

74. Barany, "Comparing the Arab Revolts," 27.

75. "Al General Rashid Ammar Yarfudhu 'Awāmir Ben Ali Wa Yanhāzu Ilā Al Sha'ab Al Tūnusī," Laha Online, 2011, accessed December 30, 2014, http://www.lahaonline.com/articles/view/%D8%A7%D9%84%D8%AC%D9%86%D8%B1%D8%A7%D9%84-%D8%B1%D8%B4%D9%8A%D8%AF-%D8%B9%D9%85%D8%A7%D8%B1-%D9%8A%D8%B1%D9%81%D8%B6-%D8%A3%D9%88%D8%A7%D9%85%D8%B1-%D8%A8%D9%86-%D8%B9%D9%84%D9%8A-%D9%88%D9%8A%D9%86%D8%AD%D8%A7%D8%B2-%D9%84%D9%84%D8%B4%D8%B9%D8%A8-%D8%A7%D9%84%D8%AA%D9%88%D9%86%D8%B3%D9%8A/37897.htm.

76. O'Donnell and Schmitter, *Transitions from Authoritarian Rule*, 45–7.

77. John Sheahan, "Economic Policies and the Prospects for Successful Transition from Authoritarian Rule in Latin America," in *Transitions from Authoritarian Rule: Comparative Perspectives*, ed. Guillermo O'Donnell, Philippe Schmitter, and Laurence Whitehead (Baltimore: Johns Hopkins University Press, 1986), 154.

78. O'Donnell and Schmitter, *Transitions from Authoritarian Rule*.

79. "Tunisie—Signature Du Contrat Social Au Bardo Entre Le Gouvernement, L'UGTT Et L'UTICA," 2013, accessed December 31, 2014, http://www.businessnews.com.tn /Tunisie---Signature-du-contrat-social-au-Bardo-entre-le-gouvernement,-l%20UGTT -et-l%20UTICA,520,35648,3.

80. Réalités, "Le Contrat Social, Un Projet Économique Et Social," April 21, 2014, accessed December 31, 2014, http://www.realites.com.tn/2014/04/21/le-contrat-social-un-projet -economique-et-social/.

81. Former government minister, Hedi Larbi, in interview with the author, April 2016, Washington, DC.

82. Padamja Khandelwal and Agustin Roitman, "The Economics of Political Transitions," IMF Working Paper WP/13/69 (March 2013), 1.

83. Noureddine Krichene, "The Arab Spring in Turmoil," *Asia Times Online*, accessed September 20, 2013, http://www.atimes.com/atimes/Middle_East/MID-01-120713.html.

84. Ibid.

85. "Tunisia: A New Confrontation between the Government and the Labor Union," *Arabic News*, May 19, 2012.

86. Ibid.

87. Ibid.

88. Noureddine Krichene, "The Arab Spring in Turmoil," *Asia Times Online*, accessed September 20, 2013, http://www.atimes.com/atimes/Middle_East/MID-01-120713.html.

89. Jaridat al Riyadh, "Tūnus: 'Ihtimāmāt Mutabadilah Bayna Al Hukūmah Al Mu'aqatah Wa 'Ittihād Al Shughl Hawla Ziyādat Al Ujūr," 2012, accessed December 31, 2014, http://www .alriyadh.com/737387.

90. Ibid.

91. Mohamed-Salah Omri, "The Upcoming General Strike in Tunisia: A Historical Perspective," *OpenDemocracy*, December 12, 2012, http://www.opendemocracy.net /mohamed-salah-omri/upcoming-general-strike-in-tunisia-historical-perspective.

92. Ibid.

93. Bouazza Ben Baouazza, "Tunisia Assembly Backs Central Bank Head Firing," *Huffington Post*, July 18, 2012, accessed September 20, 2013, http://www.huffingtonpost.com /huff-wires/20120718/ml-tunisia-central-bank.

94. Ibid.

95. Nizar Bahloul, "Tunisian Finance Minister Quits, Warns of Economic Crisis," Al-Monitor 2012, accessed February 7, 2019, https://www.al-monitor.com/pulse/politics /2012/07/houcine-dimassi-tunisia-is-prepa.html.

96. Ibid.

97. Ibid.

98. "Tunisia Job Protests Echo Spark for Arab Uprising," *Financial Times*, January 20, 2015, http://www.ft.com/cms/s/0/5d5eaab2-bf86-11e5-a8c6-deeeb63d6d4b.html#axzz44oNZS8MN.

99. "Tunisia Minister Retracts Promise of 5,000 New Jobs as Curfew Imposed," *Middle East Eye*, January 22, 2016, http://www.middleeasteye.net/news/promise-5000-new-jobs -quell-tunisia-protests-was-communication-error-says-minister-519993482.

100. Ibid.

101. Former government minister, Hedi Larbi, in interview with the author, April 2016, Washington, DC.

102. Sarah Mersch, "Judicial Reforms in Tunisia," *Sada*, April 10, 2015, Carnegie Endowment for International Peace, http://carnegieendowment.org/sada/59746.

103. Ibid.

104. Ibid.

105. Ibid.

106. Human Rights Watch, "Tunisia: Law Falls Short on Judicial Independence," June 2, 2015, https://www.hrw.org/news/2015/06/02/tunisia-law-falls-short-judicial-independence.

107. Ibid.

108. Ibid.

109. Ibid.

110. Ibid.

111. International Crisis Group, "Reform and Security Strategy in Tunisia," Middle East and North Africa Report, no. 161 (July 2015).

112. Ibid.

113. Ibid., 14.

114. Ibid., 9.

115. Ibid.

116. Ibid.

117. Ibid., 13.

118. Ibid., 19.

119. Ibid., 3.

120. "Jihadists Succeed in Penetrating the Tunisian Security Services," *Arabic News*, April 25, 2013.

121. International Crisis Group, "Reform and Security Strategy in Tunisia," 17.

122. Ibid., 18.

123. Ibid.

124. International Foundation for Electoral Systems, "Building Tunisia's Legal Framework for Regional and Municipal Elections," February 16, 2016, http://www.ifes.org/news/building-tunisias-legal-framework-regional-and-municipal-elections.

125. Interviews by the author with municipal officials, spring 2015.

126. Karina Piser, "Tunisia's Counterterrorism Strategy Could Fuel Extremism," *World Politics Review*, July 24, 2015, http://www.worldpoliticsreview.com/trend-lines/16312/tunisia-s-counterterrorism-strategy-could-fuel-extremism.

127. International Crisis Group, "Reform and Security Strategy in Tunisia," 3.

128. Ibid., 7.

129. Piser, "Tunisia's Counterterrorism Strategy."

130. International Crisis Group, "Reform and Security Strategy in Tunisia," 3.

131. Ibid.

9

SOCIAL AND EXTERNAL ORIGINS OF STATE COLLAPSE, THE CRISIS OF TRANSITION, AND STRATEGIES FOR POLITICAL AND INSTITUTIONAL RECONSTRUCTION IN LIBYA

Ali Abdullatif Ahmida

"You cannot take down a mountain with a hammer."
Libyan proverb

THE MAIN OBJECTIVES OF THIS CHAPTER ARE TO analyze the historical and structural causes of state collapse in Libya after the February 17 revolution in 2011 and the crisis of transition after 2013, and to propose strategies and models for political and institutional reconstruction in the short and long terms. These key questions will be investigated: First, what are the social origins of the postcolonial state and the factors behind the early success of the revolution and the toppling of the Qaddafi dictatorship, and why did the revolution result in a crisis of transition, the collapse of the state, and mini civil wars in many regions of the country despite the United Nations (UN)–brokered agreement in Morocco of December 2015? Second, who was responsible for the early success and then the crisis and failure after 2013, and what was the role of NATO, the United States, the European Union (EU), the Arab countries and Turkey, and the transnational organizations, especially al-Qaeda, Da'esh, and their local affiliates? Finally, what are the short- and long-term strategies for a new contract to fix the state, start reconciliation, and build institutions that bring peace and the rule of law for all Libyans?

I would like to make three main arguments in this paper. First, the crisis of the current state in Libya did not occur overnight but rather is structurally rooted in the contradictions of a modern Libyan state created under the shadow of settler colonialism. In addition, today's crisis was caused by the long process of undermining political and social institutions in the late 1980s and 1990s, especially with the reliance on informal institutions. Second, the leadership failed to tackle the security and arms challenge and to rebuild the army and the police forces after 2011. And third, the Obama administration, the EU, the regional Gulf States, Sudan, and Turkey played a negative role by supporting various factions and mitigating against compromise to reach agreement to disarm the militia groups and rebuild the army and police forces. These factors, combined with the lack of a clear vision that recognizes Libyan historical and cultural traditions and institutions, all contributed to the collapse of the state and the persisting crisis of transition. The problem of weak and fragmented institutions opened the doors for authoritarianism and the rise of strong leaders before 2011. Now, with the collapse of the state after 2013, there a temptation for a new strong authoritarian leader, which would explain the rise of General Khalifa Haftar in eastern Libya. This crisis created a Libya as a body without a head, or with three heads that are fighting each other. In short, the current crisis is one of transition, not of an old, segmented tribal society, as claimed by most Western media and policy experts of Libya.

It was not an inevitable crisis. Had the Obama administration, the EU, and the UN stopped the flow of money and arms to the various armed groups in both the east and the west, a compromise could have been reached, and the crisis could have been avoided. Instead, the two most powerful military groups became entrenched: the Libya Dawn political Islamist organization, led by the City of Misrata Brigade in the west, and the Libyan National Army, led by General Haftar in the eastern region. Consequently, without political compromise between the key regional forces, the crisis will continue, the state collapse may last longer, and Libya will become another Somalia or Iraq.

A good start to solving the problem would be an admission of responsibility by both the United States and the EU, followed by a reining in of their allies in the Gulf. Next, a firm action plan through the UN is needed to stop the flow of arms, money, and media wars between various factions in the country. Only then can one talk about institution building and national reconciliation. There is a need for a truth and reconciliation commission to heal society from the long injuries of war, repression, and the curse of revenge and retaliation, especially against the supporters of the Qaddafi regime. Severe killings and human rights abuses have taken place in all regions of the country. This chapter will address the following: the problem of institution building, the social and external origins of colonial and postcolonial Libya and the persistence of weak national institutions, the crisis of transition after 2011, and recommendations for future political and institutional reconstructions.

Defining the Problem in Libya

Two scholarly theoretical debates, on comparative social revolutions and on fixing failed states, have addressed the problem of state collapse and are relevant to the Libyan case. The literature on modern social revolutions helps explain the Libyan case from a comparative perspective. This literature evolved from theories on the national history of revolution, social mobilization and institution building, and the structure of revolution (which includes the impact of war and outside forces), which help us understand the stages of institution building after civil strife. Since the French Revolution in 1789, five stages have been recognized, including the crisis of the state, alienation, coalition building, the struggle over the future, and pragmatism. The twenty-first-century Arab Spring revolutions and uprisings have introduced new factors, such as the roles of social media, demography, youth, and transnational communication. While these factors are useful and highlighted in the analysis in these uprisings, the literature and the media coverage ignore the fact that revolutions have been defeated and appropriated by counterrevolutions.

The Libyan case is unique given that the revolutionary coalition succeeded in defeating the old regime, whereas in the other cases in Syria, Tunisia, Egypt, and Yemen, the old regime is still a factor in the conflict. On the negative side, the Libyan uprising started with the rebellion in the city of Benghazi, when it became militarized. The failure of all the leaders who managed the transition can be seen in their inability to disarm the militias and their becoming hostage to these interest groups. The number of these armed militias increased from 20,000 to 30,000 in 2011, to at least

200,000 to 250,000 in 2014. Consequently, despite the remarkable Libyan participation in the 2012 and 2014 national elections, elected officials, were unable to represent their constituencies because the armed groups did not recognize the results of those elections. I would argue that the failure that produced the crisis of transition and state collapse can be attributed to, first, the leaders who led the transition inside Libya, and, second, the United States and the EU, who stood by silently while regional powers and transnational extremist organizations filled the vacuum and blocked the Libyan democratic transition to state and institution building.

One has to keep in mind that the current analysis of the state's collapse and narrative of the simplistic invention of tribal ideology is misleading. It is an easy excuse to cover up the lack of knowledge and lack of a deeper understanding of the complexity of the Libyan social and historical reality. The tribal-based narrative fails to make sense of the participation of the Libyan people in the 2012 and 2014 elections and the fact that society has been managed remarkably well by the 113 elected municipalities in the absence of police, security, and armed forces. Again, a serious national dialogue and building a lasting constitution with good governance will not work without understanding the social origins of the state and public institutions based on Libyan political traditions, especially the strong values and culture of decentralization, regionalism, and local Ottoman and Sanussi public institutions. Above all, one must consider the Libyan living memory of the brutal genocide under Italian colonialism between 1929 and 1934, when sixty thousand Libyans died in horrific concentration camps before the Holocaust. Libyan independence under the Libyan Sanussi monarchy in 1951 was a major achievement for the Libyan people, despite the fact that it created a client state dominated by Western powers.

The Libyan Sanussi monarchy created new Western-like institutions, such as the parliament, the federal system, the civic courts, the army, and the police forces. At the same time, indigenous institutions were based on local traditions, such as the *majlis al-shukh*, the *zawya*, the Islamic Sanussi schools and universities, Islamic family courts, and traditional *urf majlis*, that reflect the autonomous decentralized traditions of the hinterland.

The Qaddafi-led anticolonial, Arab nationalist coup in September 1969 broke the silence on the genocide and violence under Italian colonialism. This populist coup became a dictatorship by 1977. In short, understanding the social and political origins of the Libyan state is an essential context for capturing the history of the current state collapse.

State collapse takes place when institutions, authority, and legitimate power, law, and political order fall apart, leaving civil society to fill the vacuum. The decline of the state is linked to the breakdown of social order. Without the state institutions and the ability to use legitimate violence, as Max Weber argued, society breaks down. Contrary to public perceptions, state collapse does not happen overnight, nor is it caused in the short term. Rather, it is the result of an accumulative, long-term process, like an illness. Consequently, when a state becomes unable to satisfy its citizen's basic social demands, rival groups try to fill in the vacuum, as in the case of Libya today, when in the last three years armed groups and criminal elements have used illegal activities such as kidnappings, ransoms, smuggling, and imprisonment as a source of revenue to satisfy their followers.

The next question is, what are the historical and structural causes of the February 17, 2011, Libyan Revolution, its early success, and the current crisis of transition since 2013? I will make three arguments to analyze the causes of the current revolution and its success in liberating Libya from the control of the Qaddafi forces. These arguments consider the Qaddafi regime's failure to address the question of political reform and its alienation of important elite groups; the impact of demography, urbanization, and global social media; and the success of an enterprising rebel leadership that was able to obtain diplomatic and military support from the United Nations, the Arab League, and NATO.

The inability of the Qaddafi regime to make serious political reforms appropriate to the changes in the economy, education, and society eventually led to conflict between a dynamically changing social structure and a rigid political system that in turn inhibited new social forces—especially unemployed youth—from having their social demands and grievances met. The gap between the Libyan youth and the ruling elite undermined all the gains achieved by the regime during the 1970s and eventually led to the formation of a revolutionary coalition that became alienated from the regime. Had Colonel Qaddafi responded with openness to the calls for reform and not overreacted to the uprisings in Tunisia and Egypt, the urban elite in Libya might have been placated, and the violent rebellion might have been avoided. Qaddafi miscalculated and overreacted. Once his army and police shot at protesters, the pent-up disaffection of Libyan society was unleashed, and it was too late for the regime to bottle it up.

In August 2011 the revolutionary forces liberated the southern region of Fezzan, which historically was both rural and pro-Qaddafi, and only two cities remained under his troop's control: his home city of Sirte and the city of Bani Walid. The regime lost moral, diplomatic, and military battles, leading to ultimate defeat in war by the end of October 2011. Furthermore, the revolutionary coalition that led the opposition and was supported by regional Arab countries, NATO, and the American military created a proxy war inside Libya's civil war. This compounded Libya's crisis of transition, which made Libya an open country for jihadi and Salafi groups ranging from al-Qaeda, to Ansar al-Sharia in Benghazi, to Derna and Subrata, to ISIS, which took over Sirte in early 2014.

The irony is the regime could have been spared if reform had been serious and if the regime had addressed the key popular social, political, and human rights abuses. Instead of implementing real reform, the regime fired on peaceful protesters in Benghazi and Biada on February 15, 2011, and Muammar al-Qaddafi and his son Saif al-Islam Qaddafi made speeches declaring war against the protestors, even calling them rats, drug addicts, and brainwashed by Osama Bin Laden. By then the majority of Libyans realized the regime was hopeless and needed to be removed by force.

The Long Specter of Settler Colonialism

Libyan history has been affected by colonialism beginning with the colonial state that was imposed by the Italians from 1911 to 1943, and that was followed by British and French administrations from 1943 to 1951. Two postcolonial states followed: the Sanussi monarchy that lasted from 1951 to 1969, and the Qaddafi regime that lasted from September 1, 1969, to February 14, 2011. The February 17, 2011, revolution opened a new era.

The Italian colonization of Libya may have been comparatively brief, but it was exceptionally brutal and bloody. Its brutality cast a dark shadow across the decades that followed. Half a million people were killed as a direct result of the prolonged military campaigns across the country, including the sixty thousand who perished in the concentration camps set up as part of Italian counterinsurgency programs. The accomplishments of Italian fascist colonial rule were quite mixed. The Italians destroyed longstanding institutions of governance and education and utterly degraded life in agricultural areas. However, they also unified the three former Ottoman provinces of Fezzan, Tripolitania, and Barqa into a single state, which is, of course, modern Libya.

Libya won its "independence," if that is the right name for it, only with the Allied military advances across North Africa in 1942–43. Even after the war, the British and American military presence became a central fact of post-Italian Libyan history and provided the necessary force and support for the installation of a pro-British and American monarchy under King Muhammad Idris al-Sanussi (1951–69).[1] The upper class that led Libyan independence made a compromise with the UK and United States. In exchange for security, economic assistance, and independence, the royal elite signed agreements granting military bases to the United States and UK in 1954. Also, this elite, which included some collaborators with the colonial state, such as the first prime minister, Mahmoud al-Muntasar, overlooked Italian colonial atrocities such as the genocidal internment of over one hundred thousand Libyans, the death of sixty thousand among them, and the exile and uprooting of over sixty thousand Libyans outside of Libya. In other words, King Idris's rule did not end the trauma of the colonial period, since his policies—mirroring those of his British and American benefactors—suppressed the more difficult questions of the past.

This colonial history, and the neocolonial rule of the Sanussi monarchy of King Idris, which attempted to impose a collective amnesia about that history, is the immediate backdrop to understanding the anticolonial populism that has been at the core of the postmonarchy regime from the outset. Outside observers might be surprised by the regime's tenacious focus on events of a colonial past that ended nearly seventy years ago. But it is crucial to understand that Libya's stubborn anti-imperialist ethos is rooted in the modern colonial experience of the Libyan people, and their very reasonable feeling that their suffering has yet to be recognized.

Populism, Cult of Hero, and the Marginalization of Institutions

On September 1, 1969, twelve young Pan-Arab and Nasser–inspired officers in the Libyan Royal Army were led by a charismatic twenty-seven-year-old officer named Muammar al-Qaddafi to overthrow the monarchy of King Idris in a bloodless coup d'état. The officers came from lower-middle-class backgrounds and represented the three regions—that is, the formerly separate Ottoman provinces—of Libya. This group had formed the central committee of a secret organization within the Libyan army called the Libyan Free Unionist Officers Movement. It subsequently renamed itself the Revolutionary Command Council (RCC) and declared the creation of the Libyan Arab Republic. The RCC's rhetoric was firmly anti-imperialist, anticommunist, and anticorruption, while making ideological references to Arab nationalism and Islam as well. The RCC, however, did not have clearly delin-eated policies and looked for guidance from the 1952 Egyptian revolution.

The 1969 Libyan revolution was not an anomaly, as so many Western journalists and scholars have claimed. Rather, its ideologies and style of governance were rooted in the hinterland social history of the Sanusi-yya resistance and the Tripolitanian Republic. The Sanusi movement was founded by an urban Algerian scholar, Sayyid Muhammad, born Ali Al-Sanusi (1787–1859). It was a reformist movement built on modernist Islamic interpretation and two innovative institutions, trade and education, which continued until 1911, when Italy invaded Libya. The Italian colonial forces faced a well-integrated, unified, and cohesive society in eastern and south-ern Libya (and northern Chad), and hence the Libyans were able to resist the modern Italian armies until 1931. In western Libya the leaders of the region organized their groups under the first republic in the Arab world, the Tripolitanian Republic, in 1918. This republic had a four-leader collec-tive leadership, a Shura or parliament council, a flag, a newspaper, and an army. But the Italians managed to defeat it by 1922, when Mussolini and the fascists decided to reconquer the colony and abrogate all agreements with the resistance. These two early cases of state formation, the Sanusi move-ment and the republic, provided the genesis of Libyan modern nationalism.

After the 1969 revolution, Libyan society experienced major social, political, and economic advances, but the new government initially enacted its policies without significant popular participation. Qaddafi's faction within the RCC did not consolidate its power until 1976. At that point, it began to experiment with creating what it called an "indigenous pastoralist socialist society." While trying to attain this objective, the state benefited from significant petroleum revenues that provided steady employment not only to Libyans but also to a large ex-patriate workforce.

If Qaddafi can be credited with anything, it was that he was able to create a state ideology that resonated strongly with the entire spectrum of pan-Arab, pan-African, and third-world national liberation movements. He did all this while employing language understood by ordinary Liby-ans and while referring to a common history that could be understood by all. Qaddafi was able to mobilize nationalist cadres effectively and attack his opponents and rivals inside and outside the country. At the core of his self-presentation was the image of the Bedouin tribesman. He spoke, ate, and dressed like a Bedouin from the hinterland. He led prayers like an imam.

The new regime also began to pursue a cultural policy of "Bedouiniza-tion" by attacking urban culture and encouraging rituals based on "tribal values," as evidenced in dress, music, and festivals. Students, intellectuals, and the urban middle class in the big cities were compelled to shift their own self-presentation as they found themselves on the cultural defensive. They were not wrong to imagine that the regime's Bedouin policies were aimed at undermining their prestige in society. As a result of deliberate deurbanization policies, for instance, the city of Tripoli (the most urban and cosmopolitan in the country) lost much of its relative importance even while its population increased to two million.

Behind the rhetoric of a pure Bedouin identity unsullied by Western modernity, however, lurked a more mundane reality. The Libyan popula-tion had increased from one million in 1950 to six and a half million with a very large youth cohort—the median age was twenty-four. Sixty-five per-cent of the population was under the age of thirty, and the unemployment rate was very high at 30 percent. Today the vast majority of Libyans (80%) live in towns and cities. The supporters of the regime—like those of the democratic uprising—include lawyers, judges, journalists, engineers, writ-ers, academics, officers, and diplomats. The oil-driven economy is complex, and Libyan citizens participate fully in it. The literacy rate is the highest in Africa (68.05%), and life expectancy is seventy-eight, years ahead of life expectancy in Tunisia. The UN 2010 Human Development Index ranked Libya as the first in Africa and number fifty-three in the world. In other words, those who want to talk about tribalism in Libyan society will have to account for the disconnect between the official regime image of Libyans as timeless Bedouins, and the more complex reality on the ground. Moreover, they will have to confront the fact that the representation of Libya as inher-ently tribal has its roots in the Qaddafi regime's battle to ideologically dis-enfranchise the urban middle classes of the country—that is, the majority of the population. The anti-Qaddafi revolution included 6.5 million people who were globally connected to international education, travel opportun-ities, social media, and international TV stations such as Al-Jazeera and Al-Arabia. These factors of globalization played important sympathetic roles in supporting the revolution.

Qaddafi's regime was able to restore its standing in the international community in 2003 by providing reparations to the families of those mur-dered in the bombing of Pan Am Flight 103 over Lockerbie, Scotland, but the regime was failing domestically. Despite being allegedly strong militarily, the regime was domestically weak because of internal dissent. Qaddafi's core of support came from his diehard allies, foreign mercenaries, and the loyalty of the residents of the two central cities, Sirte and Bani Walid.

The revolutions that occurred in neighboring Tunisia and Egypt may have been precipitating events for what occurred in Libya, but the Libyan revolution drew its core motivation from Libya's brutal experience of colonialism. The young protesters in Benghazi raised the independence flag and the photo of Omar al-Mukhtar, the hero of the anticolonial resistance. Other young men in western Libya raised photos of their own local anticolonial resistance leaders in Nalut, Zentan, and Misrata. What is most striking about the rhetoric of the Libyan Revolution is how Colonel Qaddafi's anticolonialist themes, such as statements from Omar al-Mukhtar before he was hanged, were turned against him in mass text messages, TV clips from Al-Jazeera, and posts on Facebook. Even while assaulting Colonel Qaddafi's forces, the rebels resisted calling for forceful Western intervention, although they did ask for the imposition of a no-fly zone. Libya's history explains the reasoning behind this decision. Colonel Qaddafi's nationalist populism was rooted in the traumas of the colonial era, traumas that were papered over during the modernizing but out-of-touch monarchy that ruled from 1951 to 1969.

Processes of modernization, urbanization, and especially education began as early as independence in 1951 with the support of the UN, which helped accelerate social change. In 1954 a new Libyan university with two campuses in Benghazi and Tripoli created new educational opportunities, which then led to the expansion of colleges and universities all over the country. New educational policies led to the rise of a salaried middle class, a student movement, a small working class, trade unions, and modern intellectuals by the late 1960s. The number of students increased from thirty-three thousand in 1952 to three hundred thousand in 1970. By 2010 there were two million students in all levels of education in Libya, including three hundred thousand at the college and university levels.

Gendered Nationalism

The role of Libyan women in the revolution is the most remarkable. This is a country that was one of the poorest in 1943 with illiteracy rate as high as 98 percent. Thanks to Libyan women's social movements and the spread of education since independence, millions of Libyan women are educated today. Such progress in Libyan women's education made it possible to see active young women in the February 17, 2011, revolution. In fact, the revolution began when mothers of political prisoners killed in the massacre of Abu Salim demanded justice and information about the twelve hundred loved ones killed in 1996. This protest was the start of the revolution. Libyan women contributed many services such as taking care of the wounded, documenting the regime atrocities, making videos and sending messages over the internet, cooking for the fighters, taking care of the children, speaking to the media, and sewing the revived independence flag of the monarchy. Today there are more women in Libyan higher education than men. In the humanities and social sciences departments in Libyan universities, the students are 80 percent female.

Populism

Well-paying jobs in Tripoli, Benghazi, and the oil fields attracted many rural people to move north to these cities. The population of Tripoli increased from 130,000 in 1951, to 213,000 in 1964, to 400,000 in 1970. Benghazi grew from 70,000 residents to 137,000 to 300,000 during the same period. By 2010 Tripoli had 1.8 million and Benghazi 650,000 people. But one has to be aware that thousands of poor rural immigrants lived in shanty towns outside these two cities, such as Bab Akkara, the Brareek, the Campos outside Tripoli, and al-Sabri in Benghazi.[2] In summary, whereas 80 percent of the population lived in the countryside in 1951, this statistic had reversed by 1967, with 80 percent living in urban areas. A small but well-organized working class emerged in the cities and near the oil fields.

In its first two decades, the Qaddafi regime brought many benefits to ordinary Libyans. The Jamahiriya government received wide public support from the lower and middle classes, which allowed the government to engage in a major transformation of the economy as well as social and political structures. Education and health care were free, and energy, basic food materials, and water were subsidized by the state for all Libyans. Women in particular benefited, becoming ministers, ambassadors, pilots, judges, and doctors. But these educational and social achievements were contradicted by excessive political control and the development of a cult of personality centered on "Leader-Brother" Qaddafi, who became president for life. Power became a personal matter.

Beginning in the 1980s, excessive centralization, greater repression by security forces, and a decline in the rule of law undermined this experiment in indigenous populism. Institutions such as courts, universities, unions, and hospitals weakened. Civic associations that had made Libyan society seem more democratic than many Persian Gulf states in the 1970s withered or were eliminated. A hostile international climate and fluctuations in oil revenues added to the pressures on the regime.

The regime responded by transforming its rituals of hero-worship into a rhetoric of pan-African ideology and turned to violence to repress dissent. After repeated coup attempts, it tortured, imprisoned, and exiled dissidents. The regime staffed security forces with reliable relatives and allies from central and southern Libya. During the 1990s, as economic sanctions took their toll, health care and education deteriorated, unemployment soared to 30%, the economy became ever more dependent on oil and the regime grew increasingly corrupt. Qaddafi's sons dominated the oil industry, communications, and most of the state-controlled contracts. His sons, including Mu'tasim, Hanibal, and Sa'adi, spent millions on wild parties that many young Libyans viewed through the internet and YouTube videos, while at the same time most Libyan educated professionals were paid a mere $300 a month and had to borrow money to travel to Tunisia for medical treatment. In 2010, Transparency International ranked Libya as one of the most corrupt countries in the world, at 146 out of 178. While the use of social media in Libya is not as wide as in Tunisia, Egypt, and the rest of the Maghreb, thousands of people still used cell phones, had access to independent websites, and relied upon Al-Jazeera and other TV stations. Also, after the resolution of the Lockerbie crisis and Libya's renewal of contacts with the international community, more media and newspapers were allowed to circulate, helping to accelerate reformist and dissident forces within Libya, especially among the youth who interacted increasingly with the outside world.

The move towards centralization and reliance on informal and security organizations such as the security apparatus, revolutionary committees, al Rifaq, Ahl al-Khaima, and invented tribal unofficial organizations, at the expense of formal institutions and the rule of law undermined earlier reforms and led to the decline of the experiment in indigenous political populism. A hostile international climate, as well as declining oil revenues from the late 1970s onwards, compounded the crisis of legitimacy for the regime and further weakened important public institutions such as courts, universities, unions, hospitals, and banks. Thus, a confluence of internal and external dynamics weakened the state's ideology, which had been based on populist authoritarianism and a cult of personality based on Qaddafi's persona. These changes primarily began after Libya's defeat in its war with Chad in June 1983, when ten thousand Libyans were killed. Also significant in this process was the regime's confrontation with the United States in April 1986. Conditions worsened after 1992 when the UN Security Council imposed sanctions against Libya, after evidence was produced linking Libyan agents to the terrorist bombing of Pan Am flight 103, which exploded over the town of Lockerbie, Scotland. Furthermore, the regime killed twelve hundred Islamist political prisoners in the massacre of Abu Salim in Tripoli in 1996. According to human rights organizations, the victims were Islamist political prisoners who had opposed the Libyan regime in the early 1990s. When they protested against their guards, General Abdullah al-Sanusi, head of intelligence and brother-in-law of Colonel Qaddafi, ordered these troops to open fire. The regime buried the corpses in a secret location and refused to say anything about their faith. This horrific massacre haunted the regime and was one of the leading issues in the 2011 revolution.

As discussed, The 2011 revolution started as the families of the victims of the 1996 massacre protested in Benghazi. Many residents in the city of Benghazi joined the original group of protestors. Fathi Terbal, the lawyer representing the aggrieved families, was arrested February 15, 2011. His arrest led to a social media announcement asking for the Day of Rage on February 17. When the regime's troops fired on the peaceful demonstrators, the cities of Baida and Benghazi rebelled, and those protesting stormed the Qaddafi security garrisons. Many soldiers and officers defected to the side of the protestors, including General Abdulfattah Younes, the minister of interior, and Judge Mustafa Abduljalil. The minister of justice, Younes, and Judge Abduljalil would become leaders of the newly formed Interim Libyan Transitional Council in Benghazi.

Libya under Qaddafi's leadership was an authoritarian state that relied on income from petroleum and natural gas rents. Like other petroleum-producing states such as Algeria, Iraq, and Syria, Libya has attempted to deploy both formal and informal institutions to address their citizens' material and moral demands in return for a modicum of allegiance and obedience.[3] After 1986, the Libyan regime used corporal punishment, incarceration, and forced exile for thousands of dissidents to maintain its power; it staffed its security forces with reliable relatives and longtime allies so that their interests became intertwined with Qaddafi's aspirations to stay in power. The regime also employed legitimizing strategies in order to rule;

this is what some social scientists consider the "normative" dimension of compliance.[4]

The new regime consisted of institutions and forces such as the Inner Circle of Rijal al-Khaimah (his trusted close advisors and confidants), the Revolutionary Committees (the feared zealous ideologists), tribal alliances of Sufuf (the tribal allies from central and southern Libya), and the al-Rifaq organization, which included most of Qaddafi's classmates in the southern city of Sabha and his friends from before the revolution in the early 1950s. Qaddafi invented a policy of "retribalization" and used a divide-and-rule strategy of traditional rural institutions such as Mi'ad (tribal negotiating forum), Jabr al-Khawatir (traditional Libyan conflict resolution form), and Sufuf (nineteenth-century tribal alliances). The institution of Mi'ad is a meeting of tribal leaders to deliberate; Jabr al-Khawatir is a tribal meeting to reconcile differences and make peace.[5] Qaddafi often mobilized tribal support or made peace with rivals by informally sending his kinsman and tribal advisor, Colonel Khalifa Hnaish, to these institutions to resolve differences. In the Libyan hinterland, peasant and tribal alliances functioned to fill a political void where the colonial state lacked a real presence. Despite the fact that Libyan society is detribalized and most people live in cities, Qaddafi revived old tribal alliances to recruit his troops and security forces from Sirte and Sabha to ensure loyalty to the regime.

From 1975 to 1993, the regime sustained itself by creating a military force with officers recruited from three important tribes: the Qaddafa, Migarha, and Wurfalla. When a plot to overthrow the regime was discovered in 1993, Qaddafi reduced the size of the Libyan army to fifty thousand men; only ten thousand were trained and equipped.[6] Instead of strengthening a central army, the regime increasingly relied on the security brigades that were trained, equipped, and paid by Qaddafi. These brigades and security forces were led by his brother-in-law General Abdullah al-Senusi; his sons Khamis, Sa'adi, and Mu'tassim; and his cousins including General Mus'ud Abd Hafidh, Mansur Dhawu, Ahmad al-Dumm, and Sayyid Qaddaf al-Dumm. In addition, Qaddafi created a two-thousand-person Islamic African legion with recruits from Chad, Niger, Mali, and Sudan. Qaddafi's second wife, Safiyya Farkash, was from the powerful Sa'adi tribe Bra'ssa, which gave him some support in the home region of the Sanussi monarchy.

What went wrong? There were at least three original sins: (1) the dominance of security and informal institutions, such as the leadership and Revolutionary Committees, over formal institutions; (2) the lack of a national constitution; and (3) hostility toward institutionalization. The cult of personality, corruption, the abortion of political reform, and the focus on security over institutional building all contributed to the alienation of lower- and middle-class Libyans and the defection of many reformists, military officers, and diplomats who led the democratic uprising. The Jamahiriya experiment was over. The fight was almost over. Colonel Muammar al-Qaddafi's regime lost moral legitimacy when it fired on the peaceful protesters in Benghazi, Baeda, Midrate, and Zintan; then it lost its regional, UN, and international support; and then it lost its military support. The courageous Libyan youth confronted the regime, and the whole world watched it through Al-Jazeera, Al-Arabia, and then CNN. The Arab League had to condemn the killing of the civilians, and the UN Security Council resolutions 1970 and 1973 had to protect civilians and destroy the regime forces. That was crucial in preventing the Qaddafi army from crushing the uprising and saving Benghazi from a possible massacre. In other words, the NATO forces led by the UK, France, and the United States allowed the uprising forces to survive, organize, and fight the battered and demoralized Qaddafi forces.

The history of Libyan opposition to the regime goes back to the early 1970s, and the strongest regional base for opposition was in the eastern region of the country. The regime repressed various opposition movements, including the military and student opposition of the 1970s, the opposition in exile of the 1980s, and the Islamist-inspired opposition of the 1990s. During the 1970s it first retaliated against those who led a failed military coup by executing over 120 junior officers. Second, on April 7, 1976, the regime suppressed the Libyan Student Union at the main university campuses in Tripoli and Benghazi, executing the leaders of the student revolt and torturing and purging dozens of students and faculty. During the 1980s resistance to the regime was led by an opposition group in exile that was called the Libyan Salvation Front, which allied with the governments of Sudan, Morocco, Saudi Arabia, Iraq, and the United States.

Finally, during the 1990s a new wave of opposition arose: a radicalized Libyan youth who had fought in Afghanistan, Bosnia, and Iraq and who expressed a more militant form of political Islam. The Libyan Islamic Fighting Group (LIFG) and other Islamist groups in eastern Libya initiated armed struggle and challenged the regime. Most of the radical Islamists came from the eastern cities of Ajdabiyya, Benghazi, Baida, Derna, and Tobruk, which also had been the traditional geographic base of both the Sanusiyya movement and the Sanussi monarchy. Some residents from this region had viewed Qaddafi's 1969 coup as illegitimate. Yet by 1998 the regime had managed to crush this armed Islamist insurgency. The consequence was that by early 1990 there were approximately one hundred thousand exiled Libyans living abroad.

In February 2011 the Qaddafi regime's brutal reaction to the peaceful protesters in Benghazi, Baida, and other eastern Libyan cities led to moral outrage among many people including military officers, diplomats, and even ministers. Minister of Justice Mustafa Abdel-Jalil, Minister of Interior General Abdul Fattah Younes, ambassador to the UN and longtime Minister of Foreign Affairs Abdul Rahman Shalgham, and ten other Libyan ambassadors quickly rejected the regime. Two months later more members of the elite defected, including Musa Kusa, a longtime intelligence chief and foreign minister; former minister of energy Fathi Ben Shitwan; governor of the Central Bank, Farhat Ben Gadara; and former prime minister and head of the Libyan National Oil Company, Shukri Ghanim. In addition, many soldiers and army officers defected not only in the eastern region but also throughout the rest of the country. The sole exception was Libya's southern region, where many communities were isolated and without allies in Egypt or Tunisia.

This combination of opposition forces that arose in the eastern region of the country was subsequently joined by defectors and exiled groups who all formed the revolution's new leadership: the Interim National Transitional Council. The uprising leaders met in Benghazi in March 5, 2011, and created the Libyan National Transitional Council (NTC). The council had over forty members representing all regions of the country, including professionals, academics, doctors, lawyers, reformers, defectors, Islamists, royalists, and a few traditional tribal figures from rural areas. For a listing of the known members of the NTC, refer to appendix A. The chair of the council was Judge Mustafa Abdel-Jalil, who was the justice minister under the old regime. His deputy was Abdel Haidh Ghoga, a lawyer and former head of the Libyan Bar Association. The youth were represented by lawyer Fathi Terbil, the women by Professor Salwa Deghaily, and the political prisoners by Ahmed Zubair al-Sanusi, who spent thirty-one years in a Libyan prison.

The NTC established military and judicial committees and an executive board chaired by Dr. Mahmoud Jibril, an American-educated political scientist who until early 2011 was the head of the Libyan Planning Council.

Dr. Ali Tarhouni, an exiled Libyan and a professor of economics at the University of Washington in Seattle, became the NTC's finance minister. Mahmoud Shamam, another exiled Libyan who was educated and lived in the United States, became the press and communication minister. The NTC began functioning as a parliament. The social base of the uprising that the NTC came to lead was the urban youth who joined the rallies and became the voluntary liberation army fighting the regime troops and security brigades. These young recruits were trained and led by the defected Libyan soldiers and officers.

Revolutionary Symbols and Counter Institutional Mobilization

Three symbols were used to mobilize popular support against the regime: the image of anticolonial resistance hero Omar al-Mukhtar; the old Libyan flag of the monarchy, which was adopted and viewed as the flag of independence; and the old national anthem, which was adopted after the name of the king was replaced by Omar al-Mukhtar. This is remarkable after four decades of the Qaddafi regime's rituals of presenting itself as the legitimate culmination of the Libyan anticolonial movement. In other words, the national question, which is linked to the brutal colonial period, is still persistent in Libyan society. Yet this successful mobilization was followed by a military civil war against the regime with unexpected consequences, especially the spread of arms that came to the cities of Misrata and Zentan. Groups such as jihadi and militant Libyan fighters from Afghanistan, and the previous Islamist fighters such as the Libyan Islamic Fighting Group, all turned to force. The armed militias became the power brokers in Libya despite the fact that the Libyan people participated in two impressive civil elections in 2012 and 2014. These groups had no interest in giving up their arms and found Arab and Western allies who supplied them with arms and media support.

Libya has two parliaments, one in Tobruk in the east, and one in Tripoli in the west. On December 15, 2017, the UN brokered an agreement signed in Skhairat, Morocco, that unified the two parliaments. However, the Tobruk Parliament has not voted on the Fays al-Sarraj government of National Accord yet, and the Libyan Army, led by General Khalifa Haftar, who controlled most of the eastern region including the region known as the "oil crescent" complex, rejected the political agreement. Haftar became a force in the Libyan conflict to the point that he visited Russia, Egypt, and Algeria as a Libyan statesman. I argue that the rise of a new strongman like General Haftar is problematic.

His army is popular in the eastern region as people are eager to have security and stability. Yet his history and lack of clarity in assuring Libyans of his support for the democratic process should worry the majority of Libyan people who revolted against the Qaddafi dictatorship in 2011.

The Crisis of Transition: The Struggle over the New Libya

The recent upsurge in fighting in Libya after 2013 has been the most intense since the overthrow of Muammar al-Qaddafi in 2011. In addition to pitting various militias against each other, General Khalifa Haftar has proclaimed his intention to seize power throughout the country. General Haftar is a serious player, and his operation, Karama ("Dignity"), has gathered broad support both inside Libya and abroad. He expresses the frustrations of many Libyans. Public opinion has become disillusioned with the elected General National Congress and the government of National Accord, or parliament in Tobruk; with high levels of corruption; and with the violence and lawlessness of unrestrained militias competing for resources and positions. In other words, Haftar is riding a wave of public frustration inside Libya despite the fact that his motives and integrity are questionable, particularly given his past work for the CIA and the fear of the rise of a new strong military man. Haftar did not create the crisis; the crisis created Haftar.

General Haftar has a controversial history. He is originally from the eastern city of Ijdabia. He graduated from the Royal Military Academy in Benghazi after Libya's independence in 1951 and later joined the Unionist Free Officers Organization led by Qaddafi that toppled the Libyan monarchy in 1969. In 1986, he was appointed military commander of the Libyan army in Chad. Libya was supporting the government of Goukoni Oueddei, but after his rival Hissène Habré seized power in 1982, the Libyan Army was perceived as an enemy.

General Haftar's military career ended in disgrace in 1987 when the Chadian army, aided by the United States and France, defeated the Libyans, killing seventeen hundred and capturing three hundred, including General Haftar himself. The regime in Tripoli blamed Haftar for the defeat, and while in captivity he defected and joined the CIA-backed National Front for the Salvation of Libya (NFSL). He was given political asylum in the United States, where he lived for the next twenty years.

The NFSL subsequently experienced internal fragmentation, particularly after the end of the Cold War. General Haftar left the NFSL and made peace with the regime in Tripoli, but he did not return to Libya. When the uprising against Qaddafi erupted on February 17, 2011, he joined the revolt. Haftar was eager to be its military commander but was rebuffed by the revolutionary forces, which chose General Abd-al-Fattah Younes instead. That February, Haftar tried to lead a rebellion against the increasingly weak central government in Tripoli, but he lacked support. This time is different.

This time around, General Haftar has received support from the old army command and air force; the Zintan Brigade; the eastern region of Barqa; the National Democratic Coalition; former prime ministers Mahmoud Jibril and Ali Zaidan; Libya's ambassador to the United Nations, Ibrahim al-Dabbashi; and most exiled Libyans. One has to keep in mind there are at least one million Libyans who left for Tunisia and Egypt after 2011, most of whom are supporters of the old regime. They are sympathetic to Haftar because he was a member of Qaddafi's military, at least until his defection, and he still regards the September 1969 coup as a revolution.

Saudi Arabia and the United Arab Emirates are supporting Haftar's movement, as are Egypt and Algeria. The Saudis and Emiratis consider Haftar the Libyan arm of their regional campaign against the Muslim Brotherhood, while Egypt and Algeria—both of which share long borders with Libya—have more pressing security concerns such as arms smuggling, terrorism, and stemming the flow of jihadists. A number of groups, such as the Egyptian Muslim Brotherhood and al-Qaeda in the Islamic Maghreb, have established a presence in Libya.

On the other side of the equation, Qatar, Turkey, Sudan, and the Egyptian Muslim Brotherhood are supporting various Libyan Islamists. These include a broad range of organizations and militias such as the Libyan Muslim Brotherhood, the jihadist Wafaa' block, and the old National Front for the Salvation of Libya. This broad coalition of Islamists has become more powerful despite the fact it lost the July 2012 elections to the "liberal" National Democratic Coalition.

The Islamists achieved these gains by relying on the power of regional and religious militias who exercise real power on the ground. They were further assisted by the resignation of over forty members of parliament, most of whom belonged to the National Democratic Coalition. Consequently, the General National Congress is dominated by Islamists, and they were able to oust Prime Minster Ali Zeidan in March 2014 and replace him with the Islamist-leaning Ahmed Maitig, and later with Omar al-Hassi and Ibrahim al-Ghwail. This is the larger context of General Haftar's movement.

The question is, why now? I raised this with a relative who lives in Tripoli. She responded that one should look at where Libya is today. The revolution has been hijacked by extremists, armed militias, and warlords who publicly oppose rebuilding the army and the police and who have created a climate of fear, kidnapping or assassinating anyone who opposes them and their Salafi jihadi agenda. We support Haftar, she said, and for that matter anyone who helps us create an army and police force capable of fighting terrorism and ending lawlessness. A Libyan friend who edits a leading newspaper told me around 512 people have been assassinated so far, including journalist Muftah Abuzaid in Benghazi and Nasib Karfada, a female correspondent for the Libyan al-Wataniyya television station, in Sabha.

The defeat of the old regime, the opening of Libya's borders, and intervention by militant jihadi groups enjoying Arab and international support have blocked the transition. There is a refusal to rebuild the armed forces and police. An unintended consequence of the uprising has been the rise of regionalist militias such as the Misrata and Zintan brigades, as well as jihadist groups who are powerful in cities such as Derna, Sirte, and Benghazi.

Back in 2012 these armed groups used their power to force a weak parliament to approve the Exclusion Law, which they have used to remove rivals and opponents from the political process. Thus Mahmoud Jibril and Muhammad al-Magariaf were ousted from office, as were most top officials who worked for the Qaddafi regime between 1969 and 2011.

Weak governments are effectively held hostage by armed groups who control key ministries and demand salaries for their 250,000 members—even though only 20,000 people fought the old regime in 2011. In other words, weak postuprising governments created this problem by appeasing armed groups who for economic reasons oppose efforts to rebuild the army. At the same time, groups such as Ansar al-Sharia have publicly proclaimed their opposition to elections, democracy, and a standing army.

Libya currently has three contending governments: one led by Fayez al-Sarraj, who was appointed by the Sikhairt political agreement and claims to be the legitimate prime minister; another led by Colonel Abdullah al-Thinni, who has been at this post since March 2014 in the east at Baida; and a third led by Ibrahim al-Ghwail, the Islamist-leaning leader who remerged this year, supported by the Islamist political groups from the old but expired 2012 National General Congress.

Haftar has denounced the parliament as an illegitimate body and asked the Constitutional Assembly and Supreme Court to govern the country.

When both declined, he asked the Supreme Legal Counsel to manage the country. The General National Congress in turn accused him of staging a coup to depose an elected parliament. The country is split right now.

The larger dynamics driving what is almost a civil war are a fractured political process, incompetent leadership, and a weak formal government while regional, religious, and clan-based militias and political groups fight for power, positions, oil, and money. Corruption and patronage became endemic. The elected leaders became tools for the armed militia, who demanded salary and money. The actions of many Libyan exiles were negative as well after they returned in 2011 to Libya. Some of these exiles were hungry for power, positions, and money, which led many Libyans to react negatively to all Libyans exiled in Western countries today. This reaction is understandable but often unfair because not all returning exiled Libyans participated in corruption after 2011. However, some offered their children full government scholarships to study abroad for college educations, and many of them appointed themselves to ambassadorships and cultural attaché positions. Also, some paid themselves salaries retroactively for the years they had spent in exile since 1969.

The country needs new leadership and desperately requires national dialogue and reconciliation. Without this, Libya will descend further into the abyss and become a failed state. If polarization continues, there will be a split, and it will get very ugly.

Yet this terrible scenario is not the only one. Libya's future is contingent on whether the leadership can establish stability, restore order, collect arms that are in the hands of civilians, and reconcile and unite all Libyans while learning from the mistakes made in Iraq, Afghanistan, Somalia, and Iran. Libya could be a new model for stability and democracy, and the revolution could finally build a state with strong, stable institutions and civil associations to include all Libyans. Libya has an educated modern society, and the oil and gas revenues can rebuild the country and recover the lost three decades of waste, corruption, and dictatorship. The fight now will be over the new order, on the role of Islam, the status of women, regionalism, and the relationship with NATO, the United States, and other Arab and African countries.

Both the elected leaders and the Libyan civic activists who have been the driving force for this early democratic uprising must learn from the mistakes of the post-2011 failed transition. These leaders failed to resolve the security and military problems and compromise for the sake of the entire country, an essential foundation for building state institutions. General Haftar and the powerful Misrata militias have to compromise, recognize the GNA, respect the voters' choices, and rebuild the national army and the police force, after dismantling the armed militias, and they must open the process for national reconciliation, including the supporters of the old regime inside and outside Libya. Libya is a case of failed transition, not a failed state. The Arab Gulf states, Turkey and Sudan, the United States, and the EU have been guilty as well, and they can help the process by putting a lid on the flow of arms and jihadists into the Libyan civil war, directly or through their allies and client states. The challenges of building a stable civil and pluralistic democracy are indeed formidable and much harder than defeating the Qaddafi dictatorship.

Conclusion: Strategies for Political and Institutional Reconstruction in Libya

The lessons for resolving the Libyan crisis of transition require a deep knowledge of the scholarship on comparative social revolutions and failed states and, above all, a deeper grasp of the Libyan social, institutional, and political struggle for national independence from colonialism and for the rule of law and democratic governance. Libya is not an isolated island; it is integrated in the regional Arab, African, and Mediterranean worlds. The problem of transition is complex and formidable and requires a bold new leadership and creative solutions. The lure of authoritarianism and support for a new strongman in the name of law and order are real. But this is only one option—there are alternatives to this old form of leadership and governance. The UN can play a constructive role if it realizes the obstacles and the negative factors behind the persisting paralysis of the crisis and the stalled process of rebuilding the state and civic institutions after 2012.

Political Reconstruction

The rest of the current crisis of state collapse is political due to the leadership's failure to disarm the militias, especially now in the western and the southern regions. These armed groups dictate their will, and the leaders of the three governments after 2011 could not resolve the problems, especially after the NATO bombing of the Qaddafi forces. These forces withdrew from the country and left it to the new forces such as the Misrata and

Zintan militias in the west and the returned Islamic mujahideen radicals from Afghanistan, Iraq, and Syria and Libyan armies in the east under the leadership of General Khalifa Haftar. In addition, transnational organizations such as al-Qaeda, Daesh, and Ansar al-Sharia that oppose elections and a democratic process took over cities such as Darna, Sirte, and Sibratha and cut them off from the Libyan state. Ethnic groups such as the Tibbeu, who live near the southern borders of Libya and were armed by both the Qaddafi regime and the Transitional National Council in 2011, took advantage and asserted their presence in Fezzan as a major political and military force. The Libyan Tibbeu live in Kufra, Tigirhi, Qatrun, and Al-Wagh. Their number is around sixty thousand members. But due to the collapse of the Qaddafi army, they joined the February 17 revolution and played a bigger role in the politics of Fezzan when they took over many towns and cities. Most of the Tibbeu live in northern Chad, not in Libya. That created a new problem, as thousands of illegal immigrants crossed the borders into Libya and complicated the security problems of the state crisis.

The first step to resolve the current crisis is to stop the flow of arms and aid to the armed groups. The UN can play a constructive role in this regard. The second is to correct the errors of post-2011 leaders who appeased armed groups and militias, especially their disastrous policy of rewarding them with positions and money to buy off their support. The armed militias have to be given options of either civilian or military jobs in the army and police forces as individuals, not as collective groups. Third, emerging from crisis will require a conference that includes military and radical groups, including the supporters of the old regime, and let them come to a resolution to key principles. The conference would provide a chance to overcome the original sin of the 2011 coalition, the lack of a clear program for state-building and an awareness of the negative role of outside intervention in the country. However, a national dialogue of this type must be inclusive to work. All members of Libyan civil society must be invited; this includes elders, ulama, Sufi shaykhs, trade unions, intellectuals, poets, exiled Libyans, professional associations, and women. Women's associations still face the heavy burden of patriarchy. They still carry the task of facing the crisis, and there is a need for respecting their dignity, voices, and equality, which will be critical for national peace and stability.

Attempts have been made to address the thorny issues of compromise and political reform. The Misrata military force, its political Islamists, the Muslim Brotherhood, and the Haftar Libyan army in the east and the south have agreed to give up their arms and accept political reform by calling for rebuilding the Libyan National Army and the police force. Under this compromise there would be no defeated group, and everybody is a winner—no warlords but statesmen, no revenge but justice for survivors, and rights of citizenship for all Libyans. Thus, in the future, Libya will need an effective commission for truth and reconciliation to record the facts about all abuses from 1969 until today, in exchange for pardoning and forgiveness. Only then will Libya be able to heal the open wounds of the past and achieve the survivors' justice.

Success at a strategy of unifying the armed forces in Libya and addressing transitional justice and national reconciliation will not be easy, but without it, the proxy wars in Libya will reproduce the current catastrophic situation, and the Libyan people's suffering for lack of food, health, and security will continue. Placed in comparative perspective, such a strategy is not an idealistic wish; it is based on positive examples: the modern history of Nigeria after the 1967 civil war, Mozambique in 1994, El Salvador and Uganda (1980-86), Bosnia, Columbia, and South Africa. As Mahmoud Mamdani argued in his assessment of the South African transition, "The real breakthrough represented by the South African case is not contained in the TRC but in CODESA talks that preceded it, which so far has been dismissed as nothing but hard-nosed pragmatism. Mamdani refers to the political compromise between all opposing sides and the acceptance of political reform that led to the breakthrough and ushererd in the process for a transition.

To some extent, the Tunisian opposition to the Ben Ali dictatorship is a good example of building a coalition and compromise when they met in 2003 and agreed to have a unified goal for transition after the fall of the regime. To date, no similar compromises have been made by the Libyan opposition. The only meeting was dominated by the exiled Front for the Salvation of Libya, which was tainted by its close ties to Western and Arab State Alliances.

Institutional reconstruction in Libya will have to be deliberate and pragmatic. Two strategies seem promising. First, the UN should assist the existing forces by providing mediation among the various factions. Second, the UN should encourage the building of new institutions by providing consulting and professional help. The crisis is more acute in Western Libya, where creative work is needed, while the east and the south are under the Libyan "national army" led by General Haftar. Haftar must respect the democratic process and temper his ambition to be the next strongman.

One major fact that is overlooked by most experts on the Libyan crisis is the existence of ninety thousand army members and thirty thousand police officers who are not active but still receive their salary from the state. Recalling all of them back to active service is essential. At the same time, the Libyan state leaders should reach out and offer the current militias the choice of joining the army, the police, or civil service. They can also offer scholarships to entice fighters back into productive society.

Libya must also lean on its history. The contributions of the Sanussi monarchy from 1951–69 and of the 1969 populist coup, especially in the first decade, are instrumental to making peace with history and achieving some consensus instead of rupture and silencing, as has been the pattern for all Libyan elites that ruled the country since 1969. Libyan independence is a good example to look to for lessons. The Libyan leaders in the three regions and in exile disagreed over how to imagine Libya and who is a Libyan. Their contribution rests on agreeing to focus on the national good and including all political groups, such as the ones who collaborated with the genocidal Italian settler colonial state. That is how Libyan independence was made. It was achieved by Libyans with the support of the UN and the Western powers. The weakness of the monarchy's state building was its silence on the national Italian genocide and atrocities and its close ties with the Western governments, which led to the wave of anticolonial populism in 1969. The authoritarian Qaddafi regime weakened these institutions under the monarchy and rising civil society up to the late 1960s. Yet the Qaddafi regime was successful in asserting national independence, protecting Libyan borders, and expressing Libyan grievances against Italian colonial atrocities. It is time for Libya to make peace with the history of the two states and their contribution to national and institutional building.

In the current context, Libyans deserve and need better leadership. Here the challenge is not to find charisma and ability to mobilize, but to find leaders who are willing to serve people and be part of a talented management team. Libya needs a leadership that is able to serve the people with accountability and management of public finances, with no tolerance for corruption or seeing the state as booty and a source of enrichment. Furthermore, the new leadership must invest in human capital and shared values and support public institutions such as schools and universities. Leadership must not just focus on the state level, but on local, decentralized institutions. The 113 Libyan municipalities are critical for good governance. Libya does have institutions that were built under the two regimes

In summary, the challenge is formidable, but with the right leadership and international unified support, success in building durable democratic institutions in Libya is possible.

ALI ABDULLATIF AHMIDA is Professor of Political Science at the University of New England. His books include *Forgotten Voices: Power and Agency in Colonial and Postcolonial Libya* and *Post-Orientalism: Critical Reviews of North African Social and Cultural History*.

Appendix A

1. Mustafa Mohamed Abdul Jalil, president of the NTC. Mr. Jalil was Mr. Qaddafi's minister of justice when the uprising began in February, and he defected quickly, becoming the first senior official to abandon Qaddafi. From the eastern Green Mountains town of Baida, he had a reputation for piety and honesty while serving Qaddafi and tried to bring some independence to Libya's judiciary. Once well-known case is when he resigned in protest for not releasing three hundred political prisoners despite the fact the court made a ruling in their favor in 2007.

2. Abdul Hafidh Ghoga, deputy president of the NTC. Mr. Ghoga has often acted as the NTC's chief spokesman in Benghazi. Ghoga, a lawyer and human rights activist, was among a group of lawyers representing the families of the victims of the 1996 Abu Salim massacre, in which twelve hundred political prisoners were murdered at the Tripoli prison. Demands for justice over that issue helped spark the uprising against Qaddafi in February.

3. Ahmed al-Zubair al-Sanusi, a member representing political prisoners. Mr. Zubair is a grandson of Sayyid Ahmad al-Shareef al Sansui, the third leader of the Sanusiiya, and a cousin of King Muhammad Idris al-Sanusi.

4. Othman Magairhi, Tobruk.

5. Ashur Burashad, Derna.

6. Ahmad al-'Abar. Mr. 'Abar is a businessman from Benghazi.

7. General Amr Al Bihairy. Mr. Bihairy is a member for military matters.

8. Abdallah al Maihub, Qaba.

9. Salwa al Dighaily. Ms. Dighaily is a constitutional law professor from Benghazi. She is the only woman known to be on the council.

10. Fathi al Ba'ja. Mr. Ba'ja is a well-known academic and anti-Qaddafi activist from Benghazi.

11. Fathi Terbil. Mr. Terbil is a human rights activist and lawyer from Benghazi. He was briefly detained in Benghazi on February 15 while petitioning the local court on behalf of victims of the Abu Salim massacre. That detention sparked mass demonstrations in Benghazi, the first step of the Libyan revolution.

12. Sulyaman al-Furtiyah, Misurata.
13. Abdul Magid Saif al-Nasr, Sabha.
14. Hassan all Drua'y, Sirte.
15. Hassan al-Saghiir, al Al-Shatii.
16. Farhat El Sharshary, a businessman from Sarman.
17. Mustapha El Salhiin al-Huni, Jofra.
18. Ali Qlma Muhammad Ali, Marzuk.
19. Fawzy Abdul Ali, Misurata.
20. Abdel Nasir Abu Bakr Na'ama, Tarhouna.
21. Abdul Raziq Mukhtar, Tripoli.
22. Abdul Razaq Abdul Salam al-Aradi. Mr. al-Aradi is a businessman from Tripoli who used to live in Vancouver.
23. El Sadiiq Amr al-Kabiir. Mr. al-Kabiir is a banker with ABC Bank from Tripoli who has lived outside Libya.
24. Al-Amin Belhaj. Mr. Belhaj is a past leader of Libya's Muslim Brotherhood from Tripoli and a longtime exile in the United Kingdom. His brother is Abdel Hakim Belhaj, the military commander the NTC appointed to run operations in Tripoli.
25. Muhammad Nasr al-Hariizi, Tripoli.
26. Khalid Muhammad Nasrat, Zawiya.
27. Imad Nur al-Din Nasiir, Zawiya.
28. Salim Qnan, Nalut.
29. Khalid Ali Zakri, from Jadu.
30. Ibrahim Bin Ghashir,from Misurata.
31. Abdullah al-Turki, Zintan.
32. Ahmad Miftah Hassan al-Zuwii, Kofra.
33. Uthman bin Sasi. Mr. Sasi is a businessman from Zuwara who has lived in the south of France for decades.
34. Muhamed al-Sa'ih, Zahra.
35. Mussa al-Kuni, Ubari.
36. Tahir Salim Thiyab, Al Merj.
37. Muhammad Zin al-l Abdiin, from Western Jabl.
38. Ali al Mania, Ghadames.
39. Idris Abu Fayed, Gharyan.
40. Mubarak al-Fatmani, Bani Walid.

Notes

1. I. R. Khalidi, *Constitutional Development in Libya* (Beirut, Lebanon: Khayyat's College Books, 1963), 62–3. For UN commissioner Adrian Pelt's own account, see his book, *Libyan Independence and the United Nations* (New Haven: Yale University Press, 1970).

2. On the impact of oil on Libya, see J. A. Allan, *Libya: The Experience of Oil* (Boulder, CO: Westview Press, 1981); D. Vandewalle, "The Libyan Jamahiriyya Since 1969," in *Qadhafi's Libya*, ed. D. Vanderwalle (New York: St. Martin's Press, 1995), 3–46; S. Birks and C. Sinclair, "Libya: Problems of a Rentier State," in *North Africa: Contemporary Politics and Economic Development*, ed. R. Lawless and A. Findlay (New York: St. Martin's Press, 1984).

3. Ibid.

4. Ali Abdullatif Ahmida, *Forgotten Voices: Power and Agency in Colonial and Postcolonial Libya* (New York: Routledge, 2005) 65–85.

5. J. Davis, *Libyan Politics: Tribe and Revolution* (Berkeley: University of California Press, 1991), 71–91.

6. Ali Abdullatif Ahmida, *The Making of Modern Libya*, 2nd ed. (Albany: State University of New York Press, 2009), 51–4.

10

FROM AUTHORITARIAN PLURALISM TO CENTRALIZED AUTOCRACY IN MOROCCO

Abdeslam M. Maghraoui

Like other Arab monarchies, the Moroccan regime weathered, with minor concessions, the 2011 mass protests that shook the MENA region. Almost a decade after constitutional reforms and two general elections that were supposed to open up the political sphere, the monarchy's stronghold remains unscathed. King Mohammed VI dominates single-handedly the essential centers of power. The same tight circle of royal advisors exerts tremendous influence behind closed doors and quite openly.[1] The extensive network of senior administrative, judiciary, military, and security officials, known as the Makhzen, is in full control. The elected municipal or parliamentary bodies, and the governments that emerged after the 2011 reforms, have been in every meaningful way subservient to the Makhzen.[2] And the regime's handling of a year-long social movement in the Rif, as well as protests across Morocco during 2016–17, suggests a new confidence in the classic authoritarian tactics. Measures included mass arrests, physical intimidation by regime thugs, tainted legal proceedings, the shutting down of social media, and the harassment of independent journalists and human rights activists. King Mohammed's dismissal of three cabinet members and a handful of senior officials for "negligence" in late October 2017 was a de facto and de jure confirmation of monarchic absolute power, not a political concession to the street.[3]

The slide to absolute monarchy in Morocco is pertinent to understanding authoritarian institutions and stability because the switch defies three intuitive explanations: (1) neither social handouts nor systematic repression seem to be at the center of the backslide; (2) the rejuvenation of noncompetitive authoritarian politics is driven neither by pressure from regime hard-liners nor by some change in the structure of the Moroccan political opposition; and (3) the regime's benefits from authoritarian backsliding are not obvious, and the risks are high. So why did the monarchy give up competitive authoritarianism? And how does it stay on top of the political game when financial resources are limited and a young and restless population is growing?

This chapter argues that the monarchy's slide to tighter authoritarianism while keeping a semblance of competitive institutions allows it to shift the blame for failed human development policies to other actors. In the Moroccan context, then, parties, elections, and parliaments are neither for democracy "window dressing" nor for accommodating the opposition. There is no obvious popular support for democracy, and the traditional opposition political parties, including the Party of Justice and Development, are discredited. In the Moroccan political system, major policy decisions in the most strategic sectors are still made by an executive monarchy. When policies succeed, the palace takes the credit; when they fail, the blame goes to "elected" institutions. But as the social movement in the Rif demonstrates, this strategy has its limits. Increasingly the monarchy finds itself in direct confrontation with new and young actors who demand bluntly to negotiate with the king, not the widely discredited intermediaries. More broadly, this means that the distinctions political scientists have drawn between different types of authoritarianism are conceptually useful but cannot predict institutional change or the actors' behavior. Autocrats, like the king of Morocco, are much less constrained by their institutions than the theory of competitive authoritarianism allows.

Scholars of Middle East politics are divided on why monarchies faced a different fate than the republics during the Arab Spring. The most compelling explanation has been the flexibility of monarchical institutions in comparison to the rigidity of republican authoritarianism. But authoritarian regimes in the Middle East have grown to resemble each other because they face similar challenges, draw on similar resources and institutions, and mimic the same upgrading strategies.[4] Hence, institutional differences between monarchies and republics, especially those with no oil resources, cannot by themselves provide an adequate explanation.

Beyond institutional flexibility, this chapter links the Moroccan monarchy's survival to the paradoxical benefits of facing recurring political and social shocks over time. I argue that while the monarchy uses political institutions to manage political elites and maintain cohesion, surviving challenges from below has to do with how it responds to those challenges. Timing, contingency decisions, social ties, and personal judgment seem to be more important to the monarchy's endurance than the institutional fabric. In fact, democratic-looking but discredited institutions can be a liability in times of acute crises because they expose the elites' divisions and lack of autonomy, and they erode public hope that the system can ever be reformed from within. Drawing lessons from the Arab Spring, the Moroccan regime is cynically shifting from authoritarian pluralism into plain centralized autocracy where the Makhzen flaunts its design unapologetically. In the context of this book, the implication of this argument is that no set of institutions can guarantee authoritarian stability in North Africa. A chain of unpredictable events, a major natural disaster, bad timing, or ill-conceived decisions can plunge the countries in the region into turmoil. More broadly, the chapter's argument speaks to two areas of research: the role of political institutions in authoritarian context and the puzzling survival of Arab monarchies.

This chapter is divided into four sections. The first provides the broad theoretical and empirical context of my analysis of Moroccan politics. The main contention here is that the theories underlying the study of institutions in an authoritarian context are elites-focused and hence overlook the process that helps regimes diffuse threats from street contestation. Success in the former (i.e., the co-optation of elites in functioning legislatures and active political parties) does not necessarily entail success in the latter. The second section considers the scale and intensity of protests in Morocco in 2011. I discuss the level of pressure the Moroccan regime faced to underline similarities with other protest movements in the Arab world. The third section analyzes the regime's response process to highlight timing and contingencies. I argue that promises to make formal institutions more accountable had a palliative effect on protests only insofar as the main political actor responded in an opportune fashion (i.e., when and how the king addressed the public). The last section provides evidence for the institutional unraveling of authoritarian pluralism and the emergence of centralized autocracy in Morocco.

Authoritarian Institutions and Monarchical Resilience

The study of authoritarian institutions coalesced into a distinct field of research after the proliferation of hybrid regimes that became neither fully authoritarian nor democratic after the Cold War.[5] Rather than focusing on the origins of authoritarianism, political scientists began to investigate how "democratic-looking" mechanisms sustain authoritarian rule.[6] But this body of research is by and large elites-centered and concerned primarily with the question of elites' defection. In other words, the collapse or survival of an authoritarian regime depends on its ability to provide incentives to key political players within the system.

The other relevant debate centers more specifically on the question of why no Arab monarch was deposed during the Arab Spring. There are four main perspectives on the puzzling resilience of monarchies in the face of popular protests. The most prevalent, articulated by Christopher Davidson, holds that Arab monarchs would eventually succumb to popular pressure because they face similar problems as the Arab presidents.[7] The main reason why the monarchies have been able to hold until now, the argument goes, is accessibility to considerable resources and Western support. But mounting population pressure, strenuous social demands, unemployment, and sectarianism are undermining the domestic social contract that has been in place for decades. And the lack of a coherent regional security strategy exposes the monarchies to the risks of instability in a region where Western influence is declining. In other words, the demise of Arab monarchies is a matter of time: oil prices are falling, domestic contestation is mounting, and Western priorities in the region are shifting. Davidson's argument concerns the Gulf States mainly, but it should apply more forcefully to Jordan and Morocco. Because the monarchies lack the resources to buy out political dissent and strike a "ruling bargain," they should have disappeared or become more democratic. But this is obviously not the case. Even with falling energy prices, which consumes a huge portion of Morocco's budget, the current government has continued to cut public spending and increase taxes on working people.[8] And Mohammed VI is still at the center of a political system that is hard to characterize as a constitutional monarchy.

On the question of Western support in particular, it is conceivable that Morocco's strategic partnership with the European Union has been a mitigating factor. Western support is often advanced as an explanation of monarchical survival in the Arab world. Arab sultans and princes have historically tied their faith to Western powers. From the anti-Ottoman revolts and the Cold War era to the US wars on Iraq and global terrorism, Arab monarchies have bet on the winning horse. In the case of Morocco, ties with the West may be less dramatic but no less profound due to history, geography, and demographics. Morocco's proximity to Europe and its significant immigrant populations in France, Spain, Belgium, and the Netherlands make it a particularly important partner. Morocco's stability is key to Europe's security strategy on the Mediterranean front. Certainly, European partnerships since the 1995 Barcelona Process focused mainly on border controls, human trafficking, and terrorism. But the partnerships also included political, economic, and cultural "baskets" to encourage political reforms, respect of human rights, and social development. Yet twenty years after the launching of a dozen initiatives, agreements, and partnerships, European support didn't lead to a democratic transition pact guided from above, nor did it prevent the emergence of popular contestation, Islamic movements, and radical groups that could destabilize the regime from below. If anything, Mohammed VI seems to have moved away from reforms his father initiated in the 1990s. So it is hard to evaluate exactly how Morocco's partnership with the European Union mattered in the Arab Spring.

But more importantly, the quintessential partners of Western powers in the region, Mubarak in Egypt, Ben Ali in Tunisia, and before them, the shah in Iran, lost power after only a few weeks of sustained contestation. Tunisia and Egypt are particularly relevant because they were no less pampered or pressured by Western powers than Morocco. The United States' reticence or even refusal to defend Mubarak, given his regime's cooperation in security matters and centrality to Arab-Israeli peace, reflects the limits of the Western support thesis.

A second perspective emphasizes the legitimacy assets of monarchs.[9] The general argument here is that the monarchies draw on broader local networks of support and more traditional religious norms than the republics. Hence, although by no means democratic, monarchies allow a degree of cultural and political pluralism, which lets them act as arbitrators above the fray. As such, there are limits monarchs cannot transgress lest they risk losing their status as neutral arbitrators. Certainly, monarchs are rarely exposed to the charge of sectarianism and tribalism, as was the case in Hussein's Iraq, Assad's Syria, and Qaddafi's Libya. But political legitimacy, minimally defined as the sense of obligation and willingness to obey the sovereign, is tricky to measure. In the case of Morocco, the king's religious legitimacy has often been exaggerated, based on soft evidence, or simply reflected official discourse. There is no doubt that many Moroccans identify with the monarchy and love their king. But the ultimate test is whether Moroccans would mobilize to resist another ruler should the monarchy collapse. The passivity of most Moroccans during the 1971–72 military coup attempts and various opposition movements to the monarchy under Hassan II does not gibe with the legitimacy thesis. Like Arab presidents, monarchs are the country's first leaders, artists, jurists, farmers, and educators—until they fall. Fear, more than legitimacy, kept the country in line under Hassan II.[10] Today, Moroccans are probably less fearful than before, but that does not mean that the monarchy's legitimacy has saved it from the Arab Spring. In 2013, the public outrage over Mohammed VI's pardon of a Spanish citizen accused of raping eleven children in Morocco revealed surprising feelings and attitudes about the young monarch.[11]

Yet another view holds that the monarchies, especially resource-poor Jordan and Morocco, survived popular contestation because they had already reformed their political systems.[12] No doubt, under domestic pressure and changing global norms and economies, Jordan and Morocco relaxed some state controls and allowed greater political participation. But these reforms affected neither the executive vocation of the monarchies nor the extensive power of the monarchs. Moreover, both monarchies and republics, including Tunisia, Egypt, and Syria under Bashar Assad, pursued "authoritarian upgrading" strategies to adapt.[13] If anything, processes of political liberalization and economic opening since the 1990s have narrowed the governance differences between the Arab authoritarian regimes.[14] So why would limited reforms help withstand protests in some cases but not others when the end product is structurally and institutionally the same: "liberalized autocracy"?[15]

Combining elements of the resources, legitimacy, and reform arguments, a fourth perspective links monarchical survival specifically to the type of political coalitions monarchies pursue.[16] According to this argument, the Moroccan monarchy survived because it mobilized political groups and networks that support nationalist causes. It associated itself with the struggle of independence in the 1950s, it led the recovery of the Western Sahara in the 1970s, and it remains the symbol of national unity and the protector of minorities. Such coalitions allowed the Makhzen to mobilize vast resources to sustain its formidable patronage networks. The problem with this argument is that political coalitions can be very unstable, especially those based on abstract notions such nationalism and national unity. Certainly, King Hassan's father, Sultan Mohammed V, was a symbol of independence and nationalism, but soon after independence monarchic rule was seriously contested. How else would we explain the resistance of significant sections of the National Liberation Army to disarm in defiance of Mohammed V's orders after independence (1956)? What about the Rif rebellion (1958–59), the radical nationalist opposition to the monarchy (1960s), the military coup attempts (1971–72), or the nationalists' resistance to Hassan's acceptance of a vote on self-determination in the Western Sahara (1984)? In short, Morocco's recent political history is a history of coalition failures and instability. But it is precisely that kind of instability, I argue, that allowed the monarchy to develop a degree of immunity against unforeseen events such as the Arab Spring.

In sum, the four perspectives shed light on aspects of authoritarian endurance that guarantee maximum control but miss an important dimension: the paradoxical benefits of turbulence and uncertainty.

At a press conference in July 1971, King Hassan II snapped at a reporter who seemed to probe his hold on power, "I am more royal today than ever before." Hassan wanted to dispel the slightest hint that he was an enfeebled king. The previous day, while celebrating his forty-second birthday, the king had miraculously survived a military coup. He had saved his life by inviting mutinous cadets standing guard to recite the first verse of the Quran and pledge allegiance to the throne. A year later in August, King Hassan astonishingly survived another military coup. As he was flying back from France, four F-5 military jets from the Royal Air Force intercepted his Boeing 727 in Moroccan air space and opened fire. During the attack, Hassan grabbed the radio as if he were the pilot speaking, and he announced that the "tyrant [king]" was dead. The Boeing fuselage was badly damaged and eight passengers were killed, but the plane landed safely. Hassan lived to rule for another rough twenty-seven years. Under his rule (1961–99), the monarchy faced all sorts of challenges, from stern political opposition and military coups to urban riots and rural rebellions. Whether it was good luck or survival skills that saved the king from his military, the monarchy's trajectory and how it handled the latest round of popular protests give new insights on authoritarian persistence. Authoritarian regimes that face frequent political turbulence are more likely to survive popular contestation than sturdy authoritarian regimes. It could be the accumulated experience of confronting shocks that gives certain authoritarian regimes a political edge. This chapter explores this proposition to explain King Mohammed VI's response to the 2011 popular protests associated with the Arab Spring.

The general question of why and how some authoritarian regimes handle political challenge better than others has come to the forefront after the burst of popular uprisings that shook the Arab region since 2011.[17] In the eight Arab countries that experienced significant protests, four presidents lost power (Tunisia, Egypt, Libya, and Yemen), one president lost control over much of his nation's territory (Syria), and three monarchs survived (Bahrain, Jordan, and Morocco). The case of Morocco is particularly revealing. The regime weathered mass demonstrations with no external intervention, minimal violence, limited financial resources, and no political concessions. This is surprising given the ostensible social success and political stability of authoritarianism in Syria and Tunisia, and the alleged frailty of young monarchs ruling over impoverished countries.[18] Why has the Moroccan monarchy emerged unscathed in the face of popular protests?

Scale of Protest

To tackle this question, it is important to probe first whether the monarchy was at all challenged during the protests. If the protestors' demands and social mobilization were too modest, that would provide a reasonable enough explanation of the monarchy's survival.[19] Certainly, unlike in Tunisia, Egypt, or Libya, demonstrators in Morocco didn't call for regime change (*isqat al-nizam*), and the agenda was reformist rather than revolutionary. The main political demand of the "February 20 movement"—the Moroccan version of the Arab Spring—was the establishment of a constitutional monarchy with limited powers. The movement's social claims were employment, the end of corruption, and better access to social services. These are old and familiar demands, unlikely to intimidate a 350-year-old monarchy. Also significant, the movement did not generate the emotional impact of a million demonstrators converging on a single public space.[20] There were simply no "Fridays of Furry" or collective prayers, and nothing that closely resembles the manning camps and barricades in Cairo's Tahrir Square.

Nonetheless, the regime was rattled.[21] Crowds chanted slogans such as "down with autocracy," and posters pointed the finger directly at Mohammed VI, holding him responsible for the country's epidemic corruption, political nepotism, and human rights violations.[22] The king's tight network of business partners, political advisors, and heads of security became a rallying cry. Their effigies were scornfully displayed during demonstrations. Such a public implication and direct indictment of the king is politically and psychologically significant. It desacralized the king as a person and, like elsewhere in the region, broke the "wall of fear" that protects the regime.

Furthermore, the movement did not trust the existing government institutions to carry out reforms. Activists demanded the dismissal of the parliament and the government and called for the establishment of a transitional administration, which would be charged with organizing new elections and drafting a new constitution. Clearly, although the monarchy was not called into question, the reform movement had no faith whatsoever in the political system. Protestors called for dismantling the king's powerful patronage system, the Makhzen, and warned the king to heed the voice of the people (*sma'a saout al-shaab!*). This "reformist" platform is not substantively different from the revolutionary agenda protestors across the region articulated.

But there are two other reasons why the monarchy was under pressure: the scope of mobilization and the impenetrability of the actors. Although social and political activism is hardly new in Morocco, it has been largely contained in time, space, and sectors.[23] The February 20 movement not only drew large crowds from across sectors but also organized large marches in different parts of the country for an extended period (February–June 2011). The exact number of people who joined the movement's calls is in dispute. According to Moroccan government figures, the first demonstrations, held on February 20, 2011, in fifty-three cities and towns, drew thirty-seven thousand protestors. Organizers claimed three hundred thousand people demonstrated that day. Their estimate is based on reports from local branches in the fifty-three locations. Mamfakinsh, a Moroccan Facebook group that advocates democratic change, put the number at 122,000.[24] If we accept the average of the three estimates as a reliable number, the first protests in Morocco would have drawn proportionally larger crowds than the initial protests in Tunisia,[25] Libya[26] and Yemen[27] combined. According to local media reports, the second and third demonstrations drew even larger crowds in more than one hundred cities and towns. How, then, can we explain the different outcome in Morocco?

Most ominous for the regime was that the movement was difficult to infiltrate and neutralize. The organizing nucleus and its wide and diverse supporters were not the usual actors that could be easily co-opted or intimidated. Like in Tunisia and Egypt, Moroccan activists were not well known, didn't constitute a coherent collective, and had no stakes in the existing system. Broadly speaking, the movement comprised three main circles. The dynamic core was a diverse group of web activists who had been incubating in cyberspace for years on the margins of state-monitored political and civil society. "Stealthy" individual blogs or group websites with thousands of young followers took on sensitive issues such as the king's excessive wealth, the monarchy's budget, freedom of conscience, gay rights, torture in secret detention centers, and sexual tourism in Marrakesh. When street protests began in Tunisia and Egypt, Moroccan cyber activists responded swiftly.

During the first week of February, with surprising speed and technical dexterity, dozens of uplifting videos surfaced on YouTube. They showed young men and women from different social and cultural backgrounds, calling for mass demonstrations in colloquial Moroccan and Tamazight dialects. Their message why Moroccans should demonstrate was slick, universal, and nonpolemical.

The second component of the movement was a broad coalition of some forty leftist parties, young Islamists, students' and workers' unions, various professional associations, and human rights organizations. These groups endorsed the movement's general demands and agreed that no partisan banners from any particular group would be displayed during the demonstrations. The endorsement gave the movement timely access to seasoned cadres across the country with invaluable local networks and field experience. Backing from independent civil society and combative parties culminated in the establishment of the National Support Council with branches in every major city, town, and large village. The council provided nationwide logistical, legal, and moral support to demonstrators, especially in remote areas where local authorities could repress with impunity.

The third circle of the movement was no less challenging to contain. It included tens of thousands of unstructured or unaffiliated demonstrators from all walks of life. Also significant, it included adherents of al-Adl wal-Ihsan, the largest Islamic organization and political opposition group in Morocco today. Al-Adl's endorsement and participation were particularly menacing to the regime because of the group's formidable mobilization capacity, its radical contestation of the monarch's religious status, and its apparent willingness to cooperate with secular groups.[28]

Although the movement's three circles agreed on a broad platform, like elsewhere in the region, there were basic ideological, generational, and ultimately strategic differences. During the first months, cooperation among the movement's heterogeneous components was based on two fundamental principles: (1) that members of organized associations, parties, and groups would participate as individuals, not as members of their groups; and (2) the decisional autonomy of the youth core, which was the obvious moral custodian of the movement, was to be preserved. These two principles allowed Islamists and leftists, two long-sworn ideological enemies, to come together, and moderated conflicts between cautious old guards and young militants within organized groups. In practice, the movement empowered local branches with the autonomy of decision-making to minimize the risks of infiltration and take-over. And instead of voting, the movement opted for deliberation and consensus to avoid alienating supporters. But this of course created other practical problems such as lengthy meetings and deferred decisions.

In sum, evidence suggests that the Moroccan monarchy faced at least as much pressure as the other Arab authoritarian regimes. If there was any doubt about the movement's significance and potential danger, the king didn't want to take that chance. On March 9, that is, a few days before the second planned demonstration, Mohammed VI abruptly announced sweeping constitutional reforms. Among other things, the monarch promised a new constitution that would reinforce the rule of law and separation of powers, guarantee gender equality, and give Amazigh culture and language an official status. It looked like an unprecedented political concession of a monarchy under popular pressure.

Preserving the Status Quo

By June, however, it became clear that the king's proposed reforms would not affect the dominant role of the monarchy. Aided in part by divisions within the movement and by the inability of mainstream political opposition to seize the opportunity, the king backtracked because he sensed he was still the only game in town. The palace handpicked a nineteen-member consultative commission to be in charge of revising the constitution. The designated members were independent jurists, scholars, and civil society activists, but they were defenseless in the face of royal pressure. For its part, the youth movement was uncertain whether the proposed reforms were a historic victory or a political trap. But quickly, divisions transpired on whether the movement should participate in the national consultations on the constitutional reform and make propositions to the commission. The question was never clearly settled even though the movement continued to demonstrate. In the end, mostly parties' old guards, heads of toothless trade unions, and the Islamist Party of Justice and Development (referred to here by its French acronym, PJD) relayed timid suggestions. The royal cabinet interfered in the revision process in two ways: by probing members of the constitution commission directly on specific clauses that seemed to limit the king's powers, and by playing conservative against liberal parties on the questions of identity, gender equality, and freedom of conscience. In mid-June, Mohammed VI invited Moroccans to vote "yes" for a revised constitution draft that his cabinet had filtered and approved. The not-so-new constitution was ratified by 98.5 percent of voters in a popular referendum on July 1, 2011.

In another unprecedented political development, expedited parliamentary elections in November 2011 brought Islamists to power. The PJD, the main Islamist competitor of the semiclandestine al-Adl wal-Ihsan, won the largest number of seats in the first legislative election organized under the new constitution. But in accordance with the spirit and letter of the constitution, the king appointed Abdelilah Benkirane, the head of the PJD, as prime minister. The move sucked the wind out of the February 20 movement.

None of this is meant to suggest that the regime didn't resort to repression. A nationwide crackdown that involved the security forces and pro-regime thugs (Baltaiya) was launched before the disclosure of the revised constitution and the referendum. Attempts by the police to disparage and intimidate known activists and their families were frequent. And the Moroccan security forces deployed numerous ploys on the web to confuse dates, slogans, and places of public gatherings. But between February and May 2011, the security forces generally withdrew from the demonstrations' routes to avoid confrontation. This may explain why casualties were relatively low. Throughout the protests, nine people were killed, but only three died because of lethal police force.[29]

Quite clearly, the Arab Spring protests in Morocco were serious enough to rattle the regime, and the formal political process was of little use. The monarchy found itself face-to-face with new actors that were not part of the political system, and those within the system were simply following its lead. Mohammed VI gambled with a constitutional reform proposal and a soft approach to the protests, but it was not clear where those steps might actually lead. The capacity to improvise and act under uncertainty saved the monarchy, but this runs counter to the fundamental claims of existing perspectives on monarchical resilience.

From Authoritarian Pluralism to Centralized Autocracy

When King Mohammed VI came to the throne in 1999, he had two political options to anchor his rule: total control and stability or serious reforms with potential risks. Hassan II left with the means to pursue either. From his father, Mohammed inherited a well-oiled and tested political machine. In different iterations of the Moroccan constitution, the king, as head of the state, enjoys vast powers and protections akin to those of Europe's medieval kings. Soon after independence from France, a 1958 law declared that the king and the monarchy could not be criticized or represented in comedy or caricature. The law is still enforced today, and many Moroccan artists, activists, and independent reporters have served prison terms on the basis of the law. The Moroccan king is also "commander of the faithful," or the "shadow of God on earth." The title invests the king's words, decrees, recommendations, appointments, and business interests with a sacred status. No judiciary, legislative, or executive authority can challenge the king's personal entitlements, political powers, or religious title.

Mohammed VI also inherited from his father a formidable repressive-administrative apparatus to subdue opponents. While still crown prince, Hassan personally led thousands of troops to suppress Berber revolts in the Rif mountains during 1958–59. When he became king in 1961, nationalist and leftist parties with deep urban support immediately confronted him with the question of power sharing and constitutional rule. He responded swiftly by having radical party members, trade unionists, and rural dissident leaders arrested, tried, jailed, or simply driven into exile. Four years later, youths' and workers' protests in Morocco's major cities culminated in urban riots in Casablanca. It took days and hundreds of casualties before government troops could control the situation. After the riots, Hassan dissolved the parliament, declared a state of emergency, and tried political opponents for instigating the riots. The same year, an exiled leftist leader, Mehdi Ben Barka, was kidnapped and assassinated in France by the Moroccan secret police. The following two decades were no less turbulent. In addition to unrest within the military and the Western Sahara challenge, urban "bread riots" over cuts in subsidies imposed by international institutions in the 1980s poisoned relations between the monarchy and the opposition parties. King Hassan arrested the leaders of the main opposition party, the Union Socialiste des Forces Populaires (USFP), after accusing them of instigating the riots.

Along with the authoritarian fabric, Mohammed VI inherited a great potential to transform Morocco into a full-fledged constitutional monarchy. Despite all the repressive capabilities of Hassan's regime and the central role the monarchy carved out for itself in the political system, Hassan was never tempted by the single-party model in neighboring Algeria,

Tunisia, or Egypt.[30] There is no doubt that Hassan ruled like a despot and his regime committed serious human rights violations, known in Morocco as the "years of the lead." But Hassan keenly understood that a political system that allows for risks, uncertainty, and open dissent is a better insurance for the monarchy's longevity than total domination. He deployed authoritarian strategies that mixed traditional with modern forms of control,[31] but he also hoped that the Moroccan monarch would, one day, rule over a constitutional monarchy. It couldn't be him, but he prepared the groundwork for his successor.[32] In the 1990s, at a moment of virtual national consensus around the monarchy with no serious competitor, the king ushered in a series of far-reaching reforms. Focused on sensitive areas such as human rights, gender equality, freedom of expression, business transparency, the electoral system, and the alternation of power, the reforms revived many old political wounds but inoculated the body politic.[33] The reforms culminated in the historic alternation of power in 1998, when Hassan II (one year before his death) appointed a socialist, Abderrahman Youssoufi, prime minister. These steps may not qualify as democratic openings, but there is little doubt that total monarchical control was no longer viable.

Although King Mohammed VI is credited for responding swiftly and intelligently to mass demonstrations during the Arab Spring, the praise, or blame, should go to Hassan II's flexible institutional legacy. When the Arab Spring protests began in 2011, the monarchy had taken an authoritarian turn toward the dominant one-party system that seeks total control. Such a system, as we have seen, proved inefficient in confronting mass protests in neighboring countries.

At some level, the new king seemed to expand on his father's reformist agenda. "Democratic transition" with all the related accouterments continued to be a buzzword in political and civil society.[34] But except for the "2004 Forum for Truth and Justice," which led public hearings on past human rights violations, most of Mohammed VI's steps and gestures fall under the category of "authoritarian upgrading." Even in the area of human rights, Morocco's diplomatic crisis with France during 2014–15 over torture cases shows that the "years of the lead" are not so distant.[35] Two significant changes indicate Mohammed VI's fascination with authoritarian stability characteristic of dominant one-party systems. The first is the increasing "securitization" of politics.[36] Under King Mohammed VI, conventional political leaders and state cadres virtually ceded power to new technocratic elites.[37] Prominent among the technocratic elites are the heads and senior cadres of the Ministry of Interior and the alphabet soup of security agencies. Just like in Tunisia's Ben Ali or Egypt's Mubarak government, intelligence agencies, or *mukhabarat*, filter and monitor all sensitive sectors in Morocco, from university deans and heads of political parties to appointed governors and elected local and national bodies. The other significant authoritarian development was the establishment of the Party of Authenticity and Modernity (PAM) in 2008.[38] The founder of the party is Fouad Ali El Himma, the king's closest advisor and childhood friend. Within six months of its creation, the PAM became the strongest political party in Morocco, sweeping the 2009 local and national elections. The new party borrowed the methods, rhetoric, justifications, and ambitions of Tunisia's "successful" Democratic Constitutional Rally under Ben Ali.

In sum, it was not the monarchy's alleged legitimacy, exceptional regional stability, or preventive democratic reforms that saved it from the Arab Spring. Quite the opposite, the Moroccan monarchy was able to survive popular protests in large measure because of political experience accrued through turbulence and uncertainty.

The surprising stabilizing impact of instability applies to monarchies as well as republics. Jordan's chronic political vulnerability, Lebanon's civil wars, Algeria's war against the Islamists, and Iran's fractured politics perhaps explain regime endurance in these cases. The question is what level of instability is no longer a "good thing" for political stability, and how external factors transform the nature of crises within authoritarian systems. These are empirical queries that require further research. But at the conceptual level, the great diversity of popular contestation, regime response, and outcome during the Arab Spring raises questions about the determining impact of structures, institutions, or culture alone. No doubt, these variables are relevant to understanding why some regimes resisted protests while others collapsed quickly. The role of the military, for example, was determinant in all cases. The strength of state institutions explains the different outcomes between Tunisia and Libya. And the sectarian nature of politics explains the civil war in Syria. But while structural, institutional, and cultural conditions may set the stage for a movement's direction, ultimately it is the regime's experience and flexibility that determine how well it absorbs the shock. Syria's repressive capacity, Egypt's deep state, and Tunisia's cultural homogeneity didn't seem of much help when confronted with mass protests. The dosage and timing of repression matter, the nature and scheduling of political concessions matter, and the language and justification of pace of reforms matter. These modalities have more to do with "street smart" experience than with coercive capacity, available resources, or past reforms. In general, a seemingly unsteady but flexible authoritarian regime is more likely to survive a challenge from below than a seemingly robust but inflexible one.

ABDESLAM M. MAGHRAOUI is Associate Professor of Political Science at Duke University. He is author of *Liberalism without Democracy: Nationhood and Citizenship in Egypt, 1922–1936.*

Notes

1. As a gauge of regained monarchical confidence and power, consider the remarkable change of tolerating criticism of the monarchy. In the 2011 protests, the king's closest two advisors were the symbols of power abuse and corruption and crystalized public anger. Their names and photographs were displayed for months in virtually every march organized by the February 20 movement, forcing them to withdraw completely from the public scene. In 2016, the head of a political party known for its unwavering loyalty to the monarchy was harshly and publicly reprimanded by the palace for merely mentioning, without naming, the discretionary powers of a king's advisor. Local observers predicted that the party would lose seats in the October 2016 parliamentary elections due to its leader's veiled criticism. It did.

2. As of January 2017, months after the 2016 legislative elections, which the Party of Justice and Development (moderate Islamist) won, its leader, Abdelilah Benkirane, had yet to form a government. The party has been unable to form a governing coalition due to the obstruction of political parties with close ties to the Makhzen.

3. Saeed Kamali Dehghan, "Au Maroc, la répression du Hirak provoque un nouvel exode de migrants vers l'Espagne," *Le Monde*, November 2, 2017, http://www.lemonde .fr/afrique/article/2017/11/02/au-maroc-la-repression-du-hirak-provoque-un-nouvel -exode-de-migrants-vers-l-espagne_5209309_3212.html; Charlotte Bozonnet, "Le pouvoir marocain ébranlé par un an de révolte dans le rif," *Le Monde*, October 26, 2017, http://www.lemonde.fr/afrique/article/2017/10/26/le-pouvoir-marocain-ebranle-par -un-an-de-mouvement-social_5206040_3212.html; "Crise dans le rif : Le roi du Maroc décide de limoger trois ministres," *Le Monde*, October 24, 2017, http://www.lemonde.fr /afrique/article/2017/10/24/crise-dans-le-rif-le-roi-du-maroc-decide-de-limoger-trois -ministres_5205425_3212.html; "Dans le sud Marocain, des «manifestations de la soif» contre les pénuries d'eau," *Le Monde*, October 13, 2017, http://www.lemonde.fr/afrique /article/2017/10/13/dans-le-sud-marocain-des-manifestations-de-la-soif-contre-les -penuries-d-eau_5200650_3212.html; Charlotte Bozonnet, "Au Maroc, les délicats procès des militants du Hirak," *Le Monde*, October 6, 2017, http://www.lemonde.fr/afrique /article/2017/10/06/au-maroc-les-delicats-proces-des-militants-du-hirak_5196989_3212 .html#w1Os3OgLwwd24Vz2.99.

4. See, for example, Daniel Brumberg, "The Trap of Liberalized Autocracy," *Journal Of Democracy* 13, no. 4 (2002): 56–68, doi:10.1353/jod.2002.0064; Steven Heydemann, *Upgrading Authoritarianism in the Arab World* (Washington, DC: Saban Center at the Brookings

Institution, 2007), https://www.brookings.edu/wp-content/uploads/2016/06/10arabworld
.pdf; Stephen J. King, *The New Authoritarianism in the Middle East and North Africa*
(Bloomington: Indiana University Press, 2009).

5. Barbara Geddes, "What Do We Know about Democratization after Twenty
Years?," *Annual Review of Political Science* 2, no. 1 (1999): 115–44, doi:10.1146/annurev
.polisci.2.1.115.

6. Steven Levitsky and Lucan A. Way, *Competitive Authoritarianism* (Cambridge:
Cambridge University Press, 2010); Beatriz Magaloni, *Voting for Autocracy* (Cambridge:
Cambridge University Press, 2008).

7. Christopher M. Davidson, *After the Sheikhs*, 2nd ed. (London: Hurst, 2015).

8. Mustapha Maghriti, "La politique budgétaire au Maroc, un joker du gouvernement
Benkirane: À quel dosage?," *Les Echos*, January 27, 2014, http://archives.lesechos.fr/archives
/cercle/2014/01/27/cercle_89655.htm.

9. Zoltan Barany, *The "Arab Spring" in the Kingdoms* (Doha: Arab Center for Research
& Policy Studies, 2012), http://aihr-resourcescenter.org/administrator/upload/documents
/kingdoms.pdf; Victor Menaldo, "The Middle East and North Africa's Resilient Monarchs,"
Journal of Politics 74, no. 3 (2012): 707–22, doi:10.1017/s0022381612000436.

10. Henry Munson, *Religion and Power in Morocco* (New Haven: Yale University Press,
1993).

11. "Fury in Morocco after King Pardons Spanish Paedophile Who Raped 11 Local
Children," *Daily Mail*, August 1, 2013, http://www.dailymail.co.uk/news/article-2382628
/Fury-Morocco-king-pardons-Spanish-paedophile-raped-11-local-children.html.

12. Frédéric Vairel, *Politique et mouvements sociaux au Maroc* (Paris: Presses de Sciences
Po, 2014); Menaldo, "Resilient Monarchs"; Béatrice Hibou, *Le mouvement du 20 février, le
Makhzen et l'antipolitique. L'impensé des réformes au Maroc*, Dossiers du CERI (Paris: Centre
d'études et de recherches internationales, 2011), https://hal-sciencespo.archives-ouvertes.fr
/hal-01024402/document; Michael Herb, "Monarchism Matters," *Foreign Policy*, November
26, 2012, http://foreignpolicy.com/2012/11/26/monarchism-matters/.

13. Heydemann, *Upgrading Authoritarianism*.

14. King, *The New Authoritarianism*.

15. Brumberg, "The Trap of Liberalized Autocracy."

16. F. Gregory Gause III, *Kings for All Seasons: How the Middle East Monarchies
Survived the Arab Spring*, Brookings Doha Center Analysis Paper (Doha: Brookings Doha
Center, 2013), https://www.brookings.edu/wp-content/uploads/2016/06/Resilience-Arab
-Monarchies_English.pdf; Sean L. Yom and F. Gregory Gause, "Resilient Royals: How
Arab Monarchies Hang On," *Journal of Democracy* 23, no. 4 (2012): 74–88, doi:10.1353
/jod.2012.0062.

17. Eva Bellin, "Reconsidering the Robustness of Authoritarianism in the Middle
East: Lessons from the Arab Spring," *Comparative Politics* 44, no. 2 (2012): 127–49,
doi:10.5129/001041512798838021; Ludger Kühnhardt, "The Resilience of Arab Monarchy,"
Policy Review, no. 173 (2012): 57–67; Barany, *"Arab Spring" in the Kingdoms*; Gause III,
Kings for All Seasons.

18. Jean-Pierre Tuquoi, *Le dernier roi* (Paris: Grasset, 2001); Curtis R. Ryan, *Jordan in
Transition* (Boulder, CO: Lynne Rienner, 2002); Davidson, *After the Sheikhs*.

19. Gul Tuysuz, "Morocco Protests Fail to Take Hold," *Washington Post*, February 28, 2011,
http://www.washingtonpost.com/wp-dyn/content/article/2011/02/28/AR2011022805300.html.

20. James M. Jasper, "The Emotions of Protest: Affective and Reactive Emotions in and around Social Movements," *Sociological Forum* 13, no. 3 (1998): 393–424.

21. Marc Champion, "Morocco Joins In, Defying Predictions," *Wall Street Journal*, February 20, 2011, https://www.wsj.com/articles/SB10001424052748703498804576156180408970252.

22. "Morocco Protestors Demand Political Change," BBC, February 20, 2011, http://www.bbc.co.uk/news/world-africa-12518116; Souad Mkhennet, "Moroccan King Opens Door for Change," *New York Times*, April 28, 2011, https://www.nytimes.com/2011/04/28/world/africa/28iht-morocco28.html.

23. Vairel, *Politique et mouvements sociaux au Maroc.*

24. Mamfakinch, Bilan Statistique #Feb 20, https://www.mamfakinch.com/.

25. "Tunisia Struggles to End Protests," Al Jazeera, December 2010, https://www.aljazeera.com/news/africa/2010/12/20101229122733122341.html; Bilal Randeree, "Violent Clashes Continue in Tunisia," Al Jazeera, January 2011, https://www.aljazeera.com/news/africa/2011/01/201114101752467578.html.

26. Al Arabiya, "Clash Breaks Out as Libya Braces for Day of Danger," 2011.

27. Lina Sinjab, "Yemen Conflict: Protests Continue across the Country," BBC, May 30, 2011, http://www.bbc.co.uk/news/av/world-middle-east-13595745/yemen-conflict-protests-continue-across-the-country.

28. Al-Adl wal-Ihsan is not an officially recognized party, but it has mobilized hundreds of thousands of people in support of the Palestinian cause or in opposition to the war in Iraq. The group withdrew from the February 20 movement in December 2011, while still supporting its main objectives.

29. On February 20, five bodies were found inside a bank in the northern town of Al Hoceima after protestors allegedly set it on fire during protests. Three protestors died in separate confrontations with the police between February and October 2011 in Safi, Sefrou, and Ait Bouayach. One protestor died on October 13 in Safi after falling from a high building while running away from the police. Human Rights Watch also reported several beatings during the Arab Spring protests in Morocco.

30. Abdeslam Maghraoui, "Political Authority in Crisis: Mohammed VI's Morocco," *Middle East Report*, no. 218 (2001): 12, doi:10.2307/1559304.

31. Guilain Denoeux and Abdeslam Maghraoui, "King Hassan's Strategy of Political Dualism," *Middle East Policy* 5, no. 4 (1998): 104–30, doi:10.1111/j.1475-4967.1998.tb00372.x; Abdeslam Maghraoui, "Depoliticization in Morocco," *Journal of Democracy* 13, no. 4 (2002): 24–32, doi:10.1353/jod.2002.0070; Abdeslam Maghraoui, "The Perverse Effect of Good Governance: Lessons from Morocco," *Middle East Policy* 19, no. 2 (2012): 49–65, doi:10.1111/j.1475-4967.2012.00535.x.

32. The logic is strangely similar to Don Corleone's failed schemes to gain public respectability by gradually extricating his shadowy businesses from New York crime families (The Godfather movie series).

33. Frédéric Vairel, "La transitologie, langage du pouvoir au Maroc," *Politix* 80, no. 4 (2007): 109, doi:10.3917/pox.080.0109; Sabine Planel, "Transformations de l'etat et politiques territoriales dans le Maroc contemporain," *L'Espace Politique*, no. 7 (2009), doi:10.4000/espacepolitique.1234.

34. *Une décennie de réformes au Maroc, 1999–2009* (Paris: Karthala, 2009).

35. A systematic documentation of Morocco's continuing human rights violations can be found in Human Rights Watch reports (http://www.hrw.org/middle-eastn-africa/morocco/western-sahara).

36. On the securitization trend in Arab politics, see Mouin Rabbani, *The Securitization of Political Rule: Security Domination of Arab Regimes and the Prospects for Democratization*, Perspectives (Heinrich Böll Stiftung, 2011), https://ps.boell.org/sites/default/files/downloads/Perspectives_02-40_Mouin_Rabbani5.pdf.

37. Pierre Vermeren, *Le Maroc de Mohammed VI* (Paris: La Découverte, 2009); Saloua Zerhouni, "Morocco: Reconciling Continuity and Change," in *Arab Elites: Negotiating the Politics of Change*, ed. Volker Perthes (Boulder, CO: Lynne Rienner, 2004), 61–85.

38. Ferdinand Eibl, "The Party of Authenticity and Modernity (PAM): Trajectory of a Political Deus Ex Machina," *Journal of North African Studies* 17, no. 1 (2012): 45–66, doi:10.1080/13629387.2011.582698.

11

THE POLITICS OF MAURITANIA'S ARAB UPRISING AND AFTERMATH

Matt Buehler and Mehdi Ayari

Across the Arab world, the Arab uprisings have resulted in few cases of genuine democratic reform and many more instances of violence, instability, and economic disruption. Syria, Libya, and Yemen evidence the worst, most destructive outcomes of the Arab uprisings. Yet even the countries that witnessed the most democratic reform, Tunisia and Egypt, also encountered concomitant decreases in stability and economic health. The upshot is that citizens of North Africa feel internally divided after the uprisings. On one hand, they desire the greater freedoms and democracy these mobilizations represented, but on the other hand, they also seek the enhanced stability that a robust state and strong leader furnish. The result is that many Arab autocrats continue to keep their regimes resilient while promising piecemeal reforms and palliative concessions that do not equate to serious democratization.

These trends appear clearly in one understudied North African country, Mauritania. A complex and fascinating country, Mauritania lies stuck in a geographic gap between the Middle East and sub-Saharan Africa. With nearly four million citizens, Mauritania is an Arab country. A good case can be made for including Mauritania in the Middle East, as 85 percent of Mauritanians speak Arabic as a native language and Modern Standard Arabic is the country's official language.[1] It is also a member of the Arab league, thus self-identifying as an Arab state. Yet a strong case can also be made for including Mauritania in sub-Saharan Africa, given the country's substantial non-Arab African population—speakers of Pulaar, Wolof,

Soninké, and Bambara. Further, the historical fact that the French admin-istered Mauritania from Senegal during the colonial period, and not from Casablanca or Algiers, also orients the country toward sub-Saharan Africa. Yet Mauritania's linguistic diversity differs little from that of other Arab states with substantial non-Arabic speaking populations, notably Iraq and Syria, considered solidly within the Middle East and North Africa region. Moreover, the fact that the British colonialists administered the Persian Gulf kingdoms—once known as the Trucial States—from Delhi does not, today, shift them into the region of South Asia.

Unfortunately, the fact that Mauritania geographically straddles the Middle East and sub-Saharan Africa does not mean that researchers and scholars examining both regions have studied the country intensively. Rather, it has resulted in neglect. A quick scan of English-language works on Mauritanian politics turns up five books,[2] authored in 1967, 1990, 1995, 1996, and 2011.[3] Even fewer books have sought to view Mauritania through a comparative lens, examining its differences and similarities with other Arab states. In part, this stems from the fact, as Michael Willis explains, that Mauritania's ethnic politics are a "complex and pivotal" force shaping its politics, with "no immediate parallel in the rest of the Maghreb."[4] Yet although Mauritania appears an exceptional country, its citizens—similar to those governed by other authoritarian regimes of North Africa—face a dilemma common in neighboring Arab states. Whereas Mauritania's autocrat (Mohamed Ould Abdel Aziz) maintains a regime that traps cit-izens in an authoritarian system that limits their rights and voices, it also courts their political support by proffering greater predictability and stability.

This chapter shows how this trap or lure of stability has manifested in Mauritania, and how it emerged from the political dynamics of unrest that occurred during and after this country's Arab Spring. The chapter begins by introducing the facets and characteristics of the main movements, actors, and structures that shape Mauritanian politics, and how they developed after the critical postcolonial years. Then, the chapter moves from the postcolonial period to the contemporary era, analyzing Mauritania's Arab Spring and its aftermath of authoritarian regime reconsolidation. While Tunisia transitioned to democracy and Syria and Libya descended into chaos, Mauritania followed the pathway of Jordan, Morocco, Bahrain, and other Arab states, whose regimes did not collapse. Although major pro-tests on behalf of democratization and against authoritarianism did occur within Mauritania's borders, the regime of autocrat Mohamed Ould Abdel Aziz did not falter. Rather, it undertook numerous measures that ensured it would secure authoritarian resilience in the aftermath of the Arab uprisings. To reinforce his regime's rule, Abdel Aziz bolstered the underlying tribal and ethnic structure of the state, instituted limited changes to cultivate a (largely faux) reformist image, and increased direct repression of the opposition, especially representing ethnic groups, political parties, and critical journalists.

Finally, the chapter concludes with a discussion of how phenomena from Mauritanian politics—rarely put into a comparative framework—could be usefully compared with analogous developments in Arab countries more common in scholarship, such as Egypt, Algeria, and the Persian Gulf states. By comparing Mauritania with its neighboring Arab regimes in North Africa and beyond, future studies could help highlight how Mauritanian citizens—like those of other Arab states—often face a trade-off between supporting an authoritarian system that provides security and remaining trapped in an undemocratic society.

The Tribal and Ethnic Structure of Mauritanian Politics

Much like other states in North Africa, tribe has traditionally served as the center of society in Mauritania. It is pivotal to understanding politics both within Mauritania's different ethnic groups and between them. Because full colonial pacification never occurred in Mauritania, tribes have retained considerable control over society and continue to influence its politics. According to Ould-Mey, for example, approximately 230 different tribal groups remain active in Mauritania with a semblance of tribal organization.[5] Roughly speaking, they divide into four constellations of allied tribes living within Mauritania's four main geographic regions—the North, the Center, the East/Southeast, and the South.[6] The French never fully pacified Mauritania or broke its tribal political system because the territory held little value to them. The French called Mauritania *la vide* (or the "void"), intimating its perceived worthlessness.[7] Although discoveries of precious metals increased foreign interest in Mauritania later, and this interest grew exponentially after the discovery of oil deposits in the late 2000s, the French only initially expressed interest in Mauritania for geostrategic reasons. It connected France's prized possession in sub-Saharan Africa, Senegal, with the country's settler stronghold in North Africa, Algeria.

Beginning in the precolonial era, a distinct system of tribes existed in Mauritania. There were warrior tribes, intellectual tribes, craftsman tribes, and herdsmen tribes.[8] These tribes often traded goods and services—for example, intellectual tribes sent imams to warrior tribes, and warrior tribes deployed fighters to protect intellectual tribes. This tribal system overlays ethnic politics. Within Mauritanian society, tribes were often multiethnic, including both "dominating" and "dominated" social groups.[9] Arabs within tribes included both white and black Arabs, with the former known by Mauritania specialists as Moors and the latter called Haratines. Since both Moors and Haratines are native Arabic speakers and embrace Arab cultural traditions, this study terms them white and black Arabs. Indeed, these terms may be more accurate than the Moor-Haratine dichotomy employed by most Mauritania specialists, as white and black Arabs exist throughout the Arab world. Indeed, countries such as Egypt, Morocco, and the Persian Gulf states exhibit considerable racial diversity among Arabs.[10]

Traditionally, black Arabs served as slaves for white Arabs. Some black Arabs remain enslaved in Mauritania, especially in its isolated interior. Officially abolished by law in 1961, in 1981, and again in 2007, slavery persists, and approximately 340,000–600,000 black Arabs remain enslaved.[11] Eschewing chattel slavery, white Arabs typically compress black Arabs into subtler forms of forced labor, such as domestic servants, sharecropping peasants, or livestock herdsmen. Despite the exploitative labor relations between them, white and black Arabs join forces in opposition to Mauritania's non-Arabic speaking black African minority, the Afro-Mauritanians. While sectarianism sows conflict in other Arab states, especially those with a Sunni-Shia cleavage, this tripartite ethnic divide underlies Mauritanian politics.

After colonial independence, some North African leaders—notably Habib Bourguiba—sought to break their countries' underlying tribal social structure. Mauritania's postcolonial president, Moktar Ould Daddah, took the opposite tack: he retained the tribal system and integrated it into his dominant party, the Mauritanian People's Party.[12] Thus, from independence until Daddah's ouster by way of a 1978 coup, a coalition of intellectual tribes including both white and black Arabs ruled Mauritania. Daddah was a Francophile and sought to draw Mauritania closer to France. Historically, Mauritania's southern tribes—especially Daddah's Oulad Birri clan—had assisted French forces stationed at the colonial outpost of St. Louis at the mouth of the Senegal River, from whence Mauritania was governed.[13] Because Daddah's father, grandfather, and uncles had assisted French colonialists, he too gained their favor. He was sent to France to be trained as

Mauritania's first lawyer. Along the way, he also earned the titles of Mauritania's first college graduate and first newspaper editor.

Daddah's postcolonial rule set an important precedent: tribal and ethnic politics infused all aspects of Mauritanian politics related to parties, movement, state agencies, and other formal institutions. The informal, personalist politics of tribal life shaped the formal politics of governmental institutions. Even campus life in Mauritania at the University of Nouakchott, for example, exhibits traits of tribal politics with tensions between tribes over appointments within the college administration. In opposition to Daddah's southern tribes, northern tribes fiercely resisted French colonial influence (although it was minimal in Mauritania). These northern tribes—more predominately white Arab and nomadic—were considered warrior tribes. Early leaders of the northern tribes pledged loyalty to Morocco's sultan and claimed lineage to the Idrissi dynasty of Meknes. In future years, Mauritania's northern tribes would unseat Daddah's southern tribes as core leaders of the country's autocratic regime.

Gradually, parties and movements emerged to counter Daddah's rule, including both Marxist and pan-Arab parties. Many of these parties were, in reality, embodiments of northern tribes and marginalized ethnic groups excluded from power under Daddah's reign. The Marxist Kadahine— or "toilers'" movement—grew from a teachers' union in the early 1970s. The party emerged after a 1968 strike in a French-controlled copper and iron mine outside of Zeourate.[14] In addition to Marxist parties, pan-Arab parties—often constituted from northern tribes—called for unification with Morocco and opposed Daddah and his southern tribes, which had amicable relations with some Afro-Mauritanian tribes. Other groups such as the Freedom Movement (*harakat el-hor*) agitated for the abolishment of slavery of black Arabs, integration of former slaves into Mauritanian society, and reparations for past slavery.[15] Although Daddah was no democrat and favored his tribe over others, he was also a refined intellectual who genuinely sought compromise and peace between Mauritania's different tribes and ethnic groups. He realized harmony among these groups would create stability and enhance prospects for economic development.

The Reign of Ould Taya: Increasing Ethnic Conflict

As Mauritania moved into the 1970s, a new force appeared in politics: the military. Politics by the sword replaced dialogue and consensus. In 1978 the military, advancing the interests of northern tribes, ousted Daddah.[16]

Maaouya Ould Sid'Ahmed Taya spearheaded the coup and took the reins of government, ultimately ruling from 1984 to 2005. Between 1978 and 1984, Mauritania teetered on the brink as several coups and countercoups rocked the country, creating an atmosphere of instability and low-level violence in the capital city.

Unlike Daddah's, Ould Taya's regime trumpeted its Arab nationalism and brooked little compromise with parties or movements representing black Arabs or Afro-Mauritanians. Members of the black Arab antislavery movement were imprisoned, including its leader, Messoud Boulkheir. Afro-Mauritanians began to pick up arms in underground resistance movements, such as Les Forces de Libération Africain de Mauritanie (FLAM).[17] Working from exile in Senegal and later in New York and Europe, the movement criticized the Ould Taya regime's oppression of the African minority. The Afro-Mauritanians took action due to events surrounding what became known as the "years of ash," a period in which over six thousand Afro-Mauritanians were expelled to Mali and Senegal during border skirmishes between Mauritanian and Senegalese forces.[18] The conflict began with competition over grazing rights and unresolved ethnic tensions between Arabs and Africans living on both sides of the Senegal River. Large Arab populations residing in northern Senegal, likewise, were deported to Mauritania. In response to Mauritanian repression of black Africans, riots engulfed Dakar, Senegal, in April 1989, with violence directed at Arab merchants from Mauritania working in the city.[19] Tens of thousands of Arab merchants were forced to abandon their shops and flee, and more than forty died in public lynchings and other grotesque acts of violence.[20] This conflict climaxed in 1990 when Arab military commanders in Mauritania ordered the execution of at least twenty-eight Afro-Mauritanian soldiers in the remote village of Inal, a stronghold of the northern tribes. In this context of conflict between Arabs and non-Arabs, Ould Taya sought to further emphasize his Arab nationalist bona fides. To this end, he decided in 1991 to endorse Saddam Hussein's decision to invade Kuwait. While Daddah had worked to cultivate harmony between ethnic groups and draw Mauritania closer to France and the West, Ould Taya marginalized ethnic minorities and asserted Mauritania's Arab identity.

Other politicians and activists also mobilized against Ould Taya's rule. In 1991, they converged into one party—the Union of Democratic Forces (Union des Forces Démocratiques, or UFD). Led by former president Moktar Ould Daddah's half-brother, Ahmed Ould Daddah, the UFD mobilized political forces from across the ideological spectrum. It included centrists, leftists, Marxists, and, for the first time in Mauritanian politics, activists associated with Mauritania's Muslim Brotherhood, the Islamists (known as the *Islahiyoun* or Reformists locally). Although these activists had different ideologies, they predominantly hailed from nonnorthern tribes and sought to limit the increasing influence of Ould Taya's northern tribes. Ould Taya reacted harshly to their dissent. He used the pretext of a failed military coup attempt in June 2003 to repress and imprison many of the UFD activists, in what became known as the Wad-Naga trials. Although they were eventually acquitted of charges, Ahmed Ould Daddah and other UFD activists spent months in prison living in bad sanitary conditions and suffering from torture. Some activists in the UFD, notably the Islamist leader Jamil Mansour, fled the country clandestinely.

After multiple arrests in the 1990s and 2000s, Mansour was ousted from his high-profile elected position as mayor of Arafat, Nouakchott's most densely populated ward district, which was inhabited by white and black Arabs. Despite his exile, Mansour had successfully increased the influence of Mauritania's Islamist party, especially after Ould Taya's controversial decision to open official diplomatic relations with Israel. While Ould Taya's decision made Mauritania a darling to the United States, it became a pariah state in the Arab world. Ould Taya seemed to trade the Arab nationalist credentials he had built up in the early 1990s for closer relations with the West by the 2000s. Thus, as Ould Taya's reign advanced into twenty years of rule, his policies and decision-making became more erratic and unpredictable without a clear ideological or strategic trajectory.

Failed Democratization of 2005–2008 and the Arab Uprisings of 2011

In 2005, Ould Taya's twenty-one-year reign ended. Like his predecessor Moktar Ould Daddah, Ould Taya was removed by way of military putsch. A group of generals and other high-ranking military officers ousted the autocrat and pledged reform.[21] This time, however, the coup came from deep within the bowels of Ould Taya's regime, from some of his most trusted military advisors.[22] These included the generals Mohamed Ould Abdel Aziz and Ely Ould Mohamed Vall. Abdel Aziz had served as head of Ould Taya's presidential guard, whereas Vall had acted as his director for national security. Immediately, international observers questioned whether the generals sought to implement real change or simply shift corrupt benefits away from Ould Taya and toward themselves. Indeed, as one report issued after the coup stated: "That Vall and Abdel Aziz belong to the same tribal group, one which was highly privileged under the old regime, raises the question whether they truly intend to change its clientelist patterns."[23] Specifically, both generals hailed from the Oulad Bou Sbaa, a clan within the larger constellation of northern tribes allied with Ould Taya. As the postcoup situation solidified, some analysts hypothesized that the generals ousted Ould Taya as a stratagem to attract new US democratization funding that had materialized during the George W. Bush administration.[24]

Despite this initial skepticism, the generals took steps toward reform. In 2006 and 2007, they organized legislative and presidential elections, whose results were largely deemed free and fair. They unseated Ould Taya's autocratic dominant party, the Democratic and Social Republican Party (Parti Républicain Démocratique et Social)[25] and converted it into a normal party within a multiparty framework. A new period of optimism and hope emerged, which suggested Mauritania would become the first Arab state to make an indigenous transition to democracy.[26] In some ways, these changes augured democratization that would occur in Tunisia and failed attempts in other Arab states during the 2011 uprisings. But they also reflected changes that had occurred in sub-Saharan Africa during the 1990s and early 2000s. Many speculated that democratizing changes in Mauritania's southern neighbor, Senegal, inspired its push toward democratization.

After the first round of the 2007 presidential elections, in which over twenty candidates competed, including historic oppositionists such as the Afro-Mauritanian and black Arab leaders, Ibrahim Saar and Messoud Boulkheir, two presidential candidates faced off in the second and final round. These were Ahmed Ould Daddah—the half-brother of postcolonial president Moktar Ould Daddah—and a dark horse candidate, Sidi Ould Cheikh Abdallahi. A trained economist, Abdallahi had served as a minister to Ould Taya in the late 1980s and as an advisor to the World Bank in neighboring African countries. In the end, Abdallahi defeated Daddah in a competitive race, in which the latter ultimately accepted the results and conceded to the former. This electoral outcome pleased Generals Mohamed Ould Abdel Aziz and Ely Ould Mohamed Vall, who had favored Abdallahi and surreptitiously supported his campaign. Whereas a victory of Daddah would have shifted power back toward Mauritania's southern tribes and allies of former president Moktar Ould Daddah, Abdallahi's win kept power in the hands of the northern tribes and the allies of former president Ould Taya.

International organizations from the United States, Europe, and Africa celebrated Mauritania's elections as free and fair—a definitive step toward democratization. But this buoyant optimism turned to despair. With little practical governing experience, Abdallahi encountered difficulty managing his administration, and corruption proliferated among his political appointees. Using these corruption allegations as a pretext, Mauritania's generals from the Ould Taya era took action: On August 6, 2008, they arrested Abdallahi and suspended his government. Quickly, General Mohamed Ould Abdel Aziz surfaced as the putsch leader. He announced an initiative to clean the Mauritanian state of corruption and pledged also to organize a multicandidate presidential election in 2009 (which he won handily with over 50 percent of votes cast). Abdel Aziz's closest competitors, Ahmed Ould Daddah and Messoud Boulkheir, finished with only about 14 percent and 17 percent of votes. The opposition parties decried the electoral conditions as neither free nor fair, but they begrudgingly accepted the final results to maintain social peace. Like Egypt's coup-cum-president Abdel Fattah el-Sisi, Abdel Aziz had used elections—though clearly rigged in his favor—to electorally legitimize his rule after his 2008 coup.

The uprisings of 2011 provided an opportunity for Mauritanians to voice their concerns, especially after the failure of democratization in 2008. The events of Mauritania's Arab Spring paralleled those in other Arab states but particularly modeled those in its northern neighbor, Morocco. In addition to a similar Arabic dialect and culture, the two countries both feature robust tribal social structures and striking differences in development between rural and urban areas. On February 20, 2011, protests began in Morocco under the auspices of the February 20 Movement for Change. In Mauritania, an analogous group took to the streets on February 25, 2011, in Nouakchott, the February 25 Movement. In Mauritania, the youth movement's protests started small—with only two thousand participants—but they grew larger as semiregular demonstrations occurred throughout 2012, with the largest in July 2012 numbering ninety thousand participants. Some opposition parties participated in the protests beginning in 2012, and they also put out statements warning the Abdel Aziz government of the urgency of the situation in the wake of two self-immolations—one of an unemployed man and the other of an Afro-Mauritanian of Senegalese decent, as reported by the Mauritanian press. The protesters warned that Mauritania might follow the trajectory of protests in Tunisia and Egypt.[27]

The February 25 Movement's protests centered in Nouakchott and never penetrated tertiary towns or rural areas. Ojeda Garcìa maintains that the low level of internet connectivity in Mauritania—estimates range between 2 and 11 percent[28]—hindered the diffusion of protests, especially in the countryside.[29] In Morocco, by contrast, some of the most violent protests occurred in smaller, tertiary towns marginalized by the regime.[30] It may be that the Mauritanian regime's close relations with northern tribes and rural elites stifled protests that may have otherwise sprung up in rural areas.[31]

Aftermath of Mauritania's Arab Uprisings, 2012–2016

After the height of Mauritania's Arab uprisings in 2011 and 2012, the Abdel Aziz government undertook distinct measures to weaken the opposition and enhance regime resilience. These included dividing the February 25 Movement, introducing constitution revisions, selectively repressing some activists, and holding new (though uneven) elections. At the same time, Mauritania's opposition—especially the black Arab movement, Islamists, and the opposition parties—mobilized to contest Abdel Aziz's government. Whereas in some instances these opposition movements directly confronted Mauritania's authoritarian regime, other times they sought to indirectly delegitimize its rule through electoral boycotts and other subtler tactics. While ordinary citizens continued to desire the greater rights and freedoms that the popular mobilizations of 2011 had embodied, they also realized that the continuing resilience of Abdel Aziz's regime helped ensure that Mauritania would not witness the costs of instability incurred by Syria, Egypt, and other states.

As a first step, Abdel Aziz made overtures to the February 25 Movement. He invited some of the group's leadership to his presidential palace and offered to negotiate with them. Some of the group's leaders accepted this overture, while others rejected it as a thinly veiled attempt at co-optation. Importantly, Abdel Aziz managed to convince some of the white Arab members of the February 25 Movement to defect and join a new pro-regime youth party, the Youth Movement for the Nation (*al-hara-k al-shaba-bi min ajil al-watan*). Headed by a former youth organizer for Abdel Aziz's 2009 presidential campaign, this new party emerged in April 2011 to draw youth discontent away from the streets and into an organization under the regime's tight control.[32]

Several groups opposed the government on its approach to the treatment of black Arabs and Afro-Mauritanians. Among these was the Initiative for the Resurgence of the Abolitionist Movement in Mauritania (Initiative pour la Résurgence du Mouvement Abolitionniste en Mauritanie, or IRA), which started its grassroots campaign for equal rights and the abolition of slavery in 2008.[33] IRA mobilizes through a network of over nine thousand activists and has successfully liberated thousands of former slaves in Mauritania.[34] Although slavery exists in Mauritania among both Arabs and non-Arabs, IRA has targeted and achieved most of its success in freeing black Arab slaves. IRA's leader, Biram Dah Ould Abeid, a black Arab whose parents were slaves, has chosen a confrontational approach to combat slavery in Mauritania. Abeid challenged Abdel Aziz's regime for its lax approach regarding the enforcement of slavery laws. Furthermore, he criticized establishment figures such as religious scholars, the police, and judges for contributing to the intimidation of slaves to remain in their condition of subservience and servitude. Working through IRA, Abeid in the late 2000s organized small marches and rallies that demanded police intervention to arrest slave owners and also urged imams in the High Islamic Council to address a "misinterpretation of Islam" that justified slavery in Mauritania.[35] Collaborating with international organizations, such as Amnesty International and the United Nations, Abeid also worked to raise global awareness of the slavery crisis in Mauritania and received the 2013 UN Human Rights Prize. Given every five years, this prestigious award recognizes only a handful of activists and leaders in the domain of human rights and has also been bestowed on political visionaries such as Martin Luther King and Nelson Mandela.[36]

Emboldened by the Arab uprisings of 2011, IRA began to mobilize more forcefully in Mauritania and sought to shift domestic politics through public protests. In April 2012, Abeid was arrested along with seven other members of the IRA movement for the public burning of a scared Islamic Maliki religious text, the Mukhtashar Khalil. Abeid and the IRA activists disseminated images of the book burning via social media websites such as YouTube and Facebook, reaching audiences in Mauritania and beyond. According to Alice Bullard, passages of the Maliki Islamic text describe slaves as "talking animals" and state that "slave women are consigned to the sexual license of their masters."[37] In Mauritania, white Arab clerics and tribal leaders have used these religious texts to justify the continued enslavement and social subordination of black Arab Mauritanians. While illegal de jure, slavery persists in Mauritania in part due to a strange legal loophole. Because Mauritania is constitutionally an Islamic republic, in which Islam is the official religion, certain Islamic texts are considered outside the regulatory power of temporal law, including the Mukhtashar Khalil. The fact that nearly 100 percent of Mauritanians are Sunni Muslims following the Maliki religious rite gives this text great social influence. Thus, by interweaving constitutional law and Maliki religious edicts, Mauritania's regime has—whether intentionally or accidentally—aided and abetted the institution of slavery within its borders.

Between April and October 2012, Abeid and other IRA activists remained in prison. Although a religious court determined that Abeid could not be persecuted under the apostasy law, Mauritania's regime continued to keep him imprisoned under pressure from white Arabs who feared this open resistance might provoke black Arab unrest. The imprisonment of Abeid and his allies became a cause célèbre among international human rights organizations, notably Amnesty International. Amnesty interpreted the case as one of free speech and slavery abolition, not as one of religious apostasy. In a press release, the group declared that Mauritania's regime had made Abeid and other IRA activists "prisoners of conscience" who were "detained for peacefully expressing their views" and were at "risk of ill-treatment."[38] Succumbing to international pressure after six months, Mauritania's regime released Abeid and the other activists from prison.

As a second step, Abdel Aziz's regime—modeling strategies in Morocco and Jordan—introduced incremental reforms to cultivate a reformist image, seeking to pacify protestors who demanded political change. This approach reassured citizens that Mauritania would experience some incremental change and progress after the uprisings, while it maintained the stability absent in other Arab states, such as Syria and Libya. The regime schedule planned for new legislative elections in fall 2011, and in late 2011, the regime announced plans for revisions to the existing 1991 constitution, which had originated during a brief period of political liberalization at the outset of Ould Taya's reign. These revisions aimed to formalize many of the agreements of mutual recognition and social tranquility reached between Abdel Aziz's regime and the opposition parties set after the 2009 Dakar Accord. Outside actors, notably the Senegalese government and the African Union, had encouraged and convened these talks between the regime and the opposition to de-escalate the tensions and "constitutional crisis" caused by Abdel Aziz's 2008 coup.[39]

The regime championed three major revisions to the 1991 constitution, which it promoted as important reforms that advanced change in the context of maintaining stability. The first revision addressed the topic of military coups. Henceforth, all military coups would be banned in Mauritania—an interesting yet hypocritical move for the regime, given that it had seized power through a 2008 putsch. De facto, this revision benefited the regime by legally outlawing any future military officer who might try to oust it, and also empowered the regime with a legal justification for purging suspicious officers. The second important revision introduced the "decriminalization of defamation" clause, which sought to expand press freedom for Mauritanian journalists.[40] Journalists would gain wider freedom to criticize elected officials both in print and on television. The regime agreed to end its monopolization of television news media licenses, which it had controlled for fifty-one years.[41] The third revision called for a national census in order to increase the accuracy and fairness of citizen representation in political institutions. In particular, the revision advocated the application of new biometric measures in national identity cards to ensure a comprehensive account of all ethnic groups, both black Arabs and Afro-Mauritanians. To appease black Arabs, who continued to organize protests through IRA and other antislavery movements, the regime also agreed to create an agency to investigate slavery cases, prosecute slave owners, and rehabilitate former slaves. The regime set up the agency in 2013 and gave it a long-winded name—the National Solidarity Agency for the Fight against the Vestiges of Slavery, for Integration, and for the Fight against Poverty.

The opposition parties were skeptical of these constitutional revisions. In the end, the revisions were largely superficial, a ruse meant to undermine popular opposition to Abdel Aziz's rule. The main criticism levied by the opposition parties related to the constitutional convention itself. They alleged that the convention had operated illegally. Because the regime had not held a legislative election since 2006, all legislators participating in the convention had exceeded their terms, and their electoral mandates to govern had expired. The opposition parties used this legal quandary to criticize the regime and to prod Abdel Aziz to expedite new legislative elections.[42] But the regime circumvented this problem by instructing the Supreme Court to extraconstitutionally extend the legislators' electoral terms, a legal maneuver that had never before been done in Mauritanian history. The opposition saw this as Abdel Aziz's stratagem to bypass their presence in the legislative chambers to spearhead the enactment of his proposed constitutional revisions.

On a practical level, on-the-ground facts about Mauritanian politics obstructed potential benefits from the 2012 constitutional revisions. In the end, these facts left the reforms largely superficial in nature. Although the constitutional revisions sought to increase the de jure legal status of black Arabs and Afro-Mauritanians, they continue to hold little de facto political power. Although black Arabs and Afro-Mauritanians constitute over 70 percent of the total population, they hold few political offices or appointments. White Arabs hold thirty of thirty-five ministerial posts, fifty-two of fifty-four prefectures, and twelve of thirteen governorships.[43] Moreover, although the regime created an agency in 2013 to combat slavery, it has not aggressively investigated or prosecuted cases. According to its minister, Hamdi Ould Mahjoub, no citizen reported a case of slavery to the agency until late 2015.[44] Moreover, the agency has done nothing to raise the educational level or political consciousness of liberated slaves and their descendants, which often causes them to get drawn into in-kind working relationships with their former masters in which food and shelter are exchanged for labor.

Additional caveats obstructed potential benefits from the new constitutional revision that aimed to increase freedom of political expression. The regime undermined the decriminalization of defamation clause by exempting cases related to national security. What constitutes a case of national security was left undefined, however. An ad hoc committee of the president's security advisors would determine these instances case by case after the media infraction had been committed. The upshot was that Abdel Aziz's regime retained considerable discretionary power to pursue and prosecute journalists whom it found threatening. The constitutional revisions granted the right of private individuals to purchase media licenses, but the regime also retained the power to levy exorbitant fines that could shutter media outlets easily. Even journalists using unrestricted news mediums such as blogs and YouTube could receive fees or jail time for articles deemed formally legal but dangerous to national security. While Abdel Aziz lauded the benefits of the constitutional revisions, describing them as building "a state of law and liberties in Mauritania" modeling other "democratic steps in our Arab neighborhood," reality belied his rhetoric.[45] Using the fight against terrorism as a pretext, Abdel Aziz also began to emphasize themes of national unity and national security in speeches related to his constitutional revisions. This helped the autocrat and his party—the Union for the Republic (Union pour la République)—undermine the popularity of opposition movements, such as IRA and the opposition parties of the Coordination of Democratic Opposition (Coordination de l'Opposition Démocratique, or COD).

Reacting to these reforms, citizens expressed mixed views. They likely realized that Abdel Aziz's constitutional revisions represented only minor changes, yet they truly feared that Mauritania might descend into the instability spreading across the Arab world in the aftermath of the Arab uprisings. The increasing number of sectarian, ethnic, and tribal conflicts erupting in countries like Syria, Iraq, and Yemen could easily spread to Mauritania, which suffered from its own deep cleavages.

Despite Abdel Aziz's military pedigree, not everyone in the armed forces appeared happy with his rule after the Arab uprisings. In a situation Abdel Aziz described as an unintentional accident in October 2012, Mauritanian soldiers shot the autocrat's caravan while searching cars for illicit weapons and terrorists. Seeking to reassure the public while recovering in a French hospital, Abdel Aziz asked one of the soldiers to appear on public television and attest to the fact that the shooting was accidental, not intentional.[46] Witnesses at the scene recalled, however, that they saw soldiers purposefully shoot at the autocrat's vehicle and flee when they realized he had not been killed. Nevertheless, while Abdel Aziz recovered in a French hospital, an interim committee of military leaders carried out his presidential duties.[47] Whether the shooting was truly an intentional assassination attempt or an accident remains unclear, but the incident suggests that Mauritania's instability made the president a target for someone with political ambitions for the office he holds.

Beginning in January 2013, a new level of instability rocked Mauritania due to activities of al-Qaeda in the Maghreb in Mali and eastern Mauritania. Although Abdel Aziz told French president François Hollande that Mauritania's army was "not ready" to "engage in war" alongside French troops in Mali, he pledged logistical and intelligence support for the French campaign (which became known as "Operation Serval"). As the French ousted the armed militants from their strongholds in towns north of Mali's Niger River, notably Gao and Timbuktu, Mauritania supported France indirectly by increasing security in territories east of Walatah and sealing its Malian border. By aiding the French army in combating the militants, Mauritania's military elite (constituted predominately of northern warrior tribe members) sought to earn back its credibility in the eyes of France, one of Mauritania's largest aid donors. The military elite also sought to regain favor by assisting the approximately one hundred thousand refugees displaced by the conflict.[48] By the end of Operation Serval, many of the armed militants had evaded capture by following smuggling routes that crisscross Mauritania and Libya.[49]

Since the conflict's outset, Mauritania's army still has not shuttered these routes, leading to a drastic increase in cocaine smuggling across the country and into Morocco and Europe. Between 2005 and 2009, studies estimate that forty-six tons of cocaine passed through Mauritania and other Sahel countries.[50] Since the violent clashes between Islamist militants and governments engulfed the Sahel, this region with its unpatrolled deserts and coastline has become the main entry port for most cocaine coming from Latin America to Africa (and ultimately to Europe). This parallel black-market economy in the smuggling of drugs and other illicit items provides financial support for terrorist and other armed groups in the region. Instability in Libya, in particular, provides a northern coastline from which such materials can be smuggled into the Mediterranean ports of Southern Europe.[51]

After several delays, which the regime attributed to war instability, it organized new local and legislative elections in July 2014. Originally planned for 2011, the elections contributed to the regime's strategy to cultivate a reformist image while it retained tight control over politics. Given the increasing instability in neighboring Mali and the escalating bloodshed and conflict in other Arab countries across the region, citizens welcomed these elections even though they would likely be slanted to favor Abdel Aziz and his allied parties.

Before the elections could take place, Abdel Aziz's regime planned to conduct a national census to issue identity cards and register valid voters. His administration trumpeted this as a modernizing initiative, arguing that Mauritania lacked the basic citizen registration records of most modern states. Some observers alleged this census had other intentions, however. Having come to power by coup in 2008 and legitimized by elections in 2009, Abdel Aziz now wanted to fortify his rule through electoral gerrymandering. He aimed to increase registration of voters from northern tribes and white Arabs allied with his regime, while depressing registration of voters hailing from black Arab and Afro-Mauritanian groups.[52] After the elections' final round in December 2014, Abdel Aziz's Union for the Republic dominated the polls. It secured 74 of the 147 national assembly seats, and its allied parties garnered another 34 seats. In total, political parties aligned with Abdel Aziz controlled nearly 74 percent of legislative seats.

The opposition reacted to these elections negatively, deeming them neither free nor fair. Of the eleven major opposition parties within the COD, ten chose to boycott. They refused to submit candidates for the elections. The one party that defected from this electoral boycott and chose to compete was Mauritania's Islamist Muslim Brotherhood, the Tawassoul Party. Observing the recent electoral success of Islamist parties in Tunisia, Morocco, and Egypt, Mauritania's Islamists predicted that they too would secure victory. In fact, the party secured second place, winning sixteen of the thirty-seven legislative seats captured by opposition parties.[53] Because the COD's boycott had fragmented, their political action did little to undermine Abdel Aziz's perceived electoral legitimacy. In the end, the legislative elections helped reinforce Abdel Aziz's regime and his control over politics in advance of the next major round of elections, the 2014 presidential elections. The Tawassoul Party appears to have broken ranks with COD in a bid to increase its influence through seats in the next legislative session.[54] Yet, at the end, the Islamists' electoral gamble largely failed, as they possess too few seats to enact meaningful legislation or drive political change.

As the security situation deteriorated in the Arab world, with bloodshed increasing in Libya, Syria, and elsewhere in 2014, the regime expedited the presidential elections. In doing so, the regime implied to citizens that Mauritania could incur the instability of other Arab countries if the internal stalemate between the regime and the opposition parties continued unabated. This time, however, the Islamists rejoined the COD and chose to boycott the presidential elections. After competing in the legislative elections, which were marred by fraud and unfair conditions, the Islamists realized their electoral participation had not only generated few benefits for their party but also undermined the opposition's broader solidarity.

Although the traditional opposition parties chose not to compete in the presidential election, the contest revealed the emergence of a new political party: Biram Dah Ould Abeid's IRA movement. After spending six months in prison in 2012, Abeid emerged from his cell to compete as a presidential candidate, facing off as Mohamed Ould Abdel Aziz's chief rival. Traveling from town to town and garnering support from slaves and their descendants, Abeid exclaimed: "I will free the slaves and bring them with me to the presidential palace."[55] Another candidate who drew attention was the first female presidential contender in Mauritanian history, Mariam Bent Moulay Idriss. Under conditions widely considered disadvantageous for these opposition candidates, the elections were held in July 2014, and Abdel Aziz won handily with 81.9 percent of votes. Coming in second place, Abeid garnered 8.7 percent of votes.

Although Abeid's participation in the election suggested that IRA had transitioned into a legal and tolerated opposition party, the regime's actions shortly afterward indicated the opposite. In November 2015, Mauritania's regime arrested Abeid and ten other IRA activists for organizing a peaceful demonstration in Rosso, a southern town on the banks of the Senegal River. Abeid hoped, according to Amnesty International, to "raise awareness about land rights for people of slave descent."[56] Rosso's governor ordered the activists arrested for protesting without authorized documents and belonging to a legally unrecognized organization. In a subsequent trial, they each received a two-year prison sentence.[57] Thus, although Mauritania's regime had permitted IRA to participate in the presidential elections, likely to cultivate an image of electoral pluralism and competition, the end result was that through repression the regime stifled the opposition group's capacity to mobilize for reform. Once a candidate for president, Abeid today sits behind bars.[58]

Any movement toward reform introduced because of the 2014 elections and 2012 constitutional revisions was a short-lived mirage. Abdel Aziz continued to run his regime following clan and ethnic loyalties, making appointments based on communal ties. Criteria such as administrative professionalism and noncorruption of appointees were less important in filling administrative posts. Moreover, some of the regime's anticorruption initiatives were politicized and used to discredit key opposition figures. In one incident in March 2014, Abdel Aziz's regime launched an anticorruption campaign that targeted a human rights activist—Mohamed Mkhaitir.[59] Similarly, the regime accused Nouakchott's opposition mayor—Ahmed ould Hamza—of embezzling the equivalent of $1.2 million from city hall. Although Hamza denied the charges as politically motivated and still maintains his innocence, he eventually agreed to pay money back in installments to avoid imprisonment.[60] Such monkey trials discouraged new challenges from opposition party members and other marginalized groups.

In addition to these efforts to undermine potential opposition to his rule, Abdel Aziz has moved to regulate the media and punish online dissent.

This repression of dissent has occurred under the guise of national security or public decency. Hanevy Ould Dehah, the editor of the Progressive or "Taqadoumy" blog, was prosecuted for offending public decency laws when he posted a sex education article.[61] Moreover, after serving his six-month sentence in 2009, the same blogger was sentenced in retrial of the same case with new charges of inciting rebellion for being critical of Mauritania's military in previous blog posts. In its actions, Abdel Aziz's regime has gone against the optimistic goals outlined by Mauritania's 2005–07 democratic transition period.

Through these political maneuvers, both constitutional revisions to cultivate an image of reform and repression to undermine the opposition, Abdel Aziz's autocratic regime has remained robust in the aftermath of the Arab uprisings. For Abdel Aziz and his advisors, staying in power has high stakes. Society remains polarized by ethnic and tribal tensions, which work to enrich and empower Abdel Aziz and his allies from the northern tribes. Through their influence in politics, President Abdel Aziz's Oulad Bou Sbaas tribe has gained control over Mauritania's major economic assets, specifically mining, oil, and gold. Indeed, since his 2008 coup, the heads of Société Mauritanienne des Hydrocarbures (the national oil and energy company), Tullow Oil (Mauritania's main private oil company), and Kinross (Mauritania's main gold-mining company) have been either direct blood relatives or distant cousins of President Abdel Aziz. Under the previous regime of Ould Taya, members of his Smassides tribe had held these posts and enriched themselves. Similar to Tunisia's Ben Ali family, Abdel Aziz's Oulad Bou Sbaa clan has been relentless in their efforts to insert themselves into the most profitable areas of Mauritania's political economy. Indeed, in order to keep himself and his tribe profiting, Abdel Aziz has large incentives to keep this "Republic of Cousins" functioning.[62] Abdel Aziz has supported this system through the preferential hiring and promoting of his allies and the exclusion of other tribal and ethnic groups. Whereas Abdel Aziz, the Oulad Bou Sbaa, and other northern tribes benefit from this arrangement, Daddah, the Oulad Birri, and southern tribes lose from it.

Conclusion

Cases such as Syria and Libya demonstrate that the Arab uprisings initially produced hope in democratization, which ultimately devolved into situations of instability and bloodshed. Instability in Egypt, likewise, has increased since the uprisings, leading to stricter authoritarianism as a countermeasure after the 2013 coup of Abdel Fattah el-Sisi. Although Mauritania's unrest during the Arab uprisings was far less contentious than that of neighboring states, the country witnessed major popular protests that had not occurred in nearly a decade (i.e., during the country's experiment with democratization in 2005–07). This unrest—and unrest witnessed in neighboring Arab states—increased the lure of authoritarian stability in state and society among ordinary Mauritanians. For now, it seems likely that Mauritanians would rather accept the leadership of autocrat Mohamed Ould Abdel Aziz with imperfect elections and corruption than invite instability, as occurred in Syria, Libya, and elsewhere.

At first glance, major differences make Mauritania seem like an exceptional political system. Many Arab states feature considerable ethnic and linguistic diversity with large numbers of non-Arabs living within their borders, but Mauritania's heterogeneity is striking. Moreover, the fact that Europeans never secured a major foothold or left settlements in Mauritania also makes the country seem different from other Arab states that fell under intense colonial rule.

Yet the fact that many Mauritanians would likely prefer autocratic stability to the instability of potential democratization makes it similar to many Arab states in North Africa and throughout the Middle East. Indeed, Mauritania's recent political events have many similarities with those of other Arab states. Because many Arab states also have non-Arab minorities living within their borders, it may be analytically productive to compare the activism of Mauritania's ethnic minorities—especially Afro-Mauritanians—with that of other marginalized non-Arab populations, say the Kurds or Amazigh. In several states, such as Syria and Iraq, such minority groups have mobilized in the aftermath of the Arab uprisings. This has produced instability and encouraged some Arab citizens to rally around autocrats and the lure of stability they provide. In addition to the status of non-Arab minorities, future research might examine how differences between white and black Arabs in Mauritania compare with similar diversity in other Arab states. Why have the descendants of slaves in Mauritania—the Haratine Movement—successfully formed civil society associations to advocate for their rights and reparations, whereas similar descendants of slaves have not organized in other Arab states? For example, few recall that extensive slavery existed in the Persian Gulf region, and Oman and Saudi Arabia abolished slavery relatively recently (in 1970 and

1962, respectively). Why have organizations advocating for the interests of former slaves not emerged in these states? Mauritania could serve as a useful comparative case to better understand how non-Arab ethnic minorities and black Arabs organize politically and contest authoritarian regimes contrary to their interests.

Another way scholars may usefully compare Mauritania with other Arab states is in the area of civil-military relations, and how these relations intersect issues related to the lure of authoritarian stability. Like in the states of Egypt and Algeria, Mauritania's military plays a large role in shaping politics. Coups and countercoups come to Mauritania frequently and have left a discernable (and largely detrimental) mark on politics. Like in other Arab states, they have been a key source of instability. Much like the case of Egypt in 2011–13, where a democratically elected leader was ousted by military generals, Mauritania's democratic transition was halted abruptly. Here also, a military general removed an elected leader, citing administrative mismanagement and corruption allegations as a pretext.

A better understanding of the Mauritanian military's role and embeddedness in the political economy could also contribute to academic conversations on the "deep state" in Egypt and Algeria. It would be interesting to know whether Mauritania's military benefits from similar military-industrial enterprises and public industries as those active in Egypt and Algeria, for example. Although the military's role in politics is often detrimental in these states, and particularly in Mauritania, future scholars may examine the security and military economy trade-off. It would be interesting to investigate whether Mauritanians, Egyptians, and Algerians will continue to accept the military's large role in the political economy (and its associated material spoils) if it simultaneously leads to greater stability. This issue intersects the lure that autocrats can provide to citizens by creating internal stability, even if negative consequences (such as corruption in the military economy) accompany this process.

While commonalities in Mauritania's seemingly exceptional politics can be found and compared with other Arab states, the clearest common thread is the apparent political trade-off Mauritanian citizens must make between stability and possible democratization. Like citizens of other Arab states, they seek a greater voice in politics, more representative institutions, and more serious liberalization. The importance of these values was stressed at the height of the Arab uprisings. But on the other hand, Mauritanian citizens have seen how the aftermath of the Arab uprisings has produced instability, bloodshed, and economic collapse in neighboring Arab states. Only in the coming years will it become clear whether Mauritanian citizens favor the lure of stability under their current autocrat or are willing to risk instability under a new and uncertain democratic order.

MEHDI AYARI is a former doctoral student of political science at the University of Tennessee. His research has appeared in *Political Research Quarterly*.

MATT BUEHLER is Assistant Professor of Political Science at the University of Tennessee and a global security fellow at the Howard H. Baker Jr. Center for Public Policy. His research has appeared in *Political Research Quarterly*, *Mediterranean Politics*, and *British Journal of Middle Eastern Studies*.

Notes

1. E. A. Albaugh, *State-Building and Multilingual Education in Africa* (Cambridge: Cambridge University Press, 2014).

2. A. Gerteiny, *Mauritania* (New York: Praeger, 1967); R. E. Handloff and B. D. Curran, *Mauritania, a Country Study* (Washington, DC: Government Printing Office, 1990); M. M. Mohamedou and S. E. Ibrahim, *Societal Transition to Democracy in Mauritania* (Cairo: Ibn Khaldoun Center for Development Studies, 1995); N. Foster, *Mauritania: The Struggle for Democracy* (Boulder, CO: First Forum, 2011); M. Ould-Mey, *Global Restructuring and Peripheral States: The Carrot and the Stick in Mauritania* (Lanham, MD: Rowman & Littlefield, 1996).

3. Books appearing in French and Arabic, of course, are much greater in number. Some prominent works include P. Marchesin, *Tribus, ethnies et pouvoir en Mauritanie* (Paris: Karthala Editions, 1992); Z. O. A. Salem, *Prêcher dans le désert: islam politique et changement social en Mauritanie* (Paris: Karthala Editions, 2013).

4. M. J. Willis, *Politics and Power in the Maghreb: Algeria, Tunisia and Morocco from Independence to the Arab Spring* (New York: Oxford University Press, 2014), 5.

5. Ould-Mey, *Global Restructuring and Peripheral States*, 111–2.

6. Ibid.

7. Gerteiny, *Mauritania*, 5.

8. Ould-Mey, *Global Restructuring and Peripheral States*, 113–6.

9. Ibid., 7.

10. For a discussion of white and black Arabs outside Mauritania, see E. H. Chouki, "'Race', Slavery, and Islam in the Maghribi Mediterranean Thought: The Question of Haratin in Morocco," *Journal of North African Studies* 7, no. 3 (2002): 29–52; E. Alpers, "The African Diaspora in the Northwestern Indian Ocean: New Directions for Research," *Comparative Studies of South Asia, Africa, and the Middle East* 17, no. 2 (1997): 62–81; B. Lewis, *Race and Slavery in the Middle East: A Historical Enquiry* (Oxford: Oxford University Press, 1990).

11. J. D. Sutter and E. McNamee, "Slavery's Last Stand," CNN.com, March 2012, accessed February 20, 2016, http://www.cnn.com/interactive/2012/03/world/mauritania.slaverys.last.stronghold/index.html.

12. C. H. Moore, "One-Partyism in Mauritania," *Journal of Modern African Studies* 3, no. 3 (1965): 409–20.

13. D. Robinson, *Paths of Accommodation: Muslim Societies and French Colonial Authorities in Senegal and Mauritania, 1880–1920* (Athens: Ohio University Press, 2000).

14. M. Bennoune, "The Political Economy of Mauritania: Imperialism and Class Struggle," *Review of African Political Economy* 5, no. 12 (1978): 31–52.

15. Z. O. A. Salem, "Militants aux pieds nus: Les transformations du mouvement des Haratines de Mauritanie," *Canadian Journal of African Studies/La Revue canadienne des études africaines* 44, no. 2 (2010): 283–316; Z. O. A. B. Salem, "Bare-Foot Activists: Transformations in the Haratine Movement in Mauritania," *Movers and Shakers: Social Movements in Africa* 8, no. 3/4 (2009): 156.

16. A. Antil, "La chef, la famille et l'État Mauritanie, quand democratization rime avec tribalization," *Politique Africaine* 72 (1998): 187.

17. L. Kinne, "The Benefits of Exile: The Case of FLAM," *Journal of Modern African Studies* 39, no. 4 (2001): 597–621.

18. "Opposition Movement Denounces 'Arabization' of Mauritania," December 4, 2006, accessed February 24, 2016, http://www.panapress.com/Opposition-movement-denounces-Arabization-of-Mauritania-13-501789-17-lang1-index.html.

19. S. Haggard and S. B. Webb, eds., *Voting for Reform: Democracy, Political Liberalization, and Economic Adjustment*, vol. 94 (Washington, DC: World Bank Publications, 1994), 344.

20. K. B. Noble, "Senegal Strife Leaves Air of Menace," *New York Times*, May 5, 1989, accessed February 11, 2016, http://www.nytimes.com/1989/05/05/world/senegal-strife-leaves-air-of-menace.html.

21. Foster, *Mauritania*; D. Zisenwine, "Mauritania's Democratic Transition: A Regional Model for Political Reform?," *Journal of North African Studies* 12, no. 4 (2007): 481–99.

22. B. N'Diaye, "Mauritania, August 2005: Justice and Democracy, or Just Another Coup?," *African Affairs* 105, no. 420 (2006): 421–41.

23. International Crisis Group, *Political Transition in Mauritania and Horizons*, report no. 53, April 24, 2005, executive summary.

24. D. M. Girod and M. R. Walters, "Elite-Led Democratisation in Aid-Dependent States: The Case of Mauritania," *Journal of North African Studies* 17, no. 2 (2012): 181–93.

25. R. Ojeda García, "La derrota del antiguo partido autoritario dominante (PRDR) en las elecciones legislativas de 2006 en Mauritania," *Revista de Investigaciones Políticas y Sociológicas* 11, no. 4 (2012). Also, see A. Antil, "Le PRDS: Etude de l'implantation d'un parti au pouvoir en République Islamique de Mauritanie," *Politique Africaine* 65 (1997).

26. R. O. García and A. L. Bargados, "¿E pur si muove? Logics of Power and the Process of Transition in the Islamic Republic of Mauritania," *Political Regimes in the Arab World: Society and the Exercise of Power* 45 (2012): 104.

27. Sharif Nashashibi," Mauritania's 'overlooked' Arab Spring," The Guardian, 2012. Accessed February 7, 2019. https://www.theguardian.com/commentisfree/2012/may/26/mauritania-overlooked-arab-spring.

28. Freedom House, "Mauritania," Freedom in the World 2015 series, accessed February 20, 2016, https://freedomhouse.org/report/freedom-world/2015/mauritania.

29. R. O. García, "Mauritania tras la primavera árabe: posicionamiento de Tawassoul en las elecciones de 2013," *Revista de Estudios Internacionales Mediterráneos* 15 (2013).

30. K. Bogaert, "The Revolt of Small Towns: The Meaning of Morocco's History and the Geography of Social Protests," *Review of African Political Economy* 42, no. 143 (2015): 124–40.

31. M. Buehler, "Continuity through Co-optation: Rural Politics and Regime Resilience in Morocco and Mauritania," *Mediterranean Politics* 20, no. 3 (2015): 364–85. Also, see C. Jourde, "'The President Is Coming to Visit!': Dramas and the Hijack of Democratization in the Islamic Republic of Mauritania," *Comparative Politics* 37, no. 4 (2005): 423–5.

32. Buehler, "Continuity through Co-optation," 364–85.

33. Z. O. A. Salem, "Militants aux pieds nus: Les transformations du mouvement des Haratines de Mauritanie," *Canadian Journal of African Studies/La Revue canadienne des études africaines* 44, no. 2 (2010): 283–316.

34. A. Okeowo, "Freedom Fighter: A Slaving Society and an Abolitionist's Crusade," *New Yorker*, September 8, 2014, accessed February 27, 2016, http://www.newyorker.com /magazine/2014/09/08/freedom-fighter.

35. Ibid.

36. Unrepresented Nations and Peoples Organization, "IRA President Biram Dah Abeid Wins UN Human Rights Prize," December 2, 2013, accessed February 26, 2016, http://www .unpo.org/article/16654.

37. A. Bullard, "Religion, Race, and Repression in Mauritania: The Ould Mkhaitir Apostasy Affair," May 29, 2014, accessed February 28, 2016, http://www.jadaliyya.com/pages /index/17914/religion-race-and-repression-in-mauritania_the-oul.

38. Amnesty International, "Activists Held in Unknown Location," May 4, 2012, accessed February 26, 2016, http://www.amnestyusa.org/sites/default/files/uaa12712.pdf.

39. A. S. O. Bouboutt, "La révision constitutionnelle du 20 mars 2012 en Mauritanie," *L'Année du Maghreb* 10 (2014).

40. Ibid., 25.

41. Ibid., 25.

42. K. Esseissah, "'Paradise Is under the Feet of Your Master'" The Construction of the Religious Basis of Racial Slavery in the Mauritanian Arab-Berber Community," *Journal of Black Studies* 47, no. 1 (2016): 3–23.

43. Ibid., 25.

44. Bouboutt, "La révision constitutionnelle," 31.

45. Deutsche Welle Arabisch, "The Start of Elections in Mauritania," June 21, 2014, accessed February 19, 2016, http://www.dw.com/ar/a-17726352.

46. "Mauritania Leader Abdelaziz 'Accidentally' Shot," BBC News, October 14, 2012, accessed February 24, 2016, http://www.bbc.com/news/world-africa-19938905.

47. "Mauritania's President Heads to France for Treatment after Shooting," CNN, October 15, 2012, accessed February 12, 2016, http://www.cnn.com/2012/10/14/world/africa /mauritania-president-shot/.

48. Ibid.

49. O. Taramond and P. Seigneur, "Operation Serval: Another Beau Geste of France in Sub-Saharan Africa?," *Military Review* 84 (2014).

50. A. Antil, "Trafic de cocaïne au Sahel," *Études* 417, no. 10 (2012): 309.

51. Ibid., 307–16.

52. OFPRA, "Informations sur le mouvement 'Touche pas a ma nationalite' qui s'oppose au recensement tel qu'il est conduit actuellement," April 23, 2012, https://www.ofpra.gouv.fr /sites/default/files/atoms/files/mauritanie_mouvement_touche_pas_a_ma_nationalite.pdf.

53. Z. O. A. Salem, "The Paradoxes of Islamic Radicalisation in Mauritania," *Islamist Radicalisation in North Africa: Politics and Process* 179 (2012).

54. Ibid., 41.

55. A. Mohamed, "Slavery in Mauritania: Above the Law," June 15, 2014, accessed February 29, 2016, http://english.aawsat.com/2014/06/article55333255/slavery-in-mauritania -above-the-law.

56. "Mauritania: Jailed Presidential Candidate and Anti-slavery Activists Must Be Released," Amnesty International, January 15, 2015, accessed February 29, 2016, https://www .amnesty.org/en/latest/news/2015/01/mauritania-jailed-presidential-candidate-and-anti -slavery-activists-must-be-released/.

57. Ibid.

58. Ibid.

59. Freedom House, "Mauritania."

60. U.S. State Department, "Mauritania 2013 Human Rights Report," 2013, accessed February 29, 2016, http://www.state.gov/documents/organization/220348.pdf.

61. Freedom House, "Mauritania."

62. Africa Mining Intelligence and West Africa Newsletter, "Oulad Bou Sbaas Deep into Mining," *West Africa Newsletter*, April 2, 2013.

12

ALGERIA

Economic Austerity, Political Stagnation, and the Gathering Storm

Azzedine Layachi

ALGERIA WAS NOT DIRECTLY AFFECTED BY THE REGIONAL storm in North Africa, which destabilized Tunisia and Libya, with whom it shares long borders, and Egypt. For a variety of reasons, only a small set of riots with no major incidents and no effect marked the historic moment of the Arab Spring in Algeria. Previously, however, the country had made major headway from the days of staunch authoritarian rule that lasted from independence to the end of the 1980s. Absolute autocracy was seriously challenged and somewhat softened by societal protests and an armed Islamist rebellion, but it was not undone. Important changes in the political system took place and marked a slight departure from the traditional authoritarian model of governance. As will be discussed at length later in this chapter, it all began when, in October 1988, Algeria experienced its worst street riots since independence, which led, indirectly, to the end of the one-party system and to minimal political liberalization.

Having already gone through a sour, ill-fated "Algerian Spring" in the late 1980s and early 1990s, which was followed by a "dark decade" of bloodshed and destruction driven by a relentless confrontation between the state and an armed Islamist rebellion, most Algerians were just not up for another fight in the early weeks of 2011. The state, battle-hardened by the confrontation of the 1990s, would not have hesitated to put down such a repeat upheaval. Both society and the governing elite seemed to have opted for peace and stability over a confrontation whose outcome many presented as being inevitably similar to those of Libya, Egypt, and Yemen after the fall of their leaders. In the name of stability in a highly volatile region, both state and society eschewed democratic change, economic reform, more respect for human rights, and a needed leadership change to one that corresponds more with the current generation than the one that fought for independence more than fifty years ago and that is still in charge.

Nowadays, any discussion on Algeria must deal with the survival and endurance of its system of governance in a domestic context fraught with challenges and a regional context full of signs of impending doom. This chapter will explore in detail the reasons why the winds of change of 2011 in the Arab world did not affect Algeria, how the governing system has responded to—and resisted—calls for genuine reforms, and how the looming leadership and economic crises may play out and potentially serve as catalysts for either a much-needed positive change or a much-dreaded instability. The discussion of these issues will focus particularly on leadership, institutions, mass mobilization, and conjuncture.

The chapter starts with a necessary sketch of Algeria's historical background that begins with the first years of independence and leads up to the current condition of the country. It then addresses the nature of the Algerian governing system, its genesis, dynamics, and key players. This is done partly though the discussion of regime adaptation, a theme that is prevalent in the literature of what is called "semiauthoritarianism." In trying to understand the Algerian case of political stagnation and economic crisis after an unprecedented affluence from hydrocarbon earnings, the chapter examines the role of institutions (both as organizations and as ways of doing things) and the lack of institutionalization as a key obstacle to positive change. A section is also devoted to the Algerian claim of "exceptionalism" in reference to the spring 2011 upheavals in the Arab world. Finally, the chapter tackles the question of the endurance of Algeria's political regime and of its sustenance through a variety of means, including the rhetoric of fear of political instability as a way to dismiss and quell political opposition and to delay real democratic reforms.

Background: Essence of a Regime

Located in the center of the Maghreb region, Algeria is only a few hundred miles from the southern coast of France and even closer to Spain and Italy.

It has strategic importance due to its vast territory (the largest in Africa), which links sub-Saharan Africa to the Mediterranean; its twelve hundred kilometers of Mediterranean shoreline; its vast petroleum and gas reserves; and its important mineral resources, including phosphate, coal, iron, lead, uranium, and zinc.

The country's 91,935 square miles of land is 85 percent desert. More than three-fourths of Algeria's forty million citizens live in northern cities and towns. The rest live in the desert. The population is young, with 28.75 percent under fifteen years of age and 70 percent below thirty.

In the seventh century, the Arabs from the east conquered Algeria and made it part of the Arab-Islamic Empire. After being ruled by several Arab-Islamic dynasties, in 1518 Algeria became part of the Ottoman Empire, which united it in a loose configuration of tribes and protected it against the imperial ambitions of the Europeans. In 1830 Algeria was conquered by the French, who controlled it until 1962.

The Arab-Islamic tradition served in recent centuries as a powerful unifying tool in Algeria's struggle against foreign domination, most notably in the war for independence against France from 1954 to 1962. The colonial policy of France instilled Algeria with French values and culture and is partially responsible for the nature of contemporary Algerian politics, which is split between the masses who identify more with their Arab, Berber, and Islamic cultures, and Western-oriented elites. Today, the Algerian political culture continues to reflect the impact of these and other traditions and their impact on Algeria's history.

It took France more than forty years to conquer and subdue the whole country and colonize it for 132 years. Algerian nationalists fiercely resisted colonial rule. In the 1850s the French government declared the territory part of France, and Algerians officially became French subjects, though not citizens. The French colonization triggered nationalist revolts, which were suppressed and were followed by land confiscations, onerous taxes, and tighter control of the Algerian people. Through these and other punitive acts, France intended to terrorize Algerians into submission and to procure land and money for colonization.

On November 1, 1954, the National Liberation Front (French acronym FLN), a newly born nationalist movement, called on all Algerians to fight for their independence. In 1958, a provisional government was formed in exile. Fighting continued until March 19, 1962, when a cease-fire was concluded. In a national referendum on independence, the overwhelming majority voted on July 1, 1962, for independence, and Algeria became offi-cially independent on July 5, 1962.

Soon after independence, the nationalist leadership's unity was frac-tured by serious divisions. The first years of independence were character-ized by factional fighting and by the absence of a unifying revolutionary ideology and an uncontested leader. The unity created by the FLN in the fight for independence unraveled as a power struggle ensued. The first president of independent Algeria, Ahmed Ben Bella, was overthrown by his defense minister, Colonel Houari Boumediene. The rule of a Council of the Revolution, made mainly of military personnel, followed the coup. The constitution and the National Assembly were suspended, and Boumediene was named president, head of government, and minister of defense. The new regime, which drew support mainly from the mujahideen (veterans of the war of independence) and technocrats drawn mostly from the military, promised to reestablish the principles of the revolution, end corruption and personal abuses, eliminate internal divisions, and build a socialist economy based on industrialization and comprehensive agrarian reform.

Approved by referendum in June 1976, a new National Charter reaf-firmed Algeria's socialist orientation, recognized the FLN as the only legal party, and implicitly maintained the authoritarian system. A new constitu-tion, approved by referendum in November 1976, reestablished the national legislature, and a month later, Boumediene was elected president with more than 95 percent of the vote on a single-candidate ballot. He served as head of state and government, commander in chief, minister of defense, and secretary-general of the FLN. Boumediene died suddenly in late 1978 of a rare kidney ailment. He left a legacy of a consolidated state; a stable political system, albeit authoritarian; a rapidly industrializing economy; an exten-sive state-centered socialist program; and an expanding petroleum and gas export industry.

The military replaced Boumediene with Colonel Chadli Bendjedid, who slowly took full control of the state, party, and military apparatus and engaged in a process of "de-Boumedienization" of Algeria. However, under him, the country faced many challenges by the early 1980s, including a declining economy, rapid population growth, increasing unemployment, and, by the end of the decade, a sharp drop in energy prices. State revenues— which were highly reliant on hydrocarbons export—fluctuated wildly and eventually declined drastically when oil prices dipped by 40 percent in 1986. In response to the economic crisis, Bendjedid initiated a semblance of economic liberalization, which included a shift away from heavy industry and toward agriculture, light industry, and consumer goods. Public enterprises were broken into smaller units, and several small state-owned firms were privatized. Subsidies were reduced, and price controls were lifted. The economy was also slowly opened to limited foreign investment, and efforts were made to expand and revitalize the domestic private sector.

However, due to the combined effect of these decisions and the absence of better leadership, insight, and vision, by the mid-1980s, Bendjedid's reforms exacerbated an already difficult situation. Unemployment increased, prices rose, and industrial output shrunk. The burden of the crisis and reforms fell mostly on the masses, while the upper class profited from the relative liberalization of the economy. Furthermore, the generation gap between the ruling elite, which based its legitimacy on war credentials, and the masses, 70 percent of whom were under the age of thirty and had no memory of the independence war, heightened the tensions between state and society. By the late 1980s, with a highly polarized society, Algeria was on the brink of an explosion.

Shortcomings and Failure of a Rent-Based Economy

Many things can explain Algeria's socioeconomic problems. One factor was the development strategy adopted in the 1970s, which relied mostly on the sale of hydrocarbons instead of creating productive activities that would employ a rising population and generate income from varied sources, including exports and taxes. Under Boumediene, Algeria pursued a socialist mode of development that placed all social and economic development responsibility in the hands of the state. The state became responsible for production, employment, welfare, and social protection. The country engaged in an extensive industrialization program, and the state controlled most foreign trade, manufacturing, retail, agriculture, utilities, and banking. All major foreign business interests and most large domestic businesses were nationalized. By the early 1970s, almost 90 percent of the industrial sector and more than 70 percent of the industrial workforce were under state control.

By the end of the 1970s, the country had made noticeable progress in human development indices, especially in health, education, and poverty reduction. However, the development strategy pursued proved later to be incapable of dealing with various challenges. Several large, poorly designed industrialization projects did not stimulate national development as planned, and they became a source of financial drain. The failed industrialization program was driven more by nationalist feelings than by a rational plan for economic efficiency and development. The agricultural sector suffered from neglect and remained underdeveloped and poorly organized. The 1971 agrarian revolution nationalized the land of absentee landlords and started creating a system of cooperatives among those who benefited from donated nationalized land. However, the policy failed. Agricultural production declined. Falling energy prices in the 1980s left the country with substantial deficits and an underdeveloped agricultural sector, which, in turn, caused frequent food shortages, increasing dependence on food imports, and urban migration.

In the 1980s, attempts at economic reform, motivated more by pragmatism and populism than by a commitment to deep and well-thought-out change, failed to halt the decline and caused more problems such as high unemployment, increased urbanization, and rapidly declining export revenue. These problems eroded the state's welfare capacity and ability to maintain security and stability.

At the end of 1994, with an armed Islamist rebellion under way, Algeria agreed to an IMF and World Bank–sponsored Structural Adjustment Program (SAP) whose implementation further exacerbated the situation. Under the program, the government devaluated the currency by 40 percent, lifted subsidies on basic consumption items, tightened monetary and credit policies, started liberalizing foreign trade, lowered its budget deficit, and privatized some public enterprises. Over a few years, the country's aggregate economic indicators improved (lower inflation, balanced budget and trade, increased hard currency reserves, and lower external debt), but the "shock therapy" did not fulfill its overall promises immediately. More than five hundred thousand workers were laid off by 1998; unemployment climbed to 35 percent before falling to 11 percent in 2011; the number of people living below the poverty line increased substantially, reaching 23 percent in 2006[1] before falling to 18.95 percent in 2008; and social inequality increased markedly.

In recent years, the biggest paradox has been that, while the country's overall financial standing improved due to substantial oil and gas revenues, the social and economic conditions of most citizens worsened. The main reasons are the absence of a coherent reform strategy and an inadequate use of hydrocarbon rent.

The government's most important response to social unrest during the past decade has been the infusion of large amounts of cash into the economy in the form of infrastructure investments that do not generate long-term income and employment. Around $500 billion between 2000 and 2011 went primarily to highway construction, new low-income housing construction, and agriculture. Other amounts funded microcredits to help young people start their own businesses and financed low-paying internships. However, these efforts failed to make a dent in high youth unemployment.

An extensive informal economy, which represents approximately 40 percent of nonhydrocarbon activities, is an additional obstacle to reform. This parallel economy escapes state control and taxation. Some individuals in high public offices and the bureaucracy, as well as some retired military officers with major business interests, have vested stakes in this informal economy and resist the financial transparency and accountability required by economic reform.

The overall economic environment, regulations, institutions, and practices tend to discourage reforms and private investment. They inhibit the growth of a formal private sector and tend to encourage the predatory behavior of some private businesses that extract benefits from the rent-based and subsidized formal system. Corruption at high levels of public companies and the bureaucracy became a major problem, thereby hurting the aims of public investments and contributing to dwindling state legitimacy.

The October 1988 Riots and Their Impact

Rapidly declining export revenues in the late 1980s eroded the state's capacity to deliver on its social welfare commitments and affected its ability to maintain security. A massive foreign debt was straining the country's finances, and a high dependency on hydrocarbon exports and food imports made the country dangerously vulnerable. The explosive combination of all these ingredients needed only a trigger for the conflagration to happen. There were plenty.

People were angry at the leadership, corruption, declining living standards, increasing unemployment, food shortages, and persistent inequality and alienation. Over the years, the ruling elite had consolidated its political power through access to economic rents generated by the hydrocarbon industry. It resisted genuine economic reform. Public company managers, top bureaucrats, and powerful civilians and military officers benefited from economic protectionism and from the de facto monopolies they had created for themselves in the lucrative import-export sectors.

After weeks of strikes and work stoppages, the most violent public demonstrations since independence took place in the first week of October 1988. Six days of rioting in several cities targeted city halls, police stations, post offices, state-owned cars, and supermarkets. The young rioters focused particularly on symbols of the regime such as government cars, state supermarkets, and the FLN. In a moment of panic, the state leadership, which had never faced such a challenge, used the army to quickly and violently end the riots. Five hundred rioters were killed by the repression.

The sudden mobilization of a defiant society and its aftermath severely shook and challenged the political system and the ruling elite. As if to make up quickly for the harsh repression, on October 10, 1988, President Bendjedid promised sweeping institutional reforms. Swiftly approved by referendum, the reforms included a constitutional amendment that separated the FLN from the state, restructured executive and legislative authority, strengthened presidential powers, eliminated the ideological commitment to socialism, allowed free elections and the freedom of association (including multipartyism), and hinted at a reduced role for the military in politics. Officially, the military establishment is committed to a democratic project and a republican form of government. However, many Algerians believe that it is the backbone of the authoritarian Algerian political system; it plays the role of kingmaker, watches over the security and stability of the country, and has an overwhelming place in high state institutions.

The historic societal mobilization for change and the sweeping reforms that followed were later termed the "Algerian Spring." However, as will be discussed later, just like most Arab Spring upheavals and reforms, Algeria's events failed to dislodge authoritarian rule and its aging leadership. It just softened them a bit.

Within two years of the 1988 riots, Algeria's political structure had evolved from a strongly centralized regime to the near realization of a competitive pluralistic multiparty democracy. Civic associations proliferated and became a vibrant part of Algerian political life. Many organizations—mainly those of journalists, women, and human rights advocates—played a significant role in the first years of political liberalization. In spite of setbacks in the 1990s due to political assassinations by Islamist groups and state repression, they became a permanent fixture of Algeria's political environment. They continue to constitute today a source of challenge to the government and an imposing element of the political landscape of Algeria. Among the new political formations that mobilized the masses around several issues—including regime change—two proved to be powerful and resilient: the Islamists and the ethno-cultural Berber movement.

The Berber mobilization, which developed much later in the Kabylie region, east of the capital city Algiers, was characterized as a "citizen movement," which demanded, among other things, the recognition of Berber (Tamazight) as a national language and of the inherent Amazigh (Berber) essence of Algeria's identity. Both goals were finally achieved in 2016. It was a unique movement started in the early 2000s by traditional grassroots village and tribal leadership structures called *aarch*, which were substituted for failing formal and institutional outlets for popular demands and grievances. Notwithstanding its cultural demands, the movement was directed against the entire regime, particularly its repressive nature and its unresponsiveness to social and economic problems.

End of the One-Party System and the "Dark Decade"

The late 1980s political opening produced sixty-two parties, which participated in the country's first multiparty local elections in June 1990. The FLN was badly defeated by a new Islamist party, the Front of Islamic Salvation (FIS), which secured 853 of the 1,520 local councils (55%) and 32 of the 48 provincial assemblies (67%). The FLN won only 487 local and 14 provincial constituencies. In the first multiparty parliamentary elections of December 26, 1991, the FIS won 188 seats out of 430 in the first round, while the FLN obtained merely 16 seats. Runoff elections planned for the following month were canceled in January 1992 by a military intervention, which also banned the FIS and jailed thousands of its supporters. Its two leaders, Abassi Madani and Ali Belhadj, were sentenced to twelve years in prison, which they served fully.

After the military coup and the repression, the militants of the FIS and other Islamist groups went underground and escalated violent attacks against the state and people who disagreed with them, especially intellectuals, journalists, and academics. Among the violent groups, the Armed Islamic Groups (GIA) was most notorious for its indiscriminate violence against civilians. From within its ranks was born another violent group, the Salafist Group for Preaching and Combat (GSPC), which joined the al-Qaeda network in 2006 and then changed its name to al-Qaeda in the Islamic Maghreb (AQIM) and extended its actions to the rest of the Maghreb and the Sahel region. AQIM remains a serious security threat to Algeria and the region. The state responded to the Islamist armed offensive with a large-scale crackdown against the Islamists and anyone suspected of aiding them. From 1992 to 1999, the vicious armed conflict claimed around two hundred thousand lives, caused substantial destruction, displaced close to two million people, and isolated Algeria in the international arena.

During that "dark decade," the country was temporarily ruled by a High State Council headed, at first, by Defense Minister General Khaled Nezzar, and then by independence war hero Mohamed Boudiaf, who returned from exile in Morocco to be assassinated six months later by one of his security details in June 1992. He was followed by Ali Kafi, leader of the veteran's organization, and then in 1995 by retired general Lamine Zeroual, who was the first leader to be elected since the 1980s.[2]

A combination of improved state counterinsurgency efforts and internal dissent over leadership among armed Islamist groups led to the decline of rebellion. President Bouteflika, who came to power in 1999,[3] enacted two amnesty programs for all rebels willing to give up the fight: the National Concord in 1999 and the Charter for Peace and National Reconciliation in 2005. As a result, hundreds of Islamists surrendered, and others were released from jail. However, a small number of AQIM militants remain active and continue to commit occasional violence.[4]

While pursuing a firm repression of radical Islamists, the state gradually opened up to moderate opposition parties, both religious and secular. In 1996, constitutional amendments included a provision that Islam was the state religion, made illegal the creation of parties on a "religious, linguistic, racial, gender, corporatist or regional" basis, and outlawed the use of partisan propaganda based on these elements. However, the implementation of the religious and ethnic prohibition was not thorough, especially when the state needed legitimizing partnership with some parties.

Elections in June 1997 produced Algeria's first multiparty parliament. The main winners were the FLN and the National Democratic Rally (RND, a nationalist, conservative party created to support Lamine Zeroual's candidacy to the presidency two years earlier). The FLN, the RND, the Society of Peace Movement (MSP), an Islamist party formerly known as Hamas, and Ennahda (Movement for Islamic Renaissance) formed a progovernment coalition that controlled an absolute majority and twenty-one ministerial posts, seven of which went to the Islamists. This coalition survived until

2012, when the Islamist MSP decided to drop out and join the opposition with the hope of capturing more votes in the wake of the Arab Spring. This strategy failed, and the MSP lost substantially, decimating the number of parliamentary seats held by Islamists. By that time, the absolute parliamentary majority fell in the hands of a reenergized FLN and the RND, which constitute today a powerful conservative and nationalist coalition that supports, almost unconditionally, the president and the status quo. As the Islamists dropped out of the progovernment coalition and lost a substantial number of parliamentary seats, the combined FLN-RND legislative majority and President Bouteflika looked like a reconstituted one-party system.

Structures, Institutions, and Resistance to Change

After a decade of political violence, relative peace and stability returned to Algeria by 2000. However, since then, the state has been unable to deal effectively with socioeconomic problems and with a lasting political malaise due to the failure to bring about effective change in leadership and political institutions. Meaningful reform is resisted by power holders, and the opposition lacks the ability to mount a coordinated challenge. The state continues to exclude Islamist and secular political figures who demand radical change, who ask for the reinstatement of the FIS, or who seek direct negotiations with the government for a comprehensive political solution to the country's problems. As a result, political change in Algeria has remained a controlled political liberalization.[5]

The nonviolent Islamist political parties, which were allowed in the political arena in the mid-1990s, initially obtained respectable results at the polls, but during the parliamentary elections of 2002, 2007, 2012, and 2017, they experienced a marked decline. In 2007, the MSP lost thirty-one of its sixty-nine seats in parliament. However, a new party, the Movement for National Reform or MRN (known as *Harakat al-iIslah al-watani* or Islah), a breakaway from Ennahda, won forty-three seats. Overall, the number of seats controlled by the Islamists declined from 103 to 60. In the 2012 parliamentary elections, the number of parliamentary seats held by these Islamist parties declined further to 59—49 of which were held by the "Green Algeria Alliance," which included combined candidates from MSP, Islah, and Ennahda.

After the 2017 legislative elections, the FLN and RND maintained their dominant presence in parliament by winning respectively 164 and 97 of the 462 seats (the FLN lost 44 seats; the RND gained 29). As for the Islamists,

Table 12.1. Select results of the 1997–2017 parliamentary elections

Party	1997		2002		2007	2012		2017	
	% of votes	Seats	% of votes	Seats	Seats	%of votes	Seats	%of votes	Seats
FLN	16.1	69	35.27	199	136	17.35	208	25.99	164
RND	38.1	156	8.23	47	61	6.86	68	14.91	97
Green Alliance	—	—	—	—	—	6.22	49	—	—
MRN (Islah)	—	—	9.5	43	3	—	—	—	—
MSP	16.7	69	7.05	38	52	—	—	—	—
MSP–FC	—	—	—	—	—	—	—	6.09	33
Independents	5	11	4.92	30	33	8.79%	18		28
PT	2.1	4	3.33	21	26	3.71%	24		11
Ennahda	9.9	34	0.65	1	5	—	—	—	—
Ennahda–FJD Alliance	—	—	—	—	—	—	—	3.70	15
FFS	5.7	20	—	—	—	2.47%	27	2.36	14
RCD	4.8	19	—	—	19	—	—	1.02	9
Rally for Hope for Algeria	—	—	—	—	—	—	—	4.18	19

Note: Total seats in the APN: 430 in 1991, 380 in 1997, 389 in 2002 and 2007, and 462 in 2012 and 2017. Many parties on the list are new. MRN/El-Islah was created in 1998; the FFS and RCD boycotted the 2002 elections. The FFS boycotted the 2007 vote. For 2012, Constitutional Council proclamation of May 15, 2012, and Journal Officiel, no. 32, May 26, 2012; relayed in "Final Report on Algeria's Legislative Elections," National Democratic Institute, May 2012. The RCD boycotted the elections. Online at https://www.ndi.org/files/Algeria-Report-Leg-Elections-ENG.pdf.
In 2012, MSP, Islah, and Ennahda were included in the coalition Green Alliance, which disappeared in 2017. New MSP–FC and Ennahda–FJD alliances formed in 2017.

Sources: http://www.mae.dz, http://electionworld.org/election/algeria.htm and Algérie Press Service, http://www.aps.dz/fr/legislatives2.asp.

after the dissolution of the Green Algeria Alliance, MSP formed a new coalition with the Front for Change (FC) and won 33 seats, while Ennahda allied itself with the Front for Justice and Development (FJD)—another Islamist party created by the same leader, Abdallah Djaballah—and with the El-Bina party, a minor Islamist formation, to win merely 15 seats. All Islamist parties combined won 67 seats, which is only 8 seats more than in the 2012 elections. See table 12.1 for select results of the 1997–2017 parliamentary elections.

Some of the reasons for the decline of the Islamists' popularity include intraparty conflicts and the general irrelevance of opposition parties within the political system. A third reason given is that, "unlike in Tunisia or

Egypt, Algeria's Islamist parties do not have deep roots in society and their middle class activists cannot mobilize people the way the Muslim Brotherhood can."[6] Another reason is that "the regime has successively neutered . . . the main Islamist parties, allowing them to participate in elections and including them in governing coalitions, tempting them with the fruits of power, and then watching their support slump as they compromise to stay in parliament."[7] This strategy was also used at the level of municipal councils. "When these councils failed to deliver positive results, youth became further distanced from Islamist parties. In this process, Islamist parties have acquired the same level of disdain or skepticism that secularly oriented political parties have encountered."[8]

Arab Spring and Algerian Indifference

After a long period of turbulence and uncertainty, by the end of 2010, due to increased hydrocarbon revenue, Algeria was finally enjoying a return of political stability, relative security, and some economic prosperity. However, there was still a general malaise due to high youth unemployment rates, rising inflation, lack of government responsiveness to people's pressing demands, an inconsequential political liberalization, and an aging and disconnected top leadership. The social situation in Algeria had already been tense when upheaval began in Tunisia in December 2010. The difficult socioeconomic conditions, along with a political paralysis due partly to President Bouteflika's illness, made Algeria look ready for another social explosion.

While Tunisia's upheaval was underway, riots broke out in Algiers and other major cities on January 3, 2011, after rumors that the price of basic food staples (semolina, sugar, and cooking oil) were about to rise again due to new regulations intended to rein in the substantial informal market. The riots were spontaneous and focused mainly on the rising cost of living, diminished state subsidies, a stagnant low minimum wage, an acute shortage of affordable housing, failing educational and health systems, rampant corruption, and cronyism and nepotism in public employment. The rioters demanded the improvement of living conditions, lower food prices, jobs, and respect. However, "the riots . . . never took on a directed political character; the mobs of rioters did not become protesters. There were no marches, no shared slogans and no coherent demands."[9]

The Algerian youth, especially those with diplomas, found themselves trapped in a desperate situation where the labor market could not absorb them, and immigration laws in Europe and North America became tighter. They had little faith in formal politics and political parties, which they saw as only serving the well connected. The means of peacefully expressing their grievances and getting a response being very limited, they resorted to street violence.

This was not the first time people had resorted to this mode of expression. Violent protest has become a regular occurrence in recent years. Nowadays, whenever people face a problem that neither the local authorities nor the state addresses, they often resort to attacking government buildings, blocking traffic on main roads, and organizing sit-ins and even hunger strikes.

The January 2011 riots may have been inspired by the unfolding Tunisian mass protests, but they did not benefit from the support of labor unions, political parties, or civic associations. They lasted only four days, and the protestors did not present political demands. Protests ended when the government announced a low price ceiling on basic food, tabled impending market regulations, and enacted "temporary and exceptional exemptions on import duties, value-added taxes, and corporate taxes for everyday commodities."[10] Although they stopped the riots, the measures did not resolve the underlying problems.

On January 19, three hundred young people were invited to a parliament session to freely state their complaints and wishes. The key grievances expressed related to jobs, housing, youth marginalization in the political and economic systems, and the contempt (*hogra*) shown toward them by bureaucrats and state security agents. The state responded with modest concessions to their demands.

A month after the riots, President Bouteflika finally addressed the country and promised jobs, the lifting of the nineteen-year-old state-of-emergency law, and more political freedom. The speech was received with cynicism because similar promises had failed to deal with the fundamental problems of the entire political and economic system. The lifting of the state of emergency was carried out immediately, but the curtailment of liberties did not end because many legal restrictions remained in place.

To address the wider systemic issues, a peaceful movement of political protest began on February 12 in Algiers. Its demands included democracy, the liberalization of the political sphere and the media, and the release of people arrested during the January 2011 riots. However, the movement was short-lived for several reasons. It was organized by the National Coordination for Change and Democracy (CNCD), which was created by small political parties, the National League for the Defense of Human Rights, the National Association of Families of Missing Persons (those who had "disappeared" during the war of the 1990s), an association of the unemployed, and many other small groups. It was not supported by the country's largest union, the General Union of Algerian Workers (UGTT) or by any major political parties or professional associations. The CNCD was led by the Rally for Democracy and Culture (RCD), an opposition party with a narrow constituency of Berber-speaking people in Algiers and the nearby Kabylie region. This compromised its appeal from the start due to the fact that its key figure, Said Saadi, the head of the RCD, was perceived by many people as a co-opted opposition figure who had supported the military's cancellation of the 1992 parliamentary elections and had applauded the repression of the Islamists after their legitimate electoral victory. In the end, the CNDC protest movement failed to take off as it could not recruit more protesters and was unable to break through an overwhelming police presence in the capital.

Other types of protests and localized riots over limited issues have continued and intensified at times. These actions affected several towns and villages and many professional sectors. Several strikes were led by independent unions (i.e., those not affiliated with the UGTT) in various sectors, including education, health, the civil service, the legal profession, and several industries. Striking workers tended to demand either pay raises to keep up with inflation or parity with salaries in the public sector, which benefited a few years ago from generous pay increases of 25 to 50 percent; other demands included improved working conditions and better health insurance and retirement compensation.

Suicide, especially by immolation, has also become a prevalent form of protest in recent years, in seeming emulation of the self-immolation of Mohamed Bouazizi, the man from the Tunisian town of Sidi Bouzid, where the whole Arab Spring began in December 2010. However, the increasing rate of suicides or suicide attempts by self-immolation has generated neither public interest nor the concern of government officials.

A final form of protest in Algeria, as elsewhere in the region, is illegal migration to Europe by way of the sea. Known as *harga*, this dangerous form of exit has caused many deaths; yet it remains an attractive alternative for people with no hope of ever having a decent life in Algeria.

Economically, the state is caught in the difficult position of having to resolve serious socioeconomic problems while opening the economy to global capital, enacting more austerity measures, and maintaining strict budgetary discipline. The current 50 percent decrease in hydrocarbon export earnings makes this a daunting task. The implementation of some neoliberal reforms has caused friction between the state and society, as indicated by the recurring strikes and unrest in towns and villages throughout the country. These have become regular occurrences in an environment marked by institutional failures and by a fear of the winds of change blowing from other countries affected by the popular upheavals of 2011.

Enduring Authoritarianism in New Clothes

In light of all of the above, one may wonder why the growing socioeconomic problems and the systemic failures to adequately address them have not generated a mass upheaval against the current system of governance in Algeria. Besides some of the factors discussed above, the inability of people to mount and sustain mass demonstrations can be explained by several factors.

The first is the traumatic war of the 1990s, whose memory is still vivid and whose wounds have not healed yet. As a result, many people fear that even a peaceful protest could degenerate into an uncontrollable and lasting violence. Another reason is the widely held belief that the Algerian security forces will not hesitate to resort to violence against a popular movement deemed threatening to political stability. Furthermore, people know that the most powerful institutions in Algeria are the military and the security services (known as DRS), not the civilian leadership, which has only nominal authority. Therefore, to take on the political system would either succeed, but only with the acquiescence of the military (as in the 2011 Tunisian mass protest), or fail and bring about a harsh repression, as happened in the 1990s.

Another impediment to a mass movement against the unpopular regime has been the inability of the political opposition to create a wide and sustained coalition that could lead a mass movement of protest or revolt. Also, the leaders of the regime have, along the years, become adept at neutralizing the opposition through co-optation, infiltration, manipulation, or just plain elimination. This has prevented political dissenters from organizing and coordinating a sustained nationwide protest.

Furthermore, political opposition has been missing a staunch and widely supported leader (a Nelson Mandela, an Aung San Suu Kyi, or just an Algerian Nobel Prize winner) who would lead a relentless challenge to the system. There has also been a total absence of international pressure that could lend support to domestic demands for change.

Another important element to note is that all recent mass protests in Algeria tend not to target the head of state, as was done in Tunisia, Egypt, Libya, Yemen, and Syria. Rather, they attack an elusive *pouvoir*—the real, unelected power holders in Algeria, which, in addition to army generals and the security services, include powerful FLN leaders and business magnates who enjoy de facto business monopolies, access to state resources and protection, and a privileged relationship with the regulatory state bureaucracy.

Just like other resilient authoritarian systems around the world, the Algerian one has managed to survive numerous predictions of its demise. It has done so by adapting in form, bringing in new players at the top, co-opting some at the bottom, and repressing when needed. It has also adopted many of the characteristics of what Marina Ottaway calls semiauthoritarianism. For Ottaway, these regimes are political hybrids. "They allow little real competition for power, thus reducing government accountability. However, they leave enough political space for political parties and organizations of civil society to form, for an independent press to function to some extent, and for some political debate to take place."[11] She also notes that "tentative political openings in Algeria, Morocco, and Yemen appear to be leading to the modernization of semi-authoritarianism rather than to democracy."[12] In other words, this kind of authoritarianism "lite" is established and maintained by design, not by default.

Just like other semiauthoritarian regimes, Algeria's governing system appears to be doing much of what is expected of democratizing polities: it holds regular multiparty elections, it has a functioning parliament, and it somewhat respects the freedom of association and freedom of the press. Peaceful protests are allowed to some degree, and there is a vibrant associative life (but not civil society). However, with all this in place, those who rule remain in control and do not allow the kind of changes that might push them out of power and bring about a new generation of leaders.

Institutional Failure, the Voice of the
Street, and Political Decay

What would it take to move Algeria from semiauthoritarianism to the institutionalization of political democracy? If mass mobilization overcame the ability and willingness of the repressive apparatus to put down a popular revolt, would the political institutions under semiauthoritarianism evolve into a substantive democracy? Are there consequences for elite resistance to institutionalized rule? In his 1965 article in *World Politics* titled "Political Development and Political Decay"[13] and in his 1968 book *Political Order in Changing Societies*, Samuel Huntington warned his colleagues of the modernization school about the problems that arise when there is a lag in the development of political institutions in countries that are experiencing rapid political mobilization of the masses in the wake of important social and economic change. For Huntington, "violence and instability" can be "in large part the product of rapid social change and the rapid mobilization of new groups into politics coupled with the slow development of political institutions."[14]

The expansion of political participation in Algeria during the late 1980s, due to both socioeconomic changes and political liberalization, was not matched by the required level of political institutionalization. According to Huntington, "the level of political institutionalization of any political system can be defined by the adaptability, complexity, autonomy, and coherence of its organizations and procedures."[15] This mismatch between the expansion of political participation and a low level of political institutionalization can lead to "political instability and disorder."[16] In short, a weak level of political institutionalization may be one of the reasons why "the street" may matter more in Algeria than the failing and decaying institutions of representation and of public policy making. Instead of being channeled through established and agreed-upon political institutions that aggregate, articulate, and respond to popular grievances, people's frustration with the state, parties, and leaders is often expressed through strikes, street protests, and rioting.

In a news commentary titled "Ne voulant pas des structures officielles, les Algériens font la politique autrement" ("Not caring for official structures, the Algerians do politics otherwise"), Karim Aimeur indicated that "for many Algerians, blocking the road, burning a tire, closing a city hall, participating in a rally or any other protest action is a political act. . . . This is to say that these are all political acts that take place in the street."[17] This situation indicates that the institutionalization needed for a genuine transition and an actual change has not fully materialized in Algeria. One well-known phenomenon is that much political power in Algeria is generated and exercised outside of the formal structures, which are themselves devoid of what Huntington meant by institutionalization.

The existing structures and institutions are constantly manipulated, amended, rearranged, and even sidelined when major policies and decisions are enacted.[18] That is why, for example, the Algerian parliament is seen as a rubber-stamping institution. The constitution is amended at will to fill the needs of the moment, without guarantee that future changes will or will not undo the previous ones or twist them a bit because of a given exigency. That was the case, for example, of the president's two-term limitation that was undone by constitutional amendment in order to allow Bouteflika to run for a third and a fourth term. As people realized that the "adjustment" of the formal rules aimed only to legitimize perennial tenure in power, vocal protests against Bouteflika's fourth term finally broke out around the country. When he announced in spring 2014 that he would run for a fourth term, many Algerians and foreign observers were dismayed, especially because, after fifteen years in power, he was in very poor health and confined to a wheelchair due to the stroke he had suffered a year earlier. Almost immediately, a large movement of opposition to his reelection started. Harsh condemnations were uttered by opposition leaders and the catch-all movement Barakat ("Enough").[19] The protests targeted not Bouteflika personally but the limitless presidential term and the regime, which prevented the young generation from taking the lead and revamping the system.

However, despite the *Barakat* movement, opposition never reached critical mass. Credited for having brought about peace to the country after the two amnesty programs mentioned above, Bouteflika was elected for the second term in 2004 with 84 percent of the vote. In 2008, after the term limit was lifted, he was elected for a third time with 90.24 percent. Paradoxically, and in spite of protests, Bouteflika's election for a fourth term was widely supported (81.53%). Many people saw him as guarantor of stability, security, and national unity at a time when North Africa was marred by conflict, instability, and armed groups, although at least six opposition parties boycotted the elections, some of whom spoke of massive electoral fraud. The officials campaigning on Bouteflika's behalf—his chief of staff and the prime minister—suggested in their speeches that choosing another candidate might jeopardize security, peace, and stability.

These developments took place in a difficult context marked by the physical incapacity of the reelected president, a 50 percent drop in oil and gas revenues (98 percent of export earnings), high youth unemployment, a housing crisis, rising inflation, mounting criminality, increasing attacks by armed groups belonging to AQIM and other newly formed radical groups, a steady return of conservative Islamism wrapped in prodemocracy slogans, and violence and insecurity in neighboring Libya and Mali. In these challenging times—or maybe because of them—the call for change did not reach a level high enough to overcome the voices of the officials warning about a pseudo foreign ploy to destabilize the country at a moment when chaos was raging in Egypt, Libya, Syria, and Yemen. The Algerian regime managed to enjoy a good degree of tolerance because many people believed that it guaranteed social peace and security (in contrast to the mayhem witnessed in Libya) and that it will continue to deliver the welfare benefits on which people have grown to depend.

Except for a few vocal dissenters, both rulers and ruled seem to agree that stability and peace are now needed more than the unpredictable and probably messy prospect of democratization. The much-needed institutionalization keeps being postponed, and the exercise of political and economic power continues to rest on invisible struggles between power clans and powerful brokers.

It is worth adding that a recent opportunity to bring about useful and meaningful changes that will survive clans and individuals was missed when, in response to the protests against the fourth presidential term, the constitution was amended in 2016. Term limits were reintroduced, but they can easily be deleted again. As usual, once societal pressure diminished and the state reasserted itself, the reforms amounted to refurbishing the authoritarian system without ending it. The legislative branch continued to be at the service of whoever effectively ruled the country, the independence and impartiality of the judiciary remained elusive, and executive power continued to alternate between the formal, civilian head of state and *le pouvoir.*

Recent comments by an elected national assembly deputy reflect the institutional vacuity in Algeria:

> Can we imagine a country such as Algeria functioning without a president of the Republic, and parliament finds a way to debate bills which the executive branch does not even care to execute? Parliament has become the joke of Algerian society, considering its incapacity to discuss extremely important events in the country. . . . In this situation, I decided to no longer debate any bill or law and to no longer recognize this parliament. . . . How can we debate a bill or law when the president of the Popular National Assembly rejected the motion of 100 deputies to discuss the corruption that plagues the country? . . . How do we deal with a government and ministers who, in addition to not recognizing parliament, scorn it? . . . How do we discuss a bill when we do not even inquire about a president—elected in theory by the people—who leads the country by proxy?[20]

In sum, in 1989 Algeria's political structure evolved toward a competitive pluralist, multiparty polity, but in the last two decades, multiparty politics has been degraded. The rules and outcomes of electoral competitions are set by those in power; and the representative institutions to which people are elected do not enjoy power of their own. People's interest in parliamentary elections has declined dramatically. Many people no longer find it useful to vote for a parliament that they perceive as unresponsive to people's demands and grievances, powerless vis-à-vis other centers of authority, and full of individuals who seem focused more on their personal interests than on those of society. The formal institutions fail to live up to the expectations that people had placed in the political liberalization process. Because that liberalization has been intentionally kept to a minimum, political opposition has shifted away from the formal institutions of political transactions, including the presidency, parliament, political parties, and elections. Political action today happens in the streets.

The apathy and mistrust felt toward the formal political institutions and processes have caused a legitimacy deficit that may not be fixed with hydrocarbon rent—through short-term populist spending projects—especially now that income from such sources has drastically declined. Things can easily turn for the worse if revenue shortfalls persist or worsen, or if the state and its agents commit a major blunder that triggers another violent tragedy due to the absence of institutions people believe in and trust.

The limitations in institutional avenues and in occasions for meaningful interactions between state and society over policies and grievances have created distance, mistrust, and suspicion between government and people and have contributed to recurring clashes. The policy of putting out fires one demonstration or riot at a time sidesteps necessary discussions over a new social contract. This "firefighter" policy might become less helpful when social movements start to converge and persist and when national leadership is weak and the political elite are highly divided.

The Next Leadership Succession: An Opportunity for Change or for the Status Quo

All of the challenges mentioned above might become exacerbated by the pending leadership succession, which may or may not be smooth and peaceful. President Abdelaziz Bouteflika may not complete his fourth term due to poor health. He is one of very few remaining leaders from the successful

1954–62 war of independence against France. He is seventy-eight years old, heading a country where 70 percent of the population is under thirty. Under his presidency, the state distributed generous benefits as a response to social and economic needs and as a means to buy social peace. Close to $800 billion has been disbursed since 2000 for reforms, infrastructure development projects, paid internships for the youth, subsidies, and generous salary increases for public employees. Also, under him, a privileged class of businessmen made fortunes and started to have some political clout through the political clan of the president's brother, Said Bouteflika.

The substantial infusion of cash in the economy was largely facilitated by a dramatic rise in the price of oil and in the indexed price of natural gas during much of the Bouteflika tenure in office. However, this did not resolve the structural inadequacies of the economy, did not create enough jobs, and did not generate much-needed nonhydrocarbon sectors or production and export.

The succession to Bouteflika may not go smoothly if there is a worsening of socioeconomic conditions or if there is suddenly an open fight among the power clans as each tries to direct the succession to Bouteflika. It may also usher in a crisis if there is a return of the Islamist challenge (less likely due to dwindling support and improved security). Even if Bouteflika is replaced by a "consensus" candidate (among elements of *le pouvoir*), the system is not likely to change much. This will just be another phase in its constant adaptation. A radical transition will remain elusive as long as a clean slate is not pursued.

As stated above, power does not rest in the current formal institutions. The legislative branch is at the service of whoever effectively rules the country. The judiciary has never been an independent institution; it neither administers justice impartially nor checks the constitutionality of government laws, policies, and acts. As for the executive, since 1979, the civilian heads of state have always had to contend with the real power holders: the army and the intelligence and security services (DRS). The military still forms the core of *le pouvoir*. Bouteflika managed to wrestle some concessions from them, notably a less overt role in politics, and he finally reined in the might of the DRS in 2015 by dismissing its powerful head, Mohamed "Toufik" Mediene, and by decentralizing its functions.

Bouteflika may have revolutionary credentials, the right populist rhetoric, and a savvy grasp of Algeria's power politics, especially in his feud with the DRS, but his deteriorating health has stimulated calls for his abdication and replacement. Even assuming that he does stay on for the full term, his ability to lead and rule will continue to be severely limited. This may affect elite cohesion and consensus on policies and their implementation. In the context of decreasing hydrocarbon revenue, rising social protest, and increasing insecurity in the region, this may augur serious breakdown and instability.

Bouteflika might be removed by the military, probably less directly than Bendjedid was. The Constitutional Council may be used to declare him unfit for office. He might also be removed if protests increase, instability returns, or radical Islamists reenergize their campaigns. In these circumstances, invoking Article 88 of the constitution on the incapacity of the president to govern, the military (as in the Tunisian and Egyptian cases) would act as the saviors of the people and the country by ousting the aging and ailing leader while claiming to have saved the country from chaos and violence. In doing so, they would preserve their interests under a smokescreen of seemingly revived political liberalization and ad hoc economic fixes. The president would then be replaced by someone who would not threaten the status quo, even if some political and economic reforms are rolled out.

No matter who is picked, the president may still not rule. In the existing institutional setting and structure of power, the ability to govern and to enact sound and lasting reforms does not rest on the president alone. Other players have to be brought in line with any reform agenda, especially the unelected power holders and brokers, both civilian and military.

Prospects

Algeria needs a genuine institutional overhaul and a meaningful change of leadership at all levels that is in tune with the country's demographics. It also needs sound economic reforms that would absorb thousands of young job seekers, lessen the dependency on hydrocarbon exports, and end the predatory behavior of high civilian and military office holders. The country has all the resources needed for a positive transformation in the interest of its citizens, including a large pool of highly educated people, a sizeable force of technocrats, a thriving independent print press, and an already existing multiparty political scene that can be rendered more meaningful by democratization.

These assets cannot be put to good use without important institutional changes. The powers of the branches of government need to be revised by

Table 12.2. Detailed results of the 2017 parliamentary elections

Party	Votes	%	Seats	+/-
National Liberation Front	1,681,321	25.99	164	−44
National Rally for Democracy	964,560	14.91	100	+32
MSP–FC Alliance	393,632	6.09	33	—
Rally for Hope for Algeria	270,112	4.18	19	—
Future Front	265,564	4.11	14	+12
Algerian Popular Movement	241,087	3.73	13	+6
Ennahda–FJD Alliance	239,148	3.70	15	—
Workers' Party	191,965	2.97	11	−13
Socialist Forces Front	152,489	2.36	14	−13
National Republican Alliance	121,156	1.87	6	+4
Freedom and Justice Party	88,418	1.37	2	
New Dawn	82,993	1.28	1	
Dignity Party	81,180	1.26	3	
Movement for National Reform	77,290	1.19	1	—
El Fath	69,063	1.07	1	
Rally for Culture and Democracy	65,841	1.02	9	+9
National Front for Social Justice	63,827	0.99	1	
Party of Youth	63,682	0.98	2	
Movement of National Understanding	51,960	0.80	4	
New Algeria Front	49,413	0.76	1	
Ahd 54	42,160	0.65	2	−1
Republican Patriotic Rally	40,645	0.63	2	0
El-Infitah Movement	38,061	0.59	2	+1
National Struggle Front	34,695	0.54	2	
Union of Democratic and Social Forces	33,372	0.52	1	−2
National Front for Freedom	31,976	0.49	1	
Free Democratic Front	28,790	0.45	2	
National Party for Solidarity and Development	28,617	0.44	2	−2
Party of Algerian Renewal	24,584	0.38	1	0
National Assembly Union	17,577	0.27	1	
National Union for Development	15,037	0.23	1	
National Movement of Algerian Workers	14,369	0.22	1	
Movement of Free Citizens	14,085	0.22	1	0
Equity and Proclamation Party	13,400	0.21	1	
Algerian National Front	876,111	13.54	0	−9
Other parties			0	—
Independents			28	+10
Invalid/blank votes	1,757,043	—	—	—
Total	8,225,223	100	462	0
Registered voters/turnout	23,251,503	37.37	—	—

Source: Algeria's Constitutional Council, http://www.conseil-constitutionnel.dz
/CommuniqueFr_2_2017.htm.

ending the overwhelming and unproductive dominance of the presidential office; by allowing parliament to exercise legislative, investigative, and oversight functions; and by making the judicial system truly independent and able to guarantee basic freedoms and protection against the abuse of power and politically motivated retribution. Political parties must learn to perform their functions of aggregation and articulation of the wishes of their constituencies and move beyond the personalization of their organization. The military's role in politics, which was somewhat curtailed under the pressure of President Bouteflika, needs to be further diminished so as to allow accountable and regularly alternating civilian leaders to steer the country toward adequate political and economic development.

Economic hardship for the masses, regional insecurity, and a potential crisis over leadership succession cannot be adequately tackled by the current institutional setup. The rising tide of street protests around the country—even in the far south—indicates that the current malaise could lead to a major social explosion whose consequences may be worse than those of the 1990s.

Algeria's prospects will depend on the actions of those controlling the state and on the opposition's ability to combine its efforts, articulate a clear plan for the future, and push in unison, peacefully, for its implementation. This should be done now instead of waiting until regional insecurity and instability issues get resolved. One of the best ways to fend off real or imagined external threats is to strengthen the domestic setting by way of integrated and inclusive economic development, which does not rely on oil and gas rent, and equally inclusive political reforms.

AZZEDINE LAYACHI is Professor of Political Science at St. John's University, New York. He is author of *Economic Crisis and Political Change in North Africa* and *State, Society and Liberalization in Morocco: The Limits of Associative Life.*

Notes

1. "Algeria," CIA World Factbook, May 2012, https://www.cia.gov/library/publications/the-world-factbook/geos/ag.html.

2. President Zeroual, who faced strong resistance from the regime's hard-liners when he attempted a dialogue with the jailed FIS leaders, resigned in early 1999.

3. Former foreign minister Abdelaziz Bouteflika, upon a triumphant return from a twenty-year self-imposed exile, quickly became the candidate favored for the presidency. He won by 73 percent of the vote with the support of the military and the FLN, RND, and MSP.

4. AQIM has been attacking security forces and foreign personnel in Algeria, Mauritania, Tunisia, and Mali. The largest offensive was a massive attack on January 16, 2013, by an offshoot of AQIM led by Mokhtar Belmokhtar against a major natural gas facility near the southern town of In Amenas. A swift intervention of the Algerian security forces ended the siege and left many people dead, including thirty-seven foreigners.

5. Political liberalization is a process that gradually allows political freedoms and establishes some safeguards against arbitrary state action. At this stage, the state still resorts to governing by top-down command.

6. Nasser Djabi, Algerian sociologist, quoted in Paul Schemm, "Algerian Islamists Fall to Govt Party in Election," Associated Press, May 11, 2012.

7. Jack Brown, "Algeria's Midwinter Uproar," Middle East Research and Information Project (MERIP), January 20, 2011, http://www.merip.org/mero/mero012011.

8. Hamidi Khemissi, Ricardo René Larémont, and Taybi Taj Eddine, "Sufism, Salafism and State Policy towards Religion in Algeria: A Survey of Algerian Youth," *Journal of North African Studies* 17, no. 3 (June 2012): 553.

9. Brown, "Algeria's Midwinter Uproar."

10. Bertelsmann Stiftung's Transformation Index (BTI), BTI *2012 Algeria Country Report* (Gütersloh: Bertelsmann Stiftung, 2012) 23, http://www.bti-project.de/fileadmin/Inhalte /reports/2012/pdf/BTI 2012 Algeria.pdf.

11. Marina Ottaway, "The Challenge of Semi-authoritarianism: An Introduction," in *Democracy Challenged: The Rise of Semi-Authoritarianism* (Carnegie Endowment for International Peace, 2003), 1.

12. Ibid., 2.

13. Samuel P. Huntington, "Political Development and Political Decay," *World Politics* 17, no. 3 (April 1965): 386–430.

14. Samuel P. Huntington, *Political Order in Changing Societies* (New Haven: Yale University Press, 2006 [1968]), 4.

15. Huntington, "Political Development and Political Decay," 394.

16. Huntington, *Political Order in Changing Societies*, 5.

17. Karim Aimeur, "Ne voulant pas des structures officielles les Algériens font la politique autrement," *L'Expression*, January 18, 2012, accessed June 6, 2012, www.lexpressiondz.com.

18. Ottaway, "Challenge of Semi-authoritarianism," 16.

19. For more on the movement, as described by its members, see "Interview avec des membres du Mouvement Barakat," Tout Sur L'Algerie (TSA), http://www.maghrebemergent. com/component/allvideoshare/video/latest/interview-avec-des-membres-du-mouvement-barakat-tsa.html.

20. Quoted in Mehdi Mehenni, "Les deux tiers du parlement ont boycotté le projet de loi de finances 2015, Un député indépendant plonge l'APN dans l'embarras," *Le Soir D'Algerie*, October 22, 2014, http://www.lesoirdalgerie.com/articles/2014/10/22/article.php?sid =170027&cid=2.

AFTERWORD

Hicham Alaoui

T HE GENESIS FOR THIS VOLUME CAME IN A public lecture I delivered at
Georgetown University in March 2015 entitled, "The New Arab Cold
War and the Future of Authoritarianism in the Middle East." By that point,
it had become evident that the Arab Spring had imploded due to geopolitical rivalries, sectarian conflicts, the disintegration of some states, and the
lack of long-term vision espoused by many of the original protest movements. Even amid this admittedly bleak scenario, however, the Maghreb
had the potential to chart out its own unique course. More than other parts
of the region, these countries were relatively sheltered from confessional
politics as well as foreign interventions. States were robust, except for Libya,
and hydrocarbon rents were not present, except in Algeria. Finally, and
most importantly, there was an exemplary case of a successful democratic
breakthrough in Tunisia, which could nourish hope across the Maghreb for
the prospects of democratization.

For all these reasons, the Hicham Alaoui Foundation believed a book-
length treatment of these issues was vital. After a long gestation, the product of these efforts was this volume, which took shape under the academic
stewardship of Stephen King and Georgetown University and ultimately
matured under the meticulous and professional editorship of King and
Abdeslam Maghraoui. All of the scholarly contributors delivered struc-
tured academic analysis that fit well into the guiding framework. The foundation believes this new anthology will make an important contribution to
ongoing debates about not only the legacy of the Arab Spring but also the
future of democratic transformation in the Maghreb.

The division of the book's chapters into two categories followed a systematic and thoughtful approach. When tackling the challenges and potentialities of the Maghreb, we must focus on both country-specific parameters
and broader regional dynamics. In the category of country-specific chapters,

the scholars here provided extremely useful conclusions. Above all, these case studies highlighted the historical and cultural specificities of Morocco, Algeria, Libya, Mauritania, and Tunisia. All these countries constitute the Maghreb, and each encapsulates a distinctive part of its political heritage.

Beyond that, however, these contributions underscored that complacency about any political outcome is dangerous. Democracy was not a foregone conclusion in Tunisia after the Jasmine Revolution. It required persistent and careful craftsmanship by all political actors. Likewise, Libya also experienced revolution and regime change during the Arab Spring, but assumptions about state unity and coherence proved woefully premature. In the same way, Morocco, Algeria, and Mauritania since 2011–12 have exhibited authoritarian continuity and avoided the political dramas of domestic uprisings. Yet the status quo does not guarantee future stability and peace, as historical events have proved.

The second category of contributions to this volume, the regional chapters, also furnished several provocative ideas worth contemplating in scholarly debate. The discussions of Maghrebi economics underscored the well-known problem of unemployment and the political problems that stem from the lack of meaningful jobs for an ever-growing youthful population. These discussions also implied, however, that the solution moving forward requires going beyond macro-level statistics about GDP change or financial growth, to instead consider at the micro level how ordinary people have been excluded from grand technocratic models of prosperity and development.

The contributions on secularist and Islamist tendencies also yielded reflective implications. Maghrebi societies contain ideologically diverse sectors and movements, which compel us to move beyond Orientalist tropes about the synonymy of Islam and politics. At the same time, however, it is true that political Islam will occupy some permanent part of these societal landscapes as not only an expression of opposition, but also an alternative vision for a better future. How and why Islamism evolves remains worthy of renewed conversation.

Finally, no debate about the Maghreb can credibly exclude issues of insecurity. The discussions in this volume broached the problem of jihadist networks and terrorism, as well as effective policy responses to such extremist threats. It has become critically apparent that the Maghreb cannot be analyzed in isolation from the wider regional context. The growth of militant Salafists and other radicalized groups reflects a deeper uncertainty about modern institutions and political order reverberating across the Arab world, especially among youths.

Taking a step back, this edited volume pushes contemporary thinking about the stability and future of the Maghreb in new directions. As both an academic scholar and an advocate for democracy who has been deeply involved in regional politics for decades, I take away several insights from these enlightening discussions.

First, it is striking that unlike the other two Middle East subregions commonly invoked today, the Mashreq and the Arabian Gulf, the Maghreb elegantly serves as a microcosm for all the varied political outcomes populating the entire Middle East geographic landscape. During the Arab Spring, two of the five Maghrebi countries underwent popular revolution and regime change. Of these two, Tunisia resulted in a democratic opening and transition from authoritarian rule, while Libya's transitional process was subsumed by state disintegration and internal violence. Both struggle with their own uncertainties and challenges, but it is undeniable that both made a sharp rupture from the past.

Of the three cases of regime continuity, two, in Algeria and Mauritania, remain autocratic republics underpinned by a praetorian military that dominates political institutions. Indeed, they seem to be the most stable and peaceful of all the republics that remain in the Middle East, given the instabilities that have befallen states such as Egypt, Syria, Yemen, and Iraq. The last, Morocco, is an absolute monarchy constrained by its own position. Since independence, the Moroccan monarchy has been periodically exposed to popular pressures. However, those pressures from below, of which the Arab Spring was the latest example, have never been organized and sustained enough to induce genuine change.

Second, when discussing the persistence of authoritarianism in not just the Maghreb but the wider Middle East region today, it is useful to juxtapose past trajectories against future expectations. Autocracies usually adapt after serious crises, but the changes seen today are novel. In the first postcolonial decades, authoritarian regimes across the Maghreb were relatively closed and repressive. Starting in the 1980s, however, economic crises and popular discontent threatened to overwhelm the stability of this original model. In the period that corresponded to the end of the Cold War, these regimes adapted to new material and geopolitical conditions by undertaking political liberalization. This allowed for tightly controlled pluralism, but under the watchful eye of rulers who never surrendered ultimate financial and coercive power. By the turn of the century, some of these systems had evolved into competitive authoritarian regimes, with more institutionalized opposition parties and regularized yet hollow elections.

The Arab Spring exposed the inability of these institutional recalibrations to satisfy mass demands for participation and voice, which had not been fulfilled by past limited political openings. Thus, in the post–Arab Spring era, we see the latest iteration of authoritarian strategy. The autocratic regimes that remain have actively inserted themselves into the growing divide between secularists and Islamists. They have a two-prong goal. On the one hand, they reassure conservatives and the pious by co-opting the language of Islamism, but on the other hand, they promise secularists outright protection against an Islamist take-over. They also reassure all of society that their state apparatus will not splinter and fragment.

These regimes also more aggressively reconfigured the balance of political power, knowing that the threat to their survival from popular uprisings was no longer virtual—it was real. For instance, as Maghroui noted, in Morocco long-standing patterns of pluralism and opposition have undergone "institutional unraveling" as security and intelligence forces more aggressively permeate society and filter out dissent. And in Algeria, as Layachi observed, military and presidential power holders have tightened their stranglehold on state resources, leaving the legislature—the only institutionalized arena for opposition—"constantly manipulated, amended, rearranged." In this new logic combining divide-and-co-opt with recentralizing power, these regimes attempt to satisfy multiple sectors of society at the same time while protecting their prerogatives. The goal remains the same as always: to renew their lease on political life.

Is this sustainable? Popular demobilization has occurred in most authoritarian survivors of the Arab Spring, but especially characterizes the juncture at which Morocco and Algeria now stand. Furthermore, given its preoccupation with the spread of jihadist terrorism, the West is relying increasingly on security cooperation with these two states. Morocco's collaboration is central in the European theater, while Algeria has been solicited to stabilize the Sahel. With such dependence, however, comes the West's inherent tendency to turn a blind eye to human rights abuses within these countries. At the domestic level, the social and economic crises that gave rise to protests, uprisings, and revolutions have not improved. If anything, they have worsened: low oil prices have diminished the flow of hydrocarbon rents to Algerian power holders, while joblessness and deprivation have not improved in the face of the youth explosion in Morocco. What is fundamentally needed is a genuine commitment to political inclusion by these autocratic systems.

Yet however diminished the opportunities for large-scale political change may be in the post–Arab Spring Maghreb, it is still vital to locate the potentialities of future democratic mobilization, which undeniably exist. Tunisia offers the first example. Here, there exists popular disillusionment with the ongoing democratic consolidation, marked by the return of old authoritarian elements, the frozen pact between Islamists and secular actors, and the stifling of the reform agenda. However, the memory of the Jasmine Revolution still looms large and continues to catalyze new social movements seeking to reenact the spirit of mass mobilization. Here, Arab democracy has enjoyed great success but will also face its stiffest test in the coming years.

Mobilizational possibilities in Morocco and Algeria abide by a different logic. In Tunisia, democratic elements legally included in the postrevolutionary political order will fight to maintain pluralism. In Morocco and Algeria, however, the formal political arena no longer contains significant autonomous opposition that can exist independently of these systems' centers. As the neutralization of the PJD in Morocco illustrates, co-optation has ensured that future pressures must emanate from well outside the boundaries of institutional politics. In Morocco, such challengers will spring from the kingdom's social and economic peripheries, such as the Rif. They can also emerge from spatial peripheries, in the sprawling settlements that ring major cities and thus link the urban to the rural. In Algeria, radical opposition will originate from marginalized sectors rather than established echelons, such as the business elite. In both cases, future mobilization brings both promise and peril, because it will be antisystemic in nature. Opposition will be less patient and potentially more violent than in the past and will not tolerate superficial reforms of the political state.

Future democratic mobilization in Mauritania and Libya is perhaps the most difficult to pinpoint because these are the most fragile states in the Maghreb. Communal cleavages, fractured institutions, and diverse societies make governance difficult, but in distinctive ways. In Mauritania, grinding poverty and weak infrastructure have reinforced patterns of exclusion and obscured political forces. In Libya, there is no shortage of competition, given the ongoing civil war and deepening collapse of the post-Qaddafi state. In these countries, questions of popular mobilization are more inextricably tied to existential issues of survival than elsewhere in the Maghreb.

Only time will reveal the conditions under which these myriad possibilities of change can activate. By navigating the historical and comparative terrain of the Maghreb, this book has sought to shed light on this ongoing process.

HICHAM ALAOUI is a D.Phil. candidate in Middle East studies at the University of Oxford. He is author of numerous articles in the *Journal of Democracy, Politique Internationale, Le Debat, Pouvoirs,* and *Le Monde Diplomatique,* as well as the book *Journal d'un Prince Banni.*

INDEX

Page numbers with "t" suffixes refer to tables.

www.ingramcontent.com/pod-product-compliance
Lightning Source LLC
Chambersburg PA
CBHW071013280326
41935CB00011B/1338